FOURTH EDITION

The
Cultural World
of the
Bible

An Illustrated Guide to Manners and Customs

Victor H. Matthews

Baker Academic

a division of Baker Publishing Group
Grand Rapids, Michigan

© 1988, 1991, 2006, 2015 by Victor H. Matthews

Published by Baker Academic
a division of Baker Publishing Group
P.O. Box 6287, Grand Rapids, MI 49516-6287
www.bakeracademic.com

Printed in the United States of America

Earlier editions of this book were published as *Manners and Customs in the Bible: An Illustrated Guide to Daily Life in Bible Times.*

Library of Congress Cataloging-in-Publication Data

Matthews, Victor Harold.
    [Manners & customs in the Bible]
    The cultural world of the Bible : an illustrated guide to manners and customs / Victor H. Matthews. — Fourth Edition.
        pages cm
    "Earlier editions of this book were published as *Manners and Customs in the Bible: An Illustrated Guide to Daily Life in Bible Times.*"
    Includes bibliographical references and index.
    ISBN 978-0-8010-4973-6 (pbk. : alk. paper)
    1. Jews—Social life and customs—To 70 A.D. 2. Palestine—Social life and customs—To 70 A.D. 3. Bible—Antiquities. I. Title.
    DS112.M33 2015
    220.95—dc23
                                            2014049124

Baker Publishing Group publications use paper produced from sustainable forestry practices and post-consumer waste whenever possible.

To Carol, Peter, and Samuel

Contents

List of Illustrations

Preface to the Fourth Edition

The first edition of this volume was published in 1988. Since that time both the field of biblical studies and I have continued to change. We have learned from and weathered the storms of interpretive differences and have been amazed by advances in the analysis of archaeological data. And our heightened precision in readings of ancient texts has come through the production of image-based, digital editions. With that in mind, I continue to believe that a book detailing the social world of ancient Israel deserves a place in classrooms and for private study. The editors of Baker Academic and I have decided that we should revise and expand this new edition so that it can be more effectively used as a textbook or as a supplement to other textbooks in classes on the Bible. The result of this new focus is that we have retained the best of what has appeared in previous editions, such as the historical summaries at the beginning of each chapter and the discussion of aspects of everyday life, while significantly expanding the text and adding new pedagogical features. Rather than serving primarily as a reference work, its aim is to spark conversation and to bring the narratives and the characters to life. The Bible deserves close study, and students should have the opportunity to exercise their critical thinking skills to raise questions and to seek out a fuller understanding of how the ancient world differs from their own. While they cannot physically enter Jerusalem in the time of King David, they can explore what it is like to live in a world without automobiles, electricity, and smartphones. Even though they may not experience being taken into exile after seeing their homes destroyed, they can be made aware through reading what prophets like Jeremiah had to say about these devastating times, and they can feel the pain of musicians who no longer can sing a song to Yahweh in the temple (Ps. 137). And when they read one of Jesus's parables, they can explore his use of agricultural metaphors and social situations and gain a better sense of what he meant by the "kingdom of heaven." With that said, I commend this book to your use, and I hope it succeeds in advancing your study of the Bible and its world.

Abbreviations

Old Testament/Hebrew Bible

Gen.	Genesis	Eccles.	Ecclesiastes
Exod.	Exodus	Song	Song of Songs/Canticles
Lev.	Leviticus	Isa.	Isaiah
Num.	Numbers	Jer.	Jeremiah
Deut.	Deuteronomy	Lam.	Lamentations
Josh.	Joshua	Ezek.	Ezekiel
Judg.	Judges	Dan.	Daniel
1–2 Sam.	1–2 Samuel	Mic.	Micah
1–2 Chron.	1–2 Chronicles	Hag.	Haggai
Neh.	Nehemiah	Zech.	Zechariah
Ps./Pss.	Psalm/Psalms	Mal.	Malachi
Prov.	Proverbs		

New Testament

Matt.	Matthew	1 Thess.	1 Thessalonians
Rom.	Romans	1 Tim.	1 Timothy
1–2 Cor.	1–2 Corinthians	Heb.	Hebrews
Gal.	Galatians	1 Pet.	1 Peter
Eph.	Ephesians	Rev.	Revelation
Col.	Colossians		

Deuterocanonical/Apocryphal Works

1 Esd.	1 Esdras
1–3 Macc.	1–3 Maccabees
Sir.	Sirach

Other Abbreviations

1QpHab	*Pesher Habakkuk* (Dead Sea Scrolls)
ANET	*Ancient Near Eastern Texts Relating to the Old Testament.* Edited by J. B. Pritchard. 3rd ed. Princeton: Princeton University Press, 1969.
Ant.	Josephus, *Jewish Antiquities*
Apion	Josephus, *Against Apion*
ARM	Archives royales de Mari
ARMT	Archives royales de Mari, transcrite et traduite
AUSS	*Andrews University Seminary Studies*
b.	Babylonian Talmud
BA	*Biblical Archaeologist* (now *Near Eastern Archaeology*)
BAR	*Biblical Archaeology Review*
BASOR	*Bulletin of the American Schools of Oriental Research*
B. Bat.	*Baba Batra*
BCE	Before the Common Era
BRev	*Bible Review*
BTB	*Biblical Theology Bulletin*
BZ	*Biblische Zeitschrift*
CE	Common Era
CH	Code of Hammurabi
Cor.	Tertullian, *De corona militis* (*The Crown*)
COS	*The Context of Scripture.* Edited by William W. Hallo and K. Lawson Younger Jr. 3 vols. Leiden: Brill, 1997–2002.
EA	El Amarna tablets
Eccl. Hist.	Eusebius, *Ecclesiastical History*
FEH	*Fides et Historia*
Git.	*Gittin*
Good Person	Philo, *That Every Good Person Is Free*
Hist.	Herodotus, *Histories*
IEJ	*Israel Exploration Journal*
JANES	*The Journal of the Ancient Near Eastern Society*
JBL	*Journal of Biblical Literature*

JSOT	*Journal for the Study of the Old Testament*
JSOTSup	Journal for the Study of the Old Testament: Supplement Series
J.W.	Josephus, *Jewish War*
KTU	*Die keilalphabetischen Texte aus Ugarit*
LCMAM	Roth, M. T. *Law Collections from Mesopotamia and Asia Minor*. 2nd ed. Atlanta: Scholars Press, 1997.
MAL	Middle Assyrian Law Code
NEA	*Near Eastern Archaeology* (formerly *Biblical Archaeologist*)
Opif.	Philo of Alexandria, *De opificio mundi* (*On the Creation of the World*)
OTP	Matthews, Victor H., and Don C. Benjamin. *Old Testament Parallels: Laws and Stories from the Ancient Near East*. 3rd ed. Mahwah, NJ: Paulist, 2006.
Pirqe R. El.	*Pirqe Rabbi Eliezer*
Quaest. rom.	Plutarch, *Quaestiones romanae et graecae* (*Roman and Greek Questions*)
Sat.	Juvenal, *Satires*
Satur.	Macrobius, *Saturnalia*
Spec.	Philo, *De specialibus legibus* (*On the Special Laws*)
Ta'an.	*Ta'anit*
TAD	Porten, Bezalel, and Ada Yardeni. *Textbook of Aramaic Documents from Ancient Egypt*. Winona Lake, IN: Eisenbrauns, 1996.
T. Reu.	*Testament of Reuben*
Vita Hadr.	Dio Cassius, *Vita Hadriani* (*Life of Hadrian*)
y.	Jerusalem Talmud

Introduction

One of the real joys of studying the Bible is reconstructing the manners and customs of the peoples of ancient times. The gulf of thousands of years that separates us from them can be bridged, at least in part, by garnering insights into their everyday life. What this requires, however, is a close examination of the biblical narratives and comparison of biblical data with written and physical remains from other ancient civilizations. Modern anthropological and sociological research and the discoveries and interpretations of archaeologists and art historians are also of prime importance in the reconstruction process.

Reconstructing Israel's Social World from Context

In attempting to recreate the social world of ancient Israel, scholars draw on several sources of information. Written records from this period include the biblical text and a host of extrabiblical documents that parallel but do not always corroborate the biblical narrative. Physical remains are limited to what has been uncovered by archaeologists. These remains—tomb paintings, garbage heaps, the ruins of conquered and/or abandoned cities, as well as less spectacular bits and pieces of someone's life that have almost miraculously survived the elements and the centuries—provide only a partial picture of life in ancient times. It is also possible to reconstruct a sense of the social setting from the biblical text and, by analogy, from the study of other ancient and modern cultures. To be sure, not every aspect of life is described in detail by these ancient sources. After all, the narratives are speaking to an ancient audience that understood the nuts and bolts of everyday existence, and they did not need to have these minutiae included in order to grasp the meaning of the story. In addition, there were individual tastes in clothing, diet, and even worship practices that differed from one tribe or nation to another, and it would simply be impossible to recover every detail due to our lack of information, physical evidence, or understanding.

It is fortunate, however, that many of ancient Israel's manners and customs persist over long periods of time. Modern anthropological methods of studying the social world of ancient Israel indicate that many of the traditions operative before the monarchic period (prior to 1000 BCE) continued into later periods of Israelite history. For example, tribal associations that sustained the ancestors carried over into the conquest and settlement periods when the text indicates that the tribes assisted one another in securing the land. Tribal affiliations continued to be significant as group identity markers throughout the monarchic period and sometimes were the source of dissent against the monarchy (see 1 Sam. 10:20–21 and 2 Sam. 20:1). Given the evidence of cultural continuity, it is possible, in many instances, to apply what we know about social customs employed in one era to another.

It becomes clear when reading the biblical text that it contains a wealth of information from many periods in Israel's history. Subjects range from civil and religious law to standard building codes and typical harvesting techniques. While not always satisfying the appetites for data of modern historians, the text does provide glimpses of such things as the proper procedure for dealing with a delinquent son and the requirements for purifying a priest after he comes in contact with a corpse. And given the fact that much of what is recorded is centered on ritual and worship practices, it is not surprising that so much attention is given to specifying the proper times, places, and procedures for performing sacrifices to God as well as injunctions regarding the slaughtering of animals.

While impressive in its quantity and breadth, the sheer amount of information contained here means that the student must be careful not to miss important social clues. As with any ancient text or modern technical treatise, confusion and data overload are real possibilities. Jargon associated with professional groups often requires additional explanation for the reader. For example, the word *selah* appears in thirty-nine of the Psalms and appears to be a technical term used in community worship or as a guide for religious professionals. Unfortunately, the meanings of some of these biblical terms are still mysteries that require further research and the careful use, when possible, of extrabiblical materials. For instance, the poetic texts found at the ancient seaport of Ugarit and composed between 1400 and 1200 BCE are similar in style and vocabulary to the Psalms and the epic sections of the biblical narrative. Comparative study of these texts has, in some cases, provided the key to understanding a word that has long remained obscure.

Occasionally the text includes the smallest and seemingly most insignificant details, monotonously reciting a series of genealogical "begats" or the dimensions of the pilasters and recesses of the temple (Ezek. 41). In other cases, however, the narrative may skip over the entire reign of a king, dismissing him with the phrase "he did what was evil in the sight of the Lord" (see 1 Kings 15:26). The narrator then summarizes the remainder of the king's life in the tantalizing footnote, "Now the rest of the acts of _____, and all that he did, are they not written in the Book of the Annals of the Kings of Judah?" (see 2 Kings 8:23). Allusions to this and other lost works, such as the "Book of Jashar" (2 Sam. 1:18), demonstrate that a great deal of information was available to the ancient writers that we will never be able to consult. These citations of lost works are a ready reminder that the received text is based on a heavily editorialized version of events from which to draw a picture of life in biblical times.

The book of Judges is another portion of the biblical text that appears to have had large segments of the narrative edited out, perhaps because the stories were so well known to contemporary readers. For the modern reader, however, the biblical account of the activities of the judges and other people of this time period leaves many questions unanswered. For example, why is this premonarchic society so violent and accepting of violence? Why do the judges have to rely on primitive weapons like ox goads and animal bones while their neighbors have swords, spears, and chariots? Why are political assassinations a cause for celebration (Judg. 3:12–30; 4:17–24)? Why is obedience to hospitality laws deemed more important than the life of a host's virgin daughter (Judg. 19)? Ultimately, modern readers need to be cautioned that the culture of ancient Israel was quite foreign to our own. Sometimes it is only through the use of comparative materials from nonbiblical sources, such as texts from Ugarit or the cities of Mesopotamia, that a better understanding of life in ancient times can be obtained.

Even then it is necessary to be cautious when using extrabiblical evidence. Each of these sources of information represents another culture's social perspective and therefore provides a slightly different picture of life in the biblical period than is found in the biblical text. An eagerness to draw conclusions from documents that offer some parallels to biblical narrative can therefore lead to wishful thinking and incorrect interpretations. For instance, the ancient letters from the Mesopotamian city of Nuzi (ca. sixteenth to fifteenth centuries BCE) describe family customs regarding marriage and the adoption of an heir. Superficially at least, these customs resemble those reflected in the stories told about Abraham, Isaac, and Jacob in Genesis. However, the Nuzi texts are legal documents that record private family matters and commercial transactions. They do not attest to a **covenant** with God or any concern to maintain the cultural purity of a chosen people, two prominent features of Genesis. Without more complete evidence, one must exercise caution when using parallel materials to explain or clarify the biblical narratives.

While it has its limitations, archaeological evidence provides some of the most illuminating information on everyday life in ancient times. When archaeologists apply scrupulous methods in their excavation of ancient city and village sites, data that can aid our understanding of ancient cultures slowly emerges from the ground. Such methods include the systematic recording of finds by means of photographs and written descriptions and the sharing of this material with a wide range of experts who can draw on their specialized fields of knowledge to extract more information from the finds than the archaeologist working alone. For instance, the carbonized remains found in storage jars and on excavated threshing floors, when examined by teams of microbiologists, botanists, and paleobotanists, can reveal aspects of the diet of these ancient people. Conclusions can also be drawn about their general level of health and hygiene, as well as their methods of agriculture and animal husbandry. Careful record keeping of archaeological excavations also allows future generations of scholars to return to the evidence and perhaps, using new technologies or the application of new knowledge gleaned from other archaeological sites, draw new conclusions.

At the same time, to expect archaeological discoveries to prove conclusively "the truth of the Bible" is unreasonable. The findings of archaeologists offer only mute evidence of ancient life and cannot be forced into alignment with the biblical narratives. In other words, to say, as John Garstang did in the 1930s, that a particular wall found in the excavations at Jericho was the one that fell to Joshua's trumpet blasts without examining all of the surrounding evidence (pottery, building styles, the relative depth of artifacts within the mound) is unjustified. Improved methods of excavation since his time have proven that even Garstang's identification of the stratigraphic level of

Joshua's Jericho was incorrect. While controversy exists about this site and many others, the general consensus is that archaeological research is merely one of many sources of data for the study of the Bible.

A more scientific approach to excavations requires that all finds must be interpreted in the context of the mound as a whole. Ancient cities are layered, with each level (**stratum**) representing a different phase in the life history of the site. Generally, objects found in lower strata in the mound can be assumed to be older than those found closer to the surface. Archaeologists use the artifacts recovered from these strata to establish a relative chronology of the various levels or strata.

However, some disruption of the strata does occur due to earthquake activity, the digging of refuge and storage pits, and the sinking of new foundations by later inhabitants at the site. Moreover, archaeologists can only determine the approximate age of these artifacts based on the strata in which they lie. To resolve the confusion of strata and to establish a fixed or absolute chronology for a city site, archaeologists study pottery types and other artifacts from each layer. They then compare these artifacts with finds from sites whose chronology is better understood. **Carbon 14** dating, as well as other scientific dating methods, aids in this process of constructing an absolute chronology by establishing the approximate age of organic remains (bones, wood, carbonized grain).

Furthermore, due to the limitations of time and funding, archaeologists seldom are able or even attempt to uncover an entire mound. They carefully map out squares for excavation or dig exploratory shafts in those portions of the mound that surveys or ground-penetrating radar have shown to contain the most important structures (temples, palaces, gates) or a representative selection of objects of interest.

Modern archaeological techniques do try to obtain a broader perspective on the entire mound, but it is unlikely that every shovelful of dirt will be turned or every object uncovered. The fact that many sites were excavated before more scientific methods were developed magnifies the difficulties of obtaining a complete occupational picture. A great deal of valuable information has been lost forever due to indiscriminate digging, and unfortunately many artifacts now lie without any record of their historical context on museum shelves or in storage. Because archaeology is a destructive process, each level must be recorded and then removed to get to the level below it, and what has been removed can never be replaced. As a result, we learn through archaeology some, but never all, of what there is to know about life in these ancient cities and villages. Thus responsible archaeologists today intentionally leave some portions of a mound untouched for later generations and their more advanced excavation methods.

To complete this cautionary survey of aids to the reconstruction of life in the biblical period, it is important to point to modern anthropological research. Until the beginning of the twentieth century, tribal peoples continued to live in the Near East in much the same way that their ancestors had thousands of years ago. Following the First World War, social patterns began to change, and a greater reliance on technology transformed society in the Middle East. Even so, anthropologists and ethnologists have been able to study tribal peoples in more remote regions who still engage in seasonal migration with their flocks and herds and, whenever possible, try to avoid the central government's efforts to sedentarize them. The mutual suspicion that led Abraham to deceive Abimelech (Gen. 20) is still evident in the relations between pastoral nomadic groups and sedentary peoples.

The student who engages in comparative work, however, needs to understand that no cultural parallel is likely to be totally exact. While some customs and traditions can remain unchanged for centuries, each successive group of people inhabiting the same area and practicing the same basic economy is going to be different in some way from its predecessors. Therefore it is necessary to qualify most statements made when comparing ancient and modern peoples.

Development of Biblical Literature

Understanding the history of the biblical text is also important in exploring the information it reveals concerning the manners and customs of biblical people. The text as we have it is a compilation of narratives, stories that most likely began as oral traditions passed from one generation to the next in a fluid oral rather than written form. In their final written forms, these stories represent not only early memories of Israel's past but also the political situations and religious claims of later editors. To fully appreciate the complexity of these traditions and texts spanning at least two thousand years, a reader must understand that each period of Israel's history was marked by different events and conditions. The work of the authors and editors and the perspective of their audiences are reflected in these texts. As a result, the sometimes grand, sometimes subtle variations in the pictures painted by different authors and editors speak to the concerns of many different generations. Ultimately, these writings are the products of writers and editors trying to make sense of their national history in the light of their beliefs about their national deity.

Historical Geography of Bible Lands

In preparation for moving on to the initial chapter in this survey of the social world of ancient Israel, it is first necessary to sketch out the geographical characteristics of the area that helped shape this ancient people. Ancient Israel lay in the midst of the so-called **Fertile Crescent**, which ranged from modern day Iraq and Iran in the east to the Nile Valley of Egypt in the west. It was the place of origin for the river valley cultures of Sumer, Babylon, and Assyria in Mesopotamia and the pharaoh-dominated, **theocratic** civilization of Egypt, both of which developed around 3000 BCE. Major cities with huge palace complexes and temples, as well as the large-scale bureaucracies and commercial activity needed to support them, are hallmarks of their achievements. Very early in their history the Egyptian and Mesopotamian city-states established trade contacts with neighboring regions, and succeeding periods saw a growth in these connections and in the competition for ultimate supremacy within the region by the superpower empires that eventually developed.

Given the arid character of the lands away from the Tigris-Euphrates river valley of Mesopotamia, direct travel east was hampered by the Arabian Desert, and overland trade routes by necessity followed the coast of Phoenicia and Canaan south to Egypt. The Egyptians employed ships north along the Mediterranean coast, especially to obtain the cedar trees from the Mountains of Lebanon. They also sailed a southern route down the Red Sea allowing them to touch various points along the Arabian Peninsula to obtain spices, fragrances (frankincense and myrrh), and the indigo dyes produced in India. For most of the biblical period (post-2000 BCE), the Mediterranean maritime trade routes were controlled by middleman states such as Byblos, Ugarit, and the Phoenician coastal city states of Tyre and Sidon.

All of these geographical factors contributed to making the area of Canaan inhabited by the Israelites a crossroads and a battleground for the superpowers and their allies/vassal states. Two major highways are worth noting. The Via Maris ("coastal road") stretched from Syria eastward and cut through the Jezreel Valley in northern Canaan. The King's Highway in Transjordan extended from north to south and connected the thriving population centers of Ammon, Moab, and Edom with the Gulf of Aqaba. Both trade routes helped to promote commercial travel between regions. Living on the road between empires, ancient Israel became both a beneficiary and a victim of its geographical location.

Although Israel proper is a relatively small land (250 miles long and 60 miles wide at its broadest point), several spectacular geographical features dominate the terrain and affect the people who live there. Starting from the west, ancient Israel had excellent sandy beaches but no deep-water harbors. This prevented large-scale sea trade and made the region more dependent on the ships and merchants of Phoenicia. Immediately inland from the coast, however, is a plain that gradually merges with a plateau region to the east known as the **Shephelah** ("lowland"). Settlement was relatively heavy in this area (especially after the arrival of the Philistines after 1200 BCE), and the Via Maris ran along the coast, bringing trade as well as the armies of conquering nations.

Paralleling the Jordan River valley and bisecting the country north and south is the central hill country. While it is not a precipitous range of hills, the swift plunge eastward into the Jordan Rift (an area known as the "slopes") causes a spectacular drop in elevation. Jerusalem and Jericho serve as one example of the differences in elevation that occur within a relatively short distance in this region. Lying in the southern portion of the hill country, Jerusalem's elevation is over 2,500 feet above sea level. However, Jericho, just fifteen miles to the east and near the Dead Sea in an oasis near the Jordan River, is 840 feet below sea level. Such massive shifts in the earth's surface make travel difficult and tend to cut off direct communication and cultural interaction. There were, of course, circuitous routes through the hill country following the curve of valleys, and these, like the Valley of Elah (1 Sam. 17:1–2), had their strategic and commercial value.

Three distinctive areas further divide the central hill country. In the north, the Galilee region enjoys the advantages of having the highest annual rainfall and the most fertile soil. The central portion of the hill country, once called Samaria, with its important population centers at Megiddo, Shechem, and Bethel, supports wheat farming along with fruit and olive orchards on its terraced hillsides. The southernmost section of the hill country, known as Judea, is dominated by the city of Jerusalem. At one time, irrigation farming was common here as well as terraced agriculture on the slopes of the hills. Further south is the most uncertain and fragile environment in ancient Israel, with low annual rainfall in the areas bordering on this wilderness and in the Negeb Desert.

The heart of the Canaanite landscape is dominated by the Jordan Rift, part of a massive fissure in the earth that runs from the Lebanon Mountains in the north southward into Africa. Within Israel, the rift contains the Jordan River valley. The river winds south along its course toward the Dead Sea, providing water for crops and livestock (mostly sheep and goats). The further south the Jordan flows, the more saline it becomes, thereby contributing to the country's agricultural division, with wheat being planted in the north and more salt-resistant barley being grown in the south. What little water does finally reach the Dead Sea (1,275 feet below sea level) is so clogged with brine that plant life along its banks is limited to poplars and tamarisk trees.

Because of the dramatic geological character of the central hill range and the Jordan Rift, the climate of ancient Israel is also influenced by a north-south pattern. Temperatures follow a basic Mediterranean range, though snow does fall on the peaks of the mountains and occasionally in Jerusalem. Average annual rainfall (concentrated in the months from November to March) ranges from as much as forty-five inches in the Upper Galilee region to eight inches in the Negeb Desert around Beer-sheba and Arad. There are years when these southern areas have no rainfall at all. Rainfall also declines from west to east since the hill country blocks the path of storms moving in from the Mediterranean. The result is an extremely arid region known as the Judean wilderness, where rain may not come for years. Its remarkable barrenness has made it a metaphor in the biblical text for pain, trial, and death (Ps. 78:17–20; Mark 1:13; Heb. 3:17). The southern portion of the Transjordanian plateau, east of the Jordan River, also tends to be semi-arid, especially in the regions associated with the kingdoms of Edom and southern Moab.

Transjordan, located on the east side of the Jordan River, contained several kingdoms that had dealings with the Israelites. Running from north to south, they were Bashan, Gilead, Ammon, Moab, and Edom. In some periods they were adversaries of the Israelite tribes, while in others they were vassal states of Israel or its enemies (see 2 Kings 3). These kingdoms were also a part of the Jordanian ecosystem, drawing water from the river and its tributaries and sharing in its climatic shifts. A major trade route, the King's Highway, ran from the Gulf of Aqaba northward through Transjordan, linking the area with Syria and Mesopotamia.

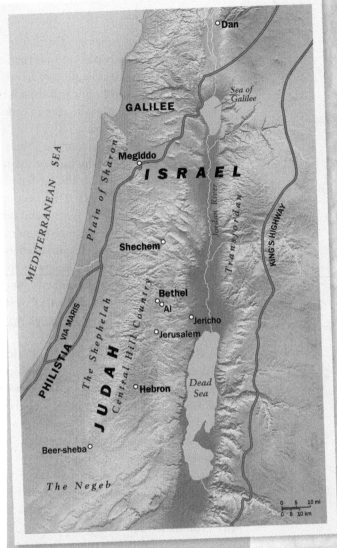

Geography of Ancient Israel
(International Mapping)

Each of the regions and geographical features described above figured into the development of the various cultures that inhabited the regions of Canaan that eventually became the kingdom of Israel. They will be referred to repeatedly in the text of this volume, and thus it is advisable to become familiar with them and their place on the map in order to understand the history and social world of the Israelites.

It is also important to note that the names assigned to the land in question change from one period of history to the next. The land originally called Canaan becomes Israel during the settlement and early monarchic periods. When the monarchy divides, the land becomes Israel and Judah. During the exilic period, the land under Assyrian and Babylonian rule was again divided and renamed Judah, Samaria, and Megiddo. These names, which change yet again under Persian, Hellenistic, and Roman rule, reflect the various political entities that governed the land during its long history. There are other geographical names, such as the **Levant** (the lands from modern Turkey to Egypt that border the Mediterranean Sea), Palestine, and Syria-Palestine, which designate areas of the land regardless of which political entities govern them at any given time.

In modern times, the names Israel and Palestine are associated with a violent and prolonged conflict over land ownership. As a result, care must be taken when applying these names to different areas of the land as it is currently divided. For example, some modern Israelis reject the name Palestine when it is applied to any portion of the land. Conversely, some modern Palestinians deny use of the name Israel to identify the land on which they live. Sensitivity should also be used when applying the names Israel and Palestine when speaking about the land in ancient times. In this textbook, the term *Israel* will be used in three ways: (1) to designate the particular group of people who settled in the land of Canaan; (2) as a label for the independent political entity established by these people; and (3) as an indicator of the land on which this group lived. The terms *Palestine* and *Syria-Palestine* will be used as geographical terms, designating the land that Israel, as well as other peoples, occupied during various periods.

In speaking about the people of Israel, it is necessary to distinguish between the terms *Israelite*, *Israeli*, and *Jew*. The first term, Israelite, designates the ancient peoples that made up the nations of Israel and Judah and who worshiped the national God, Yahweh. The second, Israeli, is the name given to modern inhabitants of the State of Israel. The third term, Jew, is used today to speak of someone who believes in and practices Judaism. In antiquity, however, the term had a series of meanings that changed over time. Before the second century BCE, the term applied to the ethnic group that inhabited the land of Judah—in other words, to a Judean (*Ant.* 11.5.173). In the mid-second century, the term began to be applied to those who did not necessarily have an ethnic or geographic connection to Judah but who believed in the God of the Judeans, Yahweh (2 Macc. 9:13; *Ant.* 20.2.38–39). This definition developed into the one used today.

Approach of This Book

This textbook is designed to assist students to more effectively read the Bible with the social world of ancient Israel in mind. In that way not only will the text come alive with the everyday activities of the characters but it will also be a further encouragement to read its stories, legal pronouncements, poems, songs, and wisdom admonitions with an eye for detail. Too often modern readers think they know what the text says without realizing that it is a product of another place and another time. That attitude is referred to by scholars as an **etic** perspective—one that applies an "outsider" viewpoint and makes little effort to be objective. What I hope will happen after you have worked with this textbook is that you will strive for an **emic** perspective—one that attempts to understand the "insider" viewpoint of the editors and storytellers who produced the biblical text. In that way, setting aside our own modern perspective as much as possible, the Bible can speak more clearly and give us a chance to look behind the text and examine the social scenery.

The biblical text is in fact a storehouse of very useful information. It can answer a variety of questions: What did they eat? What did they wear? How did they bury their dead? What forms of worship did they practice? However, it does take some delving into the stories to draw out the data it contains. And you might ask why you have to go to all this trouble. *Surely*, you might think, *I can learn all I need to know about the world of ancient Israel by just reading the text.* My answer would be that the desire to read the biblical narratives is a good first start. It is, however, not enough. If you truly wish to obtain a better understanding of the biblical world and the covenantal relationship that stands at the heart of ancient Israel's origins and identity, then you will have to dig deeper.

When you begin a study of a place and its people, the place to start is the physical and social environment in which they lived. That means that we will have to ask about the physical, economic, and social demands placed on them by geography, climate, natural resources, and their neighbors. Since there is a tendency for peoples to borrow from each other, creating a sort of cultural stew, it will be necessary in our studies to trace what may be Egyptian, Mesopotamian, Canaanite, or even Philistine about the ancient Israelites. At that point it will be possible, at least in part, to establish what was unique about Israelite culture and how they developed as a people distinct from the other nations. Of course, societies evolve over time, and therefore the answers that apply to one period of Israelite history may well change in another period. Israel did change its social attitude and customs over the two millennia of its existence before the Common Era, and thus the chapters in this volume will attempt to lay out the characteristics of the Israelites in each successive time period.

While this volume is intended for students, it should also prove useful to laypersons, clergy, and scholars in their study of the Bible. The biblical material is presented in chronological order, with chapters on each of the major periods of biblical history: ancestral, settlement, monarchic, postexilic, Hellenistic/intertestamental, and New Testament. This arrangement allows for the examination of the biblical peoples according to stages in their social development, starting with the pastoral nomadic, stateless culture of the ancestors and concluding with the subjugated, urban-based culture of Judea and Samaria in Roman times.

Each chapter provides a basic introduction to the historical and physical settings of the time period and sketches the basic elements of its social world. Specific scenes in the biblical text will be used to reveal details about everyday life in biblical times. Following the historical sketch are selected units dealing with specific social customs associated with that time period. These are divided into subheadings using examples from the biblical text, modern anthropological and sociological studies, and archaeology.

Additional aids designed to assist students include sidebars that provide extra information about the social world of the Bible, insights from other ancient Near Eastern cultures, and information about the sources of the various extrabiblical texts cited throughout the volume. There is also a set of questions designed to spark class discussion at the end of each chapter. Standard features are a glossary of terms highlighted in bold text, a select bibliography, and indexes of subjects, personal names, place names, and Scripture and extrabiblical sources. The table of contents lists the major units and comparative materials found in each chapter to aid you in finding material more quickly. Since footnotes and citations other than to the Bible or certain extrabiblical texts have been omitted, an annotated bibliography of sources is included as well as suggested additional readings.

Since this volume is not intended to be exhaustive, it will not contain explanations or discussion of every piece of information found in the biblical narratives. Instead, material has been selected to give as clear a picture of everyday events as possible while avoiding repetition. There is, however, a conscious effort to provide as much comparative evidence from other ancient

Near Eastern cultures as possible to demonstrate that ancient Israel did not exist in a social vacuum.

Discussing Aspects of Everyday Life in Ancient Israel

In addition to personal study and interaction with instructors, it is essential that students of the world of ancient Israel talk among themselves about the information they have encountered. With that in mind, I have provided below a set of terms and suggested discussion questions that will hopefully bring these ancient people to life as new ideas and perspectives are raised by the group.

Ancient Israel as presented in the biblical text, in extrabiblical documents from other ancient Near Eastern cultures, and through archaeological discoveries is only a partial picture. It is dependent upon what the biblical writers choose to include in their narratives, the purposes of ancient scribes who mention Israel in their political and economic documents, and the bits and pieces of ancient artifacts and architecture that emerge from archaeological surveys and excavations. As a result, the discussion questions listed at the end of each chapter in this volume ask you to consider larger issues rather than simply repeat what you find in the text.

Of course, there are some concrete items like ceramic remains, building foundations, ancient inscriptions, and the **stratigraphy** of **tells** that we can point to as evidence of occupation and the physical existence of inhabitants of particular places. It is exciting to be a part of an archaeological team that is carefully stripping away the layers of time that have hidden these artifacts. Still, care must be taken not to apply "wishful thinking" to our interpretations. It is best to simply say we have found an artifact whose purpose appears to be "such and such" rather than to immediately tie it to a specific biblical story and say it "proves" the truth of the Bible.

What I have attempted to do in this book is provide a means of linking what we know of the history of the ancient Near East with information on historical geography, archaeological data, and biblical references to life in ancient Israel. Sometimes these links are quite strong, and sometimes they are only speculation. Ultimately, what we know about ancient Israel is constantly evolving. New information appears every year, and new ways of interpreting this data are being developed. As a result, the answers to the questions listed below may well change, and that is something to look forward to rather than dread. There is a great deal that the Bible can tell us about the human spirit and the struggle to survive in a difficult geographic and political environment. It is therefore worth the effort to continue to explore its many facets and to look forward to what it may be able to tell us about the ancient world and ourselves.

Discussion Questions

1. What ancient resources are available to assist with the study of the biblical text?
2. What role does archaeological evidence play in reconstructing the social world of ancient Israel?
3. In what ways do physical geography and climate impact the economic and social development of a particular region?
4. How was ancient Israel impacted by its contacts with Egypt and Mesopotamia?
5. What is the difference between an emic and an etic perspective, and how does this affect the interpretation of the Bible?

Ancestral Period 1

Historical Introduction

The ancestral stories in the book of Genesis provide a legal and social foundation for much of the rest of the biblical narrative. It is important, for instance, to have a story that explains where the people came from and why they had a claim to the "promised land" that supersedes the claims of the Canaanites who occupied that territory before the arrival of Abram and his family. At the same time, it is important to explain why certain places become integral to Israel's history. The narratives draw on collective memory contained in a host of stories that were edited into their current form. These stories are not intended to serve as a history of the time period when Abram and his descendants first settled in Canaan. Instead they provide the basis for theological and traditional precedents that guide the Israelites in later periods.

In the book of Genesis, Abraham and the other ancestral figures are portrayed as pastoral nomads who travel from northwestern Mesopotamia

Precedents in the Ancestral Narratives

1. *God's covenant promise.* A conditional contract is established with Abram to receive land and children in exchange for obedience to God's command and exclusive worship of Yahweh.
2. *Altars built in Canaan.* They provide an introduction of Yahweh worship and a physical "stake" in claiming the promised land.
3. *Significant places.* Repeated visits to Shechem, Bethel, Hebron, and Beer-sheba mark them as geographic centers of importance.
4. *Circumcision becomes a mark of membership.* While not unique to the Israelites, it is sufficiently unusual (compare the "uncircumcised" Philistines) to serve that purpose.
5. *Bargaining is possible with God.* Abraham does this over the fate of Sodom (Gen. 18), and Jacob negotiates with God over becoming heir of the covenant (Gen. 28).
6. *Endogamy.* At least for the first three generations, it was important to only marry within the designated group.

Anachronisms in the Ancestral Narratives

Camels were first domesticated in the Arabian peninsula and would have been unusual among pastoral nomadic groups in Canaan prior to the thirteenth century BCE (see Gen. 12:14–16; 24:10–67; 31:17–35; 37:25).
Philistines did not arrive in Canaan until after the 1200 BCE invasion of the Near East by the Sea Peoples (see Gen. 21:34; 26:1, 8, 18).
Reference to city of Dan (Gen. 14:14) reflects the later name for a city originally known as Laish (Judg. 18:27–29).

(Haran) southwest into Canaan by way of Damascus. From there they take their flocks and families west into Egypt on two occasions, settling in the third generation in the Nile Delta region (Goshen) after Joseph obtains a royal bequest from the pharaoh. Along the way they engage in the normal pursuits of pastoral nomadic peoples, seeking pasture for their sheep and goats and interacting with the settled population. The efforts of historians and the excavations of archaeologists have yet to provide incontrovertible evidence for the historical reality of the ancestors. As a result some scholars argue that the narratives are literary recreations of tribal history compiled by scribes or priests during the monarchic or the postexilic period to provide the nation of Israel with a claim to Canaan and an origin story. According to this view, the ancestors were either folk heroes or composite characters based on the exploits of many different tribal leaders from the nation's past.

While the memories of this period are hazy, the episodes in the ancestral narratives are appealing to readers for their human interest value. They contain quite convincing and poignant descriptions of itinerant herders and their families. The attention to detail and the importance attached to certain social customs suggest that this material is more than a literary attempt to recreate an ancient era. There simply is no point in making up forms of social interaction, especially if your original audience is very familiar with tribal groups and basic family dynamics. Certainly the text does contain some **anachronisms** (elements that fit into a different time period than that of the story), and the evidence of later editing of the text is clear in many places. Nevertheless, the narratives give the overwhelming impression of a time when the ancestors of the Hebrews were new to the land and still dependent on the household and the tribe, not the nation, for their identity.

The exact dates of the ancestral period are still uncertain since we lack extrabiblical confirmation of the characters or events in Genesis. Ancient cuneiform tablets found at the northern Mesopotamian city of Mari and dated to the eighteenth century BCE do contain descriptions of tribal groups

Figure 1.1. King Hammurabi

whose activities and interactions with the urban community are surprisingly similar to those of the biblical ancestors. Of course, similar environmental and economic conditions among tribal people are likely to foster similar herding strategies and interactions with local officials. We can certainly posit that the pastoral nomadic tribes in the Mari letters operated in a similar manner, and that can assist with an examination of the setting for the ancestral narratives. Still, the use of parallel information and historical events such as those found in the Mari documents must be employed with care when drawing conclusions about the Bible. If it were possible to provide a likely time period for the ancestors, however, the turbulent centuries of the early second millennium could be a good choice.

In terms of the history of the eighteenth and seventeenth centuries BCE, it was a time of flux and transformation for the cultures of Mesopotamia. Under the leadership of King Hammurabi and his successors, Babylon conquered all of the city-states and kingdoms in the region. The kings of Babylon subjected the inhabitants of the entire Tigris-Euphrates valley to centralized rule and imposed both the benefits and the constraints of Babylonian law and administration. After 1600 BCE, the Babylonian Empire went into decline and was eventually replaced by a group of smaller states, including the Kassites in the south and the Mitanni in north-central Mesopotamia.

During the period between 2000 and 1800 BCE, Egypt also experienced internal disorder. This situation is demonstrated in the epic narrative of Sinuhe, a political refugee who fled to Canaan in order to escape being implicated in the murder of a pharaoh (*OTP*, 137–41). His joy, when he is eventually allowed to return to Egypt, is marked by a change of clothing (much like Joseph in Gen. 41:42–43) and the discarding of his "desert clothes." A further sign of political unrest in the eighteenth century BCE occurs when the **Hyksos** raiders invaded the ancient kingdom. As new leaders were installed, Egypt had little time to deal with its political and economic contacts in Canaan. The foreign invaders set themselves up as pharaohs at Avaris, their Delta region capital. Archaeological and textual evidence suggest that these foreign rulers were of Asiatic, and more specifically Western Semitic or Amorite, origin. Discovery of scarabs (images of the dung beetle that had inscriptions carved into their flat side), amulets, and other Egyptian merchandise found at Jericho, Megiddo, and other major sites in Canaan indicate active trade between the Hyksos and the Levant during this period. Some see this political shake-up as an opportune time for Joseph and his brothers to move into the area of Goshen (Gen. 46:1–47:12), also in the Nile Delta, but again we lack Egyptian sources to confirm this possibility.

> I was also given robes of purest linen, myrrh, and the scents used by Pharaoh and his court. I had slaves to perform my every wish. (*OTP*, 141)

During the time when Babylon's kings built and lost an empire in Mesopotamia, and Egypt suffered internal problems, the peoples of Canaan enjoyed relative freedom. The freedom to develop on their own continued until the rise of the New Kingdom in Egypt (sixteenth century BCE), when its aggressive pharaohs defeated the Hyksos rulers and attempted to restore their extended control over Canaan. Taken in the context of the biblical narrative, it is interesting to see that Abraham's household is able to enter and spend extended periods of time in Canaan without reference to an Egyptian presence there. If this was indeed the period associated with Israel's ancestors, then they took advantage of new opportunities for building a life in other lands distant from the conflicts in Mesopotamia and later in a region of Egypt controlled by foreign rulers.

Regardless of the degree of historicity of the ancestral narratives, the aspects of the basic economy and social life of pastoral nomadic peoples in the ancient Near East can be studied using these stories of Abraham and his descendants. Individual aspects of existence will be highlighted below, and special regard will be given to the literary construction of the narratives, archaeological discoveries, and any parallel written materials available from Mesopotamia and Egypt.

Physical Appearance and Fashion

The ancestors and their families were Semites, the dominant ethnic group in Mesopotamia and much of Syria and Canaan. There is a family of languages associated with these peoples divided into east and west Semitic, with distinctive dialectical differences but the same basic structure. Semites in the ancient Near East had black hair and a dark complexion burned even darker by the sun (Lam. 5:10). Since there are few biblical descriptions of individuals' features, the examination of burial remains and of a few surviving paintings, such as those found in the nineteenth-century BCE Egyptian tomb at Beni-Hasan, provides us with this picture. Dwellings with low roofs that stood not much more than five feet above the floor suggest that Semites were short in stature (compare the emphasis given to Saul's unusual height in 1 Sam. 9:2). Most ate meat only on festive occasions (see Gen. 18:7), and diets primarily made up of grains and goat milk contributed to their shorter sizes.

Based on what is seen in palace art and figurines, Mesopotamian men generally wore full beards that were carefully curled and squared off at the bottom. However, the West Semites of Canaan that are portrayed in both the Egyptian Beni-Hasan painting and the carved figures on the Assyrian "Black Obelisk" of Shalmaneser III (841 BCE) have short, pointed beards. These differences may be stylized artistic representations designed to distinguish between peoples. Hair was often worn shoulder length with a band of cloth or beads to hold it in place. Women's coiffures tended to be fairly simple. Their long hair was sometimes bound up with beaded ropes or intertwined with combs of bone, gold, or silver. On the road or in the pastoral encampment, however, such attention to fashion would not be possible or desirable.

In portions of Mesopotamia and other regions where the climate was extremely dry, the complexion could be easily damaged. As a result, meticulous attention was given to skin care. Both men and women regularly oiled their skin and hair (Pss. 92:10; 104:15). This gave the body a glossy appearance and also helped kill hair lice and other parasites.

By necessity, the clothing of pastoralists was primarily functional, though it was not that much different from the clothing worn by artisans and other commoners. This fashion stands in contrast to the nonfunctional, long-sleeved garment that Jacob gives to Joseph as an indication that his favorite son would not have to work with the herds (Gen. 37:3). Sturdy leather sandals protected

Figure 1.2. Semites pictured in a painting found
in the nineteenth-century BCE Egyptian tomb at Beni-Hasan

the feet of both sexes. They enclosed the heel and were fastened to the ankle by a thong that passed between the first and second toes (Gen. 14:23).

Throughout the biblical period, men wore the *kethoneth*, a knee-length wool tunic with half sleeves. This was bound at the waist with a belt. A cloak or mantle (*simlah*) was also worn as protection against the sun and during storms. In the exodus account it was used to carry bread dough and kneading bowls (Exod. 12:34). A girdle (*ezor*), or loincloth, was also worn in later periods (Jer. 13:2; Job 12:18). Women wore a similar tunic and robe that concealed the figure, although some representations in art (as in the Beni-Hasan tomb paintings) portray them with the right shoulder bare. It was customary for both males and females who were in mourning to wear sackcloth (Gen. 37:34; 2 Sam. 21:10).

Clothing not only distinguished genders but also functioned as a social marker indicating a change in status. For example, Judah's daughter-in-law Tamar wears "widow's garments" (possibly black robes). When in Genesis 38:14 she removed her widow's garb, donned normal clothing, and wore a veil, she was able to disguise herself as a harlot and fool Judah. Some scholars look to the practice of the sacred prostitutes of the Canaanite goddess Asherah, who wore veils as part of their sacred costume, as the basis for interpreting Tamar's action (2 Kings 23:7). Perhaps Hebrew women in the ancestral period generally went unveiled, and therefore Tamar was following Canaanite custom when she played the role of a veiled harlot. The issue is clouded somewhat by the action of Rebekah in Genesis 24:65. In this passage she dons her veil in expectation of meeting her future husband, Isaac, for the first time. Her act of modesty is more in line with Mesopotamian custom. This is reinforced by the Middle Assyrian law code dated to ca. 1100 BCE that required harlots to appear unveiled in public on pain of death (#40; *ANET*, 183). Ultimately, location "on the road to Timnah" and the fact that Tamar is unaccompanied may be more important to the story line than her veil.

Jewelry, then as now, was a common adornment for both men and women and also served as a visual sign of wealth. In Genesis 24:47, 53, Abraham's servant gives Rebekah a nose ring and arm bracelets as well as unspecified ornaments of gold and silver as bridal presents. Joseph, rising to his position as advisor to the pharaoh, was given a gold chain to wear around his neck and a signet ring as a symbol of his power and authority (Gen. 41:42). After the escape from Egypt, Aaron fashioned a golden calf for the people out of their earrings (Exod. 32:2–3).

Cultural Issues Faced by Immigrants

The ancestors first appear in Genesis as inhabitants of Ur of the Chaldees in southern Mesopotamia. The designation "Chaldees" is an example of an anachronism since the Chaldean people do not appear in Mesopotamian history until after 1000 BCE. Abraham, or Abram as he is originally known, and his father Terah plan a move to Canaan, but they stop in Haran, a city that is located on the Balikh River, which flows into the upper reaches of the Euphrates in what is today northeastern Syria. There they settle for a while, and Terah dies (Gen. 11:30–32). Since his origins were in Mesopotamia, that would have been the foundation of Abram's cultural heritage. During this period of his life, he undoubtedly worshiped Mesopotamian gods (see Josh. 24:14), and he would have been as familiar with Mesopotamian law and social customs as any other person of the time.

Questions Not Answered by the Biblical Narrative

Modern readers and scholars have raised a number of questions about the story of the ancestors. There are many details that do not appear in the story that would be helpful. However, since the focus of the stories is primarily theological and concerned with the inheritance of the covenant promise, mundane facts were not of prime importance to storytellers and editors.

- Is there some importance attached to having Ur of the Chaldees as the original home of Abram and his family?
- Why did Terah take his household north up the Euphrates to Haran?
- What was the political and social situation in Mesopotamia at that time, and, of course, who were the major political figures?
- Why does the biblical narrative not describe the journey from Haran to Shechem in Canaan?
- Why does Abram stop at Shechem first rather than any other city in Canaan?
- Why does the storyteller not include the name of the pharaoh?

Abram's household faces a new challenge, however, when he is directed by God to lead them away from Haran and immigrate to Canaan (Gen. 12:1–4). From this point on, they are portrayed in the text as moving from campsite to campsite and from pasture to pasture while living in goat-hair tents. According to the biblical narrative, Abram has once again left a place that had become his home, but this time he emigrates for theological reasons—God instructs him to go to a land that he will show him. Sometime later, when Abram has demonstrated his obedience, the change of his name from "Abram" to "Abraham" (Gen. 17:5) emphasizes his new status and his allegiance to the covenant with his God. On a social level, when Abram departs Haran, he and his household have to embrace the basic psychology of being an immigrant, a stranger in a foreign land. That in turn will affect nearly all of his and the other ancestors' actions during this period of Israel's history.

The journey to Canaan would have covered several hundred miles. Abraham's route, although not described in the biblical text, probably followed the international trade highway from Mesopotamia, through Damascus and Hazor, and eventually down the coast of Canaan to Egypt. The southern coastal portion of this route was known as the Via Maris or "Way of the Sea."

In preparing for his trek, a major refitting would have been necessary to equip his group for survival as they journeyed to the new land. What was required of Abram and his family was an adjustment of lifestyle from a settled, urban existence to the frequent and often meandering travels of pastoral nomads. Their new world would have consisted of setting up encampments, seeking out water sources and sometimes negotiating for their use, taking their animals to grazing areas both along their route and sometimes a distance away, and dealing with encounters with local villagers that could often be quite tense or hostile. As a result, they would have had to accommodate to a change in perspective about themselves and the peoples with whom they came in contact. That would have included a shift from being part of the group in a well-known locale to being outsiders, strangers in an alien land (Gen. 23:4).

Undoubtedly, there would have been language problems, although they are rarely mentioned in the narratives. Dialectical and inflectional differences in the pronunciation of words, even among Semitic languages, would have required some adjustments. In one instance (Gen. 42:23), Joseph spoke with his brothers through an Egyptian interpreter. But that was simply part of Joseph's disguise, and Egyptian would have sounded very different to their ears. Even when the newcomers had learned the local dialect, their accent would have marked them as strangers.

Over the years, they would have had to depend upon their own skills as herdsmen and on the produce of their flocks and herds. Life would have been dominated by the search for forage and water for sheep and goats and by the attempt to draw as little hostile attention to their group as possible. Abraham's ability to act as an intermediary with the local chieftains and village elders was therefore essential to gaining a measure of acceptance for his household in this new land (see Gen. 21:22–34).

The process of walking a social and economic tightrope caused some tensions between Abraham's immigrant group and the settled communities. A new household and its herds would place additional strain on the natural resources of the land. As a result, the attempt by immigrants to acclimate themselves to the new social and economic environment required a willingness to operate within the rules set by the people who already lived there. This social reality could well explain why so much attention is given in the biblical text to negotiations between the ancestors and the local leaders (see Gen. 23 and 26).

Another difficulty faced by every immigrant group is fitting into the legal patterns of the host group. Immigrants are seldom familiar with the laws of the land, and they are often denied the legal protection guaranteed to citizens (Gen. 19:9). This can lead to the use of deception as a defense mechanism. Assuming that survival of the group took priority over providing a potential enemy with all the facts, the morality of such a deception must not have presented much of a problem for the ancestors. As a result there are several trickster stories contained in the ancestral narratives.

Wife-Sister Stratagem

Among the most entertaining of these trickster narratives is the story of Abram's use of the wife-sister stratagem. Shortly after their arrival in Canaan, Abraham and Sarah (still bearing the names Abram and Sarai at that point in the narrative) are forced to go to Egypt to escape a famine (Gen. 12:10). This aspect of the story fits well with the ecologically fragile nature of ancient Canaan, which often was plagued with drought and then with famine. Since Abraham's household had only recently arrived in Canaan, it would be difficult to obtain food from the economically stressed local inhabitants. This meant a further trek to Egypt, where traditional wisdom indicated that food could be purchased and that transients were tolerated and occasionally used as temporary sources of cheap labor. Egyptian texts do mention "Asiatics" (*'amu*), who arrive either as prisoners of war who are sold into Egyptian slavery, or as refugees who may eventually assimilate into Egyptian society or return to their own lands.

The story of Abram's sortie into Egypt is marked by distrust and fear of the powerful Egyptians. The comic nature of the story is found in Abram's easy deception of the god-king pharaoh (unfortunately unnamed) and by Yahweh's triumph over the gods of Egypt. As Abram's household enters

Egypt, the patriarch fears that his beautiful wife Sarai may be taken from him and added to the pharaoh's harem. He is also afraid that the Egyptian king may consider killing him as a means of possessing her. Therefore Abraham devises a scheme in which Sarah claims to be his sister instead of his wife (Gen. 20:12 indicates that she is the daughter of his father but not his mother). This strategy removes him from personal danger, and when she is taken into the pharaoh's harem, it results in the enrichment of Abram's household (12:16).

Thus while the story has as an underlying theme a contest between the god-king of Egypt and Abram's God, Yahweh, it also contains elements of immigrant psychology, which always cautions them to be wary of the local people and their leaders. This attitude is also seen in the other two examples of the wife-sister motif (Gen. 20 and 26). In each of these instances, the threatening authority figure is Abimelech of Gerar. As in the Egyptian example, Abimelech is taken in by the deception. As a result, the trickster adds significantly to the household and herds (first Abraham and later Isaac), and, like the pharaoh in Genesis 12, Abimelech eventually returns the patriarch's wife unharmed after God intervenes. Clearly, the Israelite audience would have enjoyed the joke at the expense of their powerful neighbors and would have rejoiced at the demonstration of Yahweh's power.

The Purchase of Machpelah

One of the characteristics of trickster stories is that the trickster finds himself being tricked. That seems to be the case in the episode in which Abraham seeks to obtain a burial site for his wife Sarah. His household had been encamped "by the oaks of Mamre" near Hebron, and he had constructed one of his altars to Yahweh at this site (Gen. 13:18; 14:13). Repeated association with place therefore plays into both the story and the later importance of both the Cave of Machpelah and Hebron in later Israelite history. Again, as an immigrant, Abraham is constrained to obey the legal traditions of the people of Canaan. Thus when he attempts to purchase the cave of Machpelah, he has to go to the nearby city of Hebron and engage in customary procedures, all of which favor the settled community over newly arrived immigrants. First he goes to the city elders, presumably at the gate where much of the city's business and legal activities are conducted (see Gen. 23:3–10). Here he requests the elders to serve as witnesses and as advocates for him (a noncitizen) in his attempt to purchase the cave.

The owner, Ephron the Hittite, and Abraham engage in a legal dialogue, bargaining over the price and the exact parcel to be purchased. Abraham originally only wanted the cave, but since his need is pressing, he eventually is also forced to pay for an adjoining field and its trees.

The dialogue is interesting and almost comical. Ephron first offers the cave to Abraham as a gift. This haggling gambit is designed to force the buyer into being equally gracious by instructing the owner to set his own price. Once this happens, all that remains is for Abraham to count out the asking price of four hundred shekels of silver, an exorbitantly high amount (compared to Jacob's purchase of land in Gen. 33:19), and to have the transaction duly witnessed by the elders.

Two pieces of information regarding this purchase are worth noting. To begin with, this is the first piece of land owned outright by a Hebrew. God had promised the land of Canaan to Abraham and his descendants, but now the patriarch has obtained official title to a legally defined portion of it. This precedent-setting claim is then extended in later periods to the entire region of Canaan. Second, it is rather unusual for land to be sold outright in this manner to someone who lacks a kinship tie to the owner. Land was considered sacred, entrusted by a god or gods to the ruler, and he in turn entrusted it to individuals. In some cases its sale could even be considered a crime against the heirs of the owner (see Naboth's reaction to King Ahab's request to purchase his vineyard during the monarchic period in 1 Kings 21:3). One way in which this customary restriction was sometimes avoided is found in the fifteenth-century BCE *ţuppi mārūti* texts from the eastern Mesopotamian city of Nuzi. The purchaser could be adopted into the family of the owner, a legal fiction sometimes made necessary by the financial need of the land owner.

That Ephron is willing to make this sale may be due to the fact that Abraham specifically wishes to use it for his wife's burial and not as a base of operations that could threaten the local people or their economy. An even more telling explanation for the sale may be found in the title given to Abraham by the city elders, "a mighty prince among us" (Gen 23:6). Rather than being a potential threat to the peace of the area like other seminomadic groups, Abraham may have been seen as an economic asset. This does not, however, prevent his being taken advantage of in the bargaining.

The Rape of Dinah

Another example of the tensions between nomadic groups and the settled population and the ways in which they jockey for position occurs in Genesis 34. This episode describes a request by a local prince to marry Jacob's daughter, Dinah. Jacob had settled his household near the city of Shechem. To solidify his presence there, he purchases a piece of land as a base of operations for his herds and appears to be planning to settle down permanently. Jacob is in the process of sedentarization, which occurs among pastoralists occasionally, especially when they become wealthy and have holdings that require both herding and a settled location in a town.

Jacob's daughter, perhaps not showing the usual caution expected of tribal women, leaves the protection of the encampment and is raped by the son of Hamor, the king of Shechem. A Mesopotamian schoolboy's exercise tablet, written inexpertly in Sumerian and dating to the period of the eighteenth century BCE, provides a parallel to this case. According to a set of legal statements, an unbetrothed virgin could be obtained as a wife through forcible sexual relations (compare Judg. 21:19–23). The woman's parents could arrange the marriage if the rapist declared, "I will marry you" (*LCMAM*, 44; #7). The woman he had abused had no say in the matter. In the Genesis account, the king's infatuated son requests that his father negotiate a marriage contract with Jacob's household. The young man then speaks with Jacob's sons, offering for them to set the price of the *mōhar* (bride wealth that would be paid to the bride's family), which was an offer similar to that made by Abraham to Ephron in Genesis 23:13. At this point, the opportunity to gain revenge for the rape of their sister and the resulting damage to the household's honor becomes the driving force in the negotiation. The brothers state that the entire male population of Shechem has to conform to their tribal custom of circumcision before the marriage can take place.

The request for such a drastic act signals the difference in social custom and lifestyle between the two peoples. Hamor and his son try to convince their

Figure 1.3. Archaeological remains of the ancient city of Shechem

fellow citizenry to accept the Hebrews' terms; like the elders of Hebron (Gen. 23:6), they cite the wealth of the pastoral group and the resulting benefits this would have for the city of Shechem. Their argument is persuasive, and the citizens of Shechem agree to submit to the demand that they be circumcised.

Having undergone this painful procedure, the men of Shechem then become easy prey for a raid by Jacob's sons three days later. A massacre ensues, and the women and children are taken away as slaves by the Hebrews. Raids of this type were not uncommon, although they seldom resulted in the total annihilation of a city's population. Usually they only involved the stealing of animals or women (see 1 Sam. 30:1–2; 1 Chron. 7:21). The justification given by the brothers for this act of deception and carnage is to punish Shechem for the rape of Dinah (Gen. 34:31). Unfortunately, it also magnifies Jacob's fear that the stigma of being labeled unwelcome "immigrants" would once more haunt the group (Gen. 34:30). An act such as this could once again arouse suspicions and hostilities that had been dormant for years. The story thus demonstrates underlying antagonism between settled and nomadic groups that lay under the surface and threatened to disrupt their peaceful coexistence.

Burial Customs

Nomadic groups utilized a variety of burial types. These include rock cairns in which the body is interred within a mound of stones along the line of march, as is the case following Rachel's death in Genesis 35:19–20. Similarly, some are buried near distinctive landmarks or trees, which are then given a new name to mark the event (see the burial of Deborah, Rebekah's nurse, under an oak near Bethel in Gen. 35:8). In both cases, the cairn or the landmark becomes part of tribal tradition and adds to their claims on the lands through which they traveled.

Abraham's purchase of the cave at Machpelah initiates its use for both primary and secondary burial. Several members of his family in subsequent generations are buried here, and in some cases this involved the transport of their remains to the cave for secondary burial. The use of a common tomb reflects a reliance on secondary burial practices; the ancestors did not always live near Hebron, and the remains of the dead would have to be transported sometime after death to be interred at Machpelah (see Gen. 50:12–13 for the burial of Jacob).

With a common burial site available, when Abraham dies it is appropriate to say that he was "gathered to his people" (Gen. 25:8–10). Subsequently, Isaac and Jacob were also buried in the family tomb (35:29; 47:30; 49:29, 33). When social patterns are associated with particular places, a transformation process occurs in which the space (i.e., the burial cave or a city) becomes a conduit for interaction between the living and the deceased members of the household. The living are responsible for maintaining control over the household's properties and rights. The presence of the ancestral dead strengthened that heritage of ownership and made it possible to continue the tradition of interring family members in the family plot. Thus, although his bones remained in Egypt for generations, Joseph's remains eventually were transported back to Canaan during the exodus and eventually interred at Shechem (Exod. 13:19; Josh. 24:32).

Archaeologists have discovered many tombs in Canaan dated to the Late Bronze period (1500–1200 BCE) in which the burial space or shelves were utilized over and over. The bones of previous burials were simply swept to the rear of the cave or placed in ossuaries (jars for the storage of bones) along with the possessions that had been left with the bodies.

Herding Practices

Pastoral nomadism as depicted in the ancestral narratives is distinguished by preoccupation with managing herds of sheep and goats and marked by periodic shifts from one pasture area to another (see Gen. 13:5–12; 21:25–34; 26:17–33). One primary reality of pastoral life is that occasionally a group's herd becomes too large for its grazing area. Rather than let the animals denude the pasture to the extent that it would not recover by the next season, the standard practice would be to sell off a portion of the herd or divide the group, with each segment seeking pasture in a different area.

An example of this herding strategy is found in Genesis 13:2–12. The narrative tells us that Abram's herds had significantly increased during his stay in Egypt. When he and his nephew Lot return to Canaan, they discover that the region cannot support their entire herd. As a result, tensions arise among the herdsmen, and they are in danger of coming to blows. They resolve the quarrel by agreeing that Lot will choose an area in which his portion of the herds will graze, and Abram will then choose another. An environmentally safe method has been found to allow the herds to prosper. It also marks a turning point for Abram's household. Social fission has occurred, and when Lot takes his herds east into Transjordan, God's reiteration of the covenant promise (13:14–18) makes no mention of Lot as Abram's heir.

The ancestral narratives also contain evidence of **transhumance**, a practice in which a portion of the group remains anchored to a settlement, engaging in agricultural pursuits. Then, as the seasons change and local fodder is

> Concerning the cattle grazing on the stubble on the banks of the Ḥabur. . . . If the cattle are to graze on the stubble . . . my lord should appoint an overseer [*rabi Amurru*]. (ARMT 14:22.4–11)

exhausted, select members of the household take the herds on an established route to new pastures that may be some distance from their village or encampment. For instance, in Genesis 37:12–17, Jacob's sons take their father's herds north to Dothan. Jacob maintained a base camp near Hebron from which his sons took the herds to seek pasture in the hill country. They return when the seasons change and the grazing near their home base has been replenished. Jacob's sending of Joseph in search of his brothers may reflect a delay in their return or an interruption of the normal communications through travelers or other herdsmen.

The particular combination of nomadic and agricultural activities depicted in the ancestral narratives with the flexibility associated with a mixed economy meant more effective herd and land management and a safety net in times of drought and famine. The area available for grazing and watering their herds was expanded, and the means of supporting the household was diversified. The practice of allowing herds of cattle, sheep, and goats to graze in harvested fields was very common in ancient times (Gen. 37:15–16; CH 57; Mari texts: ARMT 14:22.4–11). It provided good forage for the animals, and the dung they left behind fertilized the field in preparation for the next planting season (note the injunction in Exod. 22:5 against allowing animals to break into and graze in fields not yet harvested). In addition, if the herding cycle corresponded properly with the agricultural calendar, herdsmen would be available to help with plowing, planting, and harvesting. The dependence of both herds and fields on water, however, complicated their existence and required both technical and social strategies to meet the challenges presented in the arid regions of Canaan.

Water Rights

For a herding group to survive, access to water is essential. Sheep cannot go for more than three or four days without water in cooler weather. In warmer periods they must drink every day and cannot range more than about ten miles from a water source. As a result, a basic knowledge of the location of wells, springs, and perennial streams is among the most valuable and guarded pieces of tribal information. This knowledge and the right to use water resources are shared only with close kin and allied groups. An example of the importance that water held for pastoralists and the cooperation necessitated by a common dependence on water sources is found in Genesis 29. Several groups of herdsmen have gathered around a well near Haran. The mouth of the well is covered by a large stone, and it is only when all the herdsmen have gathered their flocks around the well that they are willing to work together to roll the stone away and water their animals (29:8). In this way no accusation

Figure 1.4. Aerial view of Beer-sheba

could be made that one herder was taking more than his fair share of water, and the potential for armed conflict is diffused (see Gen. 13:7–10; 26:19–21).

When Jacob arrives at the well, he takes these herdsmen to task for gathering at the well during "broad daylight" since it is not the appropriate time to bring their flocks to the well (29:7). Their excuse that all must be gathered before the stone is pushed aside suggests both distrust and a lack of good animal husbandry on their part (compare Exod. 2:16–17). They are willing to waste a portion of the day, allow precious water to evaporate, and endanger their animals by keeping them together motionless in the heat. However, since they are there, Jacob says they may as well water the herds rather than waste any further grazing time. He single-handedly removes the stone from the well and assists his cousin Rachel to water her father's flocks (Gen. 29:9–10).

With water such a precious natural asset, it is not surprising to find two instances in the ancestral narratives in which the patriarch must negotiate with local leaders for the right to dig and use wells. In both Genesis 20 and 26, the ruler involved is Abimelech, the king of Gerar. Abraham and Isaac will obtain water rights by employing the wife-sister deception and tricking the ruler into submitting to their demands. These incidents also contribute to the development of friction between the herders and the people of Gerar, who also need the water for their own herds and fields. The tensions created are demonstrated when the men of Gerar confiscate the wells that Isaac's men have dug and his herdsmen are driven further south toward Beer-sheba. Once they are forced to leave the immediate region of Gerar, however, they are left alone, and the wells that they subsequently dig are theirs to name and use.

What this narrative tells us is that there were specific zones of pasturage designated for use by settled communities. Within these zones, outsiders were only grudgingly given even temporary water rights and grazing resources. When the leaders of a city or village felt that the pastoral nomads were threatening the welfare of their economy, it was almost certain that the newcomers would be forced to leave.

Food Preparation and Diet

The ancestral narratives provide only occasional references to food and food preparation. Melchizedek, king of Salem, welcomes the victorious Abraham by offering him bread and wine as well as a blessing in the name of El Elyon (God Most High; Gen. 14:18–20). Abraham orders Sarah to prepare a meal for his three visitors consisting of bread made in the form of cakes, milk and curds, and roasted calf (Gen. 18:6–8). Jacob offers a red lentil soup to his famished brother Esau in exchange for his birthright (Gen. 25:34). The same narrative relates that Isaac's favorite dish is freshly killed game (Gen. 27:7). To add variety to their diet, they ate fruits and nuts, considered such a delicacy that they were offered along with myrrh and balm as presents to the pharaoh's representative in Genesis 43:11.

Archaeobotany sheds some light on both the environmental conditions of various time periods and the foodstuffs grown and consumed by people in biblical times. Using dry sieving and flotation devices, carbonized seeds and other plant remains can be recovered and analyzed. The existence of certain plant types as well as evidence of plant diseases can be identified through these methods, and conclusions can be drawn about the climate and the availability of some plants in ancient times that no longer exist in the area today. Generally, every dwelling had a storage area for grain (usually kept in large pottery jars), and in larger settlements archaeologists have been able to examine the contents of ancient granaries that were associated with administrative or cultic facilities. Among the carbonized remains are wheat, barley, and date and grape seeds.

On the level of ruling elites, the cuneiform documents found at the site of ancient Nippur and dated to 1757 BCE during the reign of Hammurabi of Babylon contain menus of the food prepared for the king and his court. These include elaborate recipes for cooking stews containing various meats, leeks, and herbs like garlic and mint. The menu contained in a royal text from ancient Mari that dates to this same time period describes vast quantities of breads and cakes, bowls of dates, and a variety of concoctions made from chickpeas, semolina flour, and date syrup. Few of these items would have been found on the menu of the pastoral nomadic tribesmen who inhabited the rural districts of Mesopotamia. These tribal peoples, like those in Abraham's household, lived off their herds, the milk and meat of the sheep and goats that they tended, and the grain that they were able to obtain from villagers along their grazing route. Because the pastoralists were often on the move, permanent ovens to bake their bread would have been impractical. Therefore, like their modern descendants, ancient nomadic peoples baked their bread in small, thin cakes on a heated stone or a metal griddle. Occasionally, seasonal agriculture was practiced by pastoralists; thus Isaac "sowed . . . and reaped a hundredfold" in Gerar in Genesis 26:12.

The diet of ancient as well as modern pastoralists primarily consisted of various breads, milk and curds, and fruits and nuts gathered along the line of march or purchased from villagers. The consumption of meat, since it involved reducing the size of the herd, occurred for the most part only on important occasions, such as the arrival of visitors or as a result of an opportunistic killing of a wild animal (Gen. 27:7; gazelle or antelope). Abraham demonstrated his generosity by slaughtering one of his animals. A feast like the one Abraham prepared for his guests in Genesis 18:6–8 can therefore be compared on a smaller scale to a banquet described in a text from the ancient seaport of Ugarit (*ANET*, 146; dated to ca. 1400–1200 BCE). In this epic poem the legendary King Keret orders his wife Hurriya to have "a lamb from the flock" slaughtered to feed his guests.

A diet heavy in carbohydrates and only supplemented by dairy products, vegetables, nuts, and fruit when they become available, coupled with regular periods of famine (Gen. 12:10 and 26:1), would have caused some health problems for the people. Malnutrition would have contributed to higher infant and small child mortality rates and weakened the rest of the pastoral nomadic group. Seeing that the settled community experienced better health because of their mixed economy and access to a more varied diet, including regular quantities of olive oil, figs, and grape products, may have contributed to the sedentarization process that seems to be indicated in the biblical narratives (Gen. 33:18–19).

Marriage Customs

Marriage customs among pastoral nomadic groups are often designed to maintain social continuity as well as to perpetuate the group. As a result, marriage contracts are arranged by the father or other male kin to benefit the individual family (Gen. 24:1–9; 28:1–5; 29:1–30). This means that marriage with non-nomadic peoples or with people outside the kinship group is generally discouraged (Gen. 26:34–35; 27:46; 28:6–9; 34:14). It would not have been unusual for prospective brides and grooms never to have met prior to the wedding (Gen. 24:63–67). Although no minimum age for marriage is stipulated in the biblical text, girls were required to remain virgins prior to marriage and were usually married as soon as they reached puberty (Gen. 24:16). For economic reasons, boys often waited until they received their inheritance or were able to earn enough to establish their own household (Gen. 24:1).

Marriage within the Group

Marriage customs are highlighted in the biblical text on several occasions. Although the text may have been composed in a later period, the story of Abraham's insistence that his servant return to Haran to obtain a bride for Isaac provides insights into the negotiation process and the concept of **endogamy**, marriage within a designated group (Gen. 24:2–9). The patriarch's servant is equipped with a suitable array of gifts for the bride's family and journeys back to Mesopotamia using camels to transport his goods. It is possible that the mention of camels is an anachronism since they were not usually part of pastoral groups prior to about 1200 BCE. In any case they would be an apt representation of Abraham's wealth by the storyteller.

When the servant arrives in the vicinity of Haran, he immediately goes to the village well. It would be a place where strangers were allowed to water their animals, and at the same time he could get a good view of the local young women. At least twice a day (morning and evening) the women of the villages and

Figure 1.5. Reconstructed Iron Age well with trough at Beer-sheba

surrounding encampments came here to obtain water for cooking and washing purposes or to water their animals (24:11). The servant shows his knowledge of everyday activity by seeking a suitable bride for his master's son in this place.

The test that the servant uses to identify the proper wife for Isaac is a signal to the reader of the values expected of an ideal wife in this society (24:12–14). The inset on the Sumerian housewife shows the record keeping and attention to detail in ancient Near Eastern households expected of conscientious women. Thus the servant's plan, aside from his prayer asking God to send him the correct bride for Isaac, is to let the bride demonstrate her wisdom by offering both he and his camels a drink. In his society only a truly wise woman would show concern for another person's animals. If she knows the value of property prior to marriage, it can be expected that she will be a suitable mistress of his master's household afterward (see also Prov. 31:10–31). This dual concern with hospitality and property is so important that the narrative repeats the description of the test three times for emphasis. His joy at finding her is magnified when he learns that Rebekah is part of Abraham's extended family and therefore also fulfills the desire of immigrant groups to marry, at least for a couple of generations, within their kinship group (Gen. 24:23–27).

The actual negotiations (Gen. 24:34–50) that lead to Rebekah becoming Isaac's wife are conducted by the servant with her brother Laban and her father Bethuel. Her father, who is barely mentioned, only plays a secondary role in this scene. Laban is quite impressed by the quality of the servant's gifts to Rebekah and certainly plans to get the best bride price he can for her. The servant, however, demonstrates his own shrewdness by refusing to eat with Laban's household before beginning the negotiations. He does not wish to be unfavorably obligated to Laban within the hospitality protocol, and thus it is only after the bargain is struck and the bride wealth has been given to Rebekah and her family (24:53) that he willingly enters the house and eats a meal (24:33, 54).

While Rebekah has no direct role in the negotiations that will send her from her family and home forever, she is consulted before the departure (24:57–59). It is possible that Laban hoped to detain the servant and thus obtain even more gifts. Rebekah's willingness to leave allows the servant to depart graciously without further delay or expense. Her acquiescence in leaving may be evidence of the change in loyalties exhibited by a woman who must now be concerned with the wealth of her new household.

SUMERIAN HOUSEWIFE'S DEFENSE

To "the beloved" say: Why . . . does he demean my reputation? Have I tied up as much as one flat loaf of bread (or) 20 (liters) of flour in a leather sack? . . . There is no (cause) for worrying about his storehouse. I have not entered it. (COS 3.130)

The high value placed on endogamy is also one motivation for Jacob's journey to Haran to obtain his bride. His brother Esau had broken with custom and married two "Hittite" girls. This disappointed his parents (Gen. 26:34–35). Esau's **exogamy**, marriage outside the kinship or social group, also fits into a literary and theological pattern designed to show how Esau disqualified himself as Isaac's heir. Jacob, on the other hand, is shown to be the upholder of tradition and thus a proper heir when he obediently travels to Paddan-aram and asks Laban for one of his daughters as his wife (Gen. 27:46–28:5). While endogamy functions as one way to preserve cultural heritage in the face of potential assimilation to surrounding peoples, these stories in the ancestral narratives also provide a foundation for enforcing endogamy in the postexilic period (see Ezra 9:1–4 and Neh. 13:23–27).

> If a man hires a herdsman to herd the cattle and the sheep and goats, he shall give him 2,400 silas of grain per year. (*LCMAM*, 129 [CH 261])

Just as Abraham's servant finds Rebekah at a well, so too does Jacob meet his future bride, Rachel, at a well. However, in Jacob's case, it is the potential groom who demonstrates his worthiness by removing the stone from the top of the well and watering her sheep (Gen. 29:1–10). This shows both his physical strength as well as his wisdom as a herdsman. Although it is customary for all of the herdsmen to be present before the animals are watered, there is a point when custom must be superseded by common sense so that the animals do not become dehydrated in the heat and a day of grazing is not wasted.

Jacob's introduction to Laban is cordial enough, but it swiftly becomes evident to the crafty Laban that Jacob is not bringing gifts like Abraham's servant. As a result, Jacob has to assume the role of an itinerant herdsman in the surplus labor pool of young men who contract themselves to work for wealthy livestock owners. As a substitute for providing bride wealth (goods, jewelry, etc.) to Rachel's family, Jacob agrees to serve Laban seven years, and Laban agrees to count the wages that Jacob would have received toward this financial obligation. Laban's deception, replacing Rachel with her older sister Leah on the wedding night, allows him to extract an additional seven years of labor service from his nephew and son-in-law. Yet another seven years are expended as Jacob agrees yet again to tend Laban's flocks, but this time for a percentage of the herd. It is this final contract that enables Jacob to build up his own fortunes.

Such labor contracts for herdsmen, although not functioning as a substitute for the presenting of bride wealth, have been found among the business documents unearthed in the remains of the ancient Mesopotamian cities of Larsa and Nuzi. In these contracts, herdsmen agreed with livestock owners to tend flocks in return for a portion of the herd's offspring, wool, and dairy products.

Codes of law include references to these contracted arrangements with herds-men and their wages (CH 261). The Code of Hammurabi (eighteenth century BCE) requires negligent herdsmen to pay for animals that are lost or become diseased (CH 264–65, 267). However, if losses to the herd result from attacks by wild animals, the herders are not held responsible since that is due either to an act of God or to a poorly maintained public enclosure (see CH 266).

Importance of an Heir

The primary purpose of a marriage in biblical times was to produce an heir who would inherit his father's property and carry on the family name and traditions. Of course, social connections were also a benefit of these contractual arrangements since families in traditional societies depended upon each other to prosper and survive the difficulties of their existence. It is not surprising, therefore, that each cycle of stories about the major ances-tors shows the common theme of obtaining a male heir for the family and for the covenant with God. Long periods of infertility heighten the narrative's level of suspense. In one such instance, Rebekah finally gives birth to twins (Gen. 25:21), and a contest for supremacy ensues between her sons Jacob and Esau. Some aspects of their conflict are resolved and others created when the younger twin, Jacob, obtains a blessing and the designated heirship from his father through the use of a disguise and verbal deception. The narrative disqualifies Esau and justifies Jacob's actions by pointing out that Esau is "a skillful hunter, a man of the field," and apparently less concerned with the family's flocks (Gen. 25:27). On the other hand, the description of Jacob is of a "quiet man, living in tents." The Hebrew word *tām*, sometimes translated "quiet," can also mean "complete" or "blameless" (see Job 1:8 and 2:3). The qualities of a blameless man are extolled throughout ancient Near Eastern wisdom literature (Prov. 2:7; 13:6; 29:10); among such qualities are being thoughtful and careful of speech (Prov. 10:11–14). In addition, Jacob shows reverence for his parents by obeying their request that he adhere to the tribal marriage custom of endogamy (Gen. 28:6–7).

> The wise are soft-spoken. (*OTP*, 296; Amen-em-ope, Teaching Four)

> Speaking without think-ing causes suffering. (*OTP*, 311; Ankhsheshonq, 7:23)

There are accounts in the biblical text of daughters claiming inheritance rights (Gen. 31:14–16; Num. 27:1–11). Laban's daughters, Leah and Rachel, lament that in binding their husband Jacob to a series of labor service contracts, Laban is avoiding providing them with a dowry. As a result Laban gains both the equivalent of a bride wealth payment while retaining the dowry due to their husband for himself. The

Figure 1.6. These figurines may have been used as votive offerings.

daughters gain a measure of revenge when, as they see it, God causes Laban's flocks to dwindle while Jacob's portion of the flocks prospers. As a result, despite Laban's trickery, it is this addition to Jacob's property that they can count as their inheritance (Gen. 31:14–16). In addition, Rachel takes the extraordinary step of stealing her father's household gods (*teraphim*, vv. 19, 33–35). These sacred images were passed from father to son along with the paternal authority as heir and head of the family. By stealing them, Rachel attempts to restore her honor and correct the wrong that she feels her father had done to her and Jacob's household.

On occasion, when the wife of a patriarch is unable to produce a child, concubines (secondary wives) or slave women are used as surrogate mothers, and their children are then claimed by the primary wife. This is the case with Hagar, the maid of Sarah and mother of Ishmael (Gen. 16:2–4). Similarly, in Genesis 30:3, Rachel's maid Bilhah bears children to Jacob on Rachel's knees to create the legal fiction that Rachel has given birth to them herself (compare Ruth 4:13–17). Subsequently, both Sarah and Rachel bear children of their own, and the point is then made that God had at last provided the promised heir of the covenant (Gen. 30:22).

Another example of marriage customs that also centers on the production of an heir appears in Genesis 38. In this passage, Judah, one of Jacob's sons, marries and fathers three sons. He arranges a marriage for his oldest son, Er, to a woman named Tamar. Er dies before fathering a son, and thus the law of **levirate obligation** comes into play (see Deut. 25:5–6). According to this tradition, if the dead man has no heir, it becomes the obligation of his brother or closest male kin to marry or at least impregnate the widow. The male child born of this union will then be the legal heir of the dead man.

Above all else, control your tongue. (*OTP*, 304; Ahiqar 15)

Consequently, Judah gives his second son, Onan, to Tamar as a husband. Recognizing that fulfilling his obligation to his deceased brother will cost him a significant portion of his inheritance, Onan uses a method of birth control to prevent Tamar from conceiving. For this act of disobedience, Onan is struck down by God and the levirate obligation then falls to the third son, Shelah (Gen. 38:9–10). At that point he is too young for marriage. Therefore Judah, who has already lost two sons as a result of this unlucky marriage, promises to send Shelah to Tamar when he is grown.

Time passes, Tamar sits in her father's house (38:11; a further social slight since Judah is obligated by contract to care for her), and Judah delays the marriage fearing he also will be left without an heir. Finally, Tamar takes matters into her own hands to obtain what is her due according to the law. She removes her widow's garments, disguises herself as a prostitute, and sits beside the road at the entrance to Enaim. Judah, now a widower, does not recognize Tamar and propositions her by offering a kid from the flock. He does not have the animal with him, of course, because they have been taken to be sheared. Instead, at Tamar's urging he gives her his cylinder seal and staff as a pledge of later payment. These items are keys to a person's identity. The seal is used to inscribe Judah's name on clay tablets and personal property, and he carries the staff (probably carved and well known to his friends and family) while walking and herding the sheep. He no doubt assumes that he will get them back shortly. However, the supposed harlot mysteriously disappears by the time Judah's servant returns with the kid. Judah is forced to shrug it off. Tamar, on the other hand, has gotten what she wants and returns home to resume her status as an obligated widow (38:14–23).

Three months later, when it becomes evident that Tamar is pregnant, Judah initially—and perhaps with a sense of relief—accuses her of adultery and, based on his position as the head of household, orders that she be burned. Rather than shame Judah publicly, Tamar privately produces his cylinder seal and staff as evidence that Judah is the father of her child. This forces Judah to admit he is in the wrong, having failed to adhere to levirate custom. Tamar is cleared of the charge of adultery and gives birth to twins, finally providing her dead husband with a male heir as well as an ancestor of King David (Gen. 38:27–29; Ruth 4:18–22).

Religious Practices

Upon his arrival in Canaan, Abram's first official act whenever he established a new encampment was to build an altar of unhewn stones on which offerings could be made to God (Gen. 12:7–8; 13:18). Each of these altar sites—Shechem, Bethel, and Hebron—plays an important role in the later history of Israel, and each of these subsequent events will draw a measure of importance from Abram's foundation story. Whenever these sites form the stage for later events,

Geographic Reiteration

Both historical reality and the familiarity associated with significant sites play a role in the expected setting of a narrative in order to give it or its characters greater authority. Whether it is transformed by sacred events or its strategic qualities, it thereafter becomes in the minds of generals, politicians, and biblical writers the logical site for future significant events. The repetition of geographic citation is based on both physical realities and the desire of those producing the account to add greater importance or traditional authority to the events of the story. Over time, geographic reiteration in cultic activity, battle accounts, administrative and economic reports by bureaucrats and merchants, and the travel accounts providing intelligence for military and political activities contributes to the development of a city's or a site's physical and traditional repertoire. This data then becomes part of the repository of information employed by both scribes and kings, who wish not only to tell a story but to cast as positive a light as possible on their accounts. As a result, tradition and well-known stories indicate that monarchs, priests, and prophets should stage their coronations or other significant acts at the site of previous triumphs or turning points for the nation.

the memory of what happened there before becomes a link to the past and its authority through the principle of geographic reiteration. In addition, Shechem has yielded evidence to archaeologists of significant religious activity prior to the time of the ancestors. Such evidence adds strength to the assertion that Abram's altars were built in the vicinity of established cultic sites and indicates the desire to introduce the worship of Yahweh in this land.

Abram's altars are not only sites of worship; they also serve as a means of marking the territory that his descendants will inherit. The use of a boundary stone as an altar also seems to be described in Genesis 31:43–54, where we read that Jacob and Laban the Aramean commemorated a treaty between them by building a pillar of heaped stones, eating a meal together, and making a sacrifice. The pillar served as a boundary marker between their two spheres of influence and closes the chapter on going back to Mesopotamia to obtain a bride. The meal was an example of the use of hospitality traditions to mark their peaceful intentions, and the sacrifice invoked God as a witness to and enforcer of their transaction.

In none of these cases, however, are the details of sacrifice spelled out. The text seems to assume that readers are already familiar with the procedure, which they probably were. The only instance in the ancestral narratives where sacrifice is described in greater detail is found in the story of the binding of Isaac (Gen. 22). Here Abraham is told by God to offer his son as a burnt offering. The patriarch complies without question, as he did when told to leave his home in Haran. He gathers wood, travels to a sacred site (Moriah), builds an altar on a mountain (possibly a **high place** shrine used by the nearby village; see 1 Kings 3:4), and brings along a knife with which to slay the boy.

This story is described as a test of Abraham's faith, but it also provides an **etiology** explaining why the Israelites did not practice human sacrifice like the peoples of Canaan (compare 2 Kings 3:27). Just as Abraham is about to plunge the knife into Isaac's chest, God calls to him to stop and provides a substitute sacrifice, a ram. It seems from the story that Abraham was familiar with human sacrifice and was not completely surprised that Yahweh should demand such an offering. One point made by the text, however, is that this God, unlike those of the Canaanites, found animal sacrifices more acceptable.

While not often thought of today as a sacrificial act, circumcision as practiced by the Hebrews was just as much a sacrifice as the slaughtering of a sheep on the altar. The removal of the male foreskin was a mark of the covenant with Yahweh and served as a physical distinction from the uncircumcised men of the cities of Canaan and the Philistines who entered the land after 1200 BCE (Judg. 14:3). The practice, which the examination of mummified remains has shown, was also common among the Egyptians, but we lack documentation for why it was done. However, the command to circumcise every male "when he is eight days old," as instituted in Genesis 17:9–14, makes it clear that the circumcised are set apart, and only after may they consume portions of the sacrifice (Exod. 12:48) or be counted among the covenant community (Isa. 52:1).

Two other biblical passages stress the importance of circumcision as a rite of initiation. As noted above, circumcision is used as a ruse when Jacob's sons required the men of Shechem to undergo this painful operation before they could become members of the tribe (Gen. 34:15) and the king's son could marry Jacob's daughter Dinah. Later, at the beginning of the exodus-settlement period, Yahweh demands that Moses circumcise his son before he returns to Egypt (Exod. 4:25–26). In this case Moses has failed to conform to Hebrew custom while living with the Midianites. Zipporah, Moses's wife and the daughter of the Midianite priest Reuel (also called Jethro), rectifies the discrepancy by performing the circumcision. She uses a flint knife to cut off her son's foreskin and touches it to Moses's feet (a euphemism for his genitals), declaring him to be "a bridegroom of blood." This act, a parallel to the ritual of placing the blood of the sacrificial lamb on the doorpost before the Passover (Exod. 12:22), signals the renewal of the covenant pact and obedience to the sacred tradition. It marks the beginning of a new contractual arrangement with Yahweh as the story of the exodus begins, which is repeated when the Israelite males are circumcised prior to the conquest of Canaan (Josh. 5:2).

Legal Customs

Perhaps the most significant legal custom among pastoral nomadic peoples is that of hospitality. Once it has been offered and accepted, no hostilities are possible until the parties separate and a mutually appointed period of time has passed. Thus hospitality is neither offered nor received lightly, since it places obligations on both parties. While it most often appears in the biblical text in cases involving individuals, it also has national and international implications in the context of the ratification of treaties and other contracts.

The protocol of hospitality has already been mentioned in the discussion of the negotiation between Abraham's servant and Laban (Gen. 24:31–33) and in the treaty ceremony that marks the separation of Jacob and Laban (Gen. 31:43–54). Two quite graphic examples are also to be found in Genesis

Protocol of Hospitality

1. There is *a sphere of hospitality* that creates a zone of obligation for both the individual and the village or town within which they have the responsibility to offer hospitality to strangers. The size of the zone is of course smaller for the individual than for the urban center.
2. The stranger is *transformed* from a potential threat to temporary ally by the offer of hospitality.
3. The invitation of hospitality can *only be offered* by the male head of household or a male citizen of a town or village.
4. The invitation may include a *time span* statement for the period of hospitality, but this can then be extended, if agreeable to both parties, on the renewed invitation of the host.
5. The stranger has *the right of refusal*, but this could be considered an affront to the honor of the host and could be a cause for immediate hostilities or conflict.
6. Once the invitation is accepted, the *roles of the host and the guest* are set by the rules of custom.
   (a) The guest must *not ask* for anything.
   (b) The host *provides the best* he has available—despite what may be modestly offered in the initial invitation of hospitality.
   (c) The guest is expected to *reciprocate with news*, predictions of good fortune, or gracious responses based on what he has been given.
   (d) The host *must not ask* personal questions of the guest.
7. The guest remains *under the protection of the host* until he/she has left the host's zone of obligation.

18 and 19. These stories contain accounts of the ways in which the laws of hospitality are exercised and defended.

In Genesis 18:1–15, Abraham is visited by three "men" as he sits at the door of his tent "in the heat of the day." Abraham does not recognize that these visitors are from God, but they have entered his sphere of social obligation. Therefore he immediately acts on his customary obligation by rushing out to meet this group of strangers in order to offer them the hospitality of his encampment. In fact, his welcoming statement sounds like a formula invitation: "My Lord, if I have found favor with you, do not pass by your servant. Let a little water be brought, and wash your feet, and rest yourselves under the tree. Let me bring a little bread, that you may refresh yourselves, and after that you may pass on—since you have come to your servant" (18:3–5). Each of these comforts would have been welcome to the travelers, and there is a note of respect in Abraham's address that would please anyone's ear.

Once the visitors accept Abraham's hospitality, they are obligated to express their good wishes to him and his family. Their blessings include the prediction that Sarah will bear a child within a year. That in turn provides the basis for Isaac's name ("laughter") since Sarah is skeptical of conceiving a child long after menopause (18:11–15). Later, when Abraham and God debate the destruction of Sodom and Gomorrah (18:22–32), the "visitors'" prior acceptance of Abraham's food and attention seems to put the patriarch in a position to allow him to speak freely with God. Men who eat together in peace and enjoy one another's hospitality can thus be said to be equals.

Genesis 19:1–11 records the subsequent visit of the angels to Sodom. In this text it is Lot, Abraham's nephew, who is sitting in the gate of the city, the physical and legal equivalent of the doorway of Abraham's tent. He also goes out to meet the visitors as they approach and makes a statement similar to that of his uncle: "Please, my lords, turn aside to your servant's house and spend the night, and wash your feet; then you may rise early and go on your way" (19:2). However, Lot is not a citizen of Sodom; he is a resident alien and therefore does not have the legal right to offer hospitality within the confines of the city.

Once his visitors have eaten with him, Lot is forced to demonstrate just how seriously the obligations of hospitality are taken. During the night "all the men of Sodom" (a legal expression indicating "all citizens") come to his door and demand that the two visitors be sent out to them to be examined. Lot has violated a social protocol, and now these men wish to determine for themselves if the visitors are a threat to the city (Gen. 19:4). The possibility that there is a threat of sexual assault in their speech is based on the dual meaning of the Hebrew word yāda' ("to know"), which connotes both obtaining knowledge and sexual intercourse (compare Gen. 3:5 and 4:1). Even so, Lot's sense of duty to protect his guests is so strong that he offers instead to send out his two virgin daughters to satisfy the mob's appetite for violence or their need for hostages. The daughters are technically his property, and he can dispose of them as he wishes, but this will involve both a financial and a personal sacrifice. He is saved from taking this drastic action when the angels blind the crowd, and his family is able to escape. In this case, the violation of hospitality customs and the threats of violence function as a means of demonstrating the justice of God's intent to destroy the city.

Execution of Justice

In pastoral nomadic groups the head of the household is the absolute master of his own family and has complete legal control over its members. He arranges marriages, conducts all business transactions, and serves as the sole source of justice in legal matters involving his family. The principle of *paterfamilias*, in which the father has the power of life and death over his household, thus applies.

One example of this principle has already been mentioned. When Judah discovers that his daughter-in-law Tamar is pregnant and apparently guilty of adultery (Gen. 38:24), he immediately, without trial, orders her to be burned. That is his right as head of the household.

The father's full legal control is also portrayed in the account of Hagar's flight (Gen. 16:5–6). In this text Sarah complains of verbal abuse by her servant Hagar after Abraham impregnates her. Hagar has been used as a surrogate mother in an attempt to produce an heir, but now the servant has become contemptuous of her barren mistress. Abraham settles the matter by simply turning all punishment of the insolent servant over to Sarah. The result is that Hagar is "treated harshly," probably a euphemism for being beaten, and Hagar runs away until being sent back to the encampment by God's command to submit to her mistress (Gen. 16:7–9). After Sarah gives birth to Isaac, she becomes jealous of a rival heir that might supplant her son. Once again she calls on Abraham to deal with Hagar and her son Ishmael. This time Abraham expels them from his household, leaving it up to God to determine their fate (Gen. 21:8–14).

Weapons and Warfare

Since they had limited resources and manpower, war as practiced by the ancestors generally took the form of raids or small-scale battles. The instances in which combat is mentioned in the text point to the use of surprise attacks, such as the raid on Shechem by Jacob's sons in Genesis 34:25, or night assaults, such as Abram's mission to rescue his nephew Lot in Genesis 14:15. Abram

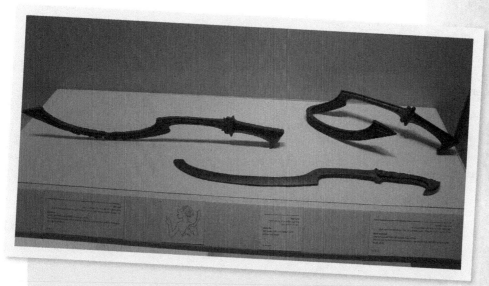

Figure 1.7. Sickle swords from the Canaanite period, designed to cut through body armor

is able to muster the largest group of men assembled by any of the ancestors. He divides his forces and attacks the camp of the invader Chedorlaomer and his allies with 318 "trained men, born in his house." Their success provides a great deal of spoil, a portion of which Abram then gives to Melchizedek, the king of Salem, in order to demonstrate his raid was not intended to serve as a preview of later hostilities against the people of Canaan (14:16, 20b–24).

The raid on Shechem contains the only specific mention of the use of weapons in the ancestral narratives (the blessing of Esau in Gen. 27:40 and Joseph in Gen. 48:21–22 does mention swords). The angry sons of Jacob take swords and kill the male inhabitants of Shechem for the rape of their sister Dinah. Archaeologists have found that the type of swords used during the Middle Bronze period had sickle-shaped blades. This style of sword probably evolved during the second half of the third millennium from the war axe, which was the most common weapon of the time. Axes of this type, with curved shafts and a narrow-edged blade, were designed for chopping and as an effective armor-piercing instrument. They are depicted in the hands of Semitic caravaneers in the Egyptian Beni-Hasan tomb paintings from the nineteenth century BCE.

Discussion Questions

1. What is it about the ancestral stories that contributed to their popularity and survival?

2. What can be learned from the narratives about everyday life in the earliest period of ancient Israel's history?

3. What is the difference between life in a pastoral nomadic group and a settled community?

4. What precedents—social, legal, or religious—are contained in the ancestral narratives?

5. How much value can be placed on the authenticity of social details contained in the stories?

6. In what ways do marriage customs, inheritance rights, and burial customs demonstrate the social character of a people?

7. How do the stories and characters presented in Genesis contribute to an understanding of Israel's history?

Exodus-Settlement Period 2

Historical Introduction

The second major historical era described in the biblical text is the period of the exodus-settlement. It includes the escape from Egypt, the wilderness wanderings, the conquest, and the period of the judges. Throughout this time, manners and customs change as the Israelites make the transition from pastoral nomadic tribal households to a settled existence in the village culture of Canaan.

Israel was not alone in its exodus and resettlement during this period. The second millennium saw mass migrations of peoples throughout the ancient Near East. Among the tribal groups that relocated themselves early in the millennium (ca. 2000–1500 BCE) were the Amorites (who would settle in northern Mesopotamia and eventually rule Assyria), the non-Semitic Hurrians, and various Indo-European groups that in time formed their own empires like Mitanni (east central Mesopotamia and Syria) and Hatti (Hittites in Turkey).

The social factors that contributed to the mass migrations of people are many and various. As city-states developed throughout the Near East and their populations were put under tighter economic control in order to support centralized governments and their bureaucracies, debt and slavery became serious problems for the common people. The poor were no longer allowed to survive on whatever land they could work. Now the land was incorporated into **chiefdoms** and fell under the control of tribal chiefs who were quickly becoming rulers over larger and larger areas. Moreover, the codification of legal statutes in these emerging city-states did not always favor or protect their citizenry from those in power. These circumstances led people throughout the Near East to seek out lands still uncontrolled by larger regimes.

By the second half of the millennium (ca. 1500–1200 BCE), groups of people who did not wish to live under the control of these emerging city-states and budding empires began another set of mass migrations throughout Canaan and adjoining regions. New patterns were set for refugee groups (Israelites as well as others from the various areas of Canaan and adjoining regions), and the newcomers were required to adjust to life within the Canaanite cultural sphere. Lacking the strength to capture walled cities, the Israelite tribes settled primarily in the hill country of central Canaan.

To give a sense of the adjustments made by the peoples that moved into Canaan during this period, a basic review of current archaeological evidence will be summarized. Syro-Palestinian archaeology is divided by major military conquests as well as changes in technology, language, culture, and religion.

TABLE 2.1. ARCHAEOLOGICAL PERIODS

Middle Bronze IIA: ca. 2000–1800/1750	Iron Age I: ca. 1200–1000
Middle Bronze IIB/C: ca. 1800–1550	Iron Age IIA: ca. 1000–925
Late Bronze: ca. 1550–1200	Iron Age IIB/C: ca. 925–586

Beginning in the Middle Bronze Age (2000–1550 BCE), political and social upheaval throughout the ancient Near East contributed to the weakening of Egypt's control over Canaan and the emergence of new powers like the Mitanni in Mesopotamia. The exact length of the Middle Bronze Age and the circumstances of the transition into the Late Bronze Age (1550–1200 BCE) are still a subject of scholarly debate. Part of the difficultly is that shifts in material culture (architecture, technology, evidence of economic change) that generally distinguish one archaeological period from another are not particularly pronounced during this transition. As a result, identifying the differences between cultures becomes more difficult. What is clear is that the period is marked by upheavals. The Hyksos invasion of Egypt around 1750 BCE and the mass assaults on several areas of the Near East by the **Sea Peoples** in 1200 BCE contributed to the opportunities for new or emerging peoples, like the Israelites, to enter Canaan as the Bronze Age transitioned into the Iron I period (1200–1000 BCE).

The uncertainties regarding the length of archaeological periods are not the only problems that make a clear historical setting for the accounts of the exodus and conquest difficult to establish. Extrabiblical sources that might indicate a clear date are scarce and subject to debate. The evidence of archaeology is incomplete and in some cases contradictory. The biblical account places the exodus in the fifteenth century BCE, 300 years before the period of the judges (Judg. 11:26) and 480 years before the fourth year of Solomon's reign (1 Kings 6:1). The strength of the Egyptian presence in Canaan during the early centuries of the Eighteenth Dynasty (1550–1069 BCE) makes this date problematic.

Egyptian sources do not mention the exodus, although there are Egyptian accounts of the use of forced labor gangs to construct the Egyptian

An Egyptian father chastises his son for traveling into the Delta Region and "consorting with the Asiatics" and another complains that his son's servant had "gone over to a life of evil mixing with the tribes of the Shasu and adopting the guise of an Asiatic" (Redford 1992, 229).

storehouse cities of Pithom and Rameses in the time of Seti I and Rameses II (ca. 1300–1250 BCE). It is possible that these construction gangs may have included Israelite slaves or groups of itinerant laborers (Exod. 1:11). Archaeologists have also found evidence of the destruction of some Canaanite sites that date to the thirteenth century BCE. However, since we lack clear extrabiblical evidence for who is responsible for these burn levels, directly ascribing them to the accounts of the conquest found in the books of Joshua and Judges is not currently possible. To be sure, Israelites may have been among the peoples who contributed to the destruction of Canaanite villages and towns, but there were other players, including the invading Philistines, who had a hand in Canaan's turmoil in that period.

'Abdi-Heba, governor of Jerusalem: ". . . send archers needed to reinforce the garrison." This is pharaoh's only hope "to keep his lands under control and end the plundering of the 'Apiru." (EA 286; OTP, 149)

While Egyptian records do not specially detail a Hebrew migration, they do provide evidence of the migration of peoples during the second half of the second millennium. These inscriptions most often refer to these disparate groups of people using social categories rather than ethnic names. For instance, Egyptian texts describe the **Shasu** not in terms of their origins but as tribes of lawless nomadic herders and sedentary farmers considered to be unsavory, rebellious, and quarrelsome. The Nile Delta region was easily accessible to the Shasu and other "Asiatics," who also inhabited the hill country of northern Canaan. These tribes fit uneasily into Egyptian culture. There are reports of numerous conflicts between the Egyptians and the Shasu between 1500 and 1150 BCE (*ANET*, 247, 254, 259).

The label *'Apiru* or *Habiru* appears to be a generic term for stateless people or tribal groups who lived in the Egyptian Delta (*ANET*, 255, 261, 483, 486) and on the fringes of the settled areas of the ancient Near East. They sometimes served as surplus labor or as mercenaries, but they appear in texts from several different historical periods (from 2000 to 1200 BCE) and are mentioned in several different areas as brigands and raiders. One large contingent of *Habiru* congregated around Nuzi in northeastern Mesopotamia. There, private contracts have been discovered binding *Habiru* to citizens of Nuzi as servants, suggesting that this group of people did not readily become members of the societies into which they moved (*ANET*, 220). The sheer numbers of these migratory peoples also posed problems for the states into which they moved and operated. The fourteenth-century Amarna texts, which contain correspondence between vassal rulers in Canaan and the Egyptian pharaohs Amenophis III (1391–1353 BCE) and Akhenaten (1353–1335 BCE), regularly mention raids and skirmishes with elements of the *'Apiru*. International treaties also included clauses requiring the regulation of migration by stateless peoples and extradition of members of groups like the *Habiru* (*ANET*, 199–203). While there is no direct linguistic connection between "*Habiru*" and "Hebrew," the description of a people without roots that live on the fringes of society and sometimes infiltrate into poorly defended areas does fit the biblical description of the early Israelites.

The only documentary evidence from Egypt of Israel as a distinct people is found on the victory **stele** of Pharaoh Merneptah dating to circa 1208 BCE. This inscription lists the peoples and cities that the pharaoh conquered in an expedition into Canaan. One line states that Israel (specified in the text by a determinative sign as a people, not a nation) was laid to waste. The mention of Israel occurs in the systematic and propagandistic description of the destruction wrought by the pharaoh's armies in the area. There is a difficulty with this interpretation, however. The language of the inscription is typical of many other similar victory announcements, and the inclusion of Israel in the list of defeated enemies may reflect some knowledge of its existence but no actual contact with it. The pharaoh may simply be reusing an earlier pharaoh's conquest list while boasting that he has subdued all of the peoples in the area. Still, it is the first extrabiblical mention of the name Israel and thus provides us with the best available evidence of the Israelites' existence in the thirteenth century BCE.

Evidence for the chronology of the conquest period as described in the book of Joshua is just as scarce and problematic. The only discussion of this holy war is found in the biblical text. Archaeological investigations of the major sites said to have been destroyed by the Israelites have provided mixed and inconclusive results, and many cities listed in the Joshua account do not contain destruction levels at the end of the Late Bronze Age. Jericho, the first city listed as being conquered by the Hebrews, has been extensively excavated several times during the twentieth century. John Garstang's early efforts in the 1930s were followed by Kathleen Kenyon, who led the

Figure 2.1. The victory stele of Pharaoh Merneptah

first scientific investigation of the site in the 1950s. Despite some early claims by Garstang that he had found the remains of the walls of Joshua's Jericho, it has been determined by most scholars that the destruction level of the city that he identified with the conquest is actually to be dated to the end of the Middle Bronze Age (ca. 1560 BCE) and probably is related to the expulsion of the Hyksos rulers from Egypt. The city walls were not rebuilt in the Late Bronze period, and the site would not be extensively reoccupied until Iron I, when pottery evidence and the excavation of tombs indicate the inclusion of the city within the kingdom of Judah. Furthermore, Kenyon's introduction of stratigraphic excavations, with careful examination of each level of the tell with thorough analysis of soil and the ceramic record, became a model for subsequent archaeological investigations at other sites.

Ai, the next site listed in Joshua's conquest itinerary (Josh. 7:2), has also proven to be a puzzle. Excavations conducted at this site by Joseph Callaway between 1965 and 1975 demonstrated that what had been a major fortified city was destroyed, possibly by the Egyptians, around 2400 BCE. The mound (**Khirbet** et-Tell, nine miles northeast of Jerusalem) remained unoccupied from 2400 to 1200 BCE, when an unwalled farming village was established housing no more than about 150 persons. It is possible that the site was used as a military outpost by the nearby city of Bethel, which does show evidence of destruction in the thirteenth century, but there was no large city at Ai such as that described in Joshua. Its name, which means "the ruin," may have led the Israelites to attach it to Joshua's list of conquests.

Other cities mentioned in Joshua's account, including Hazor (Josh. 11:13) and Lachish (Josh. 10:31–32), do have destruction levels that date to the thirteenth century. However, it is unclear whether their destruction is the work of the Israelites or other groups during this turbulent period. The destruction levels could just as easily be evidence of Merneptah's expedition as he tried to reestablish Egyptian control in Palestine or of the conquests by the Sea Peoples who raided much of the Near East around 1200 BCE.

With so many conflicting pieces of information, it is best to take a cautious view of the biblical account of the Israelite conquest of Canaan. Several theories have tried to explain the disparities between the archaeological evidence and the description of a nearly total victory sweep by the Israelites in Joshua 1–12. One possible explanation is that the book of Joshua is not as interested in historical details as it is in making the theological point that these victories are engineered by the divine warrior, Yahweh. Each battle is won because of the direct intervention of God (compare the victory over the Amalekites in Exod. 17:8–13). For instance, the fall of Jericho is not achieved by the Israelites through conventional siege warfare but through the opening given to their forces when God destroyed the city walls (Josh. 6:1–21).

The editors of the Joshua account employed selectivity in limiting the number of events described in the conquest narrative. They provide no clear indication of the time it took to complete the conquest. Possibly some cities fell to one wave of migrants while others succumbed to later attacks. The Israelite tribes may have entered Canaan over a fairly long period of time, with each successive wave of arrivals adding to their numbers and achieving new victories. Other migrating groups or even Canaanite villages (for example, the Gibeonites in Josh. 9:3–15) may have joined forces with the Israelite tribes as they began to settle in the hill country. Such allegiances could have undermined the authority and strength of Canaanite culture and eventually allowed the Israelites to infiltrate some areas with a minimal amount of armed conflict. The fact that some large Canaanite cities have no evidence of destruction during the thirteenth and twelfth centuries suggests that the region continued to support a variety of peoples. For instance, excavations at Debir (Tell Rabûd) show continuous occupation from the Late Bronze to the end of the Iron Age, and the city quite likely controlled most of the area south of Hebron.

Initially, the Israelite tribes may have settled in the underpopulated areas of the central hill country and then assimilated themselves into some aspects of the Canaanite culture. As they learned the technologies and social customs of the Canaanites, they gradually, and for the most part peacefully, merged with the dominant culture. Over time the Israelites came to control larger areas and some cities. By the time of King David only the Philistine city-states along the coastal plain and inland in the Shephelah provided a major opposition force.

The explanation of gradual infiltration is a better fit for the description of a partial conquest and settlement found in Judges 1–2. These chapters are quite open in listing those cities and regions that the Israelite tribes were not able to conquer (see Judg. 1:21). Conquest through major raids or forced entry may have augmented ongoing infiltration in cases like the destruction of Lachish (Josh. 10:31–32) and Bethel (Judg. 1:22–25). The lack of evidence at other sites such as Ai could be attributed to a later chronicling of the events or to overly enthusiastic battle reports.

Whether a swift conquest or a gradual movement of refugees and new peoples after 1200 BCE, it is apparent that groups of Israelites did eventually settle in Canaan and in portions of the Transjordan in Gilead and in territories associated with Moab. Engaging in a mixed economy of agriculture and herding, most of the Israelites would have lived in small, unwalled villages. If the episodes in Judges are to be taken into account, life was an uncertain proposition for these villagers. They had to endure frequent raids by Philistines and various Canaanite groups, who used their superior weapons to harass the Hebrews. For most of this period, social and political organization would have remained on the tribal level, and village elders exercised authority over local issues (see Judg. 11:5–11; Ruth 4:2–11).

From what can be reconstructed, the manners and customs of this era indicate Israel's shift from pastoral nomadic tribes or people seeking refuge in a new land to an independent and loosely organized group of settled tribes and villages. This transition required some fundamental changes in social life and eventually formed the basis for the covenantal community of ancient Israel in the monarchic period.

Village Life

The description of the allotment of the land in Joshua 13–17 lists the areas of Transjordan and Canaan that are assigned to the tribes of Israel. It includes a list of towns and their adjacent villages or "encampments." These smaller settlements, which also included herding enclosures, consisted of communities of around 75 to 150 persons. They are sometimes referred to as "daughters" in the biblical text (Num. 21:25, 32). The vast majority of the population during the early settlement period (ca. 1200–1050 BCE) would have been found in these villages. One reason given in the text for why the Israelites were bottled up in the less hospitable regions of the country is the "iron chariots" of the Canaanites (Judg. 1:19). This situation makes sense, even though, as the biblical writer says, "the hill country is not enough" (Josh. 17:16) to support the needs of the people as the population expanded. Very likely, the higher technology and tighter political organization of the Canaanites held the new immigrants in check for some time.

Ongoing surveys by archaeologists have traced the appearance of new or rebuilt settlements in the central hill country that date to the period after 1200 BCE. They have discovered very few Late Bronze sites (ca. 1550–1200 BCE) in the "hills of Ephraim" and the area north of Shechem and the Samaria region, and these are in valley fringes near water sources. However, during the early Iron Age (ca. 1200–1000 BCE) there is a significant upturn in settlement construction, especially after 1100 BCE. Some additional settlements were built on the abandoned ruins of ancient cities, such as Ai and Gibeon. These findings suggest (1) that there was no economic need or political impetus by either the Egyptians or the Canaanites to promote settlement in the marginal areas of hill country during the Late Bronze period, and (2) that rapid population growth occurred as the Israelites and other settlers entered the highlands of central Canaan at the beginning of the Iron Age. The factors contributing to this demographic shift are probably related in part to the destruction of Canaanite cities by the Philistines and unrest in the Shephelah and coastal areas as Egypt continued its attempt to restore its influence in the region.

Lacking the personnel to defend against a concerted attack, the new settlers depended upon their inaccessibility and did not build walls around their small villages. Extended family groups lived in multiple family compounds. These complexes may have been styled after the nomadic encampments in which the Hebrews lived while operating as pastoral nomadic groups. Villages in the hill country consisted of closely packed rows or clusters of fifteen to twenty dwellings. The primary building materials were rocks and sun-dried mud brick. Situated as they were on the hilltops, these villages seldom covered an area of more than about five acres.

Life in the village was dominated by agricultural pursuits and maintaining small herds of sheep and goats. Some domestic industries, such as pottery making, weaving garments, and fabrication of tools, were necessary for every household. Because each settlement was fairly isolated, they strove to be self-sufficient with regard to the basic necessities of life. Natural resources, such as clay for pots and copper deposits, were often available nearby (Deut. 8:9). Even by the end of the settlement period, more advanced technology and styles of workmanship, as well as rare raw materials, could still be obtained only from traveling craftsmen or in the larger cities of Canaan. For instance, 1 Samuel 13:19–20 states, "Now there was no smith to be found throughout all the land of Israel; . . . so all the Israelites went down to the Philistines to sharpen their plowshare, mattocks, axes, or sickles."

Adjoining fields provided food for the villagers and commanded the bulk of their work day. Since level ground in the hill country was at a premium, a great deal of labor went into the construction and maintenance of stone terraces on the slopes (see Job 24:11; Isa. 5:2–5). Fruit trees (olives and figs), grapevines, and some cereals were cultivated on these artificially constructed plots. The flatter areas of the plains allowed for more conventional farming methods, but they were not settled by large groups of Israelites until the monarchic period. The uncertainties of rainfall in the hill country, hungry birds and small animals, and insects also plagued farmers and severely cut into their harvests (Deut. 28:38).

Each village possessed flocks of sheep and goats that were pastured some distance from the settlement. The herdsmen sometimes kept the animals up in the higher elevations for a season, but it was also quite common to bring them back to the village folds for the night (Num. 32:24). The open "square" in larger settlements served as a common area and could sometimes be used to shelter the flocks (Judg. 19:15). However, primitive stone enclosures were more often used to prevent the animals from wandering away from encampments while in the grazing areas, and some homes were constructed with a lower stable level in which the animals could be housed. During the winter, the body heat of the animals provided additional natural warmth for their owners.

Domestic Architecture

Smaller village sites, such as that excavated at Tell Raddana (near Ai, ten miles north of Jerusalem), provided only the bare necessities of their inhabitants. Raddana, founded on a ridge top during the latter part of the thirteenth or early twelfth century BCE, consisted of six closely packed houses. The basic design of its dwellings is a simple, windowless rectangle divided into two living areas by a row of four roof-supporting pillars. These pillars are usually placed within five feet of one long wall, thereby creating a "great room" in the remaining ten-foot-wide living area. The great room, illuminated by the fire pit and sputtering oil lamps, served most of the family's indoor cooking, entertaining, and sleeping needs.

Wooden beams, set in niches cut into the walls and supported by pillars, held up the roof. Slats were made from smaller pieces of wood, brush, or thatching, which were sealed with a layer of clay. The resulting ceiling was about six feet above the floor, with the beams lowering that height by five or six inches in places.

With living space at a minimum, there was no room for luxuries or privacy. Cooking was done outside the front door in small clay ovens or in a courtyard shared by two or three other households. There was no furniture, only stone ledges built along the wall or chiseled into the bedrock, and a few flat stones spaced around the central fire pit. Lacking bathrooms, bodily needs were taken care of outdoors. If the villagers continued the pattern prescribed in the wilderness (Deut. 23:12–13), they made use of latrines outside the immediate area of the village. Some may have gone into the fields where their excrement could serve as fertilizer (Gen. 24:63).

The only innovation and true convenience designed into these homes was an interconnected cistern system that brought rainwater into the house. Chiseled out of chalk and limestone, which forms the bedrock under these hilltop settlements, bell-shaped cisterns provided a continuous supply of water. It was unnecessary to put additional lime plaster on the cisterns in the Ai/Raddana area because of the impermeability of the rock strata. Elsewhere, however, this "waterproofing cement" was used to retain the precious moisture.

Rainwater ran off the roofs and into the cisterns. Rocks were placed at the bottom to trap larger impurities, and a hole was drilled in the side, allowing water to travel into a series of adjoining cisterns and eventually into the house. This system also helped to filter the water as it passed from one cistern to the next.

There are few natural springs in the hill country, so the cistern system made life possible here for the village families. Larger springs and rivers of the plains and coastal areas supported Canaanite cities and villages. The Israelites simply had to make do with the resources in the areas where they could

Figure 2.2. Four-room house at Hazor

settle initially. Later, when judges and war chiefs like Saul and David began to conquer the Canaanite strongholds, Israelites were able to move down into more hospitable and better watered areas of the land (see Josh. 15:16–19).

Another style of house that was very common in ancient Israel during this period and into the time of the monarchy was the pillared house, also called the **four-room house**. Its basic design may have evolved from earlier structures built around an animal enclosure. Houses of this type have been excavated at Tell el Farah (Tirzah), Hazor, Shechem, and Tell beit Mirsim (east of the Jordan near the Jabbok River). They were generally two-story dwellings. The ground floor is made up of a long central room with a ceiling two stories high. The central room is surrounded by partitioned rooms on three sides. With its hard-packed earthen or plastered floor, the central room bustled with domestic activities like cooking, dining, and storytelling. Excavations of these areas reveal clay ovens, hearths, and a small group of pottery types (more than 50 percent are storage jars and cooking pots). In some cases storage jars have been found arranged around the walls of the central room. These might have contained water for cooking or the grain, oil, or olives that would have gone into the next day's meal.

The ground-floor side rooms that boxed in the courtyard provided secure stables for the family's livestock. During the winter, the body heat of the animals stabled on the ground floor of the house provided additional natural warmth for the upper story. The upper side rooms were sometimes subdivided into smaller rooms. They served as sleeping quarters, as gathering places for the family and their friends, as storage, and as spaces for cottage industries like weaving. The main hearth located in the central room could then provide heating to the entire house.

Walls in these simply constructed houses were quite thick, thereby providing good insulation against the cold and some relief in hot weather. In the hill country, where uncut stone is plentiful, the foundation and the walls were made of this building material. A mud plaster mixed with small stones was applied to the walls to smooth them over and to protect against the weather. Houses in the plains and foothills, however, would have used sun-dried mud brick for all but the foundation. These bricks, like cut stone in larger buildings, were laid in a pattern known as "headers and stretchers," which strengthened the construction and stability of the walls. Although the archaeological record can only attest to foundation patterns and the size of the column bases, the thickness of the walls and columns indicates that the standard pattern for these Iron Age houses included a second story with a sturdy, flat roof.

The roof over these dwellings was thatched with a mixture of reeds, branches, and palm leaves and then covered with earth or bricks. It provided extra sleeping accommodations (2 Kings 4:10) and served as an excellent spot for drying mud bricks or flax stalks (Josh. 2:6). As a rule, access to the upper room was provided by a staircase on the outside of the wall, although ladders may have been used within the dwelling. In warm weather the breeze on the roof relieved the family from the oppressive heat of the day, and domestic tasks could be performed in more comfort under a lean-to or awning.

Another area of the house that held both functional and traditional importance is the threshold/doorway. At first doors were simply skin coverings, but these were eventually replaced by a more permanent wattle or wooden barrier and were barred from within (2 Sam. 13:17). The threshold functioned as the legal, as well as physical, entryway to the dwelling, and in some cases may have served as the site where justice was done (Deut. 22:21) or demanded (Judg. 19:27). Sandals were removed before crossing the threshold as a sign of respect, and hospitality obligations began at this point.

Agricultural Methods and Tools

Constrained to live in the hill country, the one way the Israelites adapted to this environment was by building terraces on the hillsides. Construction and maintenance of these terraces consumed a large part of the villagers' energies, but it provided them with farmable strips of land that could support the growing agricultural needs of the people. Due to the smaller population, terracing in this period was not as extensive as it was in the monarchic period, when 50 percent of the hillsides were terraced. The gradual growth in village population, however, was one of the prime reasons for initiating such a monumental project. Since these terraces have been rebuilt and reused by villagers throughout the centuries, the primary means of determining when they might have originated is through the examination of pottery remains that appear within their soil and walls. This is not always a reliable test, but indications are that the conversion of the hills of Judea and Ephraim into farmland began in the early settlement period and continued on a larger scale throughout the monarchic period (see Uzziah's emphasis on agriculture in 2 Chron. 26:10).

The terraces are not designed to prevent erosion of existing topsoil. The hills have little soil to lose due to deforestation (Josh. 17:18) and the overpasturing of animals. Thus much of the soil found in the terraces was brought from elsewhere and was usually a mixture of different soil types. Channels were sometimes dug to direct rainwater into the terraces. These terraces were constructed all the way down the face of the hill to ensure natural filtration of the water and a better distribution of moisture to every farming strip. Since significant rainfall only occurs during five months of the year (October to February), it is essential that as much as possible remain in the soil and none of it be allowed to run off.

Grain Production

Wheat and barley were the most common crops grown in the hill country by the Israelites and their neighbors. While it comes from the tenth century BCE, the Gezer Calendar records a pattern of the agricultural year that must go back to earlier times. This schoolboy exercise, written on a broken limestone tablet, describes the seasons.

> Two months for storage (roughly corresponding to our September–November)
> Two months for planting (November–January)
> Two months for the summer planting (January–March)
> One month each to hoe flax (March–April) and harvest barley
> One month to harvest all other crops and to feast (May–June)
> One month for vine tending (June–August)
> One month for harvesting the summer fruit (August–September)

The agricultural calendar, patterned on the Mediterranean climate in this region, was thus based on the division between the rainy winter months and the dry spring and summer. Once the rains had loosened the ground, plowing and planting of various crops began in November and continued until

January (see Prov. 20:4). Wheat and barley were the first to be planted, while crops like sesame, millet, and lentils and garden vegetables like cucumbers, garlic, onions, and leeks were planted from January until March. Harvest seasons varied according to the temperature ranges of specific regions, with the warmer Jordan River valley being the first to harvest and the cooler mountain areas of the Galilee the last. This meant that barley, which ripened before the wheat, was harvested from April to May, while the latter was harvested from May to June.

To prepare the ground for planting, a wooden plow (sometimes with a metal sheath or boot attached) drawn by a team of oxen (1 Sam. 11:5) opened the furrows. Smaller villages probably shared a team of oxen or perhaps even rented one from a nearby village. A text from Mari (ARMT 14:80.4–10) mentions such an arrangement in which a village obtained the use of a team of oxen in exchange for its labor service for the government. Gideon's subsequent sacrifice to Yahweh of the precious work oxen he had used to tear down the village Baal altar in Judges 6:25–28 also may have figured into the ensuing village rage against him. In another instance, Saul's slaughter of his own oxen perhaps signaled the urgency of his demand that the tribes assemble for war against the Ammonites (1 Sam. 11:7).

A sower cast the grain into the furrows by hand, where it was trampled into the ground by foot or by the tread of the animals (Isa. 28:25). The stands of ripened grain were gathered into the harvesters' arms and cut away with sickle blades (Deut. 16:9; Isa. 17:5; Joel 3:13). These were made of bronze, although in the poorer villages wooden sickles with flint blades continued to be used. Later, when iron technology and tools were introduced into Israel, these improved farm implements were probably prized over their primitive predecessors (see 1 Sam. 13:20).

The harvested grain was taken to a centrally located threshing floor. This flattened area ranged in diameter from 160 to 320 feet (depending on the number of villages and fields it serviced), and it was located in an open place where the prevailing winds would aid the winnowing process (Ruth 3:2). The sheaves of grain were brought to the threshing floor by each farmer after the harvest (Job 5:26; Mic. 4:12). To separate kernels of grain from the stalks, oxen were driven over the piles of grain on the circular earthen floor to trample it. Israelite concern for the valuable animals that aided them in this important activity is reflected in the law of Deuteronomy 25:4, which prohibits a man from muzzling his ox while it treads out the grain. The ox was thus free to breathe and to eat a portion for its hire.

In later periods a more efficient method of threshing was developed using a threshing sledge with stone and bits of metal attached to its underside. These extra edges crushed the stalks more thoroughly than the sledge alone (see Isa.

41:15). A sledge like this is mentioned in the context of David's purchase of the threshing floor of Araunah, which eventually became the site of the temple in Jerusalem. After he completes the transaction, David uses the wood from the sledge to build a fire on the altar that he constructs (2 Sam. 24:21–24).

After the threshing, the next step in the process of preparing grain for milling was winnowing. That was done using a long wooden fork to toss the grain and chaff into the air. Then, as Psalm 1:4 says of the wicked, the chaff was driven away by the wind (see also Isa. 41:16). Jeremiah also used this common village activity to describe God's testing of the people "with a winnowing fork in the gates of the land" (15:7). Two places associated with justice are featured here: the threshing floor, where the winnowing and distribution were done, and the gate, which was used on many occasions as the center of legal and political activity in the walled cities of the monarchic period (see 2 Sam. 19:8; 1 Kings 22:10).

Sieving was the final step in separating the grain from the chaff. Small wicker screens were used to sift tiny stones or bits of pottery from the grain, which then fell to the floor where it could be collected (Sir. 27:4). Amos, an eighth-century prophet from the small farming village of Tekoa just ten miles south of Jerusalem, used this activity to describe how God in his wrath will "shake the house of Israel among all the nations as one shakes a sieve, but no pebble shall fall upon the earth" (9:9; compare Isa. 30:28).

Once the kernels of grain were swept up and collected, they were distributed to the people by the village elders. As the Egyptian sage Amen-em-ope states, each "receives bread from his own threshing floor" (*ANET*, 422). A portion was ground into flour with a simple millstone on a larger stone quern shaped like a saddle (Isa. 47:2). Then it was pulverized in a stone mortar with a rounded pestle (Prov. 27:22). Another portion was parched to be eaten as journey provisions or pressed into cakes (Josh. 5:11). The remainder was stored in plastered storage pits or in pottery jars that were stacked around the walls of homes or courtyards (1 Kings 17:14–16). Only the larger villages and towns had communal storage pits and silos for the storage of larger quantities of grain like those found by archaeologists at Shiloh.

Cultivation of Vines and Olive Trees

Every village in the hill country in this and later periods had its vines and trees. The pervasiveness of viticulture in Israelite village culture can be found in an archaeological survey of the Megiddo area. It discovered 117 winepresses of various types at small sites radiating from the urban center. Vineyards provided fresh fruit, raisins, raisin honey, grape juice, and wine. Terraces are actually better designed for these crops than for the cultivation of grain.

Methods would have had to be invented to properly cultivate and prune the vine during the growth process. Sometimes the vines were mixed with fruit trees and even trained to climb up the trees (see Ps. 128:3; Song 6:11). However, it is not clear how common such an arrangement actually was.

The vines required constant care, including pruning from June to August to remove unproductive or old vines and thus allow for new growth (compare Lev. 25:4). Supports for the vine clusters prevented bruising and rot, and the area around the vine was hoed regularly to cut back on weeds that would steal moisture needed by the fruit to ripen (Isa. 5:6; 7:25).

The grapes were harvested with pruning hooks (Isa. 18:5) in August and September. Some were dried into raisin clusters (1 Sam. 25:18), and the rest were trod or pressed into wine in a winepress (Num. 18:30; Isa. 63:2). The liquid squeezings were poured or channeled into a fermentation vat and then stored in jars or skin bags. The fermentation process was a delicate affair given the range of temperatures necessary for proper chemical transformation to take place. It seems likely that jars were stored in an upright position in order to maintain the seal (generally a clay stopper and cap). Otherwise, contact with bacteria would have turned the wine to vinegar, and contact with oxygen would have changed its color and flavor.

Because there was so much activity occurring at this installation, its importance is second only to the threshing floor as a center of community activity in Israelite tradition (Hosea 9:2). Indeed, on at least one occasion, a wine press was used opportunistically as a threshing floor. After the Midianite raiders had ravaged his village's fields, the judge Gideon secretly ground his remaining wheat in a wine press to prevent the invaders from suspecting that he was holding out on them (Judg. 6:11).

The harvesting of grapes and the production of wine was a time of great celebration, comparable to the grain harvest in the villages (Judg. 9:27). People's joy was based on the fact that wine and bread were the staples of life, and a good harvest meant their survival for another year (1 Sam. 16:20). At times the vintage festival may have gotten out of hand, leaving the village open to attack. For instance, the decimated Benjaminite tribe took advantage of the celebration at Shiloh to steal wives from among the dancers (Judg. 21:20–21).

The abundance of grapevines meant that wine was able to serve as the common beverage and also became an aspect of everyday social life (Ruth 2:14; Hosea 2:7; Dan. 10:3). It serves as a libation offering in religious contexts, although this was sometimes condemned for its association with other gods (Deut. 32:31–38). Wine also had the potential to become a source of social comment if it were used intemperately (Isa. 56:12; Sir. 31:25). Its value could also become a form of evidence of injustice to the poor, as it does in Amos's indictment of those who profit from unfair fines (Amos 2:8).

Figure 2.3. Stone watchtower

Olive and fig trees provided the chief noncereal crops. The fruit of these trees added spice and variety to an otherwise monotonous diet. The olive tree was long lived and well suited to the hot dry summers and cool damp winters of Israel and the rest of the Mediterranean basin. It was seen, along with the other produce of the land, as one of the blessings provided to the people by God (Deut. 7:13).

In the autumn, villagers gathered ripe olives by striking the tree branches with sticks and collecting the fallen fruit in baskets (Deut. 24:20; Isa. 17:6). The olives were then crushed under a revolving flat stone, and the stream of oil and juice was collected in a cistern (Job 24:11; Mic. 6:15). The remaining pulp was placed in wicker baskets to be crushed again by a stone-weighted lever. Squeezings were channeled into a larger catch basin. Gradually, the finer grade of oil rose to the top of the cistern and was skimmed off for use in lamps (Exod. 27:20). The remainder was further refined and used as a base for cosmetics, in cooking, and as medicine (Ps. 104:15; Eccles. 9:8). The residue of the inedible pulp may have been used for fertilizer or hardened into cakes that served as fuel for cooking fires. Fig trees were also among the natural resources characteristically exploited in arid farming areas like the hill country (Jer. 40:10–12). Their fruit was the last to appear in the summer, and thus figs are referred to as the "summer fruit" in the Gezer Calendar and in Amos 8:2. Apparently, crushed figs were also used for medicinal purposes as a poultice to draw infection from a boil (2 Kings 20:7). Because of their high sugar content, figs could be dried and pressed into cakes that were stored for later consumption or given as gifts in the dry, fruitless summer. Fig cakes are one of the items Abigail takes to David's camp to prevent his attack on her husband's household (1 Sam. 25:18).

This same passage provides an itemized list of the foods typically eaten by people throughout the biblical period (see also 1 Chron. 12:40). Abigail takes David's men two hundred loaves of bread, two skins of wine, five butchered sheep, five measures of parched grain, one hundred clusters of raisins, and two hundred fig cakes. With this list as a guide, it can be seen that the land did yield its agricultural wealth to the Israelites, although not without a struggle and not always in the abundance they desired (Jer. 8:13).

Weapons and Warfare

A discussion of weapons and warfare in the conquest and settlement period must take into account the differences between the historical narratives in Joshua and in Judges. The book of Joshua describes the conquest and repeatedly highlights Yahweh's role as the "Divine Warrior," who provides one victory after another to the Israelite forces. This pattern of divine deliverance is manifest in the wilderness period in the battle against the Amalekites. Moses merely has to keep his arms in the air for the Israelites to be victorious (Exod. 17:8–13). Once the Israelites enter Canaan, this principle is demonstrated in the capture of Jericho (Josh. 6:1–21) and in the defeat of the five Amorite kings when God miraculously causes the "sun to stand still" (Josh. 10:6–13).

In these battles it is God's intervention, not the strength of the Israelite tribes, that determines the outcome. They are part of a "contest between gods" motif in which Yahweh emerges the winner over the gods of the land and its people.

In contrast to this account of divinely achieved success, the book of Judges freely admits that the "holy war," or ḥerem, was a failure. Many of the Canaanite walled cities were too strong for the Israelites to capture, and the iron chariots (1:19) of the people of the plain kept the Israelites bottled up in the hill country (1:34). A rationalization or **theodicy** for this failure is spelled out in Judges 3:1–4. It states that God spared these Canaanite and Philistine cities so that "successive generations of Israelites might know war, to teach those who had no experience of it before." The plan is designed "for the testing of Israel, to know whether Israel would obey the commandments of the LORD." Through this rationalization, the Israelites can accept the reality of their political and military situation, and, in the early monarchic period, they will turn to kings and a more centralized government to assist them in expanding their territory in Canaan.

Thus during much of the settlement period, the Israelites were either under the control of the more powerful Canaanite rulers or were engaged in nearly continuous armed conflict with their neighbors and fellow tribesmen. This state of affairs can be illustrated by two passages: Judges 15:11 and 12:1–6. In the first of these texts, Samson has been pursued into the tribal territory of Judah by an army of Philistines. Eventually he is captured and turned over to his enemies. However, his captors are men of Judah who tell him, "Do you not know that the Philistines are rulers over us?"

Judges 12:1–6 shows Jephthah completing a war with the Ammonites in Gilead only to be faced with the militant jealousies of a sister tribe, the Ephraimites. Contending that they were denied their share of the glory and loot in the recent campaign, these tribesmen cross into Jephthah's territory. Unlike Gideon, who was faced with the same charge in Judges 8:1–3, Jephthah denies the Ephraimite claim, arguing that they had failed to come when called. This precipitates a civil war during which Jephthah's forces take the fords of the Jordan River to prevent the invaders from escaping and slaughter a reported forty-two *eleph* of the enemy. Though most translations render this as forty-two "thousand," an *eleph* is more likely a designation for a military unit. Whatever the actual number, it is considered a great victory over the Ephraimites.

One other portion of this narrative that demonstrates the obvious differences between the tribes in this period is the so-called *shibboleth* affair (Judg. 12:5–6). As the Ephraimites attempt to sneak across the Jordan, Jephthah's men stop them and ask them to pronounce the word *shibboleth*, which means "ear of grain" or in some contexts "stream." The Ephraimites, however, apparently speak a different dialect of Hebrew and therefore they pronounce the word as *sibboleth*, without the *sh* sound. Their inability to pronounce the term in the same way as Jephthah's people gives them away, and they are executed on the spot.

The Contrast in Weapons

Although the Philistines and Canaanites began to experiment with an iron-based military technology in the twelfth and eleventh centuries BCE, the alloyed metal of choice throughout this period remained bronze (10 percent tin and 90 percent copper). There are textual records from the late third millennium and early centuries of the second millennium from Mesopotamia indicating that tin was imported into that area, possibly from the Indus Valley or northwestern Iran. During the mid- to late second millennium, Mycenaean and Minoan traders who controlled the eastern Mediterranean trade routes brought tin ingots to the Near East, possibly from northern Europe or Cornwall in England.

The Israelites also used bronze weapons, but their lack of metallurgical knowledge and the Cyriote-Philistine monopoly over the tin trade along the

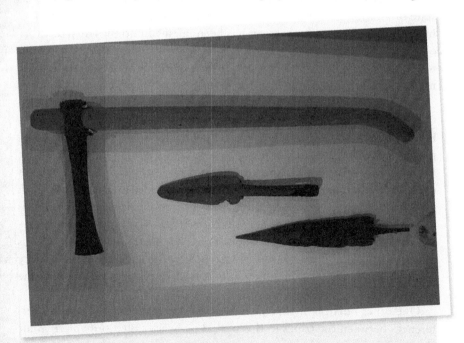

Figure 2.4. Standard equipment of a Middle Bronze Age Canaanite warrior, including a chisel type axe with concave socket, a flattened dagger with pommel and a spearhead

coast of Canaan probably forced many of their soldiers to use staffs (2 Sam. 23:21), slings (1 Sam. 17:50), and farm implements to defend themselves. Some iron weapons were undoubtedly captured during raids by Israelite forces, but without the knowledge of metallurgy to repair and fabricate new weapons out of scrap metal, they would have become pitted and useless eventually. This may explain why the forces under Joshua chose to burn the chariots of the northern coalition of Canaanite kings rather than use them themselves (Josh. 11:9). The Israelites could not repair the chariots, and they did not want to leave them behind for Canaanites to use against them in the future. Also, the chariots would have been of little use to Israelite bands operating out of the rugged hill country.

An apparent Israelite lack of skill in working metals is repeatedly mentioned in the narratives. The Israelites were deliberately denied this knowledge by the Philistines lest they "make swords or spears for themselves" (1 Sam. 13:19). As a result, Israelite tribesmen were ill equipped for war and were constantly forced to rely on inferior weapons and the element of surprise. For instance, the Joseph tribe's attack on Bethel was successful because a man of that community was captured and showed them "the way into the city" (Judg. 1:22–25).

In an episode involving the Benjaminite judge Ehud, the hero resorts to assassination (Judg. 3:15–26) to free his people from the heavy tribute demands of King Eglon of Moab. Concealing a specially designed, double-edged dagger on his person before his interview with the Moabite king, Ehud then tells Eglon that he has a message for him from God. This causes the greedy monarch to send away his guards and gives the left-handed Ehud the opportunity to draw his dagger, stab the king, and escape to rally his forces against the leaderless Moabites.

Gideon is another Israelite judge who uses trickery rather than force of arms to achieve his goals. When faced with overwhelming odds in a war against the Midianites, he divides the three hundred men that God has allowed him to bring into three companies (Judg. 7:4–7). They surround the Midianite camp, and in the dead of night wave their torches and raise such a racket by smashing pitchers, shouting, and blowing horns that the confused enemy soldiers begin fighting among themselves and flee (Judg. 7:19–22).

Other weapons mentioned in the text include very primitive items. For example, Shamgar, in Judges 3:31, is said to have killed six hundred Philistines with an ox-goad—an implement common to a hill country farmer who needed to drive his oxen. A Kenite woman named Jael kills the sleeping Canaanite general Sisera by driving a wooden tent peg through his skull into the ground in much the same way she would have used the peg to help erect her tent (Judg. 4:21). Samson, judge of the tribe of Dan, terrorizes the Philistines by using an object that simply came to his groping hand, a "fresh" (nonbrittle) jawbone of an ass, to slay a thousand men (Judg. 15:15). His rather comic exploits also include burning the Philistine fields of standing grain with torches tied to the tails of foxes (Judg. 15:5) and carrying away the doors of the Gaza city gate (Judg. 16:3).

It is unlikely that Israelite forces attempted to capture walled cities during this period before the monarchy. There are some instances when the narrative does describe ambushing forces that emerge from the city gates (Josh. 8:2–7; Judg. 9:35), but these were probably small towns with minimal defenses. At one point the text mentions that Gideon tears down the tower of Penuel, perhaps a citadel within the city. This leaves its people without a rallying point for their forces and leads to their surrender (Judg. 8:17). In Judges 9, his son Abimelech captures the city of Shechem by ambushing men as they come out to the fields and by rushing a segment of his army through the open gates (vv. 44–45).

Shechem's survivors seek refuge in the city's citadel tower, but Abimelech then builds a fire, weakening its masonry and forcing the citizens to abandon it lest they be buried in collapsing rubble. The survivors are then slaughtered by Abimelech's men (vv. 48–49). Later this wily general tries to use the same strategy at Thebez, but he gets too close to the wall of the tower and is struck by a small millstone that a woman flings down from above (vv. 50–53). Disheartened by the death of their leader, Abimelech's forces give up the siege.

While Saul, styled the first king of Israel, was actually a war chief, he did provide a measure of the centralized leadership that the people had lacked since the death of Joshua. Still, iron weapons were scarce, and the Israelites continued to have a military disadvantage when facing the Philistine armies. First Samuel 13:22 tells us that only Saul and his son Jonathan had spears and swords, most likely made of bronze. The remainder of the Israelite troops would only have had those weapons that they could swiftly acquire—probably slings (Judg. 20:16), bows, wooden clubs, and farm implements. When they manage to win a battle, it is the result of a raid that throws the enemy camp into confusion (compare Gideon's strategy in Judg. 7:19–22). Saul's son, Jonathan, and his armor bearer secretly enter the camp, causing a large enough disturbance to give his father's army the opening they need to gain the victory (1 Sam. 14:6–15).

The contrast between military technologies is graphically portrayed in the David and Goliath episode where a heavily armored knight confronts a more mobile auxiliary fighter. Goliath is described in 1 Sam. 17:4–7 as a giant soldier, clothed in a bronze helmet, bronze chain mail, and bronze greaves that protect his legs. He carries a huge spear with an iron head and is accompanied by a shield bearer. Saul offers David the use of his armor, but David has never used armor before and complains that he cannot wear it and walk (vv. 38–39). Thus he relies on his leather sling and five stones as his only weapons (v. 40).

Again, victory for the Israelites seems impossible, and the text ascribes it to God's intervention (v. 47). In any case, slingers could hurl stones with incredible force and were an important part of every army's attacking force (Judg. 20:16; 2 Kings 3:25). Portrayals of slingers have been found on the Nineveh palace reliefs of the Assyrian emperor Sennacherib. Stones flung by slingers have been found in great quantities by archaeologists in the levels of the city of Lachish associated with its capture by the Assyrians around 700 BCE. David uses his sling to good effect and opens the way for an Israelite victory against the demoralized Philistines.

Similarities in the Practice of War

The rules of warfare that were practiced by the Israelites and their enemies seem to be very similar. Warfare had its seasons (spring in 2 Sam. 11:1). It included predatory and defensive strategies, tactics, logistics, and information gathering (Josh. 2:1). And there is sometimes a disconnect between the physical remains uncovered in excavations and the description of events in ancient representations of events. Each side strove to either exterminate or subjugate the other, taking women captive as well as animals and other spoils (Num. 31:9–12).

Pitched battles in some instances were delayed when a champion like Goliath challenged the Israelites to send out their champion (compare similar challenges between Greeks and Trojans in Homer's *Iliad*). The winner of the single combat between himself and his opponent would enslave the loser's people (1 Sam. 17:9). The principle of winner-take-all is quite typical of this violent age and is even found in the Babylonian version of creation, the *Enuma Elish* (*ANET*, 67), when Marduk, the god of Babylon, challenges the chaos beast Tiamat to single combat.

Taking spoils from the bodies of the vanquished foe and cities was an accepted and anticipated practice (Judg. 14:19; 1 Sam. 17:54). In Judges 5:28–30,

---

Rhetoric of Warfare

Given the efforts of Goliath to demean and intimidate David (1 Sam. 17:43–44), it should be noted that the rhetoric of warfare also includes the real-time rhetorical displays of leaders raising martial spirit (2 Sam. 20:1), the recounting of the exploits of tribes and heroes (Gen. 49:27; 2 Sam. 23:8–39), self-justifying statements by scribes employed to express national ideology and theological underpinning for military campaigns (Judg. 2:11–23), artistic representations of warfare, ritual performances designed to raise martial spirit or invoke divine aid, and taunting by individual soldiers (2 Sam. 5:6), their commanders (2 Sam. 10:3–4), and political or clerical representatives (2 Kings 18:19–35).

Figure 2.5. Egyptian relief showing a pile of hands that have been cut from slain enemy soldiers

the mother of Sisera, general of the Canaanite city of Hazor, rationalizes that her son is late in returning because of the rich spoils he is collecting from the defeated Israelites: "A girl or two for every man; spoil of dyed stuffs for Sisera, spoil of dyed stuffs embroidered, two pieces of dyed work embroidered for my neck as spoil?"

Gideon, after defeating the Midianite kings Zebah and Zalmunna, gathers the golden earrings, pendants, and purple garments of the enemies (Judg. 8:21–26). He also takes the pendants from the necks of their camels.

Mutilation of corpses, as well as of captured enemy soldiers, was also established policy for both the Israelites and the people of Canaan (1 Sam. 31:8–10; 2 Sam. 4:12). In Judges, Adonibezek, king of the Perizzites, says that he cut off the thumbs and big toes of seventy kings whom he defeated. The same thing is then done to him when his forces are defeated by the tribes of Judah and Simeon (Judg. 1:6–7). David brings a hundred Philistine foreskins from the bodies of slain men to Saul as a bride-price for Michal (1 Sam. 18:27). In a similarly grisly vein, Nahash, king of the Ammonites, tells the Israelite village of Jabesh-Gilead that he will massacre the entire population if they do not surrender. However, submitting to his demand will cost the men of the city their right eyes (1 Sam. 11:2).

Social Organization and Administration of Law

"In those days there was no king in Israel; all the people did what was right in their own eyes" (Judg. 17:6). Written in the time of the monarchy, this observation serves as the theme of the book of Judges and a powerful argument for the establishment of a monarchy. The authority held by Moses and Joshua, and by the seventy tribal elders appointed by Moses to judge the Israelites in the wilderness (Exod. 18:21–22), seems to have disappeared during the settlement period. Even the **ark of the covenant**, the visible symbol of God's presence, is nearly absent from the Judges narrative and mentioned only in

20:27. All this points to a time of local administration of justice, not total anarchy. Individual households and village assemblies administered justice or reached consensus on issues facing the community. It was their choice to heed or to ignore the rallying calls of the judges.

The Head of Household

Israelite social organization from the time of the exodus through the settlement period was based on the extended family. A man determined his lineage first by his father, then by his clan, his tribe, and finally (if at all) by his people. That explains why when a male character enters a narrative he is usually introduced as "_____ son of _____" (Josh. 17:3). Social organization according to kinship groups is also presumed in the narratives that describe how the process of casting lots is used to identify Achan (Josh. 7:16–18) and Saul (1 Sam. 10:20–21). Each man was singled out by lot by the process of divining in sequence his tribe, clan, and family.

In the wilderness tents and in the villages of the hill country, family was the focus of life. Individual dwellings were often too small to house more than the nuclear family. Villages, however, were organized into clusters of multiple-family compounds. Thus the head of the household, in an extended family arrangement, would have been a grandfather or the oldest active male member. His home would have formed the physical and social center of a cluster of dwellings that housed his extended family. The death of the head of the family may have caused a temporary disruption of the authority structures and inheritance rights within the group, but this would have quickly ended as the family reorganized fairly quickly in the traditional pattern under the eldest surviving male or nearest male kin (see Num. 27:1–11).

> If a son has struck his father, they shall cut off his hand. (*ANET*, 175; CH 195)

An example of the way a family adapted to new leadership is found in Judges 17:1–5, where Micah is thus portrayed as living within a cluster of houses within the village. In this passage, Micah's father had apparently died. Micah moves into the position as head of the household, installing his sons in adjacent dwellings and hiring a Levite to officiate at his private shrine.

As head of the household, the eldest male is responsible for the religious practices of the family. The standard set in the "Song of Moses" in Deuteronomy 32 is that he must teach his family the proper ways to worship Yahweh. The Israelites are admonished to take the laws given at Sinai to heart and to "give them as a command to your children, so that they may diligently observe all the words of the law." Furthermore, they are reminded that this "is no trifling matter for you, but rather your very life" (Deut. 32:46–47).

The concern that each successive generation be taught not only the craft necessary to being skilled farmers and herders also extended to the elements of the law and the covenant. Methods for teaching one's children are exemplified in a series of questions that begin "when your children ask you" and end with "you shall say to your children . . ." (Exod. 12:26–27; 13:14–15; Deut. 6:20–24; Josh. 4:6–7, 21–23). As part of the educational process, the head of household would be expected to serve as a role model of right behavior and as a wise counselor (Prov. 1:8–9). Thus, in obedience to the law and custom, Elkanah takes his two wives and his children on a yearly pilgrimage to the local shrine at Bethel to offer his sacrifice to God (1 Sam. 1:3). In this way they all participate in memorializing their commitment to Yahweh, and the young are taught to keep the statutes and remember their heritage (Deut. 4:9–14).

Each family's head, in his capacity as a village elder, represented the members of the family in the assembly and in worship. In matters of law, the head of the household exercised the powers of the *paterfamilias* in much the same way as in the ancestral period. It was his right and responsibility to punish or to reward the members of his family without the interference of the other villagers. For instance, in Judges 6:28–31, when Gideon is accused by his village of destroying the Baal altar, his father refuses to punish him, saying it is a dispute between Gideon and the god Baal. The power of the father was protected by the commandment to "honor your father and your mother" (Exod. 20:12) and by the tradition of respect that was due both parents (Prov. 30:17). As is the case in other ancient Near Eastern law codes, failure to respect the authority of the father could result in extreme punishment, up to and including the death penalty (Exod. 21:15).

The corporate responsibilities of leadership and the guarantees of respect given to the head of a household, however, also brought with them an element of danger. If a man willfully broke the law, thereby endangering the survival of the community, his crime could bring destruction to his entire family group. Such a crime occurred when Achan stole from the spoils of the *herem* at Jericho (Josh. 7:1). The result of his crime against God's command to totally destroy the city, its inhabitants, and its property is a defeat in the next battle at Ai (7:11–13). As for Achan, he and his entire household are stoned for his sin to "sanctify" the people and clear them of this act of disobedience (Josh. 7:24–25).

Village Elders

Beyond the level of the individual household, authority in the village was vested in the hands of the elders. It is clear that in these small villages, each individual's and each family's actions had an effect on the entire community.

When the elders were called upon to represent their households, they did so in the interests of the village and for the good of the whole body of people. These men, all of whom were heads of households and property owners, represented the collective wisdom of the community (Prov. 31:23). As individuals within an assembly, they

Figure 2.6. The city gate at Dan. In later periods, the gate area was a place of judgment.

were responsible for formulating legal consensus based on the legal traditions and customs of the group and promoting the welfare of the whole community (Deut. 21:18–21). The Decalogue (Exod. 20:1–17), which was given to the covenant community at Sinai, would have formed the basis of their traditional legal knowledge, especially its injunctions against theft, murder, and adultery.

In the small, unwalled villages of the hill country, the elders probably met on the cleared threshing floor. Because the threshing floor was also the site where grain was distributed to the villagers, it eventually became associated with the well-being of the community and with the administration of law. This circular, open space, hallowed by its association with the harvest and the survival of the people, was the first "courtroom." In the Ugaritic legend of Aqhat (*ANET*, 151), Danil, the hero's father, sits on the threshing floor of his village deciding the cases of widows and orphans (compare Deborah's activity in Judg. 4:5 beneath a palm tree). In the Laws of Eshnunna #19 (*ANET*, 162), the statute requires that "the man who give[s] (a loan) . . . shall make (the debtor) pay on the threshing floor." These ancient Near Eastern texts may then shed light on the case of the widow Ruth, who goes to see Boaz at the threshing floor. He is spending the night there to guard his stack of grain, but it is nevertheless fitting that Ruth should approach him at this site to make what is in essence a legal petition regarding her pending marriage (Ruth 3:6–13).

During later periods, as villages acquired walls or grew into towns, the gate area became the place of judgment where cases were brought before the elders. Thus after Ruth confronts Boaz at the threshing floor, he goes to the gate and calls on the elders to sit with him and decide her case (Ruth 4:1–2). The judicial process included restating the legal situation, hearing testimony, and resolving the problem before the witnessing elders (Deut. 22:13–19).

The Judges

After the deaths of Moses and Joshua, the only other authority figures during the settlement period besides the elders (Judg. 2:7) were the judges. They are portrayed in the book of Judges as temporary leaders chosen by Yahweh to liberate the people from a specific instance of oppression. Some are distinguished by unusual physical or social characteristics (Ehud is left handed; Jephthah is an illegitimate son; Samson is a Nazirite). For the most part, the judges (with the exception of Deborah) serve as military leaders, not judicial or religious figures. Their role was to carry out a God-directed campaign against a Canaanite, Philistine, or other enemy group. The combined intervention of Yahweh and the judge then relieved the people of the burden of taxes, slavery, or oppression, which they had originally brought upon themselves by their failure to obey the covenant (Judg. 2:11–19).

Individual skills as a military leader, however, were not the chief qualification for a judge. Gideon, who was reluctant to serve and considered himself unqualified to lead men (Judg. 6:15), defeats the Midianites with a force of only three hundred men and an unorthodox strategy involving a night attack (Judg. 7:19–23). In preparing for a battle against the king of Hazor, Deborah relied upon the generalship of Barak and a promise of victory from Yahweh to inspire the troops (Judg. 4:6). Samson, the most unusual of the judges, took on the Philistines, single-handedly killing thousands of them. Eventually, however, he succumbed to his infatuation with Delilah and to his inflated ego (Judg. 16:4–22). His failure also may be attributed to the violation of his Nazirite vows to God (Num. 6:2–21).

None of the judges other than Samuel were national figures. They operated in specific, limited areas and dealt with local problems. Occasionally, the judge called on other tribes to aid in a military campaign, but it was apparently up to the tribal leaders to decide whether they would come. Thus, when Deborah called on the Israelites to join in the war against Jabin, the king of Hazor, only five tribes sent their warriors. The "clans of Reuben," as well as Gilead, Dan, and Asher, for their own reasons, chose not to respond (Judg. 5:14–18).

The narrative does not include a single example of cooperation among all twelve tribes. In fact in several instances they are described as fighting among themselves (Josh. 22:10–12; Judg. 8:1; 12:1–6). It is only during the war of extermination against the tribe of Benjamin that the majority of the tribes participate in a common effort (20:12–48).

Some tribes are not even mentioned by name in the text of Judges. It seems likely therefore that several of the smaller tribes, like Simeon (mentioned only in Judg. 1:3), were absorbed into the larger ones. As a result, when Saul was proclaimed king by the tribes of both the north and the south at Gilgal (1 Sam.

11:14–15), all twelve would no longer have existed as identifiable, independent groups. However, the tradition of Israel's original twelve tribes descended from Jacob continued to be used as an ideal expression of the nation's cultural roots.

A description of the role played by the judges in the religious activities of the people will be dealt with in the unit on religious practices. The legal function of the judge is mentioned only with regard to Deborah and Samuel. While their legal activity is not described in detail, it is interesting to note that both operated in the vicinity of the cities of Ramah and Bethel in the "hill country of Ephraim." Deborah sits in judgment over people who bring their cases to her (Judg. 4:5). In contrast, Samuel travels a circuit from Bethel to Gilgal and Mizpah, going from village to village and administering justice (1 Sam. 7:15–17). His territorial authority is widened as far south as Beer-sheba when he appoints his sons to be judges over that region, but that experiment turned into a disaster (1 Sam. 8:1–3).

Since the judges operated outside the normal structure of the village elders, the types of cases presented to them would probably include those that required an independent judgment free of local conflicts of interest. Since both Deborah and Samuel also function as prophets, it may be that the people assumed that their judgments would be based on both the legal tradition and on divine revelation.

Family Life

Marriage Customs

First-time marriages continued to be arranged by the bride's father or nearest male kin during this period. Endogamy, or marriage within the group, is not directly mentioned in the Joshua-Judges narratives, but for all practical purposes it was probably still the norm in Israelite villages simply because exogamous marriages would have been difficult to arrange with non-kin-based households. Of course, mixed marriages did occur occasionally and, while frowned on, could provide economic advantages. For example, when Samson pleaded with his father to arrange a marriage with a Philistine woman who had caught his eye (Judg. 14:3), his father does complain that his son should marry a "woman among your kin, or among all our people," but the arrangement still went forward. Similarly, there seems to be no social stigma regarding the Benjaminites' marriages to the captured Canaanite women of Shiloh (Judg. 21:20–23).

In contrast to the arranged marriage for young couples, the custom regarding widows apparently allowed for more direct contact between the two participants. The Moabitess Ruth goes directly to Boaz at the threshing floor

Marriage Rights of Widows

Given the reality that women in the ancient Near East often became widows due to disease (Ruth 1:3–5) and military activity (2 Sam. 11:17), the community had to find ways to deal with these women, who often had little means to support themselves (see Exod. 22:22; Deut. 24:19). Part of the responsibility for the widow was to provide a legal pathway for her to either remarry or obtain an heir to her former husband's property.

Levirate Obligation

The brother or nearest male kin of a deceased man without an heir is obligated to impregnate and care for his relative's widow until the son grows to maturity (Gen. 38). If the **levir** refuses, then the widow has the legal right to publicly shame him before the elders (Deut. 25:5–10).

Freedom to Marry

- In a case where her husband is held prisoner or is presumed dead in battle and two years have passed, the widow who has neither kin nor land to support her "may go to reside with the husband of her own choice" (*LCMAM*, 171; MAL A.45).
- A widow whose husband and father-in-law are both dead and has no son is declared a true widow, and "she shall go wherever she pleases" (*LCMAM*, 165; MAL A.33).
- If a widow does not receive a share of her husband's property upon his death, she may reclaim her dowry, leave his house, and marry a "husband of her choice" (*LCMAM*, 115; CH 172).

to obtain his aid in arranging their marriage. David simply sends messengers to ask Abigail, the widow of Nabal, to become his wife, and presumably it is her choice to accept his offer of marriage (1 Sam. 25:39–42).

The economic factors associated with arranging a marriage figure into several episodes during the settlement period. Sometimes the accomplishment of some great deed could substitute for the actual payment of bride wealth. For example, Caleb offers his daughter Achsah to the conqueror of the city of Kiriath-sepher (Debir). Once Othniel has accomplished this deed, however, the marriage negotiations are not yet complete. His future wife encourages Othniel to ask for an additional field, thereby increasing the size of her family's dowry payment. Achsah herself then asks for water rights, since the field they are given is in the arid Negeb region (Judg. 1:12–15). Another instance of providing a daughter as an inducement for military action occurs when Saul offers riches and the hand of his daughter to the man who is able to slay

Goliath (1 Sam. 17:25). Later, though, he demands one hundred Philistine foreskins of David as an additional form of bride wealth to complete the transaction for his daughter Michal (1 Sam. 18:25).

Childbirth and Child Rearing

When they were physically available, midwives helped with the birth of children. In addition to assisting the mother, Tamar's midwife also marked the first of twins to partially emerge by tying a crimson thread on his hand to mark the heir (Gen. 38:27–30). A team of midwives, Shiphrah and Puah, assist the Hebrew women in Egypt, including Moses's mother (Exod. 1:15–16). Probably, one aided with the actual delivery and the other supported the back of the woman on the birthing stool. Mesopotamian texts provide some insight into the elaborate set of rituals designed to deal with the difficulties of giving birth and the role of the midwife. One metaphorically describes the fetus as a boat being steered through the amniotic fluid with the aid of the goddesses Inanna and Ninhursag. In another medical text the midwife (*šabsutu*) is required to place a necklace of stones on a linen thread around the mother's neck to help precipitate the birth.

Midwives instructed the mother on prenatal care, kept a close watch on the developing fetus, and noted any unusual discharges that might signal a problem with the pregnancy. Once labor began, she sang protective chants and cleansed the birthing room of any potential threats to mother or child. When the child was born, the midwife cleaned the infant with salt and water (Ezek. 16:4) and presented it to the parents, declaring its availability for adoption. Job 3:3 depicts a birthing scene, including the statement, "A man-child is conceived," followed by a "joyful cry" that heralds the child's acceptance by the family (3:7).

The primitive medical practices, lack of basic hygiene, and the isolated environment of Israelite villages may have contributed to the high infant mortality rate as well as the death of their mothers. Even when a midwife was present, there was no guarantee that both mother and child would survive the experience. For example, Rachel dies giving birth to Benjamin as the family travels between Bethel and Bethlehem (Gen. 35:16–19). In another case, Phinehas's wife goes into premature labor after hearing the shocking news of her husband's death in the battle against the Philistines at Aphek. The double trauma to her system causes her own death, although the child survives with the help of the women attending her (1 Sam. 4:19–20).

Children had to grow up quickly in the hill country villages. As soon as they were old enough to follow directions, they were put to work in the home or the fields. As they grew older, some were sent to guard the herds (Num. 14:33; 1 Sam. 16:11) or were apprenticed to the local potter or other craftsmen in the village. Occasionally a child was also sent to be a servant in the religious shrines. Thus, to fulfill her vow, Hannah weans Samuel at the age of three or four and takes him to Shiloh as a devoted Nazirite to begin his training as an apprentice priest (1 Sam. 1:22–24).

Israelite children were expected to be respectful and obedient toward their parents (Exod. 20:12). They were to answer the call and orders of their elders (1 Sam. 3:5) and in this way become a joy and a source of honor for their household (Prov. 10:1). Disobedient or self-indulgent children, such as the sons of Eli (1 Sam. 2:22–25), were considered a disgrace to the family and the community. In some cases, the shame they had brought upon their household required the ultimate price (see the stoning of the rebellious son in Deut. 21:18–21). The ultimate expression of obedience by a child is found in the case of Jephthah's daughter (Judg. 11:34–39). She willingly submits to being sacrificed so that her father's foolish vow can be fulfilled.

Inheritance Practices

As was the case in the ancestral period, during the era associated with the settlement of Canaan, land continued to pass from father to son. The congratulations given to Naomi by the women of Bethlehem upon the birth of her grandson through Ruth stresses the importance of a male heir: "Blessed be the LORD, who has not left you this day without next-of-kin. . . . He shall be to you a restorer of life and a nourisher of your old age" (Ruth 4:14–15). Even for a man who had died without an heir, as Ruth's first husband had, the law of levirate obligation provided that the widow be impregnated by his nearest male kin so that there would be an heir for the dead man's property (Deut. 25:5–6).

Should the male line fail completely, provisions were also made for at least temporary female inheritance. The precedent is set when the five daughters of Zelophehad, who had died in the wilderness without producing a son, ask Moses and the elders, "Why should the name of our father be taken away from his clan because he had no son? Give us a possession among our father's brothers" (Num. 27:4). The solution is for the daughters to inherit from their father's estate. However, they must marry within the clan of their father to ensure that his property and land remains within the extended family (36:1–13).

Symbolic gestures sometimes play a part in the resolution of legal cases, and they often involve the use of clothing. In the book of Ruth clothing is combined with a gesture as a way of communicating a legal and socially recognized point. Thus after lying down at his feet, Ruth asks Boaz to "spread your cloak over your servant" as a ritualized gesture of contracting a marriage (Ruth 3:7–9; compare Ezek.16:8). In this scene two legally symbolic acts are

Figure 2.7. Threshing floor near Bethlehem

employed in a legally significant place, the threshing floor. It is possible that lying at Boaz's feet is a signal of subservience, but more important are her words suggesting that Boaz initiate the legal step of officially taking her into his household. Later, when the unnamed man, who is Ruth's nearest male kin (her levir), declines his responsibility of levirate obligation, he removes his sandal before the assembled elders and offers Boaz the opportunity to acquire Elimelech's field and the widow, Ruth (4:8). By removing his sandal, this man confirmed transferal of responsibility and completed the transaction that would "maintain the dead man's name" (4:10).

While some families struggled to produce even one male heir, in cases of polygamous marriages, a father may produce too many sons to adequately provide them with an inheritance. That was the source of tension in the story of Gideon, who is said to have had seventy sons by many wives (Judg. 8:30). Abimelech, Gideon's son by a concubine from Shechem, had little hope of inheriting his father's estate (Judg. 8:31). Therefore, he raised funds from his mother's kinsmen, killed seventy of his brothers, and set himself up as a warlord for three years (Judg. 9:1–6).

In less dramatic situations, the law prescribed a solution when a man had two wives and he loved one and not the other (Deut. 21:15–17). If the unloved wife bore his first child, the husband could not treat a younger son born of the beloved wife as his first-born heir or deprive him of his rightful inheritance (compare Elkanah's treatment of his two wives in 1 Sam. 1:2 and the legal solutions provided by CH 167, 170–71; *ANET*, 173).

Burial Practices

Abraham's purchase of the cave of Machpelah established his claim to a defined plot of land in Canaan. Subsequent narrative accounts of burials during the settlement period serve a similar purpose. Descriptions of burials from this period generally function as a means of establishing or solidifying claims to tribal territories. For instance, the bones of Joseph, which were carried by the people out of Egypt at the time of the exodus, were finally interred in a plot of ground near Shechem (Josh. 24:32). This piece of land had been purchased centuries earlier by his father Jacob from King Hamor (Gen. 33:18–20). By this action one of the Joseph tribes (Ephraim) legitimized its claim to that area. Similarly, Joshua is buried "in his own inheritance at Timnath-serah" in the hill country of Ephraim (Josh. 24:30). The tradition of his burial there solidified future land rights in that region when it became a part of the northern kingdom of Israel.

In contrast to the proprietary burials mentioned above that take place in new tombs, two of the most prominent of the judges, Gideon and Samson, are interred in family tombs. Gideon is buried in the "tomb of Joash his father, at Ophrah of the Abiezrites" (Judg. 8:32), and Samson's mangled body is placed "between Zorah and Eshtaol in the tomb of Manoah his father" (Judg. 16:31). As in the case of the ancestral tomb at Hebron, the cave of Machpelah, these burial places imply multigenerational residency in the area.

The burial caves or rock-cut tombs were located outside the village proper. Some personal possessions were buried with the corpse, usually to serve as symbols of who the person was in life. While there is uncertainty about the actual beliefs in an afterlife during this period, there may have been some form of ancestor worship or concern with providing items among the grave goods that were designed as comforts to the spirit of the deceased or as charms to drive away evil spirits. Archaeological evidence from the Late Bronze tombs found at Ugarit (1400–1200 BCE) suggests that a strand of popular religion involved communication with the dead and a sense of kinship with past generations. Concerns about the spirits of the dead and the popularity of ancestor worship may be the basis for laws strictly forbidding this practice (Lev. 19:31; Deut. 26:13–14). However, the fact that legal strictures were necessary to prohibit it suggests it continued to exist. The only narrative that contains evidence of the ancestor cult and the practice of communicating with the dead, or **divination**, is found in the story of Saul and the witch of Endor in 1 Samuel 28:3–19.

Various biblical texts do speak about **Sheol**, a deep and shadowy abode inhabited by the dead, both the good (Gen. 37:35) and the evil (Num. 16:30). It is not a place of punishment, but those in Sheol are cut off from the "living God" (Pss. 6:5; 88:3–5; see Deut. 5:26; Josh. 3:10). Sheol is closely connected to the grave, and the dead seem to inhabit both places at the same time (Ps. 49:14). This concept is similar to that described in the Mesopotamian *Epic of Gilgamesh*, which describes the underworld as a "House of Darkness" or the "House of Dust," from which none return and in which the spirits of the dead consume only dust and clay and are "clothed like birds" (*ANET*, 87).

By caring for the tombs of their ancestors, family members were able to maintain a link with the past and in turn secure their inheritance of the land and their membership in the ongoing society. Those whose burial spots went untended were not only exiled from God but were also cut from the inheritance of the living. Thus when Achan stole from the "devoted things" after the capture of Jericho (Josh. 7:1, 19, 21), he and his entire family are stoned to death and buried under a great heap of stones (Josh. 7:25–26; compare Josh. 8:28–29). While the stones marked the place, they did not memorialize those interred there except as a warning to future lawbreakers. Note, however, that even in the case of a crime punishable by death, it was considered dishonorable to leave the bodies unburied after death (see Rizpah's plea to David to bury her sons in 2 Sam. 21:8–14).

Religious Practices

Israelite religious practices in the settlement period range from the mass assembly of people confirming their covenantal obligations at Mount Sinai (Exod. 19:17 and 24:3–8) to private family worship at the shrine of Micah's graven image (Judg. 17:4–5). Coming out of Egypt's polytheistic environment, the Israelites were not immediately able to adapt themselves to a strict monotheism. According to the exodus narrative, the signs of power displayed by Yahweh and his spokesman Moses were enough to convince the people to leave Egypt and return to Canaan. Nevertheless, once they arrived, many found the lure of other cultures and other gods irresistible (Judg. 3:5–6).

Altars

Altars served a variety of purposes. They were sometimes built as expressions of thanksgiving for a military victory (Exod. 17:15–16) due to—or as a memorial or "witness" of—the faithfulness of the people to the covenant (Josh. 8:30–35; 22:10–34). For the most part, however, altars were used to make animal and grain sacrifices to God. The altar built for the **tent of meeting** (**tabernacle**), before which Israel worshiped during its desert wanderings, is described with four horns, or raised areas, on its corners (Exod. 27:1–2). Horned altars like this have been discovered at Arad and Beer-sheba, but they date to the

Figure 2.8. The remains of the Chalcolithic-period altar at Megiddo

later monarchic period (beginning in the tenth century BCE), not to the settlement period.

According to the **Covenant Code**, altars were supposed to be constructed of mounded earth or uncut stone (Exod. 20:24–26; Deut. 27:4–6). This injunction reflects the nomadic character of the Israelites during the wilderness period; a temporary altar implies God's presence is also mobile. It complements the command that there should be no steps going up to the altar so as not to expose "your nakedness" (Exod. 20:26; compare Exod. 28:42; Lev. 6:10). Both instructions probably also reflect a distinction between Israelite sacrifices and those of the Canaanites. For example, the magnificent Early Bronze circular altar uncovered at the Canaanite city of Megiddo has several steps going up to the top of the platform.

The further stipulation (Exod. 20:24) that their altars were to be built "in every place where I cause my name to be remembered" links particular altars to specific events in the nation's history and perhaps to sites with a long cultic history. Thus Gideon builds an altar after experiencing a **theophany** (a physical manifestation of God's person) and a command to liberate his people from the Midianites (Judg. 6:22–24). In Judges 21:4–23, the tribes gather at Bethel, a site associated with Israelite worship as far back as Abraham and Jacob (Gen. 12:8; 28:18–22), build an altar, sacrifice, and ask God's guidance in preparation for the upcoming battle against the tribe of Benjamin.

Types of Sacrifices

There were two major types of sacrifices made on these altars: burnt offerings of animals, and freewill or thank offerings of animals or cereal. Greater authority is attached to the detailed instructions provided for these offerings and the construction of the tent of meeting when Moses is recorded as receiving them directly from God (Exod. 25–40; Lev. 1–10).

The instructions for burnt offerings differ, depending upon the animal selected for sacrifice. When a bull from the herd is chosen for a burnt offering, it must be without blemish or disease. The person bringing the sacrifice must lay hands upon the head of the bull in order for it to be accepted as an atonement sacrifice for the sins of the household (see Job 1:5). Once the bull has been slaughtered, Levitical priests dash its blood against the sides of the altar. The bull's carcass is flayed and burned in its entirety (Lev. 1:3–9). If the offering is from a herd of sheep or goats, the process is the same, except that hands are not laid upon the animal (Lev. 1:10–13). When turtledoves and pigeons are offered, the bird's neck is wrung and its blood drained against the side of the altar (Lev. 1:14–17). The "pleasing odor" of the sacrifice is designed to draw the attention of the deity (see Gen. 8:21; Num. 23:1–2).

Unlike the burnt offerings, freewill and thank offerings only burn the fat of the sacrificed animal (Lev. 3:15). The household making the offering is allowed to cook and eat the remainder of the animal (7:15–18; see Elkanah's apportioning of the meat in 1 Sam. 1:3–5). Grain mixed with oil and frankincense, or baked into unleavened cakes or wafers, may also be given as freewill and thank offerings. A portion of these sacrifices is burned on the altar, while the remainder goes to the priests performing the ritual (Lev. 2:1–16; 7:11–14). These offerings are not designed to provide atonement but are intended to share the firstfruits and to express joy for a good harvest or some other blessing from God (Exod. 22:29; 23:19).

On those occasions when someone "sins unintentionally" and breaks one of God's commandments, a sacrifice can be made to expiate that sin (Lev. 4:2). Offerings are also given when a person needs purification from disease or when a vow has been fulfilled (Lev. 6; 12; 15). Purification rituals must be customized to the individual who brings the sacrifice. For example, if it is an anointed priest who has sinned, he must lay his hands on a male bull without blemish, whereas a ruler who sins is to lay his hands on a male goat (Lev. 4:3, 22–24). After the laying on of hands, the priest slaughters the animal, dips his finger into the blood, and sprinkles it seven times before the Lord. The remainder of the blood is poured on the base of the altar, and the fat is burned (Lev. 4:4–10, 15–20, 24–26, 29–31). For those who could not afford the prescribed sacrificial animal, special provisions are provided for the use of other, less expensive animals (Lev. 5:7–13).

All sacrifices expressed the people's respect for the power of their God. Failure to show proper respect for the laws and rituals associated with sacrifice could be fatal. For instance, Aaron's sons Nadab and Abihu are consumed by fire after performing a sacrificial act not commanded by the Lord (Lev. 10:1–3). Similarly, in stealing from the portion of the sacrifice that was set aside as God's alone (Lev. 7:1–21), Eli's sons condemned themselves and subsequently died in battle (1 Sam. 2:12–17).

Some sacrifices are associated with national gatherings (Judg. 2:5) or communal events like the Passover (Exod. 12:1–28 and Josh. 5:10). Such communal celebrations took shape in the context of the development of a calendar of religious holidays. Feasts centered on the major events of the agricultural year: planting season, wheat harvest, and the autumn ingathering of fruit, grapes, and olives (Exod. 23:14–17). The number of feasts and the rituals associated with them became more elaborate after the settlement period, as the legislation in Leviticus 23:1–44 and Deuteronomy 16:1–17 attests.

Spontaneous sacrifices, which do not involve an officiating priest, also occur in the narrative. Sometimes these events occur in the context of hospitality offered to a "visitor" who is only later recognized to be God or an angel. In Judges 6:17–21, Gideon is visited by an angel. He does not trust at first that his visitor is divine, and asks for a sign before offering him a "present" of a prepared kid, unleavened cakes, and a pot of broth, just as he might offer to a human guest. The angel instructs him to place the food on a rock and to pour the broth over it as a libation. After the angel touches it with his staff, flames consume the offering and he disappears.

A similar case occurs in Judges 13:15–23. Samson's parents were visited by a "man of God" who foretells the birth of their son. When he appears a second time to Manoah and his wife, they offer him a meal as an expression of hospitality and thanks for his good news. The angel refuses their food but suggests that they offer the kid as a burnt offering on a rock. When this is done, the angel ascends in the flames from the makeshift altar.

One final example of spontaneous sacrifice occurs in 1 Samuel 6:14–15. Here the people of Beth-shemesh are surprised by the return of the ark of the covenant from its Philistine captivity. They demonstrate their thanksgiving by breaking up the Philistines' wooden cart for fuel and sacrificing the two cows that had drawn it to their fields. Two local Levites take advantage of a large stone lying in the field and elevate the ark during the sacrificial ceremony.

The only example of human sacrifice by an Israelite in the settlement period is found in Judges 11:30–39. In preparation for a battle against the Ammonites, Jephthah, the Gileadite judge, takes a vow that he will sacrifice the first person who comes out of his tent to greet him upon his return. This turns out to be his unnamed virgin daughter. He is probably reluctant to carry out his promise since she is his only child, but she insists that he fulfill his oath. All she asks for is a two-month period to mourn her unfulfilled life and untimely death.

This practice seems uncharacteristic of Israelite society (compare its prohibition in Gen. 22:1–19) and therefore may be an example of a Canaanite practice that the Transjordanian tribes had adopted. It does, however, fit into the thematic pattern of the Judges period, in which the people repeatedly break faith with God or do things that are contrary to the law (Judg. 2:11–15). Jephthah's oath may be another sign of cultural borrowing, although breaking a vow violates God's law (Num. 30:2). His oath is similar to the one taken by Saul in 1 Samuel 14:38–39—also during a war against the Ammonites.

Places of Worship

A few sites occupied in the settlement period have regional religious significance. Some, like Shechem and Bethel, have a previous history of Israelite religious and social activity. Others, like Shiloh and Kiriath-jearim, are marked as significant by the presence of the ark of the covenant and have no pre-settlement background as an Israelite cultic site. In no case, however, is there one site that is preeminent over the others as Jerusalem will be in later periods. This situation was probably due to the politically fragmented nature of the tribes during the time of the settlement. Travel to a central shrine would have been difficult since the Israelite tribes did not control the entire country.

Therefore gatherings of the tribes at local sites signaled significant events in the history of Israel. According to Joshua 18:1, the "whole congregation of the Israelites assembled at Shiloh, and set up the tent of meeting there." The tent of meeting and the ark had traveled with the people during the conquest. Now that the conquest was over, the ark was brought to a central location in the hill country where distribution of the land could be made to the tribes. Since Shiloh had no previous ties to Israelite history, it was an ideal neutral site for the distribution. Shechem is where Joshua gathered the

---

Geographic Reiteration in the Settlement Period

The reuse of particular geographic locations for major staged events continues in the settlement period and adds further authority and significance to these places.

Bethel: Mentioned seventy-one times (second only to Jerusalem), Bethel is located ten miles north of Jerusalem on the Ephraim-Benjamin border (Josh. 16:2). It is situated on a hilltop with nearby perennial springs and is strategically placed at a crossroads between the Judean Plateau and the Ephraimite hill country. Tied to both Abram and Jacob, it also appears as one of the cities in Samuel's judicial itinerary (1 Sam. 7:16).

Shechem: Located forty miles north of Jerusalem at Tell Balatah, Shechem is strategically placed in the Ephraimite hill country. It was Abram's first stop in Canaan (Gen. 12:6), the site of Dinah's rape (Gen. 34:1–2), and in the settlement period is both the site of Joshua's assembly of the Israelites at the conclusion of the conquest narrative (Josh. 24:1) and his burial place (Josh. 24:32).

tribes and performed a **covenant renewal ceremony** (Josh. 24:1–28). As part of this staged ritual he recites the epic history of the people from the time of the ancestors through the conquest, and he demands that they put away their old gods and old religious practices and worship only Yahweh (compare Ps. 78:5–55). To register their assent to the covenant, he wrote down the statutes and ordinances on a stone and placed it as a memorial stele "under the oak in the sanctuary of the Lord" (Josh. 24:25–26). Shechem's association with the very beginnings of Yahweh worship, when Abram constructed an altar there (Gen. 12:6–7), provided the proper symbolic background for this ceremony and another example of the scribal practice of geographic reiteration.

Bethel is added to Israelite territory when it is captured by the Joseph tribes (Judg. 1:22–25). The city serves as an important religious gathering point in Judges 20:27 during the civil war between the tribes. With the ark standing in their midst, the tribes gather here to plan strategy in their war against the rebellious tribe of Benjamin. The tribes are initially defeated by Benjamin and must come "weeping" before the Lord at Bethel to seek guidance. This scene is reminiscent of Judges 2:5, where God tells them he will no longer drive the Canaanites out of the land on their behalf, and they weep—an action that gives their location its name, Bochim, meaning "weepers."

During the late settlement period, Shiloh once again enters the narrative and is described as the residence of the ark of the covenant. The people of the hill country journey here once a year to bring their sacrifices (1 Sam. 1:3). This narrative presupposes a fairly long residence (at least two generations) for the ark and a temple or shrine to house it (1 Sam. 3:3). The yearly pilgrimage by Elkanah and his wives may reflect the injunction in Exodus 23:16 to keep the feast of ingathering, and it implies that the Israelites held fairly tight control over the area around Shiloh. Even so, it seems unlikely that all of the villagers throughout the hill country would have made the trip each year.

After the Israelites were defeated by the Philistines at Aphek (1 Sam. 4:5–11) and the ark was captured, Shiloh was probably destroyed. Archaeological excavations at the site show a massive destruction level around 1050 BCE and a lack of occupation until the eighth century BCE. The story of the transference of the ark to Kiriath-jearim (1 Sam. 6:21) implies that Shiloh's shrine no longer existed. Immediately after this, Mizpah (Tell en-Nasbeh), in the territory of Benjamin just north of Jerusalem, functions as a gathering site for the tribes (1 Sam. 7:5). On this occasion Samuel purifies the people through fasting and a libation of water. He completes the ritual by sacrificing a whole nursing lamb as a sin offering for the people (v. 9) and by setting up a memorial stone (v. 12). Throughout the remainder of Samuel's career as a judge and during Saul's early kingship, the Benjaminite Mizpah serves as the site for national gatherings (1 Sam. 10:17–27). It is one of the places on

Samuel's judicial circuit (1 Sam. 7:16) and the place where he calls the people together to choose a king by lot (1 Sam. 10:17).

Local Shrines

Since the tribes were scattered throughout the hill country and travel was difficult at best, cultic activity at local shrines and observance of local religious customs were the norm for the majority of Israelite villagers. As noted in Judges 3:5–6, the Israelites dwelt among the Canaanite people "and they took their daughters as wives for themselves, and their own daughters they gave to their sons; and they worshiped their gods." Religious and cultural pluralism is not unexpected in these circumstances.

Despite the injunction against sacred images (Exod. 20:4–5), several of the narratives in Judges mention them as accepted objects of worship. In Gideon's village, his father builds an altar to Baal and sets up a sacred pole, or Asherah (Judg. 6:25–26). Gideon reluctantly tears this altar down, but only because of God's insistence (6:28–32). Later he has a golden ephod fabricated from spoils taken in a war against the Midianites (Judg. 8:24–28). The ephod was a garment worn by Israelite priests, and the term also designates a garment used to adorn idols in Canaanite worship. Gideon sets up the ephod in his hometown of Ophrah, and as an adornment for an idol or a cult object itself, the ephod eventually becomes an object of idolatrous worship.

The most blatant example of the worship of sacred images within a household shrine appears in Judges 17:3–5, 7–13. Micah, a man of the hill country of Ephraim, receives a large quantity of silver from his mother; he uses a portion of it to create a graven image, an ephod, and other sacred images known as *teraphim*. Micah installs these objects in a shrine in his housing cluster and designates one of his sons as officiating priest. Later, an itinerant Levite from the city of Bethlehem is hired by Micah as his official priest. Micah is sure he has done the right thing and says, "Now I know that the LORD will prosper me, because the Levite has become my priest" (v. 13).

Micah's shrine and images clearly transgress the bounds of Israelite law. But this offense is practically excused with the statement, "In those days there was no king in the land; all the people did what was right in their own eyes" (v. 6). This same statement (18:1) is also used to justify the subsequent theft of the images and the hiring of the priest by the migrating tribe of Dan in 18:14–31.

The question then arises, why did a Levite, a man charged with teaching and maintaining the law, consent to serve a group of sacred images? Why did Micah set them up in the first place, and why did the Danites jump at the chance to steal them for themselves? The answer almost certainly is that popular

Figure 2.9. Cult incense stand

religion, the religion of the local villages, was not the pure monotheism required by the law at Mount Sinai. Excavations at Tell Qiri, a settlement dating to the period of the judges, revealed a similar household shrine with incense burners and a large number of animal bones. A substantial percentage of the bones proved to be the right forelegs of goats. This is reminiscent of the law in Exodus 29:22, which calls for the sacrifice of the "right thigh" of the ram.

Evidence such as this suggests that the Israelites found it hard to give up household gods and were attracted to the agricultural gods and ritual practices of the Canaanites. The original ritual behind the **Day of Atonement** (Lev. 16:7–10), with its use of a sacrificial goat upon whose head the sins of the people are placed, may have a Canaanite or pre-Yahwistic background. Driving it out into the wilderness as an offering to the demon Azazel also seems out of character for Israelite worship.

Much of what the later biblical writers described as Canaanite worship practices was also common to the Israelites throughout their history (Deut. 12:2–3 and 2 Kings 17:7–18). That is especially true of the use of the local shrines known as "high places" (*bamôt*) for worship. For instance, in 1 Samuel 9:12–13, Samuel goes to a city to bless a sacrifice being made on the "high place" (NRSV, "shrine"). In later periods, when efforts were being made to centralize worship in the Jerusalem temple, many of the kings of the northern kingdom are condemned for failing to outlaw the high places (2 Kings 12:3 and 16:4).

So many examples of idolatry and the adoption of Canaanite rituals suggest that during this period the people were still polytheistic, or at best **henotheistic**, in their beliefs. Henotheists recognize a supreme god as well as a number of lesser divinities. Thus the Israelites may have accepted Yahweh as their chief God but still continued to believe in the existence of other gods (see Exod. 20:3). Joash's statement to his friends after Gideon destroyed their Baal altar suggests as much: "Will you contend for Baal? Or will you defend his cause? . . . If he is a god, let him contend for himself, because his altar has been pulled down" (Judg. 6:31).

A similar henotheistic note surfaces in Jephthah's reply to an Ammonite demand that he return the land "from the Arnon to the Jabbok and to the Jordan" (Judg. 11:12–24). He first recites the history of how Yahweh had given the Israelites victory over Sihon, king of the Amorites (see Num. 21:21–32). Then, summing up their right to keep these captured lands, he states, "Should you not possess what your god Chemosh gives you to possess? And should we not be the ones to possess everything that the Lord our God has conquered for our benefit?" (Judg. 11:24).

Circumcision

Circumcision, like sacrifice and fasting, functions within the biblical narrative as a means of rededicating the people. It is a distinctive sign of the covenant with Yahweh, differentiating the Israelites from the "uncircumcised" Philistines (Judg. 14:3; 15:18). However, circumcision's reintroduction at crucial points in the narrative suggests that it also has a role in ritual purification.

This practice was first introduced in the time of Abraham (Gen. 17:10) and appears as part of the strategy used by the sons of Jacob to capture the city of Shechem (Gen. 34:14–29). At the beginning of the exodus-settlement narrative, Yahweh threatens Moses because he has not circumcised his son before he started his journey back to Egypt (Exod. 4:24–26). Moses's failure to conform to Israelite custom endangered the success of the people's liberation from Egypt. Zipporah, Moses's wife and the daughter of a Midian priest, rectifies the discrepancy by performing the circumcision. She uses a flint knife to cut off her son's foreskin and then touches the bloody object to Moses's feet (a euphemism for his genitals), declaring Moses to be a "bridegroom of blood." This act, a parallel to the ritual of placing the blood of the sacrificial lamb on the doorpost before the Passover (Exod. 12:22), signals the renewal of the covenant pact. It marks the beginning of a new contractual arrangement with Yahweh that is repeated when the Israelite males are circumcised prior to the start of the conquest of Canaan (Josh. 5:2–7). In this last instance, circumcision is further tied to the Passover ritual, which is performed before their departure from Egypt (Exod. 12:1–28) while they wait to heal before entering the promised land (Josh. 5:8–10).

Discussion Questions

1. Why is the story of the exodus so important to the identity of the ancient Israelites?
2. What can archaeology tell us about the exodus and settlement period?
3. What role do Moses and the events at Mount Sinai play in the foundational story of ancient Israel?
4. What role does the invasion of the Near East by the Sea Peoples play in the transformation of Canaan after 1200 BCE?
5. What would have been necessary for small villages to survive in the Canaanite hill country?
6. What demands would have been placed on the villagers in cultivating their fields, vines, and fruit trees, and to maintain small herds of sheep and goats?
7. What can be learned about social customs and everyday life from the stories in the book of Judges?
8. How did the religious practices of the Israelites differ from those of the surrounding peoples in Canaan?

Monarchic Period 3

Historical Introduction

The transition from a loose confederation of tribes led by a war chief to a centralized, urban-based monarchy was the single most important political event in ancient Israel's history. It also functions as the basis for the political and theological agenda of the **Deuteronomistic Historian** (a label applied by some scholars to a group of sixth-century BCE editors who used a variety of sources to shape the material found in Joshua through 2 Kings). As recorded in the text, the monarchy and its attendant bureaucracy was not established overnight, nor did it begin without dispute or dissent. Once it was instituted, however, a new social and religious phase began for Israel. While Saul will be the first "king"

Figure 3.1. This stepped stone structure provided foundational support for a monumental structure that initially may have been part of the Jebusite fortifications of Jerusalem.

chosen by God, he and his family will, according to the Deuteronomistic Historian, fall into abusive and corrupt practices that disqualify their continuing rule. As a result, David, who in many ways is portrayed as an ideal king, will be the leader who establishes Jerusalem as the capital of his kingdom. His son Solomon will lay the foundations of a centralized, bureaucratic state and construct the temple of Yahweh to serve as the focal point of worship and the symbol of God's presence. In addition, the covenant made at Mount Sinai was expanded to include obedience to the king, and Yahweh's shift to Mount Zion led to the foundation of a priestly community that would orchestrate the rituals of sacrifice and define for all what obedience to Yahweh entailed.

Gilgal (unknown site probably northeast of Jericho) is identified as the place where the Israelites miraculously cross the Jordan River as they begin the conquest of Canaan (Josh. 3:7–4:19). It is also a cultic site where Samuel instructed the elders to assemble to recognize Saul as their king (1 Sam. 11:14–15). A political link is thus formed between Joshua and Saul as national leaders.

It took a variety of social, economic, and political factors to bring the monarchy into being, none of which could have been the single cause. These factors included the growing population of the Hebrew tribes in the hill country as well as continued hostilities and economic competition with the city-states of the Philistines and Canaanites. Put simply, the Israelites were running out of room to expand. They needed space to grow more food and create more settlements, and they needed to be able to establish their own trade links with other peoples. Fortunately, their efforts to break out of the stranglehold of **circumscription** (a physical circumstance that limits a group's expansion beyond its boundaries) were aided by a lack of outside interference by the superpowers of Egypt and Mesopotamia due to the incursions of the Sea Peoples. Finally, the emergence of several charismatic military leaders (chiefs), whose exploits built them a reputation and a following, served as a springboard for national leadership and consolidation of power.

The elements of change that eventually led to the establishment of the monarchy began in the late settlement period (ca. 1050 BCE) when it became evident to tribal elders that the only way to meet the threat of Philistine and Canaanite domination was to unite the tribes under a centralized leadership. As the last of the "judges," Samuel had had some success in joining the central hill country of Ephraim into a loose confederation. The towns and villages in this area formed into his "circuit" within the region (1 Sam. 7:15–17). In the course of his movements from Bethel to Gilgal to Mizpah, the text describes how Samuel exercised his judicial powers to settle tribal and clan disputes that might otherwise have torn the area apart (compare Deborah's judicial role in Judg. 4:4–5).

Still, Samuel's efforts are only marginally more successful than those of previous judges. The difficulties of dealing with a larger territory are demonstrated

From Tribal Alliances to Chiefdom

A series of military crises coupled with the frustrations associated with the temporary leadership of the judges provided strong support for the idea of appointing a single individual leader as a war "chief." His authority initially comes from the acquiescence of the tribal elders and is reinforced through the intervention of Samuel as God's representative and the anointing ceremony that marks him as divinely chosen to lead the people (1 Sam. 9:19–10:1). Since this position is designed initially to deal with the military crisis facing the tribes, Saul must first marshal the forces of the tribes and protect Israelite territory from invasion by the Philistines and other neighboring peoples (1 Sam. 11:1–11; 13:2–4; 15:4–9). Given sufficient military success and the time to consolidate his power, a chief could build a political base as a stepping stone to the establishment of a centralized monarchy. Saul attempts to do this from his central power base at Gibeon, gradually expanding his influence as chief while nudging the Israelite tribes toward unification. Furthermore, continuous clashes with the Philistines reinforced the fact that centralized leadership that could force the tribes to participate in the common defense made it less likely that the elders would return to their former level of autonomy. However, Saul will never obtain the full support of the elders and, as is characteristic of chiefdom, they will eventually throw their support to a more successful chief (David; 2 Sam. 5:1–5), who is finally able to craft the tribes into a more cohesive political unit.

when Samuel attempted to expand the range of his authority into Judah and appointed his sons to judge the southern region of Beer-sheba. Despite his best intentions, Samuel's sons, like Eli's (1 Sam. 2:12–17, 22), proved to be corrupt (1 Sam. 8:1–5). They took bribes and "perverted justice" to such an extent that the elders of the tribes called Samuel to a meeting at his base in Ramah (just north of Jerusalem) and asked him to appoint a king to rule them instead. From that point on, the text contains two strands of tradition: one that favors the idea of a monarchy and the other that strongly opposes it. This dispute, which began with the inception of the kingship, continued even after the monarchy ceased to exist in the postexilic period.

Early Monarchy

Saul's rise to power as the chief over the Israelite tribes, like David's a generation later, hinged upon his influence and ability as a war leader. His command of a professional force of fighters and his initial success against the Ammonites and Philistines gave him the credentials that tribal elders needed to name him as their king (1 Sam. 11). The support he received from the priestly community in the person of Samuel gave his leadership position the sanction of Yahweh. The fact that his final assumption of power at the behest of the elders took place at Gilgal added even greater authority, since it is also associated with the beginning of the conquest under Joshua (Josh. 4:19–24; 1 Sam. 11:14–15).

However, since a chiefdom is not a nation, Saul quickly encounters difficulties in maintaining the loyalties of the tribes. The petty jealousies and concerns over the loss of tribal autonomy appear in the biblical narrative in the complaints of "worthless fellows" who questioned Saul's leadership from the start. The potential for political fracture is clearly demonstrated in their defiant query, "How can this man save us?" (1 Sam. 10:27). These dissident sentiments stand in the face of what at first seemed like firm support for Saul. Further unrest will become increasingly evident when Saul is unable to win every battle against Israel's enemies (1 Sam. 14:29–46; 18:6–9).

Saul's growing frustration also damages his relationship with Samuel, and the conflicts over who is in charge cause matters to deteriorate. Of prime importance here is Saul's attempt to usurp Samuel's cult functions. On three separate occasions (1 Sam. 12–15) the narrative describes how Saul failed to follow tradition regarding sacrifice and the rules of the *herem* ("holy war"). A case based on a disqualification theme is built against Saul by the Deuteronomistic Historian to justify his and his family's replacement on the throne by David. A signal that Davidic or pro-Davidic scribes are shaping the narrative is found when several times Saul is even portrayed as admitting to David that his rival is destined to take the throne from him and his sons (1 Sam. 24:20; 26:25).

> Wisdom literature points to right behavior and right speech as the qualities most to be valued. Thus "the prudent are restrained in speech" (Prov. 10:19b), and "the one who heeds admonition is prudent" (Prov. 15:5b).

Saul's uncharacteristic admissions are just one indication that there is a political and theological agenda behind the retelling of the nation's history. This agenda can also be seen in the book of Joshua, where the method of storytelling emphasizes the theological significance of obedience to the covenant and God's command more than a strict recounting of historical events. In examining the record of the history of monarchy, it is plain to see that the editor's (or editors') wish is to tie the successes and failures of individual kings to their allegiance to Yahweh. Those kings who "did what is right in the sight of the Lord" and followed the path of obedience like their ancestor David helped the nation prosper (see 1 Kings 15:11–15). Conversely, those who "did evil in the sight of the Lord" opened the door to personal and national failure (see 2 Kings 16:2).

Given this political agenda, it is not surprising that the manner in which Saul's reign is described would be from the perspective of the Davidic monarchy. Written and edited by priests and scribes serving as court historians long after David becomes king and his dynasty is well established, the narrative makes every effort to legitimize the Davidic dynasty's right to the throne. Still, it is quite likely that Saul did, in fact, overstep the bounds set by the priestly community. As a result, the priests chose a successor whom they thought they could control. David is described as the youngest of seven sons from an undistinguished clan of the tribe of Judah (1 Sam. 16:3–13). By choosing him, Samuel and the Shiloh priesthood could not be accused of favoring their own Ephraimite region. Plus, David's lack of experience and political connections would make it more likely that he would look to Samuel and the priests for support and advice.

David, however, quickly proves to be his own man, perfectly capable of acquiring the leadership and military skills necessary to become a rival chief to Saul. He initially enters Saul's royal court as a musician (1 Sam. 16:18–23). David's skill as a musician is enhanced by, or eventually serves to enhance, his status as "a man of valor, a warrior, prudent in speech, and a man of good presence" (16:18). These qualities aid David in rising to the position of royal armor bearer and later to a leadership position in Saul's army (1 Sam. 18:5).

Most important to later events is David's marriage to Saul's daughter Michal. This tie to the royal household gives David a legitimate claim, however remote, to the throne. Just how important she is to him becomes clear after Saul's death. David insists on Michal's return, despite the fact that their marriage was annulled by Saul many years earlier (1 Sam. 25:44). He forces Abner, Saul's old general, to bring her to him as a prerequisite to joining David's

Mercenaries, Bandits, and Traitors

Ancient Near Eastern records contain references to men who for political or other purposes have been forced to flee authority and are labeled as bandits or traitors. Some, like David, become mercenaries, while others are mentioned as a nuisance and a menace to ordered society.

The fifteenth-century BCE inscription of Idrimi describes how he and his royal family are forced to flee from Aleppo. He spends seven years among the Hapiru warriors in Canaan as their chief and eventually becomes king of Alalakh where he is able to pass his rule on to his sons (Greenstein and Marcus 1976, 67).

The fourteenth-century BCE El Amarna texts describe political and social unrest in Egypt's lands in Canaan (Moran 1992, 137–43):

- EA 67:17 characterizes a political opponent as "like the 'Apiru, a runaway dog."
- EA 71:21 mentions 'Apiru mercenaries, who aid a rebel leader against a faithful ruler, and EA 73:28 contains a message from the rebel leader to other towns to "kill your lord and join the 'Apiru," which inspires them to join the rebels (EA 74:29).

command (2 Sam. 3:13). To encourage the northern tribal leaders to join him, David needs some genealogical link with Saul's rule. This marriage will ease their acceptance of David as the legitimate successor of their former king.

The final break between Saul and David is caused by the king's awareness of David's increasing popularity (1 Sam. 18:7–8). Certainly the popular chant "Saul has killed his thousands, and David his ten thousands" (1 Sam. 18:7) must have heightened Saul's royal jealousy. What results is a period of conflict between them that sees David branded as an outlaw. He eventually even joins the Philistines as a mercenary chief (1 Sam. 27).

Like Jephthah in Judges 11:3–11, who became an outcast from his tribe and formed an outlaw band, David builds a following of his relatives and those discontented with Saul's rule (1 Sam. 22:1–2). As a "masterless man" or bandit, David fits the accusation made by Nabal in 1 Samuel 25:10 that "there are many servants today who are breaking away from their masters." David subsequently plays a cat-and-mouse game with Saul's army. Operating on the fringes of society, several of these bandits, including Joab and Abiathar, stay with David throughout his career and form the nucleus of his advisory circle when he becomes king.

While operating as a dissident/outlaw, David makes a name for himself by protecting the city of Keilah from the Philistines (1 Sam. 23:1–5) and by helping shepherds guard their flocks in the hill country (1 Sam. 25:7–8). Marriage alliances during this period also solidify David's position as king of the tribe of Judah after Saul's death (Abigail, 1 Sam. 25:39–42, and Ahinoam, 1 Sam. 25:43).

David's service with Achish, the Philistine king of Gath, seems to be an attempt on his part to remove himself from Saul's area of effective control as well as an opportunity to acquire skills and knowledge that will help him when he becomes king. While employed by the Philistines, he builds support with the tribal chiefs of Judah by sending them portions of the spoil he takes in raids (1 Sam. 30:26; compare Josh. 22:8). Also during this period David learns Philistine military tactics, strategies, and possibly some knowledge of their use of iron technology. Such an intimate knowledge of the enemy will prove invaluable when he leads his armies against them as king of Israel.

David the King

With the death of Saul and most of his sons in battle against the Philistines at Gilboa (1 Sam. 31), David is free to establish himself as a political force within the tribes. At first, however, he does this only with his own tribe of Judah. Political loyalties among the Ephraimite tribes continue to center on Saul's family, and Abner successfully installs Saul's son Ishbosheth (or Ishbaal) as their king. Because the Philistines gained effective control over Ephraimite territory in Canaan after Saul's defeat at Gilboa, Ishbosheth had to move his

Hebron and Geographic Reiteration

Hebron (Tell er-Rumeide) is centrally located nineteen miles south of Jerusalem and twenty-three miles northeast of Beer-sheba. Narrative links tie it to Israelite history in several periods and thus establish a solid association with that city and its environs.

- Abram settles "by the oaks of Mamre" near Hebron and builds an altar there to worship Yahweh (Gen. 13:18).
- Abraham's three visitors predict the birth of Isaac at Hebron (Gen. 18:1–15).
- Abraham purchases the Cave of Machpelah near Hebron to bury Sarah (Gen. 23).
- Both Isaac (Gen. 35:27) and Jacob (Gen. 37:1, 14) spend time at Hebron.
- Caleb is awarded Hebron after the conquest (Josh. 14:6–15), although some texts ascribe it to the tribe of Judah (Judg. 1:10).
- David marries a Calebite widow, Abigail (1 Sam. 25:29–42), smoothing the way for him to install himself as king over the tribe of Judah at Hebron for seven years (2 Sam. 2:1–4; 1 Kings 2:11).
- The elders of the northern tribes come to Hebron to ask David to become their king (2 Sam. 5:1–3).
- Absalom begins his effort to oust David by first going to Hebron where he is proclaimed king and then marching on Jerusalem (2 Sam. 15:7–12).

capital to the Transjordanian city of Mahanaim (2 Sam. 2:8). David, having been proclaimed king by the elders of Judah, chooses Hebron, long associated with the ancestors and the worship of Yahweh, as his capital (2 Sam. 2:1–4).

An intermittent and bloody border war persists between the forces of David and Ishbosheth for seven years (2 Sam. 2:12–32). That finally ends as a result of a falling-out between Saul's son and his general Abner over one of Saul's concubines (2 Sam. 3:6–11). Shamed by Ishbosheth's refusal to agree to his request, Abner begins negotiations to shift his allegiance to David (2 Sam. 3:12). With Abner's help David reclaims Michal as his wife and obtains support from the elders of the northern tribes (2 Sam. 3:13–21). Unfortunately for Abner, his efforts actually result in his death when he is assassinated by David's nephew Joab for killing Joab's brother during the civil war (2 Sam. 3:22–30). Having no other alternative, the elders of Israel are forced to attend David in Hebron in order to acknowledge him as their king (2 Sam. 5:1–3).

It is this formal acknowledgment by the tribal elders that officially ratifies David's kingship and ends the political future of the Saulides. Even though David, like Saul, had been chosen by Yahweh and anointed by the prophet

Samuel (1 Sam. 9:1–10:8; 16:1–13), David will need the support of the people in order to exercise his kingly authority (2 Sam. 2:4). The loosely allied tribal confederation that made up David's "kingdom" continued to provide social and political organization at the tribal level. Village elders continued to settle local issues, although in cases of political importance David does take a direct hand (see the case between Mephibosheth and Ziba in 2 Sam. 9). Occasionally suppli- cants did try to take their legal cases to David for his ruling (see 2 Sam.14:1–20), but he did not always provide an audience or appoint judges (2 Sam. 15:2–5).

Only in Solomon's time, after Israel had experienced a degree of centralized government for almost seventy years, can Israel be considered a state similar to those surrounding it. By that time the population had more than doubled in size, and Solomon instituted a wide range of bureaucratic offices to help him support the administrative needs of the people and take advantage of their natural resources (1 Kings 4:1–21; 5:1–7:51).

Throughout David's reign a true unification of the tribes into a single kingdom remained a tenuous arrangement and required delicate political handling on his part. Perhaps to remove the hint of political favoritism toward his own tribe, David moved his capital to the more centralized and politically neutral site of Jerusalem (2 Sam. 5:6–10). This former Jebusite city with a long history as a Canaanite urban center was never captured by the Israelites until David's time (Judg. 1:18, 21). It provided a defensible location with access to major trade routes and, later, a literate population from which to draw trained scribes and bureaucrats to help manage the affairs of state (1 Chron. 11:4–9).

Jerusalem also served as virgin soil in which the Yahweh cult could grow and flourish. By bringing the people's most important religious symbol, the ark of the covenant, to his new capital (2 Sam. 6:12–19), David signals to the priests of the old cultic centers at Shiloh, Shechem, and Hebron his intent to steer an independent political and religious course. This desire is curtailed, at least in part, when he is denied the right to construct a temple for the ark (2 Sam. 7:4–16). David's disappointment is mollified when the prophet Nathan announces that God will establish a new, **everlasting covenant** with the king's dynasty that will ensure its continuance against all opposition (2 Sam. 7:11b–17). Ultimately, David's son Solomon overcomes any opposition and builds the primary Yahwist temple in Jerusalem with the help of his Phoenician ally Hiram of Tyre and the Phoenicians' technical expertise and raw materials (1 Kings 7).

Once established in Jerusalem, David and his general, Joab, consolidate Israel's political control over large areas of Canaan and Transjordan. Nearly continuous wars keep the people's sense of loyalty directed toward the capital and the king. Crisis and the success of his military campaigns work in David's favor to accelerate the decline of old loyalties to tribe and clan (2 Sam. 8:1–14). However, the concept of kingship was still fairly new in Israel, and fresh disputes arose that threatened to rip the nation apart. The question of succession within David's household was one of the primary causes of this dissension. In the last part of David's reign, Absalom precipitates a civil war in an attempt to seize the throne from his father (2 Sam. 13–19). This proves to be the severest test of David's leadership, although it also unmasks some whose loyalties are questionable (Ahithophel, Shimei, and Mephibosheth in 2 Sam. 16). Despite having to temporarily flee from Jerusalem (2 Sam. 15:13–37), the eventual squashing of Absalom's revolt gives David the opportunity to reaffirm tribal obligations to the monarchy while demonstrating the potency of his own personal army (2 Sam. 18:1–18).

> *Everlasting covenant* (2 Sam. 7:11b–17): an unconditional contract with the House of David granting them perpetual rights to rule from Jerusalem. Divine-right rule is a protection against assassination and rebellion.

One additional political repercussion of Absalom's usurpation of the throne was Sheba's revolt (2 Sam. 20:1–22). Particularly important for later developments is the cry for secession by Sheba's supporters: "We have no portion in David, no share in the son of Jesse! To your tents, O Israel!" (2 Sam. 20:1b). Although Joab is able to put down this revolt (2 Sam. 20:14–22), Sheba's rallying cry will be heard again in the time of Solomon's successor Rehoboam, and the nation will permanently divide at that point (1 Kings 12:16).

Solomon's Innovations

One positive result of Absalom's revolt is the likelihood that it smoothed the way for Solomon to succeed his father to the throne by eliminating some of the enemies of the united monarchy. Solomon begins his campaign for the throne by obtaining David's blessing (1 Kings 1:29–30), the backing of the prophet Nathan, and the support of Benaiah, the commander of the king's personal bodyguard, and of Zadok, a member of the Jerusalem priesthood. He can then argue that his power base is more legitimate and broader than that of his brother Adonijah. The tribal leaders may have feared that another civil war between claimants to the throne would weaken the nation's ability to protect itself, and they choose the course of continued stability by proclaiming Solomon king (1 Kings 1:43–48).

Solomon moves quickly to demonstrate that he is truly in charge of the nation. First, he engages in a political purge of some of David's oldest advisers, Adonijah (1 Kings 2:13–25), Abiathar (1 Kings 2:26–27), and Joab being the most conspicuous victims (1 Kings 2:28–34). The narrative then records how the new monarch made his intentions clear that he planned to rule as a true king, not just as the war chief of a sometimes rebellious confederation of tribes. To begin with, he redraws the boundaries of the twelve administrative districts of the kingdom. In this way Solomon further weakens tribal loyalties and reduces the threat of revolts (1 Kings 4:1–21; compare Sheba's revolt against David in 2 Sam. 20). Royal bureaucrats are appointed to administer the newly created political units, to collect taxes, and to provide work gangs for public works and defense projects (compare Samuel's warning in 1 Sam. 8:11–17). Each of these districts is then made responsible for supporting the royal household for one month in each year (1 Kings 4:7). Since some of these districts were larger and had more natural resources, some provision must have been made to balance the financial load.

The second major action attributed to Solomon is the effort to turn Jerusalem into a true administrative and religious center for all of Israel. He accomplishes this with the assistance of King Hiram of Tyre, who provides the building materials and trained architects to construct Solomon's palace and the temple of Yahweh (1 Kings 5:7–12). The temple, constructed in the style of Canaanite temples of the day, housed the ark of the covenant and, more important, "housed" the presence of Yahweh among his people. In this way their God, who directed them in the desert and gave them the law at Mount Sinai, is transformed into a national deity. His presence is now transferred to Mount Zion, a priestly community is formed to serve before the altar, and God's role now includes the sanctioning of the rule of the king in Jerusalem, his holy city. With king and God enthroned in a well-established capital city, Israel now joins her neighbors as a legitimate nation. And, not coincidentally, the ark of the covenant is lost to the sight of the people, never leaving the temple, in essence submerged by the new structure.

As part of the process of installing the official worship of Yahweh in Jerusalem, Solomon initiates a new priesthood to serve in the temple. His ally Zadok heads this new group. Abiathar, David's old companion and a priest of the Shiloh cultic group, is exiled from Jerusalem and sent to the nearby city of Anathoth along with his line of priests (1 Kings 2:26). This serves the king's purpose by gaining a stronger hold over the activities of the priests. However, it also sets up a competition between the Jerusalemite (Zadokite) and Levitical priesthoods that will continue until the fall of the temple in Jeremiah's time (587 BCE; see Jeremiah's complaints against the priesthood in Jer. 2:26–28; 23:33–34).

Rounding out the Deuteronomist's list of Solomon's innovations as king is the establishment of close ties with several foreign nations. His links to Hiram and Phoenicia appear to be primarily economic and are reflected in the aid for constructing the temple and palace complex. The long-standing custom of solidifying alliances between nations through political marriages is demonstrated when Solomon marries a daughter of the king of Egypt (1 Kings 3:1).

The irony of this marriage to a daughter of the pharaoh would not have been lost on the Israelites in the united monarchy period or later. As much as anything else mentioned in the text, it is intended by the Deuteronomist to testify to the fact that Israel had indeed become a nation to deal with in Near Eastern affairs. Of course, Egypt during the mid-tenth century BCE was weak and divided, with pharaohs claiming the rulership in both Upper Egypt (Thebes) and in Lower Egypt (Tanis). The political unrest of the Third Intermediate Period in Egypt may have contributed to our present lack of documentation between Egypt and Israel, but the plausibility of a royal marriage is not out of the question. In fact, Egypt may have needed an ally against the Philistine city-states, and Israel could have filled that role early in Solomon's reign.

An example of royal marriage alliances appears in the El Amarna texts (EA 29). After long drawn out negotiations, Thutmose IV (ca. 415 BCE) is given as a wife the daughter of the Mitannian king Saussatar. The marriage benefits both sides since Mitanni was threatened by the Hittites at this point and wanted to prevent a two-front war with Egypt. Thutmose in turn gained an ally against the Hittites, and this marriage led to a period of peace in the region.

Whether this marriage is an appropriate political action to be taken by an Israelite monarch or not, the theologically minded text indicates that Solomon's wives became the prime cause of his downfall and the division of the kingdom (1 Kings 11:1–13). The emergence of political rivals who flee for safety to Egypt also provides evidence that the Egyptians were not above shifting their alliances or playing both sides of the political game when it was to their advantage (1 Kings 11:14–20). Solomon's multiple marriages to foreign women also lead to the sanctioning of the worship of their gods. Dissatisfaction with foreign influences coupled with the people's deep dissatisfaction over high taxes and labor service (1 Kings 12:4) all contribute to the schism in the next generation.

The account provided in 1 Kings indicates that Solomon tries to establish a true monarchy on the foundation of the old confederation of tribes and their loyalty to David. These efforts include the refortification of the nation's borders and strategic sites with monumental defenses constructed at Megiddo, Gezer, and Hazor (1 Kings 9:15–19). While archaeological evidence of tenth-century BCE gates and wall systems at these sites remains in dispute, it would have been a wise decision for any ruler to shore up his control over cities that commanded major trade and military routes. Unfortunately, current excavations have not recovered sufficient evidence of foreign trade goods to indicate as extensive an economic enterprise as that described in the biblical narrative (1 Kings 9:26–28; 10:26–29).

In many ways, Solomon's administrative scheme justifies Samuel's warnings (1 Sam. 8:10–18) about the tyrannies of kings and makes it easier for the tribal leaders to dissolve the union when Solomon's son and successor, Rehoboam, refuses to concede to their demands for greater autonomy and shared governance at their meeting at Shechem. The cry for secession then goes out: "What share do we have in David? We have no inheritance in the son of Jesse. To your tents, O Israel!" (1 Kings 12:16).

Without the possibility of political compromise, the tribal elders look for a new leader, Jeroboam, who they hope will be more compliant. Jeroboam has some administrative experience, having served Solomon as a supervisor of forced labor (1 Kings 11:28). In addition, the prophet Ahijah, like Samuel in 1 Samuel 16:1–13, provides divine sanction for the accession to power of a rival to the sitting king (1 Kings 11:29–31). Although Jeroboam has to flee temporarily to Egypt and Pharaoh Shishak I's court

Figure 3.2. One of the Amarna Tablets, a diplomatic letter from King Tushratta of Mitanni to Amenhotep III of Egypt. It includes a greeting to his daughter, who was given in marriage to create a diplomatic alliance.

(1 Kings 11:40), once Solomon had died he quickly returned, and his accession as king of the northern tribes (1 Kings 12:20) opens a new chapter in Israel's history.

It also coincides with Egypt and other Near Eastern powers taking the opportunity to return their attention to Canaan and a divided Israel. One possible sign of this is the Canaanite campaign of the pharaoh Shishak (Shoshenq I; 926–918 BCE). Based on the list of conquered cities in his badly damaged Karnak relief, his army appears to have followed a route north from the Negeb region into the Judean Shephelah, onward north to the Sharon Plain, and finally into a portion of the Jezreel Valley. Its route indicates an effort by the pharaoh to recapture control of the coastal trade route to Egypt. The list's failure to include clear references to the Philistine cities and the lack of archaeologically verifiable destruction levels suggest that they were Egyptian allies at this time (1 Kings 14:25–26; 2 Chron. 12:2–12). Jerusalem is not mentioned as one of the 154 towns Shishak destroyed in the pharaoh's commemorative relief at Karnak. This is possibly explained by the account of Rehoboam's reign, which records that he surrendered much of the city's wealth to Shishak (1 Kings 14:25–26). Comparison of these two records does show that Canaan was periodically subject to invasion, but the traditional ideological scribal practices of both Egypt and ancient Israel lend themselves to self-aggrandizing on the part of the pharaoh and a theme of God's justifiable punishment on Israel and Jerusalem in the Deuteronomist's account (compare Jer. 25:15–26).

Divided Monarchy

His mismanagement of the Shechem conference left Rehoboam David's original kingdom—the tribal territory of Judah—plus the city of Jerusalem. Jeroboam is recognized as the monarch over most of central and northern Israel and portions of Gilead in Transjordan. However, he lacks a religious center upon which to focus the people's worship and thus restores the old cultic centers of Dan and Bethel. In these shrines, located at the extreme northern and southern borders of his kingdom, Jeroboam places the images of golden calves to symbolize God's presence and to serve as a substitute for the ark of the covenant. At the same time, he supplants the Jerusalem-linked priesthood by establishing a non-Levitical line of priests to serve in his shrines (1 Kings 12:25–33).

Jeroboam further differentiates the practice of religion in the northern kingdom by instituting a festival calendar that deviated from the one used in Jerusalem and Judah. Specifically, he sets the Feast of Tabernacles in the eighth month rather than the seventh (1 Kings 12:32; see Lev. 23:39; Num. 29:12). Although the narrative states that Jeroboam "alone had devised" the change (1 Kings 12:33), it may be that the new monarch is simply reverting to an old agrarian calendar that had been used in the northern region prior to the time when David and Solomon attempted to centralize the Yahweh cult in Jerusalem. Such a calendar would reflect the different harvest seasons in the Levant that varied according to the temperature ranges and rainfall averages of specific regions. By realigning the festival calendar, Jeroboam plays to the economic interests of the northerners, who wanted to see their traditional practices restored. In holding his own separate set of festivals, he also brings worshipers to his shrines and keeps them away from the temple in Jerusalem.

In the Deuteronomistic version of the history of the kings, these actions are condemned as the "sin of Jeroboam" (1 Kings 14:16; 16:31). However, the shrines and the revised calendar were shrewd political moves by a king trying to create a separate identity for his new kingdom and who could not afford lingering loyalties to Jerusalem. Appointing a non-Levitical priesthood made it easier for him to control the cult. He could quickly silence interference from priests and prophets, like Ahijah, who originally had helped him gain the throne. In addition, his promotion of the *bamôt* ("high places") in local villages and towns (1 Kings 12:31) gained him the support of those tied more closely to popular or traditional forms of local religion than to a national cult.

Despite his elaborate attempts to consolidate his power through political and religious reforms, Jeroboam still lacked one thing that his rival Rehoboam possessed: the sense of legitimacy that comes from multi-generational dynastic rule. Despite his mistakes, Rehoboam retained the loyalty of the people of Judah to the Davidic line, and that kept him in power and protected his descendants from political coups for the next three centuries. The tradition of an "everlasting covenant" with David's house (2 Sam. 7:18–29; 1 Kings 11:34–39) grew in importance and influence over the years. From the tradition evolved the idea of and hope for a messiah that is expressed in later prophets and the postexilic period, when the monarchy ceased to exist.

Without a tradition of dynastic rule, Jeroboam faced the same political pressures from the tribal leaders and the army that had eventually driven Saul from his throne. He also faced the wrath of the Levitical priestly community that was now excluded from the central shrines of Dan and Bethel. It is not surprising, therefore, that the pattern of succession in the northern kingdom was more often the result of assassination or military coups. For example, an Israelite general named Omri rises to power with the backing of the army and by assassinating another general who had killed the previous king of Israel (1 Kings 16:8–22). In other cases the prophets gave their sanction to a new claimant through the traditional means of anointing him. Thus Jehu was anointed king by one of

> **MOABITE STONE**
>
> Omri, ruler of Israel, invaded Moab . . . because Chemosh . . . was angry with his people. However, I defeated the son of Omri and drove Israel out of our land forever.

Elisha's associates (a "son of the prophets") and commissioned to seize the throne from Ahab's son Joram (2 Kings 9).

During the ninth century, Israel and Judah exhausted themselves in wars with other minor states in Syria, Transjordan, and Philistia. Israel also had expanded its control over Moab during Omri's reign. A resurgence of nationalism in that country during Ahab's reign is described in both 2 Kings 3:4–27 and in the Mesha Inscription, a thirty-five-line tribute praising the Moabite god Chemosh for delivering his nation from its neighbor Israel (*OTP*, 168–69). While both accounts claim victory over their opponent, the Moabite text probably reflects the end of effective Israelite rule in Transjordan.

These border conflicts often involved territorial disputes, as in the case of the war with Syria, in which Ahab of Israel and Jehoshaphat of Judah combine their forces to recapture Ramoth-gilead (1 Kings 22:1–4). In another account, the prophet Elisha bursts into tears when he tells Hazael (842–800 BCE) that he would become king of Syria and would be allowed to ravish Israel with his armies (2 Kings 8:7–15). Hazael subsequently campaigns against the Philistine city of Gath but accepts a ransom from Judah's king Jehoash to bypass Jerusalem (2 Kings 12:17–18). From Assyrian texts we learn that Hazael proved to be a very resilient and infuriating petty king on the empire's border. Another record of his efforts to consolidate his control over the Syrian tribes and establish himself and his son as their king is found in the fragmented Tel Dan memorial inscription. In what is clearly a propagandistic recitation by Hazael's son, he claims to be a legitimately appointed king and remarks that he had eliminated the seventy other claimants to the throne (see Judg. 9:5; 2 Kings 10:6–7). Also of interest here is a reference to the "House of David" as one of his opponents.

> Shalmaneser III's "Black Obelisk" inscription notes, "Having demonstrated my power, I accepted the surrender of the people of Tyre and Sidon, and from Jehu, the son of Omri" (*OTP*, 181).

The general lack of stability in the northern kingdom, combined with a monarchy that ruled without roots and without a tradition of smooth power transitions, played into the hands of the emerging superpower nations of Egypt and Assyria. Israel and Judah exhausted themselves in wars with Syria (1 Kings 20:1–34; 22:1–36; and 2 Kings 6:8–7:16) and the nations of Transjordan (2 Kings 3:4–27) with mixed results. During this same period the superpowers consolidated their control at home and prepared to expand into this strategic land bridge between Mesopotamia and Egypt. The last period of relative independence for Israel and Judah came during the long reigns of Jeroboam II (788–748 BCE) and Uzziah (ca. 783–742 BCE).

The shortsightedness of the two kingdoms' policies with regard to other nations emerges in the prophecies of Amos and Hosea and comes to full bloom

Calaḫ Bull Inscription of Shalmaneser III (841 BCE): "In my eighteenth regal year, I crossed the Euphrates for the sixteenth time. Hazael of Damascus trusted in the massed might of his troops . . . I decisively defeated him. I felled with the sword 16,000 of his troops. . . . I pursued after him. I confined him in Damascus" (*COS* 2.113C, 267).

after 740 BCE in the face of the military might of the Assyrian king Tiglath-pileser III (also known as "Pul," 2 Kings 15:19). The Assyrian war machine had first entered the area in 853 BCE when their king, Shalmaneser III, was defeated at the battle of Qarqar by a coalition of kings, including Ahab. After the Assyrians defeated Syria in 841, however, Jehu, king of Israel, was then forced to pay tribute to Shalmaneser III, according to his "Black Obelisk" inscription. The description of Jehu as "the son of Omri" follows standard Assyrian scribal tradition to label kings as "sons" of the founding ruler whether or not they have kinship ties. From that time on the Assyrians, devastating large areas and massacring entire city populations, repeatedly forced their way south and west to the Mediterranean Sea coast. Situated on the major trade route of the Via Maris, Syria, Israel, and the Philistine city-states were eventually absorbed into the growing Assyrian empire.

These newly formed vassal states of Assyria were restive under harsh foreign rule and repeatedly revolted. Seeking to create a united front, in 736 BCE Israel and Syria declare war on King Ahaz of Judah in order to force him to join their revolt against the Assyrians. Ahaz subsequently calls on the Assyrians for help (against the advice of the prophet Isaiah, Isa. 7:1–9), and this leads to the easy defeat of the rebels. However, the price Ahaz pays for Assyrian help is full submission to the stronger nation. The deep anger Ahaz incurred is found in his portrayal by the Deuteronomistic Historian. The chronicle lists such misdeeds as paying a "bribe" to the Assyrian king Tiglath-pileser III that included the bronze Sea that Solomon had erected (2 Kings 16:17–18), placing an altar of foreign design in the Jerusalem temple (1 Kings 16:10–16), and the traditional complaint of making sacrifices on the "high places" (1 Kings 16:4).

A later revolt by Israel's King Hoshea in 722 BCE finally causes the Assyrians to take the drastic measure of destroying Israel's capital at Samaria, deporting a large proportion of the population to remote locations in the Assyrian Empire, never to return (2 Kings 17:1–6), and effectively ending the political history of the northern kingdom. The kingdom of Judah also felt the effect of Assyrian displeasure. Repeated invasions and the destruction of many villages and towns left the local population impoverished and angry with their leaders in Jerusalem (see Mic. 1:8–16; 3:1–4). King Sennacherib recorded in his royal annals (*OTP*, 191–92) that during his 701 BCE siege of Judah's capital city, he held King Hezekiah prisoner in Jerusalem "like a bird in a cage" while he captured and enslaved the populations of forty-six other cities in Judah. The biblical account of the siege of Jerusalem credits the miraculous survival of the city to divine intervention (2 Kings 19:32–37). Internal politics within the Assyrian Empire may have also contributed to the lifting of the siege. Second Kings 19:37 states that upon Sennacherib's return to Nineveh, his own sons murdered him, but the chronology of these events does not coincide with the Assyrian record.

Judah's Submission and Reform

The traumatic effect of Israel's destruction and successive Assyrian invasions led Judah into a state of quiet Assyrian vassalage in the period after Hezekiah's death. No prophetic voice was heard during the long reign of King Manasseh (687–642 BCE). It was simply a time for political submission to the **hegemony** of an empire that stretched from Mesopotamia to Egypt. Only after the Assyrian Empire began to crumble under assaults from the Babylonians and Medes was Judah able to assert a measure of political independence. That is made evident when Josiah (640–609 BCE) takes advantage of the disruption caused by the Assyrian emperor Ashurbanipal's death in 627 BCE to inaugurate a religious and political reform designed to purge the people of their allegiance to foreign gods and Canaanite worship practices and to centralize all power and authority in the city of Jerusalem (2 Kings 23:1–27).

Josiah's reform begins with a renovation of the Jerusalem temple (2 Kings 22:3–7), an action that ordinarily would be construed as political rebellion against the Assyrian overlords (see Hezekiah's reform in 2 Kings 18:4–8). The king's orders are carried out by a group of priests and scribes, including Hilkiah the high priest, Shaphan (principal scribe in the king's retinue), and his son Ahikam. Their intent and that of the king is to restore the powers of the monarchy and of the Jerusalem priesthood with themselves as its leaders. To do this they will use the newly recovered "Book of the Law" and its authentication by the prophet Huldah as their authority (2 Kings 22:8–20). The practical aspects of the reform involve instituting the legal code found in Deuteronomy 12–26, a code that sets up Jerusalem as the only true place of sacrifice (Deut. 12:13–14) and commands the elimination of all vestiges of Canaanite and Assyrian worship (2 Kings 23:4–14). To ensure that this reform became a national effort, the high places and local altars are destroyed (Deut. 12:2–4), the seasonal religious festivals are centered on the capital (Deut. 16:2–17), and the Levitical priesthood is authorized to officiate only within the precincts of the Jerusalem temple (Deut. 18:6–8). In addition, the altar and shrine at Bethel were destroyed and its cultic practices eliminated. It is fair to say that Josiah's reform is the exact reversal of "Jeroboam's sin."

One further aspect of Josiah's efforts was the revival of the celebration of the Passover festival (2 Kings 23:21–23; 2 Chron. 35:1). The assertion is made in the Deuteronomist's narrative that the Passover had not been kept during the judges period or since the establishment of the monarchy. In fact the last mention of the Passover in this narrative is in Joshua 5:10–12 at the beginning of the conquest (compare the Chronicler's version that adds a Passover in Hezekiah's day, 2 Chron. 30:1–5). Its absence during the monarchic period is curious, but its revival by Josiah makes logical sense because it evokes the people's memory of liberation from foreign domination in Egypt, and it is Josiah's task to throw off Assyrian hegemony and restore the nation to independence.

Such a radical reform could not be put into effect overnight. Enforcement must have been difficult in the face of long years of polytheistic religious activity and the tradition of using local high places for worship. Archaeological findings from this period include fragments of a horned altar incorporated into a wall at Arad. That the altar had been dismantled and its stone reused in the construction of a nonsacred structure suggests a conscious attempt to eliminate sacrificial activity at Arad. Finds such as this indicate that religious reformers had some success, but the actual extent to which they were able to bring about permanent change in the beliefs and practices of the Judeans cannot be definitively determined. The fact is that Josiah's reform was only enforced for thirteen years until his death in battle at Megiddo against Pharaoh Necho II (609 BCE; 2 Kings 23:29–30).

Josiah's death spelled the end for most of his reforms and the beginning of a new era of submission to the superpowers. Egypt quickly claims Judah and the surrounding regions as a consequence of Josiah's failed campaign (see the later version of events recorded in 2 Chron. 35:20–24). In Judah, this meant a new master and the installation of a puppet king. Josiah's son and immediate successor, Jehoahaz, is taken hostage to Egypt, and his brother Eliakim is placed on the throne. The pharaoh graphically portrays Eliakim's status as a servant of Egypt by changing his name to Jehoiakim (2 Kings 23:34).

What follows are the last painful days of Judah's monarchy. A series of political mistakes and unwise revolts eventually lead the superpowers to crush the troublesome nation. The sequence of events begins with a shift of masters. In 605 BCE, Babylonian forces complete their conquest of the Assyrian forces and defeat their Egyptian allies at the battle of Carchemish. Two years later, the Babylonian king Nebuchadnezzar wrests Judah from the Egyptians, and Jehoiakim suddenly finds himself a Babylonian vassal (2 Kings 24:1). Because of a temporary reversal of Babylonian advances on the Egyptian border in 601 BCE, and promises of aid, Jehoiakim revolts, bringing the might of the Babylonian army on his people.

During this period the prophet Jeremiah condemns Jehoiakim's policies (Jer. 22:24–30; 36:30–31) and denounces the people's reliance on the temple of Yahweh to save them from any outside threat (Jer. 7:8–15 and 26:4–6). Forced to deal with unrest in this buffer zone with Egypt, the Babylonian king besieges Jerusalem and captures it in 598 BCE, taking Jehoiachin, the son of Jehoiakim, back to Babylon as a hostage along with a group of Judah's leaders and priests (2 Kings 24:10–17). Nebuchadnezzar then installs as his puppet king the last of Josiah's sons, Mattaniah, and changes his name to Zedekiah (2 Kings 24:17).

Following this initial chastisement of a disloyal vassal state, there is a period of relative quiet as Jerusalem licks its wounds. However, in the ninth year of his reign, Zedekiah revolts against his Babylonian masters (probably again at the urging of Egypt, Jer. 37:7). Realizing more drastic measures are needed, Nebuchadnezzar completely destroys this source of continual irritation and rebellion. While Jeremiah urges the people to surrender to the Babylonians and accept Yahweh's judgment (Jer. 38:17–18), Zedekiah continues to hold out until the city falls to Nebuchadnezzar's army in 587 BCE. Orders are given to tear down the city walls and destroy its buildings, including the temple (2 Kings 25:8–10). The last reigning king of Judah is forced to watch the execution of his sons and then has his eyes gouged out (Jer. 39:6–7). The only remaining member of the royal house, Jehoiachin, eventually dies in Babylonian exile without an heir, never having returned to Jerusalem (2 Kings 25:27–30).

The fall of Jerusalem and the Babylonian exile mark the end of the Davidic monarchy. The community in exile will develop a new identity that will be discussed in the next chapter. When a portion of the exiles return to rebuild Jerusalem and its region, they will be ruled by foreign officials and an increasingly rigid priesthood. The monarchic period witnessed a major social transformation and the creation of new political and religious institutions, and, in the face of political pressure from the superpowers of the day, eventually a fall into decline and near oblivion. After the kingdom was divided, Israel was conquered by Assyria, and a large segment of the people of Judah were taken into exile after the destruction of Jerusalem. The life of the people that remained included growth of an urban-based culture in Jerusalem and other administrative sites, as well as the retention of agricultural village life for the majority of the population. Both aspects of this society will now be examined.

The Israelite City

The transition during the monarchic period from essentially a village culture to one dominated by an urban-based culture with a centralized administrative structure brought enormous changes to the lives and religious practices of the people of Israel. A large proportion of the population continued to live in villages, but these settlements became linked with the life and economy of their region. These rural villages, or "daughters" (Josh. 15:47; 1 Chron. 7:28), supplied produce for the cities' markets and men for the king's armies and labor battalions (1 Kings 5:13–17). Despite some feelings of hostility, such as those expressed by the prophet Micah (3:9–12), the villagers' fate—for good or bad—was hereafter intimately tied to that of the cities.

During the monarchic period, many of the Israelite cities were built over the ruins of older Canaanite cities (Megiddo, Gezer, Bethel, Dan, and Hazor). Since there are a limited number of acceptable sites to establish a city that could support a large population, this was a common practice. However, there is archaeological evidence from Hazor that in the reconstruction process, some areas of a ruined city were avoided at least for a time, perhaps due to a religious ban. That may explain why the large mound of ruins in the center of the city, which contained the ruins of the Late Bronze ceremonial palace destroyed at the end of the Canaanite occupation, was never rebuilt. No prohibition is mentioned for Jerusalem, David's capital, which was originally a Jebusite city (Judg. 19:10; 1 Chron. 11:4–5). When David made it his capital of the united kingdom, he apparently utilized its existing features while building a palace within the old citadel, as well as an enclosure to accommodate his growing bureaucracy and house his closest followers (2 Sam. 5:9–10).

When a new city was built, certain considerations governed the choice of a site. Thus Samaria, the capital of the northern kingdom, was established on the site of a large agricultural facility owned by a man named Shemer (1 Kings 16:24). King Omri purchased the property that included a fortifiable hill, numerous oil presses, and a threshing floor (1 Kings 22:10). An archaeological survey of the site and a series of excavations have found the remains of a large Iron I estate that originally occupied the hilltop. Ceramic remains demonstrate that sustained agricultural activity took place here from at least the eleventh century BCE until it was purchased by Omri in the early ninth century BCE. Such a large operation would have required an adequate water supply for a growing population. In addition, the site has access to major commercial routes, and its distance from supporting agricultural areas was another major consideration.

City Walls

Cities in the ancient world contained several major features. Most important among these was the enclosing wall system. Iron Age cities excavated in the areas associated with ancient Israel and Judah had walls as much as thirty feet thick, rising to a height of fifty feet or more. They were constructed of a mixture of stone and mud brick, with larger quantities of stone being used in hill country and Galilean sites where it was more easily quarried. It was also a common practice for stone from earlier occupation layers to be recycled and reused in new construction. That, of course, disrupted the stratigraphy of the site and adds another factor to the archaeologist's chronological puzzle.

A common architectural feature was the use of **ashlar masonry**, which incorporated dressed stones that were then worked smooth on all six sides in the Canaanite-Phoenician style. The uniform stones alternated lengthwise (headers) along the width of a wall and crosswise (stretchers) along the length of the wall for added strength and stability. These particular styles of stone dressing and the engraving of mason marks on the stones help in unraveling some of the stratigraphy problems.

The walls served as the major defense of the city and thus were constantly maintained and refortified with towers and in some cases with the addition of a **glacis**, a clay and stone slope built up against the face of the wall. The glacis was sometimes plastered over to present a smoother, less scalable surface. It was also designed to prevent effective use of scaling ladders or battering rams against the wall face or city gate (see Joab's attack on Beth-maacah in 2 Sam. 20:15–16; Joel 2:7).

Generally, wall construction followed the slope of the hill or promontory upon which the city was situated. As a result, walls could seldom remain straight for any great distance. Eventually, these alternating protrusions and indentations were intentionally incorporated into a defensive design called an "offset-inset" or redans wall construction. The uneven face of the wall provided yet another obstacle to a frontal attack. Moreover, these features gave the defenders more protection, a better view of the enemy, and a broader field of fire from the battlements.

In peaceful periods or for cities that had natural defenses to rely upon, solid walls and extravagant battlements could be replaced with **casemate walls** that afforded more living and commercial space. Casemate walls consisted of two parallel walls connected by short perpendicular walls. This hollow-wall pattern allowed for the creation of a series of rooms, or casemates, between the two parallel walls. These casemate walls could be filled with rubble to strengthen the structure in case of a siege of the city. Casemates could also be used for storage or as back rooms for houses built within the walls (Josh. 2:15). Examples of this building style have been discovered in the tenth century BCE remains of the fortress cities at Megiddo, Hazor, and Gezer, which some attribute to the work of King Solomon (1 Kings 9:15–19). While not affording the protection of solid walls, casemates did have the advantage of a lower cost, quicker construction, and the creation of premium space within the walls for warehouses and shops in a city with a growing populace.

Figure 3.3. Excavations at the Solomonic-period gate at Gezer

City Gate

As the primary entry port into a walled city, the gate was an extremely busy and vulnerable feature. Some major cities had entry gates at various levels of the site (2 Kings 15:35), but there was always a major gate giving access outside the city. The gate provided access for the city's inhabitants and visitors, served as an assembly area for important governmental and religious announcements and activities (1 Kings 22:10; 2 Kings 23:8), and functioned as a high traffic commercial and legal center for the city (Deut. 22:15–24; 2 Sam. 15:2; 2 Kings 7:1). However, because it was a pathway through the walls, it was invariably the focal point from which troops would sally forth and the point of attack for enemy forces (Judg. 9:34–40 and 2 Sam. 10:8; 18:4). The multiple-use character of the gate required ingenious construction techniques that would provide a fairly broad entrance and activity space for the population and visiting merchants. At the same time, it had to present a significant obstacle to potential attackers.

During the monarchic period, the diagonally positioned, six-chambered gate became the norm. Archaeologists have found this type of gate at Beth Shemesh, Hazor, Shechem, Gezer, Megiddo, and Tirzah. A stepped approach, often with right-angled turns, led up to a multistoried entranceway. The towered gateway and surrounding walls would have been the first line of defense for the city (2 Sam. 11:20–24). On the inside of this first gateway sat two of the gate's six chambers, one on each side of the gate's entrance. Beyond these chambers lay second, third, and fourth gateways, each separated by two chambers and protected by a set of metal-hinged wooden doors. The last of the succession of gates was the actual entrance into the city. During times of war, the chambers that separated each of the gateways could be used as defensive positions against those who tried to breach the gate complex.

The biblical narrative suggests that the gate of Mahanaim in which David awaited word of the battle with Absalom's army was a multistoried type (2 Sam. 18:24). While the watchman went up on the roof of the first, exterior gateway, David sat between the two inner gates. A chamber inside the Iron Age II gate area at Dan contained limestone benches and a canopied platform where the king, one of his officials, or the image of a deity could sit in state.

> Dani'ilu . . . arose and sat at the entrance to the (city-) gate, among the leaders (sitting) at the threshing floor. He judged the widow's case, made decisions regarding the orphan. (Aqhat 5.5–8; *COS* 1.103, 246)

These massive structures used by judges and kings may serve as a model for David's positioning himself at Mahanaim. David's sitting between the gates signaled to the army his personal command of the city and his desire to be engaged in and informed about the battle and the defense of the city. After David hears the news of Absalom's death, he goes "up to the chamber over the gate" to mourn the loss of his son (2 Sam. 18:33). This chamber may have been located in one of the towers flanking the gate or a room in the upper story of the gateway itself. Of course, architectural features varied based on the topography, wealth, and importance of the site.

During peaceful times the gate served as a gathering place for merchants (Gen. 19:1; 2 Kings 7:1; Job 29:7a). The stalls and booths of craftsmen and hawkers as well as the produce market for surrounding villages were found here (Neh. 13:15–16). Fresh produce was bartered for bread, pottery, leather goods, and clothing. International trade is represented in texts that mention Egyptian jewelry and the many products that passed through Phoenician hands (Ezek. 27:12–24). Traders obtained perfumes and incense from Sheba and Arabia (1 Kings 10:2; Jer. 6:20), and ingots of metal from Cyprus and Anatolia were available in these open-air bazaars (see Isa. 3:18–24 for a list of some of these products).

Like the threshing floor (*gōren*) in unwalled villages, the city gate (*ša'ar*) functioned as a gathering place for legal and social activity (Ruth 3:10–14; Josh. 20:2–4; Ugaritic Tale of Aqhat). There is no law that says the elders must spend their time sitting in the gate waiting to see if a legal case would be brought before them. Instead it is clear that they often chose to sit in the gate because it was a place to transact business, share gossip, and demonstrate their status as men of property and influence (Prov. 31:23).

Each of these gate areas was intimately associated with the economic and social well-being of the community, and each would have been large enough for a crowd to gather and a trial to be held. Deuteronomy 21:18–21 provides a good example of how the gate area served as a legal forum. In this text the parents of a "stubborn and rebellious" son are required to bring him to the gate where they testify against him before the elders. Fol-lowing their testimony, "all the men of the city" certify their consensus agreement that drastic measures must be taken, and they stone the son to death. This type of communal execution was designed to bring home to the entire com-munity that crime was not just an individual matter—it was a physical and religious threat to the entire population of the city that must be "purged" from their midst and serve as an example to other miscreants (Deut. 21:21).

The gate served as one of the city's judicial centers. On a higher level of authority, the king was also supposed to listen to the cases of his people, but that would often be in a more formal setting (2 Sam. 14:2–4; 2 Kings 8:4–6; Jer. 36:22–23). David's failure to provide a hearing for the complaints of tribal officials gives Absalom an opening for his rebellion. Absalom makes his case against the king by standing "in the way of the gate" and commiserating with these men, assuring them that he would have given them a fair judgment if he were king (2 Sam. 15:1–6). The legal role of the gate continues to be found in later periods, including just before the fall of the northern kingdom of Israel (ca. 750 BCE). The eighth-century BCE prophet Amos exclaims that justice has been perverted "in the gate" at Bethel and presumably in other Israelite cities (Amos 5:10–15).

> In one of the Iron Age gates excavated at Tel Dan was a raised podium with circular stone bases at each corner that would have supported wooden posts for a canopy. Here the king or a high official could have sat to hear legal cases, preside over disputes, or witness the deployment of troops (2 Sam. 18:4).

Streets and Public Squares

Regardless of the massive battlements and walls constructed by these ancient peoples, at some point in their history every city was eventually destroyed. Rather than giving up a prime site, the inhabitants or other people who moved into the area seldom abandoned a destroyed city for long. However, they did not completely rebuild the city. Instead they recycled usable building materials in addition to bringing in new quarried stone. As a result city planning was practically impossible, because the new inhabitants simply built on top of older, destroyed layers of occupation. That is in fact how these mounds, or tells, grew in height as each successive layer of occupation was added. Originally, the city had been built on the crown of the hill to maximize its protection, but as it was rebuilt time and again on the same spot, the amount of space within the citadel or the city proper was reduced. This process of rebuilding made

Figure 3.4. Plaza outside the city gates at Dan

establishing open areas like thoroughfares and market squares difficult. Only when the site was expanded beyond its original wall system did some degree of city planning become possible (see David's expansion of Jerusalem; 2 Sam. 5:9).

The average size of a city site in the biblical period was five to ten acres. For those sites like Jerusalem that became major urban centers due to their growing political importance and expanding population, planning considerations would be possible in those sectors where new administrative and religious complexes were constructed. When a city expanded beyond its walls and down the slope of the tell or, like Jerusalem, across connecting valleys, the older cramped nature of the city could be alleviated, at least until the next destruction cycle. When resources became available, these new areas could be enclosed within the city's walls as its fortifications expanded outward. Such a process led to expansion of the site of Hazor to 200 acres in the Late Bronze period (ca. 1550–1200), and Dan eventually grew to 50 acres in size during the monarchic period. At its height in the eighth century BCE, Jerusalem covered 150 acres (compared to 37 acres in the tenth century BCE).

With space at such a premium, it is no wonder that biblical Hebrew lacks a specific word for street. *Ḥus*, which literally means "outside," is used to refer to open places or streets (Deut. 32:25; Ps. 31:11; Jer. 5:1) and to bazaars (1 Kings 20:34). Occasionally, Hebrew *šûq* is used for a "street" (Prov. 7:8; Eccles. 12:4–5), but that derives from the use of a path to drive beasts or to conduct business. Within the walls of a city, or even in unwalled villages, these "streets" would have been narrow, winding paths between buildings, many times ending in a blind alley. Often these were choked with traffic, carts, booths, and accumulated garbage. Only in well-planned cities or neighborhoods, as discovered in excavations of certain sections of Samaria, were streets a consistent width, running in straight lines parallel and perpendicular to the city wall.

What little open space that did exist in larger cities like Jerusalem for public assembly and market activity was in front of important buildings like the palace and the temple and in the vicinity of the city gate. A Hebrew term used for these relatively open places is *reḥob*, a "broad area" (Judg. 19:15; Job 29:7b). In Deuteronomy 13:16 and 2 Samuel 21:12, it can be loosely translated as "public square." The first of these texts refers to the "square" as a place large enough for the public destruction of loot following the capture of a Canaanite city. In the second instance the *reḥob* was a place within the city of Beth-shan where the Philistines had impaled the bodies of Saul and his sons and left them as a shameful exhibit. It functioned as the marshaling area for Hezekiah's troops in yet another text (2 Chron. 32:6). Since it was large enough to serve as an assembly point like the city gate, the public square could also be used as a place for public pronouncement and the settlement of legal cases (Amos 5:16; Isa. 59:14).

Considering the space limitations in most ancient walled cities, the most likely place for an army to assemble (2 Sam. 10:8) or for major public events to be staged would have been immediately outside the city gate. Evidence for the latter occurs in 1 Kings 22:10–12. According to this passage, King Ahab of Israel and King Jehoshaphat of Judah sat enthroned before the city gate of Samaria on what had been a threshing floor, surrounded by court officials and four hundred prophets. Such a spectacle would have been too cramped within the confines of the city walls and could not have taken advantage of so many symbols of royal power and judicially charged space.

Palace and Temple

The two urban structures that came to represent the power and prestige of the Israelite monarchy and the worship of Yahweh were the king's palace and the temple in Jerusalem. These buildings mark the transition from tribal to national status and from village to urban culture. Unfortunately, little remains of these monuments to the power of David's and Solomon's kingdom. Despite the fact that Jerusalem is one of the most excavated ancient cities in the world, large sections of the original city are covered by structures sacred to Islam and Judaism and cannot be disturbed. In addition, a large portion of the physical remains has disappeared as a result of repeated destruction and the reuse of materials in the construction of later structures.

What has been revealed in the most recent excavations is evidence of the establishment of an Israelite city on the site in the tenth century BCE and a succession of expansion projects that extended the original "city of David" (2 Sam. 5:7–9) over a much larger area. Should further excavations become possible, they could help reveal a more complete history of the city's life.

The detailed descriptions of Solomon's temple in 1 Kings 6 and 7:13–51 and of his palace in 1 Kings 7:1–12 suggest a drastic change of fortunes from the time of Saul and David. The biblical narrative extols the fact that in just two generations the Israelites had risen from a people subject to the power of the Philistine city-states and Canaanite warlords into a cohesive kingdom with far-flung commercial relations (1 Kings 10:22–29). Solomon also had a working arrangement with Hiram, the king of Tyre, to provide craftsmen and building materials for his construction projects (1 Kings 9:11).

One result of this reliance on foreign expertise was the use of a basically north Syrian decorative and architectural style in the temple's construction. Possible models for this temple type in the Iron I period are found at Tell Ta'yinat (twenty-seven miles east of Antioch) and the Ain Dara temple just

Sacred Architecture

The creation of sacred architecture includes recognition that there is a difference between sacred and profane space. Profane or mundane space is that in which everyday activities occur. Sacred space has been set aside, usually because of an event associated with a god. Because it has been defined as sacred and comprises a specific location, it is outside the realm of normal human activity.

When a structure like a temple is placed upon sacred space, it in turn becomes sacred through contact and as a result of sacred activities that are conducted within that structure (sacrifice, prayer, ritual). The structure itself is hierarchical in design. Its inner chambers are only open to the highest levels of the priesthood who serve in that place.

In most situations, priests or other officiants who perform tasks in sacred structures cannot be diseased, maimed, or "unclean" in any way. In the biblical text, that meant wearing the purest white linen garments (Exod. 28) and the exclusion of such persons as lepers (Lev. 13) and eunuchs (Deut. 23:1; Lev. 21:17–21). Women are excluded on the basis of the contamination from their menstrual cycle (Lev. 15:19–24) and other bodily discharge such as that associated with childbirth (Lev. 12:1–6).

Sacrificial animals, grain offerings, perfumes, oils (Exod. 30:22–33), and all other items that were brought into the sacred structure had to be without blemish and/or of the finest available (Exod. 29:1–2). Otherwise the efficacy of the sacrifice or rite would be diminished or negated.

northwest of Aleppo. Although no archaeological remains of Solomon's temple have been found, its description in 1 Kings 6–7 and 2 Chron. 3–4 provides a basic picture of its structural design.

At the entrance to the temple stood two massive, carved pillars named Jachin and Boaz (1 Kings 7:21). While they may have had a structural purpose, it is more likely that they marked the entrance to the sacred zone, beyond which nonpriests were not allowed to pass and where the king stood on ceremonial occasions (2 Kings 11:14; 23:3). They also may have stood in silent witness to the presence and power of Yahweh, like the pillar of cloud before the tabernacle (Exod. 33:9). Column bases for similar freestanding pillars have been found at the entrance to Canaanite temple sites at Tel Ta'yinat and Ain Dara. These pillars are also represented on carved ivories from Phoenicia.

Laid out on an east-west axis with its main entrance on the east, the temple was oblong with two courtyards. The outer courtyard was made up of the "lower pavement" (2 Chron. 7:3). Then, up a series of steps (Ezek. 40:6, 26) and through a succession of gates (40:19–28) was the inner courtyard, a central gallery approximately 90 feet long and 30 feet wide (40:17–19, 28). Offset-inset walls surrounded each of these courtyards (40:6–7). Burnt offerings were performed in the inner courtyard, where the altar and its accompanying set of sacrificial tables were placed (40:38–47). At the western end of the central courtyard, covering the final thirty feet and separated from the rest of the chamber by a wooden wall, was the **Holy of Holies**, where the ark of the covenant was housed (1 Kings 6:23–28). A secondary structure that abutted the main temple contained storerooms and offices for the priestly community (1 Kings 6:5).

Accompanying the construction of the Jerusalem temple and shrines at Megiddo, Lachish, Beth-shan, and other sites, new forms of worship and an expanded priesthood also came into being during the early monarchy. Along with housing the ark within the temple of Solomon, a group of priests was charged with its care and the maintenance of the continuous sacrificial routine (1 Kings 8:1–6). The religious calendar was expanded or revised to include festivals and sacrifices that were now held in Jerusalem. However, the local "high places" continued to host sacrificial rites despite attempts to officially discourage their use in favor of the national religious shrine in Jerusalem (1 Kings 3:2).

Palace and temple represented a new form of government in which the people were subject to the rule of a single king. During the early monarchy, the king had to take care to balance his efforts to create centralized rule with the continuing presence of tribal interests and loyalties. The elders and large land owners, now referred to as the "people of the land" (2 Kings 21:24), continued to exert economic, social, and military influence. Even so, social stratification did became more pronounced as the king was assisted by a new elite group composed of his advisers (2 Chron. 23:1–3) and extended family

(2 Chron. 11:23). Unlike the "people of the land," who inherited the land they owned, this new class received land by royal decree. The granting of "fields and vineyards" to loyal followers is alluded to by Saul when he claims David will not show such favor to the Benjaminites (1 Sam. 22:7). Presumably only those who have done a service (military or administrative) for the king will be marked as "his men" (see 2 Sam. 19:31–38). This "spoils" system of rewarding his supporters is reminiscent of Samuel's warning that a monarch would "take the best of your fields and vineyards and olive orchards and give them to his courtiers" (1 Sam. 8:14).

While it is uncertain whether the lists of government officials appointed during Solomon's reign are an accurate reflection of his policies, it is likely that a growing royal bureaucracy would have been necessary to manage the affairs in the former tribal districts, collect taxes, and recruit manpower for the army and labor battalions (1 Kings 4:1–19). The resources of the nation were expended in monumental construction projects and the enhancement of court powers. The citadel became an administrative nerve center with its offices and warehouses squeezing out previous inhabitants. An extreme example of this reorganization was found at Megiddo. In the early tenth century BCE, the city contained only two administrative buildings, leaving 75 percent of the

Figure 3.5. Aerial view of Megiddo

city available for private dwellings and shops. By the late tenth century, over 80 percent of the city was occupied by administrative facilities, including the city wall system and gate area, a palace, seventeen royal storehouses, open courtyards used as campgrounds by merchants and the military, and a water system to support the city. Excavations then show that by the eighth century the commoners were crowded into a few small dwellings. Presumably that meant that nonadministrative personnel were forced to dwell outside the city in nearby villages.

The imposition of zoning and the growth of administrative facilities signaled the creation of boundaries between the powerful and the powerless within the city. In Samaria, for instance, a wall was built to divide these two areas of the town, and the architecture was markedly different in each. The prophet Amos, as part of his criticism of social inequities in Israelite society, condemns the lavishly decorated houses of the rich and influential as "houses of ivory" (3:15; see 1 Kings 22:39). Excavations at Ahab's capital city of Samaria confirm the wealth of the elite, revealing numerous ivory objects and furnishings.

Such a transition from regional administration and local religious practices was not accomplished overnight. Opposition to Jerusalem and the monarchy surfaced in the next generation and contributed to the division of the kingdom. However, the kingdom of Israel in the north immediately adopted a similar form of government with a monarchy and the establishment of national shrines at Dan and Bethel as a way to focus the people's political loyalties and worship practice on their newly created nation (1 Kings 12:25–33). Clearly, once the temple/palace process had begun, it could not be reversed.

As the kingdoms of Israel and Judah gradually fell prey to the superpowers in the eighth and seventh centuries BCE, the temple and palace became symbols both of the sins of the people as well as of future hope and restored glory. Isaiah centers much of his prophetic message on the "everlasting covenant" God had established with the "house of David" (2 Sam. 7:18–29; Isa. 11:1–3). His assurance is that Jerusalem, while punished for the sins of the people, will never be destroyed (Isa. 10:24 and 29:7–8). Living at this same time (late eighth century BCE), the rural prophet Micah places the blame for destruction by invading Assyrian armies squarely on the leaders and policies of the cities of Samaria and Jerusalem (Mic. 1:5). Unlike Isaiah, he has no abiding tie to the city culture and predicts that these royal capitals will "become a heap of ruins" as testimony to God's wrath (Mic. 3:12).

After the northern kingdom had been destroyed in 721 BCE, Jerusalem and its temple became the last bastion of hope for Yahweh's chosen people. Josiah's religious and political reforms (2 Kings 22:3–24) came at a point (622–609 BCE) when Assyrian control of Judah was weakening and the empire was about to dissolve. His reforms, modeled on the laws in Deuteronomy 12–26, were designed to redirect the people's political and religious focus exclusively on Jerusalem and the Davidic monarchy. Central events such as the Passover celebration (2 Kings 23:21) were restored to prominence, and provisions were made to increase the power of the Jerusalem priesthood by eliminating all of the local shrines and by recalling all the active Levites to Jerusalem (23:8). Josiah's untimely death in battle against the Egyptians (2 Kings 23:29) ended his reform measures.

Even after most of the reforms had ended, the idea of the temple as the supreme expression of Yahweh's power and presence continued to survive. It remained a symbol of hope for the people of Jerusalem. Yet just before the fall of the city to the Babylonians (600–587 BCE), Jeremiah warns of the destruction of the temple and the city. In his estimation the temple had become an idol and a symbol of false hope for an unfaithful and misguided people (Jer. 7:8–15; 26:4–6). Like other prophets, however, Jeremiah does offer the inhabitants the hope of a restored city, complete with a new temple, after their punishment is complete (Jer. 30–31; see especially 31:23).

Private Dwellings in the City

The style and size of private dwellings in Israelite walled cities varied based on available space, construction materials, and the relative importance and wealth of the inhabitants. Excavations of Iron Age II (eighth century BCE) levels at Megiddo and Hazor reveal houses in the residential quarters of the city of a standard four-room style with a central courtyard. The fact that these sites have a long history and many previous occupation levels may explain why small, subdivided houses are found next to much larger and more complex administrative buildings. Newer homes with better construction and more installations to serve the needs of the inhabitants probably belonged to the new Israelite elite who now ruled these cities. Space limitations had squeezed the social classes closer together, while forcing most of the nonadministrative inhabitants out of the walled cities into surrounding towns and villages.

Ah, you who join house to house, who add field to field, until there is room for no one but you, and you are left to live alone in the midst of the land! (Isa. 5:8)

In newer cities like Samaria and Tirzah, there was a clearly defined distinction between the poorer areas and those of the elite. This latter area was usually on the western edge of the mound where a prevailing west wind would cool the houses and carry away cooking and human odors. These houses were much larger and better built, generally showing additions, the raising of floor and wall levels, and repairs made over the long periods of time that they were occupied. Like those in the villages, they were pillared structures with stone foundations and only a few windows for ventilation (Hosea 13:3). There was more use of tooled stone in the walls, including squared-stone corners. The central courtyard contained the oven, cooking vessels, and storage jars and served as a gathering area for the family and their friends.

The entrance to these private dwellings usually led into a cluttered alleyway, and there were stairs on the outside of the house leading up to a second story where the family or their guests could take advantage of the evening breeze (1 Kings 4:10). If the house was built next to the city wall, these stairs were built against the wall. An economy of materials can be seen in the construction of doorways at the end of the wall so that only one doorjamb was required. The ceiling consisted of log beams thatched over with several layers of a clay and straw mixture.

Sanitary conditions within these homes and in the streets continued to be unhealthy in this period. Human waste would have been burnt (1 Kings 14:10) or cast into the streets to mix with the mire and be scavenged by roving dogs and rats (Ps. 18:42b; Mic. 7:10). It would have been common practice for men to publicly urinate against walls (NRSV translates the Hebrew phrase meaning "those who urinate against the wall" in 1 Sam. 25:22, 34 euphemistically as "male"). Poor ventilation, the odor and noxious gases arising from decaying food and waste matter, and the extreme heat of the day contributed to the rampant growth of bacteria, fecal contamination of food, and the spread of parasitic infestations (tapeworm and whipworm) and diseases. Frankincense and other sweet-smelling aromatics were burned in small incense stands in these homes to mask some of this staleness. While these stands, which have been excavated in large numbers at Megiddo, Gezer, Beth-Shan, and Shechem, may have also had a cultic purpose (Jer. 19:13), their smoke helped to cover the household odors and drive away insects.

> I have hauled sand and carried salt, but nothing is heavier than debt. ("Teachings of Ahiqar," *OTP*, 306)

Excavations at Jericho, Bethel, Gezer, and other sites have revealed stone-lined drainage systems for sewage and excess rainwater. However, these and indoor toilets (a seat over a cesspit) are only associated with the houses of wealthier families. Examination of Iron II toilets in private homes in Jerusalem demonstrates that ash was spread over the deposits in cesspits to help neutralize the odor. However, references to muck and mire in the streets (2 Sam. 22:43) suggest that they were still the principal areas for waste disposal. Waste was also deposited in nearby fields (2 Kings 9:37) and in communal dung heaps.

Archaeological evidence shows that at least some houses in the urban setting served as both dwelling places and industrial and commercial establishments (see Jer. 18:2–3 for a potter's house). At the site of Shechem a house was uncovered that contained dye vats and loom weights, suggesting a clothing manufacturing enterprise. Elsewhere booths were discovered attached to the outside of a house. Inside were rows of clay storage jars containing the carbonized remains of grain. This may have been a shop selling grain to city dwellers. A similar shop unearthed at Hazor with a large number of small pottery bowls may have been a primitive food shop or market.

Social Life

Even with a more urban-centered culture emerging during the monarchic period, the vast majority of the Israelite population, like the prophet Amos in Tekoa, continued to live in small, unwalled villages and towns. Everyday life there would have remained much the same as it had in the settlement period except for the increasing demands (i.e., taxes; 1 Kings 4:27–28) and economic opportunities afforded by regional urban centers. Cities like Beer-sheba, Jerusalem, Lachish, Samaria, Megiddo, and Hazor became focal points of royal power and major defense posts for the rest of the land (1 Kings 9:15–19). They, along with bazaars established in nearby cities like Damascus (1 Kings 20:34), served as regional markets for farm produce and provided a clearinghouse for manufactured and imported goods. The profits garnered by the grain sellers also led to corrupt practices (Prov. 11:26) and a willingness to violate the Sabbath in order to continue conducting business (Amos 8:5). Farm families made the trek from their villages once or twice a year to sell their surplus grain and to buy new farm implements, pottery, and luxury goods (jewelry, perfumes, and cosmetics). They also came to Jerusalem and other religious centers to make sacrifices and to celebrate major religious holidays (1 Sam. 1:3; 1 Kings 12:27).

Until the Assyrian occupation of their country in the eighth century BCE, those Israelites who did live within the walled cities were primarily members of the elite population, as well as government workers, trained scribes (Ps. 45:1), and a growing number of prominent merchant families (see a characterization of this wealthy class in Amos 4:1). Their "service sector" jobs made it necessary for them to live close to the administrative hub. However, because the inhabitants of the walled cities devoted their full time to managing the affairs of the government and the economy, these cities were not self-supporting. They depended on the rural farm belt to supply them with food and the raw materials for manufacturing. Local villages also provided surplus manpower for construction projects (1 Kings 9:15) and military campaigns (9:22).

Growing debts among the rural farmers also led to wealthy individuals buying up their farms and abusing the poor (Isa. 5:8; Amos 5:11–12). That in turn led to a migration of the rural poor to the environs of the cities or into the hills to join groups of bandits (1 Sam. 22:2). The best that these displaced persons and their families could hope for was to glean the harvested fields (Lev. 19:10) or work menial jobs as day laborers (Deut. 24:14) or temporary debt slaves (Exod. 21:1–2).

Social Mobility

A symbiotic arrangement between the rural and urban areas is quite common in the ancient Near East. Each can benefit from the other, but interaction can also lead to social change that disrupts old patterns. While the basic traditions and loyalties of extended family relationships can remain intact in the villages, the opportunities of joining the royal elite or the military may dissolve old ties among city dwellers. The drive to advance in a period when social mobility is possible can lead to the abandonment of old values and the establishment of new loyalties to the state and to oneself.

One possible example of this may be Jeroboam, son of Nebat. This son of a widow from the tribe of Ephraim rises to a position of high authority, being given "charge over all the forced labor of the house of Joseph" (1 Kings 11:28). Solomon chooses him for this position because he has proven himself to be "industrious." That suggests a culture that is moving away from reliance on nepotism and tribal favoritism to one that links work ethic and merit as desirable attributes. Later the prophet Ahijah singles Jeroboam out to rule the northern ten tribes because Solomon allows the worship of the gods of his foreign wives (1 Kings 11:29–33). When Solomon learns of this potential rival, he attempts to have him killed, but Jeroboam escapes to Egypt where he bides his time until Solomon's death (11:40). While Jeroboam may have begun his attempt to undermine Solomon's authority prior to the king's death (as suggested by the **Septuagint**, the Greek translation of the Old Testament) or simply waited quietly in Egyptian exile, he is willing to lead the revolt against Rehoboam (1 Kings 12:12–20). Obviously, his loyalty to his former benefactor ends when the opportunity arises for him to become a king himself.

The monarchic period yields other examples of individuals taking advantage of a situation to advance socially and in rank. In the late ninth century BCE, the succession to the throne of Israel seemed to be constantly in dispute. As a result, the ambitions of military leaders, the support they could garner from the army, and a swift method of assassination were the primary means to power. A drunken King Elah is murdered by Zimri, "commander of half his chariots" (1 Kings 16:9–10). Immediately, the newly installed king solidified his hold on the throne by killing Elah's family and supporters (16:11). However, Zimri only reigns for seven days when he is overthrown by Omri, another army commander (1 Kings 16:15–20). Then Omri has to wage a brief civil war that ends when he defeats a rival claimant named Tibni (vv. 21–22).

The biblical narrative does not record the genealogy of either Zimri or Omri, which may indicate that these upstart kings came from unimportant families and rose to power on the strength of their skills as soldiers.

Clothing and Personal Adornment

Although the general style of dress did not change markedly during the monarchic period, there were some shifts in the quality of costume, jewelry, and other personal items, especially among the well-to-do (Isa. 3:18–23). Some of these changes were the result of the growth of the urban elite and the desire to differentiate between social classes. Other changes reflect increased contact and commercial activity between Israel and surrounding nations (1 Kings 10:25).

Items of clothing served as social markers, indicating a person's status, occupation (2 Sam. 20:8), and affluence. Thus the wealthy were able to demonstrate their affluence by having more than one set of clothing (1 Kings 11:29) and by wearing clothing brightened with expensive Tyrian purple dye extracted from the hypobranchial gland of the murex snail (Prov. 31:22; Ezek. 23:6). Even the poorest in society could offer their outer garment (*beged*) in pledge as a sign of their free status (Amos 2:8; Yavneh Yam Ostracon).

> Despite the fact that your servant had completed his assigned work, Hoshaiahu ... kept your servant's cloak. ... Please order my supervisor to return my cloak either in fulfillment of the law or as an act of mercy. (Yavneh Yam Ostracon; *OTP*, 355–56)

The elaborate vestments worn by priests indicated their role as intercessors in the temple and were emblems of their **ritual purity** (see Exod. 28). The *me'il*, or robe, was a loose, wide-sleeved outer garment worn by royalty (1 Sam. 18:4; 2 Sam. 13:18; 1 Chron. 15:27), priests (Exod. 28:4, 31–32), and prophets (1 Sam. 28:14; 1 Kings 11:29). Samuel is often described wearing this special garment. As a child, his mother Hannah brings him a new *me'il* each year (1 Sam. 2:19). The prophet is wearing a *me'il* when he announces Saul's loss of the kingship (15:27). Later, when a desperate Saul employs the services of the witch of Endor, the king recognizes Samuel's spirit rising from Sheol because the shade is dressed in a *me'il* (28:17).

Everyday personal garments were designed to be draped loosely around the body. They helped regulate body heat and were styled in such a way to allow for ease of movement. The garments of the common people were most commonly made of wool. Woolen garments were difficult to launder and were probably washed infrequently or for special occasions only (Exod. 19:14). They were nearly always moist with perspiration and soiled with food and dirt. This led to skin infections and the transmission of bacterially based diseases (Lev. 13:47–59).

Figure 3.6. Panel depicting Israelites
bearing tribute, from the Black Obelisk of Shalmaneser III

The basic undergarment for both men and women was the *kuttōneth*, a shirt-like garment that is depicted in ancient art in a variety of styles. Usually made of wool, it could reach as far as the ankles or just to the knees and could have either long or short sleeves (2 Sam. 13:18). The *kuttōneth* is depicted in the "Black Obelisk" inscription of the Assyrian king Shalmaneser III (842 BCE). In a series of sculpted and cuneiform-captioned registers, Jehu, the king of Israel, is shown bowing before the foreign king. In addition, his servants are shown carrying gifts as tribute payments to the emperor. Jehu is wearing a fringed *kuttōneth* tied with a girdle that also has hanging tassels. A pointed cap covers his head while his beard, like those of the Israelite porters carved on this monument, is trimmed to a point (possibly a standard feature Assyrian artists used when depicting non-Assyrians). The porters have a slightly different costume. Each is also wearing a *kuttōneth*, but it is covered by a fringed *śimlâ*, or mantle, which is draped over their left shoulders. Their beards are trimmed to a point like the king's and they are wearing pointed caps and sandals with upturned toes.

Another Assyrian monumental relief (a large, two-dimensional stone carving) and inscription dating to 701 BCE show Judean captives being escorted from the city of Lachish on Judah's western border. This inscription commemorates the conquests of Sennacherib from the period, his invasion

Figure 3.7. Replica Yavneh Yam Inscription

of Judah, and the siege of Jerusalem (2 Kings 18–19). The barefooted prisoners on the relief are wearing a short-sleeved, full-length *kuttōneth*. They are bareheaded and have closely trimmed beards. The variations in depicting these people may reflect different clothing styles popular in Israel and Judah or simply the changes in costume from one time period to the next. However, their traditional clothing continues to distinguish them from their Assyrian captors, an indication that they have not adopted the clothing styles of the superpowers that ruled over them.

The rather elaborate hems with suspended tassels found on the *me'il* and most garments in the ancient Near East symbolized the rank of kings and their advisers as well as the members of the military. The biblical narrative uses the association between royal robes and political status several times. Samuel graphically demonstrates how God will "tear the kingdom" away from Saul's family when he grasps and tears the hem of Saul's robe (*me'il*). After cutting off the hem (*kānāp*) of Saul's garment, David feels remorse, realizing that he has symbolically weakened the king's authority (1 Sam. 24:4–5). The prophet Ahijah tears Jeroboam's new linen garment into twelve pieces as a symbolic demonstration that God has granted Jeroboam the right to rule the ten northern tribes (1 Kings 11:29–31).

The girdle or belt (*'ēzôr*), which was used to tie the *kuttōneth* and *śimlâ* (2 Kings 1:8), also could function as a weapons belt and a sign of rank (Ezek. 23:15). In 2 Samuel 20:8 Joab wears a "soldier's garment" tied with a girdle, *ḥagôr*, through which he has sheathed his sword. David uses the same term in describing Joab's murderous crimes to Solomon (1 Kings 2:5–7). In this case, however, Joab's *ḥagôr* symbolically represents the blood of Joab's victims and serves as a justification for Solomon's purge of the old general.

There are instances in which clothing played a part in legal transactions or as a form of authentication. For instance, in the Mari texts it was a common administrative practice to send a lock of hair and a piece of the fringe of a prophet's garment along with a written report to the king. Since clothing was considered an extension of the person, this would be the equivalent of sending the prophet herself to the royal court. Garments or other personal items were also given "in pledge," or as collateral for a loan or other transaction (Gen. 38:17–19). Even the poorest free man could offer his outer garment to seal an agreement, but the law restricts taking a widow's garment as a pledge (Deut. 24:17). To prevent abuse by the creditor or the overseer, the law requires that a garment be returned to its owner at the end of the day (Exod. 22:26–27; Deut. 24:12–13). However, both the prophet Amos (2:8) and the Yavneh Yam **Ostracon** provide documentation that the law was not always respected. The prophet accuses the wealthy of keeping these pledged garments and sleeping on them before the altars of other gods. The ostracon contains a plea that the day laborer's garment be returned to him so he can maintain some semblance of dignity as a free man and as proof that he is "not guilty of any breach of contract" (*OTP*, 355–56).

A person's clothing was an important representation of identity and status. To have it taken away was a tragedy and a sign of loss of authority or even freedom. For instance, war captives are stripped (Isa. 20:2) and then given "captive's garb" (Deut. 21:13). Even to have a garment intentionally damaged was an insult. That is the case in 2 Samuel 10:4 when the new king of Ammon demonstrates his political independence from David's kingdom. He has his servants shave off half of the beards of David's emissaries and cut off half of their robes. This act shames the Israelites, symbolically emasculating them. It denies them the role of royal messengers, dismissing their rights to diplomatic immunity, and graphically transforms them in the sight of the people into socially damaged half-men.

During the monarchic period there were some shifts in costume and personal adornment, especially among the well-to-do. In some cases the stylistic changes were a sign of further differentiation between the classes or a reflection of commercial contact with merchants and diplomats from Egypt and Assyria. Fabrics were brightened using expensive dyes (Judg. 5:30; Ezek. 23:6), and the temple in Jerusalem was adorned with multicolored curtains (2 Chron. 2:7, 14; 3:14). Possessing more than one set of clothing also denoted a person of wealth and authority (1 Sam. 28:2; 2 Sam. 12:20; 2 Kings 5:5).

The array of garments worn by aristocratic men and women is mentioned in Isaiah 3:18–24. The list contains items that only the wealthy could afford and

> **BAḪDI-LIM TO ZIMRI-LIM**
>
> Aḫum, the priest, has brought me the hair and the garment fringe of a prophetess, and her complete report is written on the tablet. (ARM 6.45:7–10)

indicates the large variety of garments that could be found in their wardrobes. Head coverings in this list include veils, scarfs, and headdresses for women and turbans worn by both sexes. The priestly turban was a symbol of authority reserved for that profession. Sashes, mantles, and girdles would have been used to tie the undergarments, some of which are said to be made of linen (Ezek. 16:10). Special robes and festal garments with embroidered cloth (Ezek. 16:13) were used for festive occasions, weddings (Judg. 14:19), and entertaining.

Jewelry and Personal Items

The list of personal items in Isaiah 3:18–24 also includes jewelry and personal care products. While some of these pieces of jewelry were worn by men, the list in Isaiah seems to be a catalogue of what well-dressed, wealthy women wore. Various adornments literally covered the owner from head to foot. While the display of wealth is quite extravagant, in an age before coined money, individuals often wore their jewelry as a demonstration of their prosperity and economic worth (Hosea 2:13). Among the many items listed in this passage and other texts there were delicately carved, garlanded frontlets and moon-shaped crescents, drop pendants on twisted necklace cords, armlets (note Saul's armlet of office in 2 Sam. 1:10), nose rings (Ezek. 16:12) and signet rings, and tinkling anklets (Isa. 3:16), all fabricated of gold or silver (see Prov. 25:12). Engraved signet rings were used to stamp documents or as symbols of the authority of the office (Jer. 22:24). They often were encrusted with precious and semiprecious stones (Ezek. 28:12–13). Larger pieces, like the breastplate of the high priest (Exod. 28:15–21), also contained mounted precious stones (see the "crown of Milcom" in 2 Sam. 12:30). A metaphorical description of the clothing and jewelry worn by Jerusalem, here portrayed as Yahweh's unfaithful bride, includes bracelets for her arms and a gold and silver chain around her neck. Her head is adorned with a crown, earrings, and a nose ring (Ezek. 16:10–13).

Cosmetics

Jezebel's preparations before meeting the triumphant Jehu and her own inevitable death have served as the classic example of the use of cosmetics by Israelite women in the monarchic period (2 Kings 9:30). While she was a Phoenician princess who had married King Ahab, it is likely that other women of the elite class would have followed her lead in personal adornment. Her use of eye paint, *puk*, may have been a fashion borrowed from Egypt where eye makeup was employed by both sexes. Analysis of eye paint deposits from Egyptian tombs and from cosmetic palettes has shown that it consisted primarily of crushed galena mixed with gum and water. Both Jeremiah (4:30) and Ezekiel (23:40) speak of women who enlarged their eyes with eye paint, which suggests that it was a fairly common practice among the elite in Israel to use cosmetics and scented oils.

Archaeologists have also found red dyes made from iron oxide (red ochre) or crushed leaves of the henna plant (Song 1:14) in Egyptian tombs. This mixture would have been applied to cheeks, lips, finger- and toenails, and hair to add color to a woman's appearance. Other shades of color were produced with a mixture of clays or crushed plant matter. The "perfume boxes" of Isaiah 3:20 may refer to receptacles for the dried resins and powders used to make dyes and to concoct fragrances.

Perfumes of various types were used by the Israelites to mask household odors and as incense offerings in shrines and temples (Exod. 30:34–35; Jer. 6:20). Along with oils and other ointments, these scents could also be applied to the body (Prov. 27:9) as well as sprinkled on clothes (Ps. 45:8) and on room furnishings (Prov. 7:17). Soaps and lye were used to cleanse and purify the body (Job 9:30; Jer. 2:22). The Song of Songs mentions a number of the scents commonly available on the luxury market in ancient Israel. Among them are spikenard (taken from gingergrass root and imported from Arabia), myrrh, saffron (extracted from crocus and imported from Iran or Kashmir), and turmeric (Song 4:13–14; 5:5). The spices mentioned among the gifts from the queen of Sheba to King Solomon (1 Kings 10:2, 10) probably included those used for cooking as well as those that were burned as incense (frankincense and galbanum) or used as personal fragrances (such as calamus, myrrh, saffron, and nard).

Forms of Entertainment

The growth in leisure time among the elite and the standardization of the religious calendar would have contributed to the variety of entertainment options during the time of the monarchy. A larger and more diverse population in the urban centers, the significantly greater personal wealth of some individuals, and the increase in both religious and social events would have made entertaining more of a mandatory social expectation (2 Sam. 13:23–27). Of course, the exuberance of children also contributes to the creation of games that they play in the streets of the city (Zech. 8:5).

As in earlier periods, occasions for celebration, such as marriages and births, religious festivals (2 Sam. 6:14–15), and military victories (1 Sam. 18:6) all could spark individual and mass entertainment. These might include feasts (1 Sam. 20:5), singing and dancing to a variety of musical instruments (stringed as well as rattles and whistles), board games (many examples of which have been excavated in Israelite sites and Egyptian tombs), and riddle contests

Music, Dance, and Celebration

The human condition contains times of both joy and sorrow. There are a number of examples in the biblical text in which music and dance function as the opposite of mourning or tragedy.

> You have turned my mourning into dancing. (Ps. 30:11)

> For everything there is a season . . . a time to mourn, and a time to dance. (Eccles. 3:4b)

> The joy of our hearts has ceased; our dancing has been turned to mourning. (Lam. 5:15)

(Judg. 14:12; 1 Kings 10:1). Additional forms of entertainment were borrowed from neighboring countries or the encroaching empires. While the Assyrians were particularly fond of physical contests involving hunting and archery, as well as javelin and stone throwing, the Babylonians enjoyed wrestling (see 2 Sam. 2:14) and more intellectual games such as deciphering cryptograms and crossword puzzles.

During the monarchy, however, these events were probably more common and more elaborate as the king, the nobility, and the priesthood drew the people's attention to themselves and to the Yahweh festivals. Many of these celebrations were enhanced by musical performance. For instance, when Jehoshaphat returned with his army to Jerusalem after a victory over Moab and Ammon, his victory processional marched to the temple accompanied by individuals playing harps and lyres and trumpets (2 Chron. 20:28). Similarly, the wine and merriment of the feast described in Isaiah 5:12 was heightened by musicians playing the lyre, harp, timbrel, and flute. The text also indicates that the royal court was entertained by professional musicians and singers (2 Sam. 19:35 and Eccles. 2:8).

Dancing would have been a natural accompaniment to many celebrations in all of the ancient Near Eastern cultures. Cylinder seals from Mesopotamia have been found that depict dancers performing a variety of dance steps, for example, as part of a religious ritual such as the whirling dance (*gūštu*) at the feast of the goddess Inanna. The book of Psalms provides information on ritual activity within the Jerusalem temple and shows that

An Assyrian text lionizes the reign of the emperor Ashurbanipal (668–627 BCE):

The old men dance, the young men sing, the women and girls are merry and happy; women are married and provided with rings, boys and girls are brought forth, the births thrive. (Gabbay 2003, 104)

worship was regularly accompanied by praise in the form of "tambourine and dance" (Pss. 149:3; 150:4). There also seems to be a tradition of young women singing, dancing, and rattling their tambourines in celebration of military victories (Judg. 11:34; 1 Sam. 18:6–7; Jer. 31:4).

The **superscriptions** contained in many of the Psalms provide information on orchestration and tunes composed to accompany temple ritual. For example, the superscription for Psalm 54 instructs the choirmaster to use stringed instruments when performing this hymn of praise, and in Psalm 56 the appointed melody to sing this hymn is "The Dove on Far-off Terebinths." The superscription to Psalm 22 instructs the choirmaster to perform this song according to a popular tune of the time, "The Deer

Figure 3.8. Bell-shaped terracotta female musician figurine

of the Dawn." These instructions also include specific instrumentation and some technical terms, such as *Selah* (Ps. 32:4, 5, 7), whose exact meanings are still unknown to modern scholars.

Temple rituals also included the singing of psalms in procession by pilgrims and priests. Psalm 24 and the "songs of ascent" (Pss. 120–134) are good examples of hymns that might have been used in public processions either within the city of Jerusalem or on the road to the temple from other towns. Chronicles systematically emphasizes the cultic use of music, especially in terms of David's role as institutor. Thus, David is said to have appointed men who were "in charge of the service of song in the house of the Lord" (1 Chron. 6:31–48). Choirs or pious individuals sang psalms on particular occasions (Ps. 92, a song for the Sabbath) and as continuous praise to Yahweh (Ps. 66, a hymn of one who has come to fulfill a vow).

Health Issues

It is often difficult to identify specific diseases or the manner in which they were treated in ancient Israel. The biblical text describes quite a number of medical problems that afflicted the people, but in many cases epidemics or other afflictions are ascribed to the contaminating influences of other nations (Num. 25:1–9) or God's anger over inappropriate behavior (Num. 12:10; Ps. 38:2–3). In other cases, physical conditions, such as a man with crushed testicles or one who has become a eunuch, cannot be repaired, and the individual is declared unclean and forbidden to enter the temple (Deut. 23:1; compare, however, Isa. 56:3).

Some were treated with herbal remedies (mandrake for infertility, Gen. 30:14). In other cases topical salves, referred to as "balm," were used to cover or soothe a wound (Jer. 46:11; 51:8), while injuries were "wrapped with a bandage" (Ezek. 30:21). More serious problems included a disease of the bowels (possibly amoebic dysentery, 2 Chron. 21:15, 18–19), boils or tumors (perhaps bubonic plague in 1 Sam. 5:6–12), and various plagues (2 Sam. 24:13–15; 1 Kings 8:37).

The common denominator for many of these diseases and their diagnosis was attribution to divine causes. When the Philistines captured the ark of the covenant in battle, they brought it to the city of Ashdod (1 Sam. 5:1–5). However, they then connected the outbreak of tumors in Ashdod and other Philistine cities to the ark's presence and the wrath of the God of the Israelites (5:8–12). David and Israel are punished with a three-day decimating plague when David sinned by conducting a census (2 Sam. 24:10–17).

Leprosy (probably a general term used for several different skin conditions, none of which were Hansen's disease) appears in several narratives and in legal texts (Lev. 13–14). The law prescribes a complicated set of procedures in which the afflicted person must go to the priest to be examined. Certain primary appearances of eruption or discoloration of the skin are listed as well as several secondary features. A waiting period in increments of seven days is set for the disappearance of these outward symptoms. If the outbreak is still present after that time, the priest declares the individual unclean and an outcast from the community and the temple (Lev. 13:1–11; see the lepers forced to live outside Samaria's gate in 2 Kings 7:3). The contagion was considered transmissible through clothing, which was burned if washing did not remove the stain (Lev. 13:47–59).

Physicians are mentioned in a few scattered instances in the biblical text. Even then, they seem to be associated with illegitimate practitioners such as magicians and pagan priest-healers (Deut. 18:10–12). This is apparently the case when King Asa is condemned for consulting physicians instead of Yahweh (2 Chron. 16:12) and when King Ahaziah seeks to consult the priests of Baal-zebub of Ekron (2 Kings 1:2). Jeremiah, in speaking of spiritual healing of the people, mentions the "balm of Gilead" and physicians to administer it (Jer. 8:22). The prophet also indicates that herbal medicines were known and used (Jer. 51:8). Similarly, Isaiah prescribes a "cake of figs" poultice to be applied to a boil troubling King Hezekiah (Isa. 38:21).

For the most part, medicine and the treatment of disease remained a primitive business, with the biblical writers describing some health problems as incurable (Deut. 28:27; 2 Kings 15:5). Still, afflicted persons or a relative could seek out a holy man or prophet whose intercession with a god might affect a cure. For instance, a distraught woman asks Elijah to restore her comatose son to life (1 Kings 17:17–24). The prophet lies on the boy three times and calls on God to "let this child's soul come into him again" (v. 21). Once the boy is revived by this procedure, his mother testifies that "now I know that you are a man of God" (v. 24). Similarly, Naaman, a Syrian general, has to cross into hostile territory to be "cleansed" of his leprosy by Elisha's intercession. The rather outlandish cure involves having the general "wash in the Jordan seven times" (2 Kings 5:10). Given no option if he wished to be cured and return to his former life as the king's advisor, Naaman follows the instructions. After being cleansed of his disease, he states, "I know that there is no God in all the earth except in Israel" (5:15).

Conceptions of Death

Conceptions of the afterlife during the monarchic period center on Sheol, a poorly defined region from which there was no resurrection and in which there was no reward or punishment (Job 17:13–16). Sheol is sometimes personified with the ability to reach out to the living, entangling them in the "snares of death" (2 Sam. 22:5–6) and drawing them into a place so cut off from the world of the living that "the dead do not praise the Lord, nor do any that go down into silence" (Pss. 6:5; 115:17–18). Occasionally, Sheol is paired with Abaddon, another word for the place of destruction or the underworld (Job 26:6; Prov. 15:11).

In the only instance in the biblical narrative in which the dead communicate with the living, Saul asks the witch of Endor to bring up Samuel's shade from the netherworld (1 Sam. 28:8–19). Saul had been cut off from communication with God and therefore is willing to seek out an "oracle from the dead" using a proscribed sorcerer (Deut. 18:10–11). The woman employs a ritual pit to draw up the spirit of the dead in a manner similar to that found in the Gilgamesh epic. When Samuel's shade appears, he complains that his rest has been disturbed and prophesies the end of Saul's reign and the death, in battle, of his sons (1 Sam. 28:16–19).

Other reflections on the character of Sheol are found in the prophetic and wisdom literature. The prophet Isaiah, taunting the king of Babylon (14:4–11), appeals to the common Israelite belief that the dead go down to

Sheol where they, king and pauper alike, are all the same, lacking authority or acclaim. After being confronted by the prophet Nathan and following the painful loss of his son, David sums up the general Israelite belief concerning the dead. As the child lay ill, the king fasted and wept, lying on the ground. But after his death, David simply states, "Can I bring him back again? I shall go to him, but he will not return to me" (2 Sam. 12:21–23). Likewise, Job remarks that "those who go down to Sheol do not come up" (Job 7:9–10).

Still there is a link between the living and the dead that suggests a form of ancestor worship did exist. Jeremiah mentions to King Zedekiah the funerary practice of burning spices "for your ancestors, the earlier kings" (Jer. 34:5). More to the point, Isaiah condemns those people who "consult the ghosts and the familiar spirits that chirp and mutter" and "consult the dead on behalf of the living" (Isa. 8:19).

> Open a hole in the earth that the spirit of Enkidu may issue forth from the netherworld, that to his brother he might tell the ways of the netherworld. . . . Scarcely had he (Nergal) opened a hole in the earth, when the spirit of Enkidu, like a wind-puff, issued forth from the netherworld. (*Gilgamesh* 13:79–84; *ANET*, 98)

Mourning

Since death was common as a result of disease, famine, and the ravaging armies of invaders, various forms of mourning rituals were employed by the friends and families of the deceased. Some of these, depending upon the status of the person involved, could be quite elaborate and expressive. For example, the messenger who brings the tragic news of Saul's death has torn his clothing and placed earth on his head as a sign of the nation's loss. David acknowledges the importance of the deceased king and does him honor by also tearing his robe, weeping, and fasting until evening (2 Sam. 1:2–12). Furthermore, David composes a eulogy (2 Sam. 1:17–27) for Saul as well as for Abner (2 Sam. 3:33–34).

Another expression of mourning for the highborn dead included a funeral procession, with the mourners wearing sackcloth and making a tearful outcry at the gravesite (2 Sam. 3:31–32). While sackcloth is mentioned several times as appropriate apparel for mourners (Ps. 30:11; Jer. 6:26), there is also a recognizable mourning garment (*beged 'ēbel*) that signaled to all that the person was grieving (2 Sam. 14:2). In some instances mourners put dust on their heads (Josh. 7:6; Lam. 2:10) or shaved their heads (Isa. 15:2; Ezek. 27:30–31; Mic. 1:16). Jeremiah also mentions the custom of bringing food and drink to the mourning family and cutting oneself as a sign of mourning (16:6–8; 48:37), a practice prohibited in Deuteronomy 14:1.

Mourning rituals are also practiced when a person's identity or body has been damaged or when it is necessary to show humility as a penance or to obtain help from God. In the first instance, David's daughter Tamar is raped by her brother Amnon. Her response, when he refuses to marry her, is to put ashes on her head and tear the "long robe with sleeves" that indicated she had been one of the virgin daughters of the king (2 Sam. 13:18–19). Penitent mourning is found in the costuming of the defeated king of Aram (and his advisors in 1 Kings 20:31–32) and in Hezekiah's clothing himself in sackcloth and going to the temple to seek help from Yahweh during the siege of Jerusalem (2 Kings 19:1).

Burial Customs

During the Iron Age there were diverse burial practices. Surveys and excavations of tombs in the northern kingdom of Israel have shown the use of natural caves enlarged to accommodate multiple burials, rock-cut tombs, tumuli, "bathtub"-shaped clay coffins, and storage jars. The lack of standardized burial customs in the northern kingdom stands in contrast to those found in Judah, where rock-cut tombs are most common for family burials. The reuse or multiple use of tombs by family members is found in both regions (see 1 Kings 13:31; 2 Kings 13:20). Also typical of these tombs is an array of pottery vessels (bowls, juglets, flasks, and lamps). The location of tombs is directly related to the distance from the settlement or the size of an individual estate.

According to biblical custom, failure to be buried was anathema for the Israelite dead, shaming them and their families. Ahijah and Elijah spoke of a day of vengeance on Jeroboam and Ahab when Yahweh would destroy their families and leave their corpses unburied (1 Kings 14:11; 21:24). Elisha sends word to Jehu through one of the "company of prophets" that Jezebel's body will be eaten by dogs and "no one shall bury her" (2 Kings 9:7–10). Similarly, God's unfaithful people would be defeated by the armies of Egypt, Assyria, or Babylon, and in the midst of the national tragedy, their bodies would be left for birds and animals to consume (Jer. 16:4) or cast onto dung heaps (Amos 4:3). A similar means of dishonoring the dead was to burn their bones into lime (Amos 2:1) or ash on an altar, as Josiah does to the bones of the priests of Bethel (1 Kings 13:2; 2 Kings 23:16–20).

The law required that even executed criminals be buried as soon as possible (Deut. 21:23) and that bodies found beside the roadway be buried by the people of the nearest village (Deut. 21:1–9). On one occasion, however, David hands seven of Saul's sons over to the Gibeonites to pay "blood guilt" for Saul's attack on this non-Israelite people (2 Sam. 21:1–6). In violation of the law, David allows their bodies to remain impaled for a full season. He is eventually

Figure 3.9. Ketef Hinnom burial chambers carved in the seventh century BCE reveal benches with head niches where the deceased were placed.

shamed into burying them along with the bones of Saul and Jonathan by the faithfulness of Rizpah, mother of two of the executed men who stays with the bodies to prevent them from being eaten by animals (2 Sam. 21:10–14).

The bodies of the dead were buried in tombs that reflected the social station of the individual. Some of the kings of Judah were buried in ancestral tombs within the city of Jerusalem (2 Kings 9:28; 12:21), but most other people would have had tombs outside the city proper. Cremation was almost unknown among the Israelites, although the bodies of Saul and his sons are burned after their remains are retrieved from the walls of Beth-shan by the men of Jabesh-gilead (1 Sam. 31:12). This may be because of the dismemberment and advanced state of decay. After the cremation, the bones are buried under a tamarisk tree, and a seven-day fast is observed as a mourning period (v. 13; compare the thirty-day mourning period for Moses in Deut. 34:8). In contrast, during the Iron I period cremation is common among the Philistines and other coastal and lowland peoples, who inhumed their dead in simple or cist graves, anthropoid coffins, jar or urn burials, or bench tombs.

Burial for kings and the wealthy was in family tombs (2 Sam. 21:12–14) in caves or carved into the rock of nearby hillsides. The often-repeated phrase at the end of a king's reign, "[he] slept with his ancestors, and they buried him in the city of David" (1 Kings 15:8), is used of most of the kings of Judah.

Similar notices are attached to the accounts of the reigns of Israel's kings (2 Kings 14:16). Excavations have uncovered several Iron Age II tombs located away from human dwellings. They are rectangular in shape (about eight to ten feet on a side) with benches on three sides of the tomb. Examples of this type of rock-cut tomb have been found on the northern end of the Ophel Hill on Mount Zion, and these may be royal sepulchers. Perhaps this is the spot where Absalom prepared an elaborate monumental tomb for himself "in the King's Valley" with a pillar to mark the spot (2 Sam. 18:17–18). The reference to Manasseh's tomb (seventh century BCE) being located in the Garden of Uzzah (2 Kings 21:18) may suggest that a new site was designated for royal burials after the original area within the city was filled.

SILWAN TOMB INSCRIPTION

This is [the grave of . . .]yahu who was over the house. There is no silver or gold here, but rather his bones and the bones of his slave-wife with him. Cursed be the man who will open this.

The growth of the elite class during the Iron II period is further demonstrated by the creation of elaborate rock-cut tombs such as that identified by archaeologists as the tomb of the "Steward of the House." They generally had a single large chamber, although there are some with multiple chambers. This tomb likely had an Egyptian-style pyramidal cap like others in that area. It is located in the village of Silwan on the eastern slope of the Kidron Valley, across from the City of David. In addition to its monumental features, the tomb sports an inscription giving a partially destroyed name of the owner and cursing anyone who would disturb it. It may be the tomb of Shebna, King Hezekiah's steward, who was rebuked by Isaiah (2 Kings 22:15–16) for carving a tomb displaying Egyptian influences higher up on the hill than his social status would allow. It does not appear to be designed to contain his entire family.

Eventually, older burials could no longer remain in the principal place within the tomb but were placed in the charnel pit, sometimes in a niche below the bench where the body was initially interred. These bench-like shelves are carved into the walls to accommodate only the most recent burials. Rounded pillows are carved at one end, often with clay lamps placed at the head, perhaps to light the way to the underworld for the dead. Jars of wine, water jugs, and open-mouthed food jars designed to aid the dead in their journey are also found in these tombs. Personal items like arrowheads and seals are also common grave goods, and sometimes display foreign influences in design or manufacture.

By necessity the burial of the poor or lower classes would have been much less elaborate, perhaps involving simply the scooping out of holes in the earth. Both the Valley of Hinnom (Jer. 7:32) and the Wadi Kidron (2 Kings 23:6) may have served as common burial grounds for the poor. In some cases, their bodies may even have been placed in abandoned or pillaged tombs that once belonged to a prominent person or family (2 Kings 13:20–21). Infants were often interred in jars within the floor of the house itself. The large number of these domestic burial sites gives further evidence of a high infant mortality rate in the cities.

Following the destruction of the northern kingdom by the Assyrians in 721 BCE and the deportation of a segment of the population, the number of rock-cut tombs declined. The decline in the size of the population, even with the introduction of new peoples into the region, is indicated by the lack of rock-cut tombs after the seventh century BCE.

Law

The Bible preserves several collections of laws, with the apodictic (command law) Decalogue or Ten Commandments (Exod. 20:1–17; Deut. 5:11–21) functioning as a legal foundation for the casuistic (case law) codes that provide more detailed legal pronouncements. Although the case laws reflect legal situations and provide the answer to "but what if" legal questions, the Decalogue continues to function as a major addendum to the covenant with Yahweh. Thus Jeremiah, in his "Temple Sermon," lists many of the Ten Commandments as part of his indictment of the people of Judah (Jer. 7:8–11), and Hosea also includes five from the standard list in his indictment of Israel (Hosea 4:2).

> ### JEREMIAH'S TEMPLE SERMON
>
> Will you steal, murder, commit adultery, swear falsely, make offerings to Baal, and go after other gods? (Jer. 7:9)

The casuistic legal collections include the Covenant Code (Exod. 21–23), the **Holiness Code** associated with the priestly community in the **Second Temple period** after the return from exile (Lev. 17–26), and the **Deuteronomic Code** (Deut. 12–26). The last of these collections was implemented during Josiah's brief reform movement in the late seventh century BCE. While it does contain revisions of earlier legal pronouncements (compare the treatment of debt slaves in Exod. 21:2–6 and Deut. 15:12–18), the Deuteronomic Code also contains provisions specific to Josiah's attempt to centralize worship in Jerusalem (Deut. 12:13–14). In part these revisions were reflections of theological differences between the time of the Deuteronomic writer and his predecessors. Other revisions, such as the option of bringing "sacred donations" to Jerusalem rather than the actual "firstfruits" of the harvest if they have to travel too far to make their offering (Deut. 12:21–27), are accommodations to changing political and economic factors.

> ### HOSEA'S INDICTMENT OF ISRAEL
>
> Swearing, lying, murder, stealing, and adultery break out. (Hosea 4:2)

Of course, one of the most important of these new factors was the introduction of the monarchy and the movement of a large number of people into urban centers. This alone contributed to significant changes in legal custom and the administration of justice in ancient Israel. Naturally the Israelite kings, like their ancient Near Eastern counterparts, wished to exercise as much control over the law and its enforcement as possible in order to increase their own authority. This meant the king had to be identified with the dispensing of justice to all segments of society, especially the weak. The ideal, perhaps best exemplified in the narrative by Solomon's judging of the two prostitutes (1 Kings 3:16–28), was to create the perception that he was a "just king." With this accomplished, it would be more likely that people would look to him first for justice.

The other major factor at work is the transformation of the Covenant Code (Exod. 20:23–23:19). With its emphasis on the village culture, there was a need to meet the more complex needs of urban legal problems. New situations arose that had not been a part of their society before, requiring new or revised regulations on aspects of construction (Deut. 22:8), making loans (Deut. 23:19–20; 24:10–12), or the accuracy of weights and measures (Deut. 25:13–16). The Deuteronomistic Historian indicates the changing legal situation by having Solomon ask for wisdom "to discern between good and evil" in order to rule his people (1 Kings 3:9).

> ### PREFACE TO HAMMURABI'S CODE
>
> At that time Anum and Enlil named me to promote the welfare of the people, me, Hammurabi, the devout, god-fearing prince, to cause justice to prevail in the land, to destroy the wicked and the evil, that the strong might not oppress the weak. (*ANET*, 164)

During the early monarchy, royal judicial authority was held as a prerogative of the king, and little delegation of authority to local judges occurred (2 Sam. 15:3). However, both Moses traditions (Exod. 18:13–27) and the Deuteronomist (Deut. 1:9–18) contain details on how Israel's leaders are to appoint individuals to perform judicial roles, and that model is then idealized by the author of Chronicles in the depiction of the reign of King Jehoshaphat (ca. 873–849 BCE). Of course, the growing complexity associated with running the nation and the sheer number of cases would have led to a major overhaul of the judicial system (2 Chron. 19:4–11). It simply makes sense for the king, who has fortified the border regions, to now use these new fortress cities as judicial centers where district courts are held and judges can hear cases (vv. 5–7). While the Chronicles account postdates Jehoshaphat's by several centuries, it is possible that the appointment of Levites and priests in Jerusalem to hear appealed cases dealing with religious crimes also makes administrative sense. That is particularly true since their authority is over legal categories in which "bloodshed, law or commandment, statutes or ordinances" are involved (v. 10).

Shifts in Family Legal Customs

The introduction of royal authority forced changes in some legal customs but was unable to supersede others. Early in David's career as king at Hebron, he faced a legal problem with the potential to tear apart his political hopes for a united kingdom. His general Joab murdered Abner, the commander of Ishbosheth's army (2 Sam. 3:26–27). This was done in the name of blood revenge, since Abner had killed Joab's brother Asahel in battle (2 Sam. 2:18–23).

The blood feud was an extension of familial responsibility to protect its own. It was tied to clan affairs since it involved a dispute between two extended families (Gen. 9:6; Deut. 19:11–12). However, private feuds directly threatened the authority of a king trying to establish a system of royal justice. The solution (2 Sam. 3:29–39) was for David to disclaim responsibility for Joab's act and to disgrace Joab by forcing him to mourn publicly at Abner's funeral. The king also calls on Yahweh to insure that the "blood stain" be placed on Joab's head rather than on the king or the people (3:28–29). In resolving the fictitious case presented to the king by the woman of Tekoa, David goes a step further and invokes royal authority to protect the accused murderer from clan vengeance (2 Sam. 14:4–11).

One way of addressing this problem came with the establishment of six Levitical "cities of refuge" as described in Joshua 21:13–40. Here a man who had accidentally caused the death of another could flee from the vengeance of family and clan to a city of refuge. There he would be tried by the elders of the city and either granted asylum or punished for his crime (Num. 35:9–34). In the time of Josiah's reform (late seventh century BCE), when all worship and royal authority were centralized in Jerusalem, the number of cities of refuge remained at six, but there was no direct Levitical involvement (Deut. 4:41–43; 19:1–13). Instead, these cities would have been part of an administrative network that supported the authority of the monarchy.

Marriage and Betrothal

The more cosmopolitan atmosphere of the royal court and the increased contacts with other nations led to a greater acceptance of intermarriage between Israelites and non-Israelites during the monarchic period. For example, Solomon attempted to solidify foreign alliances through his marriages to foreign princesses, such as the pharaoh's daughter (1 Kings 3:1), and Ahab strengthened already strong ties with the Phoenicians when he married Jezebel, the daughter of the king of Sidon (1 Kings 16:31). In the text, these diplomatic marriages do have a dark side, where they are cited as prime causes for the adoption of idol worship (1 Kings 11:1–8; 16:31–33) and the suppression of Yahweh's prophets

Ancient Near Eastern Laws concerning Marriage and Familial Rights

If a man pins down another man's virgin wife who is still residing in her father's house, and they seize him lying with her, that man shall be killed; that woman shall be released. (CH 130; *LCMAM*, 106)

If a man forcibly seizes and rapes a maiden who is residing in her father's house . . . who is not married, and against whose father's house there is no outstanding claim—whether within the city or in the countryside, or at night whether in the main thoroughfare, or in a granary, or during the city festival—the father of the maiden shall take the wife of the fornicator of the maiden and hand her over to be raped; he shall not return her to her husband, but he shall take her; the father shall give his daughter into the protection of the household of her fornicator. If the fornicator has no wife, the fornicator shall give "triple" the silver as the value of the maiden to her father; her fornicator shall marry her; he shall not reject her. If the father does not desire it so, he shall receive "triple" silver for the maiden, and he shall give his daughter in marriage to whomever he chooses. (MAL A.55; *LCMAM*, 174–75)

(1 Kings 18:13). Nevertheless, with such a precedent set by the king, it is not surprising to find mixed marriages among the rest of the people. (Bathsheba's marriage to Uriah the Hittite in 2 Sam. 11:3 may be a precursor of this shift.)

The parallels between Israelite marriage laws and those found in other ancient Near Eastern law codes indicate a common Near Eastern tradition that persisted over many centuries. For instance, the sanctity of the betrothal vows is found in Deuteronomy 22:23–27 and also in the eighteenth-century BCE Code of Hammurabi (#130). The presumption in both cases is that the father contracts the marriage, and once a girl is betrothed, she technically becomes the wife of that man. Any crime against her, such as rape, is also a crime against both her father and her betrothed husband.

The Babylonian law states that a betrothed virgin who has been raped will be freed while her attacker is executed. The Deuteronomic statute is more specific, taking into consideration the location of the crime and using this factor as the basis for the punishment of the couple. If the crime took place within the city, both are to be executed, since the woman could have cried out for help. However, if the rape is committed in the "open country" where no one could hear her cries, she goes free and only the man is executed.

The Middle Assyrian Law Code (ca. 1100 BCE) also contains similarities to the biblical criminal code. MAL A.55 is concerned with the rape of an unbetrothed virgin still living in her father's house. The code states that it does

If a man intends to divorce his first-ranking wife who did not bear him children, he shall give her silver as much as was her bride wealth and restore to her the dowry that she brought from her father's house, and he shall divorce her. (CH 138; *LCMAM*, 107)

If the wife of a man who is residing in the man's house should decide to leave, and she appropriates goods, squanders her household possessions, or disparages her husband, they shall charge her and convict her; and if her husband should declare his intention to divorce her, then he shall divorce her; neither her travel expenses, nor her divorce settlement, nor anything else shall be given to her. (CH 141; *LCMAM*, 106–7)

If a woman repudiates her husband . . . her circumstances shall be investigated by the authorities of her city quarter, and if she is circumspect and without fault, but her husband is wayward and disparages her greatly, that woman will not be subject to any penalty; she shall take her dowry and she shall depart for her father's house. (CH 142; *LCMAM*, 107)

not matter whether this crime has taken place in the city or the country, after dark, or during a religious festival. The rapist must pay a fine in silver to the father for the loss of his daughter's virginity, and the father has the option of forcing this man to marry his daughter with no possibility of divorcing her later. Deuteronomy 22:28–29 is almost an identical version of this law. Here the rapist must pay a fine of fifty shekels of silver and marry the girl without later recourse to divorce.

An Israelite man may divorce his wife by giving her a formal bill of divorce. Grounds for such action would be based on her having committed some "indecency" (Deut. 24:1–2). For instance, adultery would be considered grounds for divorce (Jer. 3:8). Ancient Near Eastern law codes also list childlessness (CH 138) and taking a job outside the home (CH 141) as grounds for divorce. There is no law in the biblical text allowing a woman the right to divorce her husband. However, he may not make unsubstantiated accusations of adultery or shameful conduct against her on pain of paying a fine and being publicly whipped (Deut. 22:13–19).

Inheritance Laws

Samuel's earliest arguments against the establishment of the monarchy "like other nations (have)" included the statement that the king "will take the best of your fields and vineyards and olive orchards and give them to his courtiers" (1 Sam. 8:14). Such privileges were granted by the king of Mari to reward tribesmen for military service (ARM IV 1:10–28). Saul did attach "any strong or valiant warrior . . . into his service" (1 Sam. 14:52), and presumably he was able to do this by granting them privileges at court and tracts of land. The kings would have done this by transferring land to these royal advisers that was no longer being used or whose owners were dead or had forfeited on their service obligations. There is evidence in Hammurabi's Code of transferring feudal rights and obligations in cases of default (CH 30).

The sale of land outside the family or clan was unusual in ancient Israel. Even during the siege of Jerusalem by Nebuchadnezzar in 587 BCE, Jeremiah's cousin offered him the option to purchase a field in Anathoth. Before the land could be offered to a stranger, Jeremiah had "the right of redemption by purchase" (Jer. 32:7–9). This transaction was completed and signed before witnesses. Its stipulations were recorded on a legal contract prepared by the scribe Baruch, and one copy was then placed in a sealed earthenware vessel for safe storage (vv. 10–14).

On occasion, kings tried to exercise their powers so as to infringe upon inheritance traditions. Thus in 1 Kings 21:1–4 King Ahab attempts to purchase the vineyard of a Jezreelite named Naboth. As was his right as a member of the covenant community, Naboth refuses to sell his land to the king, citing the fact that he cannot give him "my ancestral inheritance" (v. 4). Ahab has no legal recourse and goes home to sulk. His Phoenician wife Jezebel, however, has no qualms about taking what she wants. She is not bound by Israelite tradition or the law and promptly trumps up charges of blasphemy against Naboth (21:8–12). Two witnesses, as stipulated in Deuteronomy 19:15, are brought forward to testify against him, and he is subsequently stoned to death (1 Kings 21:13–14). Naboth's sons are apparently also executed along

> These five men abandoned their territory (and) came to me because their brothers had been entrusted with wheat and a field (and) were satisfied. . . . These men should be taken and entrusted to the hand of the *sugāgum* (so that) they may be brought to me and given satisfaction. (ARM IV 1:10–28)

Reassignment of Land

If either a soldier or a fisherman abandons his field, orchard, or house because of the service obligation and then absents himself, another person takes possession of his field, orchard, or house to succeed to his holdings and performs the service obligation for three years—if he then returns and claims his field, orchard, or house, it will not be given to him; he who has taken possession of it and has performed his service obligation shall be the one to continue to perform the obligation. (CH 30; *LCMAM*, 86–87)

Figure 3.10. Stele of Hammurabi, depicting the king before a seated deity; the rest of the stele is inscribed with the Code of Hammurabi.

with their father for this crime, leaving no direct male heir to inherit the property (2 Kings 9:26).

When Ahab, as the ultimate heir of property within the kingdom, goes to take possession of Naboth's field, he is confronted there by the prophet Elijah (1 Kings 21:15–19). The king and his entire family are cursed for having "sold themselves" in order to take possession of land that is not theirs. The "King's Call to Justice" theme, employed here by the Deuteronomistic Historian, emphasizes that even the king is not above the law and will be called to justice by Yahweh, a justice that will affect his rule and that of his descendants. This same theme also occurs in the narrative of David's adultery with Bathsheba (2 Sam. 12:1–23) and of Solomon's idolatry (1 Kings 11:1–13).

Slavery

Slavery was a part of Israelite tribal society from the earliest periods. Abraham acquired at least two slaves in his travels, Eliezer of Damascus (Gen. 15:2) and the Egyptian woman Hagar (Gen. 16:1). It is unclear how many slaves were held by the Israelites during the early settlement period. The Judges narrative notes that Gideon's son Abimelech was born to a slave woman (Judg. 9:18), and it is likely that raids and warfare provided some slaves (1 Sam. 4:9). The number of slaves increased significantly during the early monarchy due to David's almost continuous wars, which provided a steady flow of prisoners. These non-Israelite men and women became perpetual household servants, wives

(Deut. 21:10–14) or concubines, and construction workers (2 Sam. 12:31). Not all prisoners of war, however, were spared to become slaves. In one instance (2 Sam. 8:2) David executed two-thirds of his Moabite prisoners, perhaps to strike terror into the people of that nation.

Solomon's public works projects were built by forced labor battalions drafted from the Israelite villages (1 Kings 5:13–18). The text states that Israelites were not to be relegated to the status of slaves since their role was to serve in the army and in positions of authority (1 Kings 9:22). By whatever title, Israelite "workers" would have been required to participate in the grandiose building programs of their kings along with the levies of captured Canaanite slaves (1 Kings 9:20–21).

Due to periodic economic downturns, droughts, or the heavy taxes imposed on them, poor Israelites occasionally were forced to become slaves, selling themselves or members of their family into slavery to satisfy a debt (see Amos 2:6). According to the Covenant Code of law, this servitude was to last only six years for males; in the seventh they were freed and their debt cancelled (Exod. 21:2). Another law protecting the rights of slaves is recorded in Exodus 21:26–27. This statute required that male and female slaves be freed if their masters had brutalized them. This early legal code (Exod. 21:7–11) also stated that daughters, sold by their father into slavery, did not obtain their freedom in the same way as males. Many of these women became concubines or wives, and thus their position as slaves or free women was determined by their eventual marital status.

> If an obligation is outstanding against a man and he sells or gives into debt service his wife, his son, or his daughter, they shall perform service in the house of their buyer or of the one who holds them in debt service for three years; their release shall be secured in the fourth year. (CH 117; *LCMAM*, 103)

The later Deuteronomic Code (dating to after 620 BCE) also required that slaves be freed after six years of service (in a similar case, CH 117 mandated only three years of service) and that they should not be sent away empty-handed (Deut. 15:12–15). In other words, former debt slaves are given some form of economic support so they do not immediately fall back into debt service. This Deuteronomic Code further simplified the law by including both men and women in this six-year, limited period of servitude (Deut. 15:12). The fact that these laws were not always obeyed, however, is attested to in Jeremiah 34:8–16. Here the prophet complained that Israelite slaves had been freed based on a decree by King Zedekiah during the Babylonian siege of Jerusalem; the people had then reenslaved them after the immediate danger passed. Such a blatant violation of the law became part of God's indictment against the city and its more affluent citizens.

> If a barber shaves off the slave-hairlock of a slave not belonging to him without the consent of the owner, they shall cut off that barber's hand. (CH 226; *LCMAM*, 124)

Legal provision for perpetual slavery for male Israelites does appear in the law in order to address those slaves who wish to remain slaves. Someone might choose slavery in order to prevent falling back into the pattern of poverty that had forced him into slavery originally or because freedom would have separated him from his family. The latter is explained in Exodus 21:4–6, where a master has given a man a wife, and they then had children while the debtor was still a slave. When his period of servitude ends, he has the legal right to go free, but not his wife and children. At that point the former slave can renounce his freedom by swearing an oath to God and having an awl driven through his earlobe into the post of his master's door (a revised version is found in Deut. 15:16–17, without reference to a wife). The mark of the awl branded him as a slave for life, and the doorpost signified he now belonged to the household within. In a further variation on this theme, the Code of Hammurabi prescribes mutilation or capital punishment for those who participate in the fraudulent removal of a slave mark (CH 226–27).

Within the biblical narrative and its legal codes, the majority of references to slaves in the period of the settlement and monarchic periods involved Israelite debt slaves. This may explain why, according to the law, both Israelite families and their slaves were included in the covenantal community's Sabbath obligations to honor the Creator's recess by resting from all work (Exod. 20:8–11). In the Deuteronomic Code, this attitude toward slaves is tied directly to the memory of Israel's enslavement in Egypt (Deut. 5:12–15). The collective memory of their own enslavement became the basis for establishing a tradition calling for a generally humane treatment of slaves under the law.

Religious Practices

The establishment of the monarchy did not initially have a dramatic effect on local and family religious practices. Popular religion remained separate and often quite different from the official religion of Jerusalem and the temple.

Legal Significance of Place

The symbolism employed to add authority to a legal decision often is tied to place. In particular, the threshold, the doorpost or doorway of a dwelling, which symbolizes the life and well-being of the persons who live within the house, is a common location to perform legal acts or to display to all a legal judgment.

In CH 227, if a person "misinforms a barber" about the status of a slave and thus tricks the barber into removing the distinguishing "slave-hairlock," then that man is to be executed, and his body is to be hung in the doorway of his own house (*LCMAM*, 124).

In Judges 19:26, the Levite's concubine, as her last living act, casts herself before the door of the house where her husband and his guest had spent the night while a mob had brutalized her. In so doing she indicts those within the house for sacrificing her life to save their own.

When the ark of the covenant was captured by the Philistines and placed at the feet of the statue of the god Dagon, God causes an earthquake to topple the statue. Its fragments are thrown onto the threshold of the god's temple, defiling that entranceway and demonstrating Yahweh's power over the gods of the Philistines (1 Sam. 5:1–5).

Political developments further complicated and added to Israelite religious practices. They continued to worship a variety of deities, including Yahweh, based on the influences of religious pluralism that had marked previous periods.

The official worship of Yahweh and the initial organization of its Levitical priesthood was part of establishing Jerusalem as the nation's capital during David's and Solomon's reigns. Shortly after the division of the kingdom, however, Jeroboam and the later kings of Israel created rival shrines at Dan and Bethel where non-Levitical priests oversaw worship (1 Kings 12:25–33). Under this new regime, the kings legitimized the use of high places in local villages. In Judah, however, the main (if not the only) cult center was the Jerusalem temple, which continued to be under the control of Levitical priests. The division between the two kingdoms contributed to differences in understanding of the proper worship of Yahweh that would continue as long as the northern kingdom of Israel existed.

In contrast, while the Assyrians and Babylonians did not impose the worship of their gods on the Israelites when they conquered the region (2 Kings 17:24–33), their destruction of many of the local shrines (2 Kings 25:9, 13–17) and their deportation of a large portion of the population made performance of many of the religious rituals and festivals difficult, if not impossible. And, of course, the peoples who were brought into what had been Israelite territory from other parts of the Assyrian Empire carried their gods with them and continued to worship them despite efforts to teach them about the Israelite god and the law (2 Kings 17:27–29).

In Judah, after suffering through the Assyrian invasion and Sennacherib's siege of Jerusalem in 701 BCE, the child-king Manasseh and his advisors choose to reconcile with their Assyrian masters rather than continue to rebel. The result, based on the indictment of Manasseh by the Deuteronomist, is the restoration of the high places, the open worship of the god Baal as well as "all the host of heaven," presumably including the Assyrian pantheon of gods (2 Kings 21:1–7).

A single pattern of worship that emphasized the Yahweh cult existed only when the monarchy was free to exercise strong control over the entire land, as in Josiah's time (2 Kings 23:1–27). The disintegration of the Assyrian Empire after the death of the emperor Ashurbanipal in 727 BCE allowed Josiah to institute a series of religious reforms based on the legal code found in Deuteronomy 12–26 and designed to reconstitute Jerusalem as the religious focal point for the nation. These reforms forbade worship of any deity but Yahweh (Deut. 12:29–13:18), outlawed shrines (including the local high places) other than the Jerusalem temple (Deut. 12:2–4), and purged Canaanite practices from official Israelite worship (Deut. 12:29–14:2). Although the reform ended with Josiah's death and the subsequent destruction of Jerusalem by the Babylonians in 587 BCE, it left a residue of religious tradition that will help spark the return from Babylonian exile and the reconstruction of the temple in 515 BCE.

Figure 3.11. Horned altar from Megiddo, tenth to ninth centuries BCE

Popular Religion

During the settlement period and the beginning of the monarchic period, the individual Israelite homes and villages continued to engage in popular expressions of religion, most of them centered on seasonal festivals (1 Sam. 20:18, 29) or annual pilgrimages to a shrine (1 Sam. 1:3). For example, the New Moon festival was celebrated monthly on the first day after the appearance of the crescent moon (Ps. 81:4; Amos 8:5). The day was set aside for rest, feasting (1 Sam. 20:18, 29), and sacrifice (Num. 28:11–15). In fact, the concept of internal religious pluralism allows for recognition of religious practice at several social levels, from the family or household level to the village level and to the national level of religious expression. Each of these levels may have shared some rites and sacred objects, but it would be a mistake to say that they are simply the same form of worship expressed in small or large groups.

These sacrifices and other rites dedicated to various gods were designed to ensure the fertility of the people, the land, and their herds. They were made on altars in private chapels (Judg. 17:5), in villages (Judg. 6:25–28), or collectively on the local village "high place" (bamah, 1 Sam. 9:19; 2 Kings 17:9–10). Excavations at Lachish and Tell Michal and other sites demonstrate that these sacred installations were marked by the construction of platforms and benches around the altar to hold sacred vessels or stands. Horned altars made of limestone, too small to be used in animal sacrifices, have been found at a number of sites, including Megiddo and Tel Miqne-Ekron, dating to the Iron II period. They were probably used for burning incense and for grain offerings by the family. Sacred household images (teraphim) in the form of the particular gods a household relied upon for protection and prosperity (Judg. 18:14) remained a part of Israelite religious custom and are even mentioned in the story of David's escape from Saul's palace (1 Sam. 19:11–17).

> **KUNTILLET ʿAJRUD INSCRIPTION**
>
> Your days may be prolonged, and you shall be satisfied . . . give YHWH of Teman and his Asherah . . . (COS 2:2.47B, 172)

Given the uncertainties of life in the ancient Near East, with the real and constant dangers of drought, famine, and war, it is not surprising to find that the Israelites chose to adopt some of the religious practices of their neighbors. That would have included the use of images (such as the terra cotta figurines found at many sites) as well as specific rituals, prayers, and sacrifices. Among the Canaanite communities, worship of fertility gods also included the use of both male and female cult prostitutes (Deut. 23:17). Sexual activity at local shrines was designed to promote the fertility of the land by encouraging the storm god Baal and his consort Asherah to engage in divine intercourse, causing abundant harvests and a growth in herds.

The exact extent to which Israelites incorporated non-Yahwist religious rituals is uncertain. However, there are a number of instances in the narrative that suggest it did occur. In 1 Samuel 2:22, Eli's sons subvert the activities of women whose job it is to clean up the debris of the sacrifices "at the entrance to the tent of meeting" at Shiloh (see Exod. 38:8). It is possible that by lying with these women, the priests are, in effect, promoting the use of

Figure 3.12. Bronze figurine of Baal, Canaanite god of war

cult prostitutes (Lev. 19:29). For this violation and others, all of the adult members of Eli's priestly clan are condemned to die (1 Sam. 2:31–34), and his sons will die when the ark of the covenant is captured by the Philistines (1 Sam. 4:11).

The adoption of particular Canaanite religious practices prompted the Deuteronomic Historian to formulate an ideal of proper behavior in the law calling for strict adherence to Yahweh's covenant (see especially Deut. 13–14). This legal prohibition was reinforced by the stern pronouncements of the prophets against idolatry (Jer. 8:19; Hosea 10:3–6; Mic. 1:6–7). The law also provides an impetus for Josiah to pursue his religious reforms in the late seventh century BCE. Among other things, he breaks down the houses of male prostitutes within the temple precincts (2 Kings 23:7).

Despite his construction of the Yahweh temple in Jerusalem, Solomon's building of temples for the gods of his foreign wives (1 Kings 11:4–8) simply serves as an acknowledgment that even the monarchy was willing to sanction the worship of other gods. The priesthood in the capital could not effectively police these illicit practices, which apparently continued throughout the history of Judah (1 Kings 14:22–24). Examinations of the ancient buildings at the caravan site of Kuntillet 'Ajrud, in the northeast portion of the Sinai Desert (thirty miles south of Kadesh-barnea), have revealed drawings and a fragmentary Phoenician inscription that add fuel to the argument that Yahweh worship shared some aspects of the Canaanite fertility god Baal and his consort Asherah.

The division of the kingdom further weakened local worship of Yahweh. In the northern kingdom of Israel, popular religion was given free rein by Jeroboam and his successors, who only demanded the people's political loyalties. Existing local "high places" were promoted by the kings as a way to curry favor with the villagers and build support for their rule (1 Kings 12:31). Worship of one deity did not preclude devotion to another (see 1 Kings 16:31; 22:1–8). While Yahweh was worshiped on Mount Carmel in Jezreel (1 Kings 18:19–45), Ahab was free to erect a temple to Baal in his capital city of Samaria (1 Kings 16:32–33). Israel's royal shrines, like Bethel, were staffed by priests loyal to the regime and served as rallying points for major festivals (see Amos 7:13). Prophets active in the north often pointed to these local and politically oriented shrines as the justification for the destruction of the nation (Amos 7:9 and Hosea 10:8).

Desecrating Sacred Space

One way that conquering armies and religious reformers try to show the failure of gods or to demonstrate complete mastery over a people is to desecrate sacred facilities (temples, altars, graves, etc.). A more recent (late eighteenth century CE) example comes from revolutionary France, when Catholic churches were transformed into "Temples of Reason" or used to house animals. Their efforts, like those of the ancients, were designed to erase the memory of a place once dedicated to worship.

In 2 Kings 10:18–28, the usurper Jehu completed his purge of Ahab's family and the worshipers of Baal in Israel by luring them to a celebratory sacrifice in the temple of Baal in Samaria and then massacring them. He also destroyed the sacred objects and "destroyed the temple of Baal, and made it a latrine to this day" (v. 27).

Psalm 74:3–8 describes the Babylonian destruction of Jerusalem and its temple (see 2 Kings 25:9–10). The lament says that these enemies of Judah "set up their emblems" on the temple site and "smashed all the carved work" of the temple. They set fire to the sanctuary and "desecrated the dwelling place" of Yahweh's name.

Standing stones (*maṣṣēbôt*) were erected on the high places in both Israel and Judah as well as in the temple of Baal in Samaria (2 Kings 3:2; 10:26; 17:9–10). These slabs of stone marked the entrance to sacred precincts or represented the presence of the deity. *Maṣṣēbôt* are also part of the regional shrine within the Iron II fortress at Arad along with incense altars and a courtyard containing a sacrificial altar. These standing stones were so closely associated with various forms of Canaanite worship that Josiah singled them out for destruction, along with the altars and sacred poles (*'ashērîm*) dedicated to foreign deities, in his seventh-century reform movement (2 Kings 23:14; see also Deut. 7:5; 12:3).

While less is known about religious practice in the southern kingdom of Judah, Jerusalem remained a major cultic center. Local shrines did exist in Judah (1 Kings 14:23), but some kings attempted to suppress their use. The royal annals describe how King Hezekiah "removed the high places, broke down the pillars, and cut down the sacred poles" (2 Kings 18:4). Archaeologists have found a horned altar that may have been associated with the shrine at Beer-sheba, which dates to Hezekiah's time (ca. 701 BCE). These well-dressed stones were reused as fill in constructing a later wall, perhaps evidencing a royal attempt to eliminate the high place at this site (2 Kings 18:22).

Josiah's seventh-century reform (2 Kings 23:4–24) actually provides a long list of Canaanite religious practices engaged in by the people of Judah. In order to strengthen the Yahweh cult and his own control over the nation, the king removed idols and banished their priests from the temple along with all sacred vessels and incense burners associated with their cult. The Asherah (*'ăšērâ*), a sacred wooden pole set up in the temple, was taken out and burned, and its ashes were made unclean by scattering them over a "potter's field" graveyard (v. 6). Cult prostitutes were banished, and the "high places" were defiled and abolished from one end of the land to the other (vv. 7–8).

In addition to these efforts to purify Yahweh worship in Judah, Josiah also eliminated religious practices and icons associated with neighboring peoples. He destroyed a shrine in the valley of Hinnom that was being used for the sacrifice of children to the god Molech (2 Kings 23:10). He removed the images of horses and chariots from the temple precincts, a vestige of Assyrian sun worship possibly introduced in Judah by his grandfather Manasseh (v. 11). Altars that had been built to foreign gods by previous kings were pulled down and destroyed (vv. 12–15), and the graves (vv. 16–20) of Baal priests at Bethel (one of the sites in which Jeroboam had placed a golden calf, 1 Kings 12:28–29) were defiled. The final expression of his clean sweep comes in 2 Kings 23:24 with the outlawing of mediums, wizards, *teraphim*, idols, "and all the abominations that were seen in the land of Judah and in Jerusalem." Josiah's efforts did not extend far beyond the boundaries of his own country, and much of what he attempted to accomplish ended with his death at the battle of Megiddo in 609 BCE.

NUR-SIN TO ZIMRI-LIM, KING OF MARI

Abiya, prophet of Adad, the lord of Aleppo, came to me and said: "Thus says Adad: 'I have given the whole country to Yaḫdun-Lim. Thanks to my weapons, he did not meet his equal. He, however, abandoned my cause, so I gave to Šamši-Adad the land I had given to him.'" (A. 1968; Nissinen 2003, 21–22)

Role of the Prophets

The office of prophet, which is held by both men and women, is present in cultures throughout the ancient Near East. Much of what was considered prophetic activity is associated with practices of divination and the interpretation of omens by professional cultic officials and priests. Their work was based on the assumption that the gods could be consulted and that omens were provided to signify whether particular actions were propitious at this time. For example, it would be unthinkable to go to war or begin the construction of a new temple without first engaging in some type of divinatory process, such as the examination of the entrails of a sheep, the flight of birds, or interpretation of dreams. Among the ancient texts from Mesopotamia that describe speaking prophets are the Neo-Assyrian inscriptions (ca. 800–650 BCE) and the letters from the eighteenth-century BCE government archive at Mari. These individuals generally spoke in the name of a particular god, sometimes in the form of an ecstatic pronouncement.

In ancient Israel, prophets are not commonly mentioned (aside from Abraham, Moses, and Miriam, Gen. 20:7; Exod. 7:1; 15:20; Deut. 34:10). During the settlement period, when "the word of the Lord was rare" and "visions were not widespread" (1 Sam. 3:1), Samuel served in a variety of capacities, as a prophet (1 Sam. 3:2–21), judge (7:17), and priest (7:3–17; 9:13–14). When he appointed his corrupt sons as his successors (8:1–3), the tribal elders demanded that Samuel ask Yahweh for a king to rule over Israel (1 Sam. 8:4–5).

Prophetic activity increases in the monarchic period. For example, there are several instances when these individuals receive word from God regarding who was to be chosen as king and who was to be rejected (1 Sam. 9:16; 15:10–11, 22–23; 16:1; compare Mari text A. 1968). On a number of occasions they anointed Israel's kings (1 Sam. 10:1; 16:13; 1 Kings 1:34, 45; 2 Kings 9:1–13) and, at times, they are instructed to anoint the kings of other nations as a prophetic sign of Yahweh's intervention in the affairs of other countries (1 Kings 19:15–16). During a king's rule, prophets provided advice on military matters (1 Kings 22:5–6; Isa. 1:1–17) and on questions about the royal succession (2 Kings 20:1). Some of the prophets who are active just before the fall of the northern kingdom of Israel (721 BCE) and the subsequent fall of Judah (587 BCE) warned kings of the dangers of yielding to their enemies (Isa. 37:5–7, 30–35). Other prophets actually encouraged surrender and stated as part of a theodicy that God would fight on behalf of the conquerors as a form of punishment for Israel's and Judah's disobedience to the covenant (Jer. 21:3–10; 38:17–23).

The biblical picture of the relationship between prophets and their audiences usually contains the seeds of conflict. Even before the monarchy was established, Samuel warns the people against kings and the power they exercise (1 Sam. 8:11–18). In another instance, the court prophet Nathan, who had previously encouraged David by proclaiming that God would grant his dynasty an "everlasting covenant" and the right to rule in Jerusalem (2 Sam. 7:8–17), berates the king for committing adultery with Bathsheba (2 Sam. 12:1–15). The Deuteronomist's version of the royal annals of King Ahab declares that this northern king "hates" the prophet Micaiah for consistently speaking against Ahab's military

> In the temple of Annunitum three days ago, Šelebum (the *assinnu* prophet) went into a trance and said: "Thus says Annunitum: Zimri-Lim, you will be tested in a revolt! Protect yourself! Let your most favored servants whom you love surround you, and make them stay there to protect you! Do not go around on your own! As regards the people who would test you, those people I deliver up into your hands." Now I am sending the hair and the fringe of the garment of the *assinnu* to my Lord. (ARMT 10.7; Nissinen 2003, 47–48)

engagements. Then, rather than listening to Micaiah's warnings, the king surrounds himself with four hundred court prophets who always tell him what he wants to hear (1 Kings 22:5–28). The biblical record then notes that King Ahab dies in a battle that Micaiah had warned him to avoid (vv. 29–40). The results of these conflicts between kings and prophets prove deadly for others beside the kings. Jezebel, Ahab's Phoenician wife, attempted to systematically exterminate Yahweh's prophets in the name of her allegiance to Baal (1 Kings 18:4). She in turn is condemned by Elijah (1 Kings 21:23), and she subsequently dies in Jehu's revolt against the house of Ahab (2 Kings 9:30–34).

Throughout the monarchic period, Yahweh's prophets deliver the dual message to obey the covenant by worshiping only Yahweh and ensure that there is social justice and equality for Israelites, both rich and poor. Faced with the disobedience of the people, the eighth-century BCE northern prophet Hosea likens Israel's worship of other deities to adultery (Hosea 2:2–13). As an **enacted prophecy** or prophetic sign act, Hosea is commanded to take a "wife of whoredom" and to father three children whose names represent the consequences of Israel's adulterous adherence to other gods (1:1–8). Later prophets echo Hosea's warnings against idolatry, reminding Israel and Judah of their deliverance from Egypt and their covenant agreement to obey Yahweh's law (Jer. 2:6–7; 11:1–8; Ezek. 20:1–21; Hosea 11:1–2; Amos 2:10; Mic. 6:4).

In order to encourage the people to be obedient to the covenant and God's law, the prophets remind them that they must stop unjust economic practices like rushing the end of the Sabbath in order to resume business and using false weights to cheat their customers (Amos 8:4–5; see Isa. 10:2; Hosea 12:7). The eighth-century BCE southern prophet Isaiah admonishes the people of Judah on God's behalf, "What do you mean by crushing my people, by grinding the face of the poor?" (Isa. 3:15). The prophet Amos travels north into Israel, where he condemns the wealthy for oppressing the poor. He tells them that the fine houses they have built and the vineyards they have cultivated will become the property of foreigners when they are taken away into exile as punishment for their unjust policies and attitudes (Amos 5:11).

Temple Worship and the Yahweh Cult

There were several shrines scattered throughout Canaan during the premonarchic period. These included the ones at Shechem (Josh. 24:25–26), Shiloh (1 Sam. 1:3), and Dan (Judg. 18:27–31), and the three corners of Samuel's circuit as a judge: Bethel (1 Sam. 10:3), Gilgal, and Mizpah (1 Sam. 7:16). Archaeological investigations indicate that after the Philistines captured the ark of the covenant (1 Sam. 4:10–11), Shiloh and the Iron I temple, which had housed the ark, were destroyed. Shiloh's prominence probably ended at that point, with the site not resettled until the sixth century BCE. The biblical account indicates that the ark went into obscurity in the village of Kiriath-jearim for a generation (1 Sam. 7:1–2). The narrative then shifts the priestly group that had served at Shiloh to the city of Nob, an unidentified location (1 Sam. 21:1–9). This was not, however, the only priestly community operating in Canaan at that time. David and his family were also associated with the cult center in Hebron (2 Sam. 2:4 and 15:7) and worshiped in Bethlehem (1 Sam. 20:6).

Jerusalem Temple

The temple most intimately associated with the Davidic dynasty was the one built by Solomon in Jerusalem. Its site, like Jerusalem itself, was on politically neutral ground—the threshing floor of Araunah the Jebusite (2 Sam. 24:18–25 and 2 Chron. 3:1). Any suggestion of previous cultic usage was supplanted by a Yahweh theophany, which marks the end of the plague of punishment that had resulted from David's illegal census-taking. King David's purchase of the threshing floor (a place associated with justice in the older village culture) and his sacrifice on the site further transform the ground into a sacred spot. King Solomon's construction of the temple on this site provided royal legitimation for the Yahweh cult and is sanctified by the Deuteronomist's assertion that this is the place Yahweh has chosen for his sacrifices (Deut. 12:13–14).

The key element that associated this site with Yahweh was the ark of the covenant. David had it brought to his new capital with great fanfare and ceremony after he became the king over all the tribes (2 Sam. 6:1–19). During his reign the ark continued to be housed in a tent, a parallel to the wilderness tabernacle (Exod. 40:1–8), and the sacrificial routine was initiated with David making burnt offerings and peace offerings before the tent (2 Sam. 6:17).

The next logical step for David would have been to construct a temple dedicated to Yahweh worship. However, the text offers a variety of reasons why David did not build a temple to house the ark. According to 2 Samuel 7:8–17, the need for a temple was replaced by the need to create a ruling house. First Kings 5:3 excuses David from this task because of the pressure of military campaigns to protect the nation. But the Chronicler, despite giving David credit for establishing the priestly bureaucracy that would supervise temple worship, says that he was denied the right to build the temple because he was "a warrior and had shed blood" (1 Chron. 28:2–3).

As a result, the task was left to David's successor, Solomon, who had the leisure time and resources to build the temple to Yahweh in Jerusalem (1 Kings 5:4–6). Even the shaping of the stones at the quarry rather than on site eliminated the warlike noises of iron tools and signaled that this was a time of peace (1 Kings 6:7). In Solomon's dedication of the completed temple, he follows

David's example, initiating sacrifices of various kinds (peace offerings, burnt offerings, cereal offerings) followed by a seven-day feast for all the people (1 Kings 8:62–66). From the beginning, then, David set the precedent: the king officiated at sacrifices and initiated national worship festivals (note that much later Josiah reinitiated the Passover; 2 Kings 23:21–23). Some of David's sons are even described as being priests (2 Sam. 8:18). The actual degree to which royalty participated in the sacrificial cult other than as sponsors or patrons is unknown.

Role of the Priestly Community

While David is credited by the Chronicler with establishing the temple priesthood (1 Chron. 15:1–24), and Solomon is recognized as significantly responsible for reorganizing it (1 Kings 2:35), the Levitical priesthood eventually disputed the idea of the king as both political and religious leader. Over time, the Levites gained more complete control of the sacrificial rituals, and the king, while still an advocate for the people with God, took a secondary, ceremonial role. For example, whereas Solomon functions in a priestly role by offering sacrifices, prayers, and blessings at the dedication of the temple (1 Kings 8:54–66), in the Chronicler's account Hezekiah offers only a brief prayer on behalf of the people while the priests and Levites actually offer the sacrifices during the reinstatement of the Passover festival (2 Chron. 30:13–27).

This struggle between the priests and king for primacy in ritual matters may have been sparked by the royal practice, starting with Solomon (1 Kings 11:6–8) and Jeroboam (1 Kings 12:28–33), of building altars to foreign gods and promoting non-Levitical priests to lead their worship (1 Kings 13:33). The result in the biblical text was to portray the kings as either evil idolaters like Manasseh (2 Kings 21:2–9) or as reformers who looked to the prophets and priests to help them cleanse the temple and renew the worship of the people (Joash, 2 Chron. 24:2–14; Josiah, 2 Kings 22:3–23:25). The biblical account produced by the Deuteronomic Historian does not take into consideration the internal political pressures that were placed on the kings to accommodate local forms of worship or to conform to the customs and religious practices of their Assyrian and Babylonian masters. Manasseh ruled for forty years as a vassal of the Assyrians, and his long reign might well be attributed to his success in compromising with his overlords and their rules.

With kings fighting for their own survival, the Levitical priests became the protectors and interpreters of the law, although it should be noted that the non-Levitical priests in the northern kingdom were condemned by the prophets as being ignorant of the law (Hosea 4:6; Amos 7:10–17). In Judah, Josiah's reform attempted to centralize worship in the Jerusalem temple, reinforcing the priests' position and strengthening their control over both established

Figure 3.13. The Islamic Dome of the Rock
probably stands on the site of Solomon's Temple in Jerusalem.

and popular religion. The Deuteronomic Code in chapters 12–26 provides a blueprint for the religious activities in Judah's villages and towns. As a revision of earlier law codes, the Deuteronomic Code updated Israel's laws for a new generation while at the same time solidifying the theological thinking behind Josiah's reform efforts. Everything from dietary laws (14:3–8) to the proper place and means of slaughtering animals (12:15–27) is found here, as well as the religious calendar (16:1–17) and the referral of difficult legal cases to the Levitical priests (17:8–13).

In Jerusalem itself, the actual routine of sacrificial offerings and temple worship was left in priestly hands. Extremely elaborate ritual and sacrificial instructions are described in the book of Leviticus, although they were designed to address worship in the Second Temple, which was constructed in 515 BCE after the return from Babylonian exile. In particular, the Holiness Code in Leviticus stresses the role of the priests to teach the people to "distinguish between the holy and the common, and between the unclean and the clean" (Lev. 10:10). Among the statutes is a list of which animals were to be used for particular sacrifices (Lev. 1:3–17), what portion of the animal was reserved for God (3:16), the use of the sacrificial blood (4:6–7), and the offerings that were acceptable from a man who could not afford the normal sacrificial animal (5:11).

Matters such as ritual purity, the interpretation of the law, and the treatment of disease (Lev. 13–14) are also found here and are reserved as the exclusive province of the Levitical priests. The Holiness Code would not have been strictly enforced until the postexilic period, when the monarchy had ended and the priests were the principal leaders of the people.

Weapons and Warfare

At the beginning of the monarchic period, the most important element in warfare was the establishment of parity between the Israelites and their neighbors. David's mercenary years with the Philistines almost certainly gave him an intimate knowledge of their battle tactics and their skill in the use of weapons (1 Sam. 27:1). Archaeological discoveries and the examination of technological innovation that eventually brought the ancient Near East into the Iron Age by the tenth century BCE demonstrate that it is unlikely that iron weapons were the predominant item in the Philistine arsenal. However, learning about the enemy from the "inside" must have contributed to the eventual Israelite victory over the Philistines and other neighboring peoples.

The establishment of the monarchy itself was another important factor in the war against the Philistines. With the tribal groups united under a single leader, they were a much more powerful and effective force. From his capital at Jerusalem, David led his armies (2 Sam. 8) or entrusted them to Joab's leadership to protect the villages and towns of his kingdom from invaders (2 Sam. 10). As the area of his effective control grew, the valley of Succoth grew in strategic importance. It guarded the fords leading into Transjordan from the invading armies of Ammon or Syria. Under Solomon, the area of Mahanaim (east of Succoth on the north side of the Jabbok River in Transjordan) was incorporated as one of the twelve administrative provinces of the kingdom (1 Kings 4:7–19).

Organization of the Army

One important innovation of the united kingdom of Israel was the organization of the army into two different units: the regular army and local militia. Naturally, most strategy was based around the professional soldiers of the regular army. Like Uriah the Hittite, many of these "Mighty Men" (2 Sam. 23:8–39) were foreign mercenaries whose loyalty was to the crown and who were expected to possess the military experience needed in the wars against the Ammonites and Syrian princes. Others, at least at the beginning of David's reign, were from his family or the group of outlaws he had led before the death of Saul (2 Sam. 21:15–22). They served as an elite shock force that could be reinforced as needed by the less experienced village militia (2 Sam. 12:26–29). From the perspective of five centuries after the time of David, 1 Chronicles 27:1–15 provides a somewhat idealized description of the command structure and size of the militia, with each formation consisting of twenty-four thousand warriors (a number somewhat high for the Davidic period). It is likely that a portion of this force was kept in reserve in case the king needed to call them into service quickly.

Weaponry

One sign that the Israelite monarchs were achieving military parity with their neighbors was the incorporation of chariotry into their armed forces. In the settlement and judges period, chariots had been a weapon of the Philistines and Canaanites, not the people of Israel (Josh. 11:4–9; Judg. 1:19). David's and Solomon's enhanced political status and military success can be gauged, however, by their acquisition of chariots (1 Sam. 8:11; 2 Sam. 8:3–4) and their building of stables to house the horses (1 Kings 4:26). Their successors in both Israel and Judah use chariots as a matter of course in every military campaign (1 Kings 22:29–35; 2 Kings 3:7; 8:21). For instance, in the Annals of the Assyrian king Shalmaneser III (858–824 BCE), King Ahab of Israel contributes two thousand chariots and ten thousand soldiers to a coalition army. The commander of chariot forces becomes one of the major military officers in Israel but also a potential threat to kings who cannot control them (see Zimri's usurpation of the throne in 1 Kings 16:9).

In the armies of Israel and Judah as well as those of their enemies, infantry was separated into fighting units and equipped with three basic weapons—spear, bow, and sling. Assyrian reliefs from the period of the divided monarchy (ca. 900–721 BCE) depict spearmen in mailed coats carrying a shield in one hand and equipped with a sword either strapped to the back or thrust into the belt (compare Goliath's armament in 1 Sam. 17:5–7; and David's followers in 1 Chron. 12:8; 2 Chron. 14:8). With weapons designed for close infighting, the spearmen formed the first wave of attack. Depending on the terrain, chariots and cavalry were used both on the flanks and in formation. Chariots were also used to conduct commanders (1 Kings 22:31–34; 2 Kings 9:21) and messengers around the field while the entire force was supported by bowmen and slingers (2 Kings 3:25b; 1 Chron. 12:2; 2 Chron. 26:14; Isa. 13:18).

> **ANNALS OF SHALMANESER III**
>
> I marched south to Qarqar and laid siege to the city. Once it was captured, I set it on fire. Irhuleni, the ruler of Qarqar, mustered only 700 chariots . . . but his twelve covenant partners also fielded armies against me. . . . Ahab, the ruler of Israel, 2,000 chariots and 10,000 soldiers. (*OTP*, 179)

Figure 3.14. Assyrian relief from Nineveh depicting Assyrians capturing a fortress in Egypt

Siege Strategies

Open-field tactics, terrain considerations, and strategies based on the number of chariots and soldiers on the field are found in a number of biblical passages (1 Kings 20:23–30; 22:29–36). However, a major challenge to military strategists in the monarchic period was the capture of a walled city. The strong points of the city (walls, glacis, moat, and gate complex) had to be overcome. Again, it was the Assyrians who perfected strategies to offset each of these challenges. Their reliefs and royal annals depict Assyrian armies employing assault ramps and ladders, wheeled tanks fixed with battering rams, sappers tunneling under walls, infantrymen with inflated goatskins crossing rivers and moats, and mobile towers bristling with archers thrust up against the city wall. These methods and structures were probably used in the Assyrian capture of Samaria in 721 BCE (2 Kings 17:5–6), Sennacherib's siege of Jerusalem in 701 BCE, and the Babylonian capture of Jerusalem in 587 BCE (2 Kings 25:1–4).

While the people of the city rained down stones and arrows on their attackers (2 Sam. 11:24), the strategy of the besieging army was to spread the defenders as thinly as possible along the walls. During lulls in the fighting, the

SILOAM INSCRIPTION

The two teams working in opposite directions were digging toward one another with picks. The workers began shouting to each other when they realized they were four and one-half feet apart. . . . Thus the water was able to flow through the tunnel. . . . (*OTP*, 194)

uncertainties of their fate and sometimes the dire words of the prophets must have caused the defenders to become disheartened (Jer. 21:1–10). Plus psychological ploys were occasionally employed by the besiegers, including stopping up springs and cutting down fruit trees as a symbol of cutting away the future of the people (2 Kings 3:25a). In 2 Kings 18:19–35, the Rabshakeh, the Assyrian spokesman, called to the people of Jerusalem to surrender and to overthrow King Hezekiah. His pleas were not answered, but Hezekiah's negotiators were clearly worried since they asked him to speak in Aramaic rather than Hebrew so that the people would not understand him (v. 26).

Famine also worked in favor of a besieging army. They could obtain food and other items from the surrounding countryside and from supply columns. However, if the siege lasted too long, the price of goods rose precipitously for the defenders (2 Kings 6:25), and they sometimes resorted to cannibalism (2 Kings 6:26–29). Water supplies were a constant matter of concern. Cisterns were dug around the city (Jer. 38:6) and built into the roofs of many homes to catch rainwater. In times of war the entrance to springs outside the city walls were concealed (2 Chron. 32:4), and a water tunnel was cut from inside the city to the spring. Hezekiah may have constructed the Siloam Tunnel to divert the waters of the Spring of Gihon prior to the Assyrian siege of Jerusalem (2 Kings 20:20). According to the inscription found in the tunnel, two teams of workmen, working from opposite directions, cut through over 1,700 feet of solid rock until "[there was heard] the voice of a man calling to his fellow" (Sir. 48:17–19). In some places this tunnel is over 155 feet below the ground. Water was stored in the tunnel and was channeled into a pool inside the city. Sometimes these tunnels were also a weak point for the city, as David's men demonstrated when they traversed the tunnel into Jerusalem to surprise and capture the city (2 Sam. 5:8).

During the fighting, forces of slingers (Judg. 20:16; 2 Kings 3:25) and archers harried both the defenders and attackers (2 Sam. 11:24). All this activity caused confusion and masked the approach of towers or reserve forces. Eventually, an attack was made at a particular spot in order to breach the wall and enter the city (2 Kings 25:4). The text indicates that breaching the wall was usually followed by a general pillaging and burning as the attacking force took out their built-up frustrations on the defenders (2 Kings 14:12–14 and 25:9–11 are two examples of this). Some prisoners were taken and led away as slaves (Jer. 38:21–23). The Assyrian king Sennacherib describes how his army captured Babylon in 689 BCE, filling the city squares with corpses

> **ANNALS OF SENNACHERIB**
>
> I laid siege to that city; with mines and siege machines, I personally took it—the spoil of his mighty men, small and great. I left no one. I filled the city squares with corpses. . . . I handed out the wealth of that city . . . to my people and they made it their own. (COS 2.305)

(compare Isa. 5:25), smashing its idols, tearing down houses and city walls, and seizing the wealth of the city. In a final demonstration of his power, the Assyrian emperor carried off the images of the city gods that the Babylonians had previously taken from Assyrian cities and restored them to their temples.

Policy of Deportation

The ultimate punishment for peoples who continued to revolt against the Assyrians and Babylonians was deportation. Many cities were destroyed and their inhabitants slain or enslaved during these military campaigns. The Assyrians in particular relished the brutal slaughter and mutilation of their victims. King Ashurnasirpal II (883–859 BCE) records in his annals that his troops suppressed rebellious cities by acts of extreme cruelty. In one text he boasts that they killed three thousand soldiers and disfigured many of the captives, cutting off arms, hands, noses, and ears, and gouging out the eyes of others. The heads of the slain were hung in trees around the fallen city. When such terror tactics were not enough and vassal kingdoms continued to revolt, the answer was to deport the troublemakers to some other portion of the empire where they would have less reason to revolt. Into the empty space created by this deportation, the kings of Assyria transported subjects from elsewhere in their realm.

Despite the fall of Samaria to the forces of Shalmaneser V in 722 BCE, Israel took advantage of that king's death and joined a league of other states led by Hamath (Syria) and Gaza (Philistia). This resulted in another Assyrian campaign in 721 BCE, led by the new Assyrian king Sargon II. When he recaptured Samaria, Sargon deported a large proportion of its people. Second Kings 17:6 states that they were "placed in Halah, and on the Habor, the river of Gozan, and in the cities of the Medes." This effectively ended the monarchy in the northern kingdom and led to the creation of a new mix of people in that area. The Samaritans, who are later identified as living in what had been the northern kingdom of Israel (Ezra 4:17; Neh. 4:2; *Ant.* 9.14.277–91), may have descended from these people imported by Assyria, who intermarried with the Israelites who were not deported.

The other major example of deportation is Nebuchadnezzar's transport of large groups of people from Judah and Jerusalem to Babylonia. This was done twice, in 597 and again in 587 BCE, following revolts by Jehoiakim (2 Kings

ANNALS OF SARGON II

The inhabitants of Samerina, who agreed and plotted with a king hostile to me, not to do service and not to bring tribute to Aššur and who did battle, I fought against them with the power of the great gods, my lords. I counted as spoil 27,290 people.... I settled the rest of them in the midst of Assyria. I repopulated Samarina.... I brought into it people from countries conquered by my hands. (*COS* 2.295–96)

24:1–16) and Zedekiah (2 Kings 25:1–11), respectively. The territory of Judah was not completely depopulated, but its capital city of Jerusalem and other major strongholds were destroyed and their inhabitants taken into exile. Unlike the Assyrian deportation of the people of Israel, however, descendants of Judah's exiles did return to Jerusalem after 538 BCE. Cyrus the Persian king made this possible when he captured Babylon in 540 BCE. He issued a decree (known as the Cyrus Cylinder) that allowed captive peoples to return to their countries and even provided funds for them to rebuild their temples (Isa. 45:1).

Discussion Questions

1. What were the political, economic, and social forces that led to the establishment of the Israelite monarchy?
2. To what extent does the biblical narrative shift its focus from village life to urban life after the establishment of the monarchy?
3. In what ways are laws and forms of justice a reflection of the culture that develops them?
4. How helpful are the records from Egypt and Mesopotamia for the reconstruction of Israel's history?
5. In what ways does the establishment of Jerusalem as Israel's political and religious capital contribute to the creation of a national identity?
6. What political and religious changes resulted from the division of the kingdom?
7. How are city walls, city gates, temples, and palaces a form of architectural propaganda?
8. Who benefits the most from the creation of monumental temples and why?
9. To what extent do the prophets and the law codes emphasize issues of social justice?
10. What role do the prophets play, and do they have a real effect on the policy decisions of those in power?

Exile and Return 4

Historical Introduction

The Babylonian exile of the people of Judah begins in 597 BCE with the capture of the city of Jerusalem by Nebuchadnezzar's army and the subsequent displacement of large portions of the population of Judah. It marked a turning point in Israelite history. The political and social changes that took place markedly transformed them as a people and transformed their belief system into a monotheistic faith that allowed them to survive cultural extinction. Further changes will take place during the period of Persian rule, 540–332 BCE, including the return from exile of some of the people of Judah and the reconstruction of the temple in Jerusalem. Finally, the conquest of the Persian Empire by Alexander the Great of Macedon in 332 BCE brought even more drastic changes to the Israelite community at home and in the regions where the exiles chose to remain.

Throughout this period of their history, the people of Judah (later termed Yehud by the Persians) had only minimal control over their own affairs. The power vacuum left by the elimination of the Davidic monarchy will eventually give the priestly community a new position as the arbitrators for the nation, at least in matters of religion. In order to survive as a people, the people that returned to Judah and those who formed the exilic communities accepted some things that they could not control while clinging to those aspects of their culture that set them apart from other nations. Among these were their story of the exodus from Egypt, the covenant renewed at Mount Sinai, Sabbath observance, and the developing **canon** of law and history. Even more drastic adjustments will take place during the Hellenistic (Greek) and Roman periods, but these will be dealt with more fully in the next chapter.

Written sources for this period of Israel's history are incomplete and sometimes difficult to fit together. For example, Ezra's praise of the "wall in Judea and Jerusalem" suggests that upon his arrival in Jerusalem in the latter part of the fifth century BCE, he found the walls already under reconstruction (Ezra 9:9). Other texts indicate that the walls were rebuilt in an earlier period by Nehemiah, perhaps around 445 BCE (Neh. 2:1–6). While Ezra's return to Jerusalem is traditionally thought to have preceded Nehemiah's, it is possible that Ezra should be dated later to the reign of the Persian king Artaxerxes II

Murashû Family Archive

The Murashû firm was operated by a family of Jewish financiers in Nippur during the Persian period (464–404 BCE). They produced records of their transactions, including lease contracts, on cuneiform tablets. They also employed a labeling system using ink inscriptions in Aramaic on the tablets that provides a synopsis of the tablet's content and the names of business associates. Among the many names listed in these documents are familiar Jewish personal names, including Hanani, Shabbatai, and Jonathan. While some names are Babylonian, it is possible to establish through linguistic analysis some of the families mentioned as being Jewish, especially those that include a form of the divine name Yahweh. It is likely that many Jewish families, at least for public and business purposes, adopted Babylonian or Babylonian-sounding names to blend into their exilic environment. The Murashû documents also indicate that these Jewish exiles had business rights and opportunities similar to their non-Jewish neighbors (see Jer. 29:5–9). Below is a typical example of one of their commercial transactions.

> Yadi'-yaw, the son of Bana-'el; Yahu-natan, Shama'on and Ahi-yaw, the sons of Yadi'-yaw; Satur, the son of Shabbatai; Baniya, the son of Amel-nana; Yigdal-yaw, the son of Nana-iddin; Abda, the son of Apla; Nattun, the son of Shillim; and all their partners in Bit-gira; spoke freely to Ellil-shum-iddin, the son of Murashû, as follows: "Rent to us for three years the Mares Canal, from its inlet up to its outlet, and the tithed field which is on this canal, and the field which is to the left of the Milidu Canal, and the three marshes which are to the right of the Milidu Canal, except the field which drinks (its) waters from the Ellil Canal; and we will give you annually 700 kur of barley according to the standard measure of Ellil-shum-iddin, and, as an annual gift, 2 grazing bulls and 20 grazing rams." (9.45; Coogan 1974, 8)

(404–358 BCE). In addition to the biblical narratives in Ezra and Nehemiah, some information can also be drawn from the prophetic books of Haggai, Zechariah, and Malachi.

The material in the book of Daniel, while perhaps useful in getting impressions of court life in the Babylonian and Persian periods, has some problems chronologically, and it was probably written much later than the events it records. (Note that Dan. 2:4b–7 is written in Aramaic, the principal spoken language of the postexilic era, rather than Hebrew.) The book of Esther has similar chronological problems, although portions of the book seem to date to the late Persian period and offer some insight into life during this time. The **Deuterocanonical**/apocryphal book of 1 Esdras provides a slightly different Greek version of the narrative from 2 Chronicles 35, through Ezra, to Nehemiah 7:73–8:12. In 1 Esdras there are some additions to (see esp. 1 Esd.

3:1–5:6) and omissions from the biblical narrative, which probably reflect the changed concerns of the Maccabean community when the book was compiled in the late second century BCE.

Extrabiblical sources include Babylonian court records, official decrees of the Persian government (including the "Cyrus Cylinder," *OTP*, 207–9), and a variety of legal and business documents from Mesopotamia, including the Murashû family archive found during the excavations at the southern Babylonian city of Nippur.

From approximately this same period, there are letters from the Jewish military colony stationed on the Nile island of Elephantine in southern Egypt that tell of life during the Persian regime of the fifth century BCE. These Aramaic documents include both private and legal communications and official letters from the community and reflect some of the difficulties associated with living in a multicultural environment, including the destruction of their temple to Yahweh on the island. In addition, Josephus, the Jewish historian of the first century CE, records some of the events of the return from exile in the eleventh book of his *Antiquities of the Jews*. Generally, his chronicle is based on tradition as well as written sources available to him and thus must be treated carefully by historians.

Exilic Period

The traumatic effects of the deportations and the end of the monarchy in Judah plus the destruction of Jerusalem and Solomon's temple forced some drastic shifts in the cultural practices of the people who remained in Judah and among those who inhabited the various areas of the Babylonian exile. One of the most fundamental changes that came to Judah in the wake of the Assyrian and Babylonian conquests of that region was an end to their political independence. The northern kingdom of Israel ceased to exist after 720 BCE. A large percentage of the upper and middle class populations was deported and partially replaced by non-Israelites, resulting in a mixed population, some of whom would later be called the Samaritans. They were ruled as an Assyrian province by a succession of foreign masters and had a strictly limited autonomy in deciding local issues. Provincial boundaries apparently remained the same from the Assyrian through the Persian period. Discovery of papyri and **bullae** (seal impressions) in the Wadi ed Daliyeh cave nine miles north of Jericho provides evidence that the position of governor of Samaria appears to have become hereditary in the fifth century BCE, with four generations of rulers coming from the Sanballat family.

Judah remained an Assyrian vassal state for another century. The fall of the northern kingdom led to an influx of northern refugees who escaped south and provided the basis for perpetuating the stories of northern prophets like Elijah, Elisha, and Hosea among the people of Judah. In 701 BCE, Sennacherib ravaged the Judean countryside, capturing Lachish, deporting a portion of the population, and besieging the city of Jerusalem (2 Kings 18:13–16; *OTP*, 191–92). Gradually, however, Assyria's power over the fringes of its empire began to decline. The result was a loosening of controls over Judah, which set the stage for Josiah's Deuteronomic reform movement (640–609 BCE) with its emphasis on religious and political centralization (2 Kings 23). More than ever, Jerusalem and Solomon's temple were identified as the site of Yahweh's presence (Deut. 12:5; 16:2). The royal theology of God's "everlasting covenant" with the Davidic house of kings (see 2 Sam. 7:8–17) seemed for a brief time to once again be vindicated.

Because Hezekiah of Judah did not submit to my yoke, I laid siege to 46 of his fortified cities . . . and countless villages. . . . I conquered them, using earthen ramps and battering rams. . . . I took 200,150 prisoners of war. (Annals of Sennacherib; *OTP*, 191–92)

During the wave of enthusiasm generated by the royal reform movement, Josiah attempted to expand his political control and religious reform to Bethel in the north (2 Kings 23:4, 8, 15, 19). However, this was not to last, and ultimately Josiah's kingdom also succumbed to the superpower struggles for control of Canaan. He was killed at Megiddo in 609 BCE in an aborted attempt to prevent the Egyptian pharaoh Necho II from joining forces with the Assyrians in northern Syria (2 Kings 23:29–30). Subsequently, when the Assyrians were defeated by a coalition led by the Babylonians at the battle of Carchemish in 605 BCE, Judah was reduced once again to the status of a vassal province, first under the control of the Egyptians and then Babylon.

This period ends with successive revolts by the kings Jehoiakim (2 Kings 24:1) and Zedekiah (2 Kings 25:1). In reprisal, Jerusalem is sacked twice, and the temple is completely destroyed in 587 BCE. The Babylonians take a fairly large proportion of the ruling class, including King Jehoiachin, into exile in 597 (2 Kings 24:10–12), and then deport two additional groups in 587 and 582 (Jer. 52:30). The displaced persons were settled throughout the Babylonian Empire, some perhaps set to the task of rebuilding ruined city sites. For example, the name Tel-abib (Ezek. 3:15) means "city mound of the flood," suggesting that the site had been damaged by flood waters. Other groups were established near administrative centers such as Calah, Nineveh, Babylon, and Nippur.

Some refugees who fled during the Babylonian conquest went to Egypt, while others were scattered into the Transjordanian kingdoms (Jer. 40:11–12) and the Judean wilderness (Ezek. 33:24–27). Even with the deaths of many of the people due to war, famine, and disease (Jer. 21:9) and the removal of a portion of the population to Mesopotamia, the land would not have been emptied to the degree that is described in 2 Chronicles 36:20–21. It is possible that the compiler of Chronicles, writing in the late fourth century with access to the account produced by the Deuteronomist and other sources in the detailing of events, wished to minimize the importance or even existence of a Judean remnant left in the land during the exile. This bias is reflected in the later disputes between the returning exiles, Samaritans, and other "peoples of the land" (Ezra 4:4; Neh. 2:10).

Excavations have shown that the towns and villages in the eastern, southern, and western sections of Judah, including Jericho, Lachish, and Beth-Shemesh, have massive destruction levels and periods of abandonment after 587 BCE. However, the territory of Benjamin, north of Jerusalem, was left relatively untouched by the Babylonian armies, probably because of the pro-Babylonian tendencies of its leaders. The people who lived there were able to plant and harvest their fields and continue commerce as before. With the seat of government moved to Mizpah (probably Tell en-Nasbeh), they would have also benefited from the maintenance of order supplied first by Gedaliah's administration and then, after his assassination, by a Babylonian appointee. Babylonian provincial governance following the assassination of Gedaliah (Jer. 41:1–3) was probably exercised from Samaria (Jer. 52:30). It is quite likely that this political arrangement was subsequently adopted by the Persians. Once the exiles began to return to Jerusalem in larger numbers, the province of Yehud (Judea) is established as an administrative province separate from Samaria. Yehud became an autonomous unit reporting directly to the **satrap** (or provincial governor) and the Persian emperor.

One sign that the general makeup of the population of this region remained virtually the same between 587 and 535 BCE is found in the ceramic record and other evidence of the material culture. Surveys demonstrate that 70 to 80 percent of the pottery forms that had previously been used in Judah continued to be used. Those people that remained behind in Judah were ruled by Babylonian-appointed governors and were expected to pay tribute from their harvests (Lam. 5:1–6). For Judah to be able to pay this tribute, however, attempts were made to stabilize the economy by redistributing farmlands to the poor (Jer. 39:10) and rebuilding a few city sites (Gibeah, Gibeon, Mizpah). This did not extend, however, to rebuilding Jerusalem. Other than the temple complex that was restored in 515 BCE, much of

VERSE ACCOUNT OF NABONIDUS

Charges include:

- Made an image of a deity that nobody had ever seen in this country.

- Built a temple as a holy seat for this deity.

- Ordered the New Year's Festival to cease.

- Conquered the Arabia trading center at Tema and remained there while his son ruled in Babylon. (ANET, 312–15)

the rest of the city remained in ruins until the time of Nehemiah in the mid-fifth century.

An indication of the indignation that the people of Judah felt immediately after the fall of Jerusalem for their foreign masters was the assassination of the Babylonian-appointed governor, Gedaliah. Although he was a member of the prominent family of Shaphan, which was previously involved in government affairs (2 Kings 22:3, 12; Jer. 36:10–12), apparently the people were angered because he was not a member of the Davidic royal house. His movement of the political capital from ruined Jerusalem to Mizpah also may have increased their antagonism. As a result, a faction headed by Ishmael son of Nethaniah and other members of the royal family took out their frustrations by killing Gedaliah (2 Kings 25:22–26; Jer.

Figure 4.1. The Babylonian Chronicle includes the military campaign of the Babylonians against Jerusalem in 597 BCE and the capture of its king.

41:1–3). Although most of the rebels apparently escaped to Egypt taking the prophet Jeremiah with them (Jer. 43:5–7), this act became the justification for a third deportation (2 Kings 25:26).

The biblical text passes over the historical events during most of the remainder of the exilic period. Babylon went into a swift decline after the death of Nebuchadnezzar in 562 BCE. His immediate successor, Amel-Marduk (i.e., Evil Merodach of Jer. 52:31; 562–560 BCE) is mentioned in 2 Kings 25:27–30 when he frees King Jehoiachin from house arrest. According to this account, Jehoiachin, as a ruler in exile, sat at court in a place of honor and received a regular daily allowance of food. A fragmentary text from the Babylonian Chronicle (*ANET*, 308) contains a notation that Jehoiachin received a ration of oil from the king's storehouse.

However, this Babylonian king was assassinated after only two years, and his two successors ruled only five years between them. A palace revolt then placed Nabonidus, a son of a priestess of the moon god Sin, on the throne. The polemical "Verse Account of Nabonidus" (*ANET*, 312–15), which dates to the period from 555 to 539 BCE, when the city fell to the Persians, is filled with references to his neglected duties as the chief officiant at national religious festivals. This may have been due to his allegiance to family gods, especially the moon god Sin. Failure to support the chief gods of the pantheon angered the powerful Marduk priesthood in Babylon and contributed to his overthrow and the capture of the city by the Persian king Cyrus.

Nabonidus made the political situation even worse by his long absences from the capital. He spent ten years (553–543 BCE) fighting the Arab tribes for control over the Arabian trade routes and engaged in archaeological projects from his base at Tema in northern Arabia. During this time his son Belshazzar ruled as his co-regent in Babylon. As a result, opposition grew among the priesthood as well as the general population even though Nabonidus did restore the New Year's festival upon his return to the capital. If Cyrus's claims in his victory inscription (Cyrus Cylinder) are to be believed, the priesthood and people of Babylon actually welcomed the Persian king in 539, turning the city and the empire over to his rule with only a minimal amount of fighting.

> **CYRUS CYLINDER**
>
> I returned the images of their gods to their sanctuaries which had been in ruins for a long period of time. . . . I also gathered all of the former inhabitants of these places and returned them to their homes. (*OTP*, 209)

Postexilic Period

Technically the Babylonian exile ended in 539 BCE when Cyrus issued a decree allowing all captive peoples to return to their homelands. For example, textual evidence shows that exiled inhabitants of Neirab, a settlement in Mesopotamia named for its original site in Syria, took advantage of this opportunity to return to their country. However, there does not appear to have been a mass exodus of the Judean people from the various exilic communities in Mesopotamia. Still, the decision on the part of some to return divides the community into returnees and inhabitants of **Diaspora** communities (no longer as forced exiles). Initially (Ezra 2:64–65) only a small group returned to Jerusalem with Sheshbazzar, the new Persian governor of Yehud (Judea). One tradition suggests that he was one of Jehoiachin's sons, if he is the "Shenazzar" mentioned in 1 Chronicles 3:18. However, it is just as possible that he was a non-Judean Persian appointee. He is credited with laying the foundations for the new temple and returning the sacred vessels taken by Nebuchadnezzar when he sacked the temple in 587 BCE (Ezra 5:14–15).

> **CYRUS CYLINDER**
>
> Marduk allowed Cyrus to enter Babylon without a battle . . . and delivered Nabonidus, the king who would not revere Marduk, into the hands of Cyrus. (*OTP*, 208)

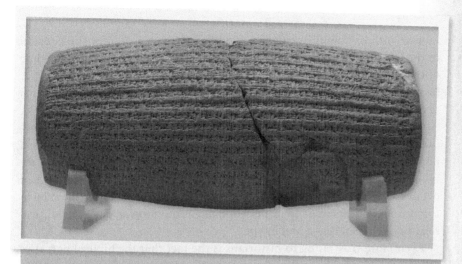

Figure 4.2. The Cyrus Cylinder, one of the Persian
official decrees that are a valuable source for this period

A few years later, a second and larger group of exiles returned to Jerusalem under the leadership of Zerubbabel (Jehoiachin's purported grandson) and the priest Joshua/Jeshua (Hag. 1:1; Ezra 2:2). They also experienced some difficulties in rebuilding the temple and the ruined portions of the city. The Samaritan governor was suspicious of the returnees, feeling that they might be a threat to his authority in the area. The Samaritans were further angered when Zerubbabel rebuffed their request to help with the rebuilding process (Ezra 4:3). Tattenai, Persian governor of the province "Beyond the River," and his associates apparently saw these activities as a disruption to the peace of the region and sent letters to the Persian king trying to delay or end further construction in Jerusalem (Ezra 5:6–17). These tactics worked during the confusing period after the death of Cyrus (530 BCE) and the reign of his son Cambyses (530–522 BCE), but eventually the inhabitants of Yehud received official sanction from the new Persian king Darius and completed construction of the temple in 515 BCE.

Once the temple is completed, Zerubbabel disappears from the text despite the royal (Davidic) titles given him by the prophets Haggai ("signet ring"; 2:23) and Zechariah ("the branch"; 6:12). He may in fact have died or been recalled by the Persian government. However, it is also possible that the biblical writers considered that his mission was fulfilled with the rebuilding of the temple. As a result, his narrative ends, and the next stage in the restoration process, rebuilding the walls of Jerusalem, is then addressed.

One conclusion that might be drawn from this sequence of events is that political realities and a full recounting of details are of less concern to the biblical authors than their emphasis on religious matters. The possible revival of the Davidic monarchy takes second place in the narrative to the rebuilding of the Jerusalem temple and the reestablishment of the priestly community. A further sign of this shift in priorities is found in the book of Malachi, which may be dated to the period immediately after the rebuilding of the temple. Attention is given by the prophet to improper sacrifices (1:6–14) and unlawful mixed marriages among the people (2:10–12). However, neither the real picture of political events nor the exact relationship between the Persian administration and Yehud can be reconstructed from this book. This absence of detail sets aside the strategic importance of Samaria and Yehud to the Persian Empire as elements in its trade network and as monitoring posts of political relations between Persia and Egypt.

Even more frustrating to historians is the fact that the biblical narrative tells us very little about the crucial period in Persian history from 515 to 445 BCE, when the empire was engaged in international conflict with the Greek city-states. All that the biblical text contains is reference to a succession of governors (Neh. 5:15). No chronological scheme can be determined using this evidence, although it is interesting to note that some of these governors do have Jewish names (Elnathan, Yehoezer, Ahzai). There are no details of the administration of this long period of time until the appointment of Nehemiah as Persian governor (*peḥâ*; Neh. 5:14) of Yehud by Artaxerxes I (ca. 445 BCE). The archaeological record is also scanty, yielding only a few ring seals, clay bullae (hardened seal impressions), and stamped jar handles that contain the names of provincial governors and the term Yehud. However, the large number of Yehud stamp impressions found at Ramat Raḥel (located on a hill midway between Bethlehem and Jerusalem) may indicate that that site served as the administrative center for Persian tax collection.

From ancient Greek sources (Herodotus and Thucydides) it is possible to learn that during the sixth and fifth centuries, the Persian government concentrated its efforts on an attempted conquest of Greece. Those hostilities were concluded between the Greek Delian League and Persia in 461 BCE with the Peace of Callias. The energies of the Persian Empire were also required during this period to suppress revolts in Egypt and in Babylonia (486–484 BCE). Darius and Xerxes, his successor, spent huge sums of money raising and equipping armies for these various military enterprises. As a result, little time was left to consider minor political matters in outlying provinces. Jerusalem's problems were virtually ignored until the war with the Greeks was over. Only then did it become possible to obtain the king's attention for local concerns on the fringes of his empire.

Perhaps taking advantage of this reemerging concern for matters within the empire, Nehemiah sought the support of the king to stabilize the growing tensions in Jerusalem personally (Neh. 2:1–8). He had received word of its ruined walls and difficulties in dealing with the neighboring provinces and used his rank within Artaxerxes I's court to obtain permission to rebuild them. Nehemiah is described as the "cup-bearer" of the king (Neh. 1:11). This was a title given to a trusted and generally high-ranking official responsible for tasting the king's food and drink to guard him against assassination by poisoning. It is also probably a ceremonial title, since Nehemiah himself most likely delegated the actual testing to others. It should be noted that Nehemiah's request is not to immigrate back to Jerusalem (Neh. 1:6) but only to fulfill a specified administrative function as a member of the Persian bureaucracy. His role is similar to that of another Persian official, an Egyptian named Udjahorresnet, who served the Persian kings Cambyses and Darius in the late sixth century BCE as their representative in Egypt. Among his administrative projects was the restoration and cleansing of the temple of Neith in Sais and the creation of a network of bureaucrats whose task was to teach the Egyptians "everything useful to them." That work included the codification, interpretation, and enforcement of traditional Egyptian law in order to minimize corruption and support the local cult community.

> I did as his majesty commanded me. I furnished them with all their staffs consisting of the well-born. . . . I placed them in the charge of every learned man [in order to teach them] all their crafts. . . . I supplied them with everything useful to them, with all their equipment that was on record. (Udjahorresnet Inscription; Lichtheim 1980, 36–41)

The fact that Nehemiah, a Jew, was in such a high position demonstrates the degree of social mobility within the Persian Empire. Apparently, those who chose to remain in exile could find opportunities to advance to even the highest levels of government, and there is nothing in the biblical text that condemns those who chose to remain in the Diaspora. The Persian king also showed good sense and follows a pattern used elsewhere by sending a representative to Jerusalem whose cultural and ethnic background was the same as that of the people he was to investigate.

Upon arrival Nehemiah makes a personal inspection of Jerusalem's damaged wall system before meeting with the political representatives of the provinces of Judea and Samaria (Neh. 2:11–16). Despite the threats of Sanballat, the Samaritan governor, Tobiah, the Ammonite official, and Geshem, the Arab tribal leader, he makes the decision to restore the walls. Nehemiah brushes aside their opposition, saying, "You have no share or claim or historic right in Jerusalem" (Neh. 2:20). This may be his assertion of the full independence of the province and of the role of the governor of Yehud as well as an attempt to separate the religiously suspect Samaritans and other "foreigners" from connection with Jerusalem and the temple. While it is unlikely the partially restored walls could serve as a real protective barrier, their symbolic value asserts that Jerusalem is indeed the capital of a province and its inhabitants are a separate and distinct people.

Sanballat and his allies continued to plot against Nehemiah and the construction in Jerusalem (Neh. 4:7–8). While these may have been idle threats, it is likely that any construction project during this period could attract attention and become a target. Excavations at several sites in central Judea have revealed destruction levels dating to the period around 480 BCE. This evidence may reflect the clashes between Persia and Egypt during this period. It could also explain the abandonment of indefensible sites in the absence of garrisons of troops to defend them from lawlessness or attack. Persia's conquests of Egypt in 525 and 343 BCE, and the constant skirmishes in between, left few resources for mediation between the returned exiles (*bene ha-gola*) and the Samaritans. In any case, Nehemiah is said to have completed the project and prevented an attack by the Samaritans or others by arming his workers and posting guards on the walls at night (Neh. 4:10–23).

After fifty-two days of hard labor the city walls were restored, at least to the extent that a case could be made that they encompassed the inner city of Jerusalem (the old City of David), thus securing it against attack (Neh. 6:15). Sanballat and Tobiah do continue on several occasions to try to lure Nehemiah into a trap or to discredit him (Neh. 6:1–13), but he is able to survive them all (see his statement of honest administration in Neh. 5:14–19). Nehemiah then secures his position by appointing Hanani, his brother, and Hananiah, the governor of the citadel, as administrators in Jerusalem (Neh. 7:2). Because of the need to resettle the city and provide enough men to defend it (Neh. 7:4), a census is taken and lots are cast to determine the one in ten who would live within the city proper (Neh. 11:1). It is unlikely, however, that the city was fully reinhabited as it had been during the monarchic period. Its population in this period most likely was not more than three thousand persons.

According to the biblical account, the remainder of Nehemiah's administration, divided over two terms as Persian governor under Artaxerxes I (Neh. 13:6–7), concentrates on civic and religious reforms. A general remission of debts and mortgages is granted to alleviate pressures on the people who had been working on the walls (Neh. 5:1–13). Since Yehud would still be subject to taxation by the Persian government, these economic reforms could have only been temporary and may have been intended to try to end particularly egregious practices at that time. Along those same lines, Levites are appointed to oversee temple worship, and trusted officials are designated to gather taxes and tithes (Neh. 12:44). Nehemiah's emphasis on safeguarding the Sabbath as a day of rest is enforced by closing the gates of the city so that foreign traders could not do business and no commerce of any sort could be transacted during the religious holiday (Neh. 13:15–21). A further sign that Yehud is establishing itself as a separate and unique province within the empire under his leadership is a purge of foreign influence in Jerusalem. For example, Tobiah the Ammonite is expelled from his furnished room within the temple (Neh. 13:7–9), and one of the grandsons of Eliashib the high priest is exiled for marrying the daughter of Sanballat (Neh. 13:28). In addition, Nehemiah forbids all marriages between Jews and non-Jews as a further effort to separate what he conceived of as "proper Jews" (those descended from returned exiles and those like himself from the Diaspora communities) from the foreigners among them (Neh. 13:23–27).

The final stage in postexilic history chronicled in the biblical text is the career of Ezra the scribe. Although he is traditionally thought to have preceded Nehemiah, there are clear indications in the text that Ezra should be dated to the reign of King Artaxerxes II (404–358 BCE). For instance, on his arrival in Jerusalem he found the walls already rebuilt (Ezra 9:9). Whatever the actual time of Ezra, his stated purpose in bringing another recruited group of priests, Levites, temple singers, gatekeepers, and servants back to Jerusalem was to "study the law of the Lord, and to do it, and to teach the statutes and ordinances in Israel" (Ezra 7:10). In order to accomplish this goal, Ezra emphasized the religious and social reforms set forth by Nehemiah and brought about the impetus to formulate the canon of Scripture.

Both Nehemiah's and Ezra's purpose in coming to Jerusalem may have been tied to Persia's desire to control Judea in the face of growing unrest in Egypt after the revolt in 460 BCE by Inaros, a Libyan nobleman, who was able to solicit support from the Athenians. Artaxerxes I had had to marshal a major military expedition, using Gaza and Ashkelon as staging areas for his troops before defeating the Egyptians and reestablishing Persian control over Lower Egypt. Realizing that the region required additional attention, imperial representatives would have been discharged to tamp down unrest, build strong points at strategic locations, and reinforce Persian administration. Thus, by establishing a consistent legal system and a strong internal power structure based around the Persian governor and the priests of Yahweh, Artaxerxes and his successors may have hoped to ensure the loyalty of the Jews. The Persian government had previously ordered the codification of law in Egypt to prevent disputes over land. Ezra's role in codifying Jewish law could have fit into this same administrative practice.

Regardless of the reason for his coming, Ezra is given extraordinary powers to administer the province. The very magnanimous letter or edict (Ezra 7:12–26) issued to him by the Persian king instructed Ezra to (1) take with him any Jews who wished to return to Jerusalem, (2) "make inquiries about Judah and Jerusalem according to the law of your God, which is in your hand," and (3) carry with him a great sum of gold and silver with which to purchase animals for sacrifice and for the general fund of the temple. Additional funds, up to a specified limit (one hundred talents of silver = one-third of the income of the province), could also be obtained from the provincial treasurers for the maintenance of the temple and the cult, and Levites and priests were now to be exempted from the payment of tolls, customs, and other duties (Ezra 7:21–24).

Each of these royal commands was designed to give Ezra a free hand and an ability to be generous to his supporters when he arrived in Jerusalem. The large numbers of returnees (over five thousand, as the list of heads of families in 8:1–14 suggests) made an impressive entourage, and the wealth Ezra brought to the temple demonstrated the backing of the Persian government and the general regard that Persia had for the religions of its subject peoples. Such regard served the Persian government well in that it allowed Persian kings to claim the backing of a subject people's gods (Ezra 1:2–4; 2 Chron. 36:22–23). One last stipulation in the letter gave Ezra the power to "appoint magistrates and judges who may judge all the people in the province Beyond the River who know the laws of your God; and you shall teach those who do not know them" (Ezra 7:25). Those who chose not to obey Ezra and his judges were subject to punishments ranging from the death penalty to imprisonment, exile, or the confiscation of goods (7:26). Admittedly, some of the language in the king's edict may simply be an example of "high rhetoric," which aggrandizes the royal representative and demonstrates the largesse of an absolute monarch. Whether Ezra could actually draw on the stipulation in the letter seems unlikely, but it still would have bolstered his claims to authority upon his arrival in Jerusalem.

Persian adherence to the dualistic Zoroastrian religion allowed them to support the gods of the various peoples within their empire while maintaining their allegiance to the Persian god Ahura-mazda. Only in those instances where countries actively opposed Persian rule were their gods labeled "evil gods" and their worship suppressed (see Annals of Xerxes, *ANET*, 317).

Having received his orders, Ezra gathers the group of exiles who would return with him to Jerusalem. After taking a census of these people, it is discovered that there were no Levites among them (Ezra 8:15). A special effort is then made to recruit priests and temple servants "for the house of our God" (8:16–17). Once these men are gathered, they are given charge of the gold and silver donated by the king to the temple treasury. The narrative quickly passes over their journey by stating that they arrived without incident, having escaped ambushes and enemies along the way (8:31). After taking three days to recover from the trip, Ezra publicly places the contributions in the temple treasury and delivers the king's commission to the provincial officials. Sacrifices of thanksgiving and sin offerings are then made by the newly arrived exiles (8:33–36).

Once these initial steps were taken and after demonstrating the backing he had from the Persian government, Ezra sets about investigating the situation in Judah. He hears testimony from officials that mixed marriages between Jews and non-Jews were still occurring (Ezra 9:1–2). Citing the prohibition of these types of marriages as a corruption of the people (Deut. 7:3), Ezra demands that the priests and Levites take an oath to put away wives and children of improper marriages (Ezra 9:12–10:5). He follows this up with a proclamation demanding that all of the exiles assemble for a meeting within three days to deal with this troubling situation (10:7–8).

This meeting is held in the ninth month (November-December) in an open space in front of the temple. Ezra insists that the entire assemblage separate themselves from the people of the land by divorcing their foreign wives (Ezra 10:9–12). The sheer magnitude of Ezra's request causes them to ask for the appointment of a representative group to deal with this issue. These representatives investigate the situation in each of the cities and judge individual cases in the local districts (10:13–14). After two months of interviews, the names of all of the men with foreign wives were compiled, and each man is required to divorce his wife and disinherit the children of that marriage. In addition, each is forced to make a sin offering of a ram from the flock (10:16–44). The actual list of men who take the oath and put aside their foreign wives (10:18–44) only contains 112 individuals, a small number that may only reflect the more important men in the community.

The continuation of Ezra's actions in reforming the religious and social character of the people is found in the depiction of a major public event in

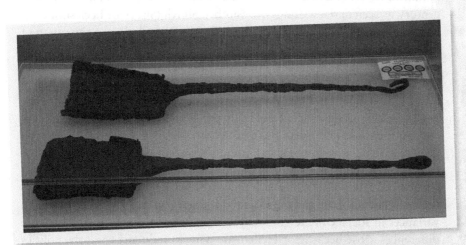

Figure 4.3. Iron altar shovels from Dan, ninth to eighth centuries BCE

Nehemiah 8. Using the Sinai tradition for a "new beginning," Ezra stages a covenant renewal ceremony (Exod. 24:3–8). This involved a public reading of the law and an oath taken by all of the people that they would henceforth adhere to that law (Neh. 8:1–6). In conjunction with the reading, however, interpreters of the law helped the people to give "the sense, so that the people understood the reading" (v. 8). This was probably due to the fact that Aramaic had become the spoken tongue of that day for the majority of the population, but the law read by Ezra was in Hebrew.

Following the initial reading of the law, the Feast of Tabernacles was celebrated for seven days. There was a reading of the law on each day of the feast (Neh. 8:14–18). Another assembly in which a collective act of penitence was made then followed their joyful celebration. Prayers were made confessing past sins while the people fasted and wore the sackcloth of mourning (Neh. 9:1–37). The scroll of the law was then signed by the priests and Levites (9:38–10:27) while the remainder of the people took an oath to obey its injunctions (10:32–39). Included in this oath was a set of special regulations involving sacrifice and the payment of tithes in support of the Levites and the temple (10:32–39; compare Exod. 30:12–16). These stipulations, as much as anything else, point to the enhanced role that the priestly community now played in the shaping of postexilic Judaism.

No further mention of Ezra or his activities is found in the biblical text. Whether he returned to Persia and the service of the king or remained to enforce the covenant is unknown. However, his reform galvanized the priests of the Second Temple into beginning a more systematic compilation of an authoritative version of the law and the history of the people. By the second century, as seen in the writings of Jesus ben Sirach (Sirach or Ecclesiasticus), this had become, by tradition, the basis for the compilation of the canon of Hebrew Scriptures.

Starting with the Assyrian conquest and deportation of the people of Israel (721 BCE) and continuing with the Babylonian destruction of Jerusalem (587 BCE), a great Diaspora, or scattering, of the Jews began. Initially they were spread throughout the Near East, and in later periods under Greek and Roman rule they were scattered throughout Mediterranean and European countries. Influences of the Persian culture during the postexilic period and the dispersion of the Jews resulted in the creation of two basic types of Judaism: Judean and **Diasporic**. While each retained a basic respect for Israelite traditions, the laws (Torah), and the sanctity of Jerusalem, language differences and variances in social climate gradually widened the gulf between them. More differences arose because of Hellenistic (Greek) influences and the politics of the Roman emperors and their administrators. These influences will be discussed in the next chapter.

Life in the Diaspora

With the rule of the monarchy having ended and the temple in ruins, many people chose or were forced to leave Judah. Some were political refugees who fled into temporary exile in the Transjordanian kingdoms. Others founded communities in Egypt (Jer. 43:1–7). Many of these people chose to remain in Egypt after the exile ended. These and other exiles that came in later periods eventually formed the nucleus of Jewish communities in major cities like Alexandria in Egypt. Some of them even served as mercenaries in the Egyptian and Persian armies. Letters and other documents confirming the existence of these communities (dating to the fifth century BCE) have been found at the Jewish military colony of Elephantine, located on an island in the Nile River near modern Aswan. These documents describe business dealings, contracts, wills for the transfer of land, and other aspects of everyday life that suggest the people had settled into their foreign existence. Of course the texts also describe the problems faced by this Jewish community, including the arrest of some individuals, sharp dealings with local merchants and officials, and, as noted below, the actual destruction of their temple to Yahweh.

A similar picture emerges from texts describing life among the exiled Jews in Mesopotamia. Some taken into exile represented the elite of Judah's society (2 Kings 24:14–16), while others were simply common citizens who were gathered up carrying few possessions (Ezek. 12:1–7) and taken as a group into the Babylonian region where they created new settlements. For some, especially those associated with the temple community, beginning a new life was a difficult task (Ps. 137), but the realities of prolonged captivity must have sobered the hope of quick return (Ezek. 24:15–24) and sparked the energies necessary to get on with life.

Despite the loss of their former status and the symbols of past glories, the people were given some hope that the exile would eventually end. For instance, the book of Kings (see also Jer. 52:31–34) ends its chronicle with the positive note that Jehoiachin (and presumably his family) was released from house arrest in his thirty-seventh year of exile. He was also given a place of honor at King Evil Merodach's (the name means "man of Marduk") table and a pension (2 Kings 25:27–30). Confirming this are Babylonian ration lists, uncovered by archaeologists, which state that Jehoiachin and his family received yearly allotments from the king (*ANET*, 308).

As the years went by, many of the exiles became more a part of the land and culture of Mesopotamia. For instance, recently published cuneiform documents dating from the reign of Nebuchadnezzar and into the Persian period contain reference to a city named āl-Yāhūdu. It was most likely located in the Babylon-Borsippa region of central Mesopotamia and contained a majority population of exiled Judeans. These texts, written primarily in āl-Yāhūdu and the nearby city of Našar, contain records of economic transactions, including loan documents and receipts. They provide evidence that by the second generation the exiles spoke the Mesopotamian dialect of Aramaic and used Aramaic script in writing. Some exiles also took Babylonian names (Zerubbabel, Mordecai), while others retained their Yahwistic personal names. Functioning as a normal part of the local economy, these individuals adopted the practice of calculating their transactions using the Babylonian month names. Unfortunately, the āl-Yāhūdu texts do not provide conclusive evidence of the social status of the exiles, nor do they contain references to religious practices.

Evidence of the cultural adaptations made by the exiled Jews is also found in the Murashû documents, discovered at the southern Mesopotamian city of Nippur and dating to the second half of the fifth century BCE. These legal texts provide documentation that life in the exile was not overly restrictive for the Jews. There is no evidence of discrimination against them in matters of business. They paid the same interest rate on loans as everyone else; participated in a wide variety of occupations, including date grower, fisherman, and goatherder; and negotiated contracts for the use of land as tenant farmers. Further signs that these communities did have some power to manage their own affairs can be seen in Ezra 8:17–20, which indicates that the temple servants had retained their former status as cultic officials and were able to resume their role on return to Jerusalem.

The apparent fullness of life evidenced in these texts may be one explanation why many of the Jews chose to remain in Mesopotamia after Cyrus's decree allowed them to return to Judea. The first-century CE Jewish historian Josephus suggests that their reluctance to return was based on their "being unwilling to leave their possessions" (*Ant.* 11.1.8). After over sixty years in exile, it would have been difficult to give up what they and their families had created.

Nevertheless, new groups continued to return to Judea throughout the Persian period. However, in recruiting returnees, leaders sometimes found it difficult to obtain a full range of skills and occupations. For instance, when Ezra was gathering the people to return with him to Jerusalem, he found that no Levites had gathered for the trip (Ezra 8:15). As a result, he sent out messengers to various towns to recruit these traditional temple servants to complete his company.

Life after the Return from Exile

Perhaps the first textual evidence of life after the exile is to be found in the census lists of those who returned to Jerusalem. The list of those who followed Zerubbabel, the Persian governor (Hag. 1:1), and Jeshua/Joshua, the chief priest, is found in Ezra 2:1–70 and Nehemiah 7:6–69. This census contains the names of leaders, clan or family members, and temple officials, men of mixed or suspect family origin, servants, and animals. A short appendix to the list is found in Nehemiah 12:1–26 and provides additional information on the priests and Levites who "came up with Zerubbabel." The total number mentioned in the text exceeds the numbers of the groups listed. However, the total probably includes unnamed or undistinguished members of the group of returnees.

Another census list is found in Ezra 8:1–14. It contains the priestly and secular clans (numbering about 1,500) who returned with Ezra. An emphasis on the priestly members of the company indicates their importance to the writer as well as to the postexilic community. Persian governors like Zerubbabel and Nehemiah came and went, but it was priests and scribes like Jeshua (spelled Joshua in Haggai) and Ezra who really shaped postexilic society and put their stamp on the development of postexilic Judaism.

We can only speculate on exactly who returned to Jerusalem after 538 BCE. Certainly, the priests and other temple officiants had a vested interest in resuming the cult, and the bureaucrats who accompanied each new governor had a specific job to perform. However, the average individual may have come either out of piety inspired by Isaiah's vision of a glorious procession through the wilderness (Isa. 40:3–5) or out of a desire to make a new life in a place where land would be easier to obtain and new businesses had the potential to flourish.

Archaeological surveys have been able to identify settlement patterns during the Persian period that indicate that the majority of the population lived in small farming villages and on individual homesteads (averaging 1.5 to 2 acres). Some of these sites were newly established on previously unused pieces of land, and they were probably settled by members of the Persian military who were given plots of land in exchange for their service. Others are built over the ruins of previously occupied villages or estates that had been destroyed during the Iron IIB destruction by the Babylonians. And in some cases there is evidence of continuous occupation from one period of time to another. There are groupings of these small settlements west of Bethel in the territory of Benjamin, in the central Judean hill country around a string of fortresses, in the Shephelah southeast of Lachish, and in the southern Judean highlands. While the typical Persian highways with way stations for travels do not exist here, the villages and homesteads form a pattern that follows normal routes from Beer-sheba in the south to Bethel in the north.

Political Conditions

Whatever their reason for coming, the former exiles found a ruined capital city and large portions of the countryside neglected and out of production upon their arrival. They also quickly discovered that Judah was only one small province (*medinah*) within the larger administrative unit (satrapy) of "Beyond the River" (Ezra 4:11). As such, they could not expect the Persian government or its powerful provincial officials to pay any more interest to them than they did their neighboring provinces. They could do nothing about the resettlement of some of Judah's former territory by Edomites and Ammonites or the control held by the Arab tribes over Gaza and the routes south to Egypt. The satraps would have watched for any signs of political disloyalty and taxed them heavily. The stream of returned exiles represented a potential political threat to these satrapal officials' influence in the region, and they would have been suspicious of any efforts to increase Jerusalem's importance. On the local level, the rivalry for political authority was especially a concern for the governor of Samaria. Thus, it is not surprising that for over one hundred years Samaritan governors and their allies among the satrapal hierarchy attempted to obstruct the rebuilding of Jerusalem as an administrative center for the fledgling province of Yehud (Ezra 4:4–6; Neh. 4:1–9).

City Planning

Since the biblical narrative concentrates on rebuilding Jerusalem's temple and walls (Ezra 3:8–6:15; Neh. 2–4), the text provides little information about the dwellings of its inhabitants. Babylonian governors probably allowed or even encouraged some small efforts at reconstruction on the ruined site as long as it served no military purpose. There are some indications that Jerusalem may initially have served as a destination for religious pilgrims after its destruction. Jeremiah 41:4–6, which describes pilgrims coming to Gedaliah's court in Mizpah, at least suggests that worship was planned, whether in Mizpah or Jerusalem.

At the end of the exile it seems reasonable, although there is no archaeological evidence to support it, that the returning Jews restored some of the buildings in the ruined portions of Jerusalem to provide themselves with housing and business space (Hag. 1:4). After a delay of over twenty years, the temple was rebuilt in 515 BCE under the direction of Zerubbabel (Ezra 6:15). At this point, however, the city walls had not been rebuilt, and the majority of people lived in nearby villages and farms. The prophets Haggai (1:10–11) and Joel (1:4, 9–12) describe the hardships faced by these farmers, who lost crops to locusts and drought. Still, no substantial number of people would have been attracted to settling in Jerusalem until its ramparts were repaired and it stood once again as a symbol of Israelite identity, if no longer as the capital of an independent nation.

An important step in Persian administrative policy that resulted in rebuilding the pride of the Jewish people occurred during the reign of Artaxerxes I in the mid-fifth century BCE. His decision to move the capital of Yehud from Mizpah to the more centrally located Jerusalem is tied into the mission of the Persian governor Nehemiah. It probably reflects the desire of the Persian Empire to bolster its defenses against further problems with Egypt and to link Jerusalem to the network of highways that supported troop movements and the lucrative trade routes to the coastal plain and south to Beer-sheba and Gaza.

Because of the limited resources and manpower available to him in Yehud, Nehemiah most likely confined his construction to repairing the damaged wall system in order to more effectively enclose the eastern hill of the city, the site of the city of David, and the Temple Mount. Modern excavations in Jerusalem have had mixed results due in part to the difficulty of excavating near the Temple Mount and the mining of materials from earlier periods by later builders. To this point, material remains from the Persian period have only been uncovered on the eastern side of the site.

Utilizing a workforce that could follow the outline of the city's wall system and assigning each group to rebuild a particular portion of the wall, they would have been able to complete a refurbishing of the fortifications and gates of the citadel area within a few weeks (Neh. 3:1–6:15). Again, it seems likely that further reconstruction took place after this, but archaeological evidence is still lacking to provide a clearer picture of what was actually accomplished. It is also unclear how many people actually lived in Jerusalem and the extent to which the city was reinhabited.

Housing for the *nethinim* (temple servants) and priests within the newly walled area was constructed on the ridge of the Ophel, near the sanctuary. Shops for the tradesmen guilds and artisans, such as jewelers, were located to the east and southeast of the walls of the Temple Mount. Other commercial and industrial districts that supplied the city's needs were probably located outside the citadel but possibly within the circumference of the ruined monarchic city walls (Neh. 3:8, 11). Evidence for this is found in Nehemiah's order that the gates of the city be closed on the Sabbath. His action prevented the entrance of Tyrian fishmongers and other merchants on this holy day and reduced their influence over the Jewish inhabitants (Neh. 13:15–21).

Most of what is known about city construction and planning outside of Jerusalem in the Persian period comes from excavations in the more heavily settled areas of the Galilee and the coastal plain. This information is limited, however, since some of the most important cities (Megiddo and Jericho) were abandoned during this period and became badly eroded as a result. Others that did survive destruction after the fall of Babylon, like Samaria and Ashdod,

Figure 4.4. A section of the "broad wall" of Nehemiah 3:8,
which has been uncovered in the Jewish Quarter of the Old City of Jerusalem

had their Persian-era strata badly damaged by construction during the Hellenistic and Roman occupation.

Relatively intact evidence of the Persian occupation has been found at the coastal cities of Tell Megadim and Shiqmona. Persian-period levels at each of these sites show at least some quarters of the city set out in a standard grid pattern. This was an obvious innovation over the narrow, twisting street patterns common to earlier periods. Here large tracts of houses were built on either side of a road that was crossed by avenues running perpendicular to it. Similar homogeneous housing patterns have been found in the Persian cities in Greece (Olynthus) and at Sardis in Anatolia. Such finds suggest that many regional satraps used a standard pattern of construction. This local pattern of strictly-organized city streets was part of a larger system of roadways built and maintained by the Persian Empire. These highways connected the capitals of the empire to the capitals of the regional satraps and facilitated trade and military movements throughout the empire (Herodotus, *Hist.* 5.52–53).

Those sites in Judah that were rebuilt and fortified by the Persians and the returned exiles were not strengthened to the extent that they had been in the past. A case in point is Lachish, which had been abandoned after its destruction by the Babylonians in 587 (see Jer. 34:7). The Persians rebuilt it as an administrative center but did not expend much effort on its defenses. For example, the threshold of its restored gateway was paved with undressed stones. The entranceway was plastered with clay and soft chalk over a gravel base to accommodate the flow of traffic to and from the city. This suggests a role for the city more commercially oriented than defensive in nature.

The excavated portion of Jerusalem's wall dating to the Persian era (summit of eastern hill) also shows signs of being built with less care than in the past. For instance, cracks in the spaces between standing stones were simply filled with rubble. Perhaps the haste with which Nehemiah restored the walls and the lack of expert workmen contributed to this style of construction (Neh. 4:21–23). It may also reflect a lack of materials or funds, as well as a decision on the part of the Persian government to prevent true refortification of these cities at the edge of the empire.

Domestic Architecture

One domestic architectural form that endures in the postexilic period was the "open-court house." Originally introduced to the region by the Assyrians in the eighth century BCE, this structure remained practically unchanged in style throughout the Babylonian and Persian occupations. It consisted of a central open court with rooms on three or four sides. Any lack of uniformity may reflect an uneven construction site or the relative affluence of the owner. Also it may have been based on a pattern found in Mesopotamian cities in which buildings are linked with units sharing a common partition wall.

The governor's residence at Lachish also contains some Persian architectural innovations. Among these are the use of drum-shaped columns on cut stone bases, which supported the porch and lined the stairways—both of which are found in Persian and Greek palaces and temples elsewhere. The building also had a vaulted stone roof and arched doorways. Rooms containing storage areas and residential apartments were arranged around a central courtyard. As is so often the case, the entire structure (except for the columns) was constructed of stone salvaged from the ruins of earlier buildings.

For those Jews who lived in the farming villages in the countryside of Yehud, housing remained much as it had in earlier periods. Depending on the relative wealth of the occupants, the courtyard house of one or two stories continued to be the principal style of construction. Excavated levels within these villages from the Persian period contain some new pottery types (some imported from Greece and Cyprus), a few Persian and Greek coins, and the usual array of domestic items common to every Israelite home.

Marriage Customs

If the book of Esther is any indication, marriage between Jews and non-Jews was not seen as inappropriate to some in the Diasporic communities (Esther 2:1–18; see Jer. 29:6). For the exiles that chose to return to Yehud, one of their chief desires was to settle quickly and profitably into community life in Judea. To achieve this, many of them married into the prominent Moabite, Ammonite, and Samaritan families of Judea and Samaria (Ezra 9:1–2). In order to make this new, more advantageous family alliance possible, it was often necessary to divorce Jewish wives (Mal. 2:13–16). This practice was apparently quite common from the beginning of the return from exile until Ezra's time at the end of the fifth century BCE. It brought with it social acceptability for the exiles, as well as assuring title to land that returning exiles would not otherwise have.

On at least two separate occasions, however, a concerted attempt was made by representatives of the Persian government, both of whom came from the stricter religious elements of the Diasporic community, to outlaw these mixed marriages. Nehemiah's ordering of strict endogamy (marriage within the group) had a variety of social causes. For one thing, these marriage alliances, especially with the noble families of Samaria, threatened the political identity and independence of the province of Yehud. If enough of the ruling class from both areas became allied by marriage, a case could be made to the Persian government to unite them under a single ruler. Thus, when he learned that the grandson of Eliashib the high priest had become the son-in-law of the Samaritan governor Sanballat, he expelled the young man as a defiler of the priesthood (Neh. 13:28–29). Elite marriages were also targeted by Ezra, whose lists of the intermarried contain a disproportionate number of elders and priests (Ezra 10:16–44).

Another reason given for banning these mixed marriages is offered in both Nehemiah's and Ezra's reform decrees. They bemoaned the fact that children of these marriages no longer spoke the language of Judah. Instead they were taught the language of their Moabite, Ammonite, and Ashdodite mothers (Neh. 13:23–24). As a consequence, the social and religious heritage of the returnees could quickly be lost in the Persian imperial melting pot. Recognizing this, Nehemiah cited the precedent set by King Solomon, who had married many foreign wives and thus brought idolatry to Israel (Neh. 13:26–27). This final argument was his justification for demanding that the people cleanse themselves "from everything foreign" (Neh. 13:30).

Ezra took the religious arguments against these marriages a step further by orchestrating a dramatic series of events. In the ninth month (November-December), some eight months after leaving Babylon to return to Yehud, Ezra learned that the "people of Israel, the priests, and the Levites" were intermarrying (Ezra 9:1). In response, he performed acts that were usually associated with mourning: he tore his garments, pulled out his hair, and fasted. Ezra further shamed the Israelites by praying and weeping in public (Ezra 9:3–10:1). The leaders then proposed making a covenant prohibiting such marriages. Ezra appeared to take this under advisement and then decreed that all of the returned exiles assemble within three days to deal with this issue (10:2–8).

The assembly of the people in Jerusalem took place in an open space in front of the temple during a rainstorm, further dampening their spirits but also making it harder for Ezra to achieve a quick solution. As a compromise, a panel of elders was created to investigate mixed marriages throughout the province, including those of priests and other temple officials. Within two months they compiled a list of those men with foreign wives and their children (Ezra 10:17). These men then pledged to divorce their wives, disinherit the children of the marriage, and make a guilt offering (Ezra 10:19). Such a radical solution was deemed necessary in order to purify the people, especially the priesthood. Only then was a covenant renewal ceremony conducted and the nation once again proclaimed to be the people of Yahweh (Neh. 8–10).

Economic Life

As might be expected, the economy of the province of Yehud continued to be based on agricultural production. The initial problems of repairing hillside terraces and reclaiming abandoned fields were dealt with by the first groups of returnees, and then by subsequent groups as more land was put back into production. It was the duty of the governor to aid them in this task, since it was his responsibility to see to it that the province became productive enough to pay its taxes (Neh. 5:15). The smaller population of Yehud after the return from exile meant a larger concentration of land in the hands of a few families and a general labor shortage. Those who attempted to work small farms ran into the double problem of paying taxes and farm debts. When a bad harvest occurred (Hag. 1:6), they were forced to either forfeit on their mortgages or sell themselves and their families into slavery to pay off their debts (Neh. 5:3–5).

Nehemiah attempted to deal with this problem by bringing charges against the nobles and officials who were demanding interest on loans and thus driving their fellow Israelites further into debt (Neh. 5:6–9). He loaned the destitute farmers money and distributed grain to their families. Furthermore, their creditors were required to return all confiscated lands and interest payments (5:10–13). Of course, these were probably only temporary fixes since they only reflect the actions of a single governor, and the economic pressures and abuses were endemic.

Other economic activities practiced in the cities and towns of Judea also benefited from membership in the Persian Empire. Most obvious among these economic benefits was the right of Judea to strike its own coinage, a privilege granted by the emperor to some local mints after 420 BCE. Among these smaller mints allowed to produce small coinage were Gaza, Samaria, Ashkelon, and Jerusalem. The use of coined money helped standardize commercial transactions and also contributed to a return of national pride. In the fourth century, coins bearing "Yehuda" were circulated within the country and the empire. A sign that these coins were a product of the Persian period, however, was the inclusion of the Athenian owl on one side.

The road system, so important to communication and commerce, was maintained and expanded by the Persian government, and caravans were protected by groups of soldiers and horsemen (Ezra 8:22). Sea and land merchants throughout the empire supplied goods for the inland markets of Judea on a regular basis and transported luxury goods and manufactured items. The traders from Tyre on the Phoenician coast brought all sorts of wares to Jerusalem (Neh. 13:16), including dried fish, perfumes, and ointments from Arabia, fine pottery and jewelry from Greece and the Persian provinces on Cyprus and in Anatolia, and metal utensils and weapons from Mesopotamia or Egypt. Such a variety of goods demonstrated to the citizens of the empire the economic advantages attendant with being a part of that international community.

Craftsmen of various types (Neh. 3:31) served the needs of the local population and produced goods that could be exported. A business district outside the restored walls of Jerusalem was apparently established where the stalls of these craftsmen and traders were constructed (Neh. 13:20). Just as King Ahab placed Israelite merchants in the bazaars of Damascus in the ninth century (1 Kings 20:34), this area near Jerusalem most likely included Jewish and foreign merchants or their representatives from throughout the empire. Having access to such a variety of goods would have raised the standard of living in the city and added to the temptations to adopt foreign customs. This concern may be one factor in Nehemiah's ordering the closing of the gates of Jerusalem on the Sabbath to prevent commercial activity on that day sacred to the Jews (Neh. 13:19). It did not prevent cultural mixing during the remainder of the week, but it did set a precedent that a certain religious and social standard was being upheld by a representative of the Persian government.

Burial Customs

Looking at the sixth century, it is difficult to discern any changes in burial customs other than in the grave goods left with the body. Rock-cut tombs with benches along the walls and a straight entrance continue to be used. While few of these tombs contain a significant assemblage of grave goods, there is some evidence in the Persian period of an increased number of metal burial offerings. These include bowls, mirrors, strainers, and bracelets. Imported Egyptian cosmetic jars made of alabaster and black kohl (eye makeup) sticks are also found in these tombs and this would represent the wealth of the deceased. There does not seem to be any evidence of the Zoroastrian practice of secondary burial in which bodies are exposed and the bones later collected for interment.

In the fifth and fourth centuries there are two main types of tombs in Judea and the surrounding lands: the shaft tomb and the pit grave. The shaft tomb, with either a vertical shaft or sloping steps down to the burial chamber, is found primarily along the coastal plain. These tombs were constructed by wealthy Phoenicians for themselves or for the Persian officials of the area. Tombs of this type have been excavated at Gezer, Lachish, Dor, Gesher ha-Ziv, as well as several other sites. Since the tombs are located fairly close to the settlement, that may reflect a family desire to keep in regular contact with the deceased and to make interment easier.

Pit graves, in which the body is buried in a shallow depression, were common among the less well-to-do. Most of these pit graves contain a single body, although a few do contain a family unit. Among the sites so far excavated that contain this grave type are Hazor and Tell el-Hesi. Grave goods in these tombs include Greek pottery, alabaster jars, Phoenician coins, and gold jewelry, but the majority, again, contain few grave goods other than a single juglet or bronze anklets.

Religious Life in the Diaspora, Yehud, and Samaria

For the initial groups of exiles and for the people who remained behind in Judah after the destruction of Jerusalem in 587 BCE, one direct sign of change came in the message of the prophets. They began to place a greater emphasis on apocalyptic themes featuring the restoration of the nation and the "reign of Yahweh." Ezekiel's visions of the "valley of dry bones" (37:1–14) and the "restored temple" (chaps. 40–48) are good examples of this theme. In addition there emerged in the exilic communities a greater reliance on the law and the priests who interpreted it. This development came at the expense of the monarchy, an institution that earlier historical events had rendered defunct.

Figure 4.5. The steps to the major shrine erected on Mount Gerizim, the worship center of the remnant of the northern kingdom of Israel

There is some evidence that initially the exiles found it difficult to worship away from the Jerusalem temple (Ps. 137). Of course, some would have chosen to assimilate to the dominant culture and accepted the worship of the Mesopotamian gods or a mixed religion including both Yahweh and the gods of their captors. Others, who wished to remain strict Yahwists, may have been reassured by Jeremiah's claim that they could worship God in Babylon (Jer. 29:4–7). This group, when they realized that the return would not occur as soon as they had hoped, placed greater emphasis on prayer (Dan. 10:2–3; Esther 4:16) and certain aspects of the law that set them apart from their captors (Esther 3:8). These included laws prescribing ritual purity (including dietary habits), Sabbath observance, and circumcision. The prohibition against marriage outside the group was also enforced by leaders of the postexilic community (Ezra 9; 10:10–15) and may have originated among the stricter customs of the Mesopotamia exiles.

It may be that the **synagogue**, or some similar place of nonsacrificial worship and prayer, also developed during the Babylonian exile as a response to the loss of the temple in Jerusalem. Although no physical evidence has been found for a synagogue prior to the first century CE, at some point it would have been necessary for the synagogue to develop as a center of the community's religious life and assembly. Synagogues are prominently mentioned in the New

Testament period (Matt. 4:23; Mark 1:21; Luke 4:16). It is therefore generally agreed that they gradually came into existence in Mesopotamia, Egypt, and Judea at least two centuries prior to the Common Era.

Another factor that suggests the possibility of some sort of worship place being utilized in the exilic communities is the large numbers of priests and Levites (including Ezekiel) who were taken into exile. They undoubtedly continued to provide for the nonsacrificial religious needs of the people, even though they no longer had a temple to serve as the focal point for their worship activity. A nonsacrificial cult, which emphasized prayer and the study of the law, would have presented little political threat, thus accommodating the Babylonian and Persian governments. That priests and Levites still existed as something more than ceremonial titles when the exile ended and the temple was rebuilt in Jerusalem suggests that they continued to serve at least a diminished role in the religious life of the Diaspora communities.

In what had been the northern kingdom of Israel, ties to the Yahwist faith were mixed with the ideas of the new settlers who were brought in by the Assyrians after 720 BCE. These peoples included representatives from the Transjordanian kingdoms as well as Mesopotamia. Eventually, their religious practices began to center on the early history of Israel and its link to Shechem and Mount Gerizim. Their major shrine was built there (*Ant.* 11.8.321–24) in the time of Alexander the Great (ca. 330 BCE). Evidence from the fourth-century Samaria papyri and inscriptions found on coins and personal seals indicates that the majority of the people mentioned in these texts had Yahwistic names, demonstrating links with Yehud and an allegiance, at least among the elite, to the god of the Israelites. It should also be noted that when the Elephantine community sought permission to rebuild their destroyed Yahweh temple, they wrote to religious leaders in both Jerusalem and Samaria. The intermarriage between the leading families in Samaria and Jerusalem that Nehemiah condemned is further evidence of the social links between the two provinces (Neh. 13:28).

In Egypt, the refugees from Judah established communities that maintained regular contact with Jerusalem. Jeremiah spoke to them condemning their improper rituals, such as burning incense to foreign gods (Jer. 44:2–10). During the fifth century, the Jewish colony on the island of Elephantine in southern Egypt built a temple to serve the cultic needs of its community. While this

---

ELEPHANTINE PAPYRUS (*TAD* A4.7)

In the month of Tammuz, year 14 of Darius the king . . . the priests of Khnub who are in Elephantine the fortress, in agreement with Vidranga who was Chief here said: "The Temple of YHW the God which is in Elephantine the fortress, let them remove from there." Afterwards, that Vidranga, the wicked . . . said: "The Temple . . . let them demolish." Naphaina led the Egyptians with the other troops. They came . . . with their implements, broke into the Temple, demolished it to the ground. (Porten 1996, 140–41)

was a clear violation of the Deuteronomic injunction that required all cultic activity to take place in Jerusalem (Deut. 12 and 2 Kings 23:1–25), the religious authority of the priesthood had been negated by the destruction of the Jerusalem temple. In addition, the religious needs of the Jewish people in the Diaspora clearly outweighed this prohibition in the minds of the exiles (see Isa. 19:19–22 for the prophecy of an altar in Egypt). In any case, according to the Elephantine papyri, this temple was destroyed by the local Egyptians at the behest of the priest of the Egyptian god Khnub (Khum). After consultation with Bagavahya, governor of Judah and Delayah, governor of Samaria, the Elephantine community was advised that they could restore their temple, but they were only licensed to burn incense and present meal offerings. There is no mention of resuming animal sacrifice.

The influence of the polytheistic society in which this Jewish colony was living also may have softened the restrictions against the worship or recognition of other gods. The letters from Elephantine do mention worship of Yahu (i.e., Yahweh) by these Jewish mercenaries. However, they also describe sacrifices being made and oaths being taken in the name of the Canaanite goddess Anat as well as several other gods.

The Postexilic Role of the Priesthood

Priests and Levites were considered guardians of the law and officiants at all formal religious ceremonies (Deut. 17:8–13; 18:1–5). As a result, it is not surprising that when the first groups of exiles returned, the census included four families of priests, numbering 4,289, who joined the caravan (Neh. 7:39–42). What is unusual is that only seventy-four Levites were in the company (Neh. 7:43), fewer even than the number (392) of temple servants and singers who made the journey (Neh. 7:44–60). One explanation for this is that more priests were taken into exile than Levites, and these numbers simply represented the ratio of their descendants. It could also represent a preference on the part of the writer to tally the priests as a more important group.

Another argument, however, is based on the competition between priestly groups that dates back to David's bringing the ark to Jerusalem and his division of cultic responsibilities between Abiathar, a Levitical priest, and Zadok (2 Sam. 20:25). The text provides Zadok with a lineage that is traced back both to the priestly line of Eli (2 Sam. 8:17) and to the priestly line of Aaron (1 Chron. 5:29–34). However, it is also possible that Zadok was actually a Jebusite priest, serving the cultic needs of the people who inhabited Jerusalem (Jebus) before David made it his capital (2 Sam. 20:25; see 5:6–10). By assigning Abiathar cultic duties, David helped to relieve the strain put on Levitical priests caused by the decline and destruction of the sanctuary at Shiloh

Figure 4.6. During the exile, most Jewish leaders tried to protect the people's cultural identity by stressing the covenant made at Mount Sinai, shown here.

(1 Sam. 4; see Jer. 7:12). When Shiloh deteriorated after the battle in which the Philistines captured the ark of the covenant, the Levitical priests spread themselves across Israel, serving at local shrines such as Nob where Abiathar lived until the site was destroyed by a vengeful Saul (1 Sam. 22:11–20). The surviving priests existed solely on what worshipers provided for them and the support that they received from the monarchy (Deut. 14:29).

In the transition between the reigns of David and Solomon, Zadok, who had supported Solomon's claim to the throne (1 Kings 1:8), and his descendants won the chief place in the priestly community, and Abiathar was exiled to Anathoth, two miles north of Jerusalem (1 Kings 2:26, 35). The Levites were thereafter given a secondary role in the temple hierarchy behind the Zadokite priesthood and were restricted to cultic duties at local shrines. They became "temple servants" but had no claim to the chief priesthood or to the sacrificial functions of the Zadokite priests in Jerusalem. Josiah's reform brought many of the Levites back to Jerusalem and increased their status, but not to the extent that they were considered to be among the chief priests (2 Kings 23:9; Ezek. 44:10–16). The only change in this posture came after the fall of Jerusalem, when many of the priests were killed (2 Kings 25:18–21) or taken into exile. With no one else to officiate at sacrifices, Levites were probably pressed into service to maintain local religious activities in Judah, but we have no textual evidence to document these cultic practices.

When it became possible for the exiled Levites to return to Jerusalem, they may have decided that exile was better than a return to an inferior status in Judea (see recruiting difficulties in Ezra 8:15–20). The Zadokite priests could be expected to resume their position as the chief religious officials. Descendants of Levites who had led the people in worship during the exile may have had other ideas on this subject. However, when the priests arrived in Judea, some compromise must have been made with these Levites, since the text makes no mention of a conflict between them. Feelings between the two groups may have softened during the exile when they had to work together in the absence of a temple to preserve the law.

A higher regard for the Levites is also found in the books of Ezra and Nehemiah and in the account of the Chronicler (probably written around 300 BCE). This retrospective history covers the events narrated in the books of Samuel and Kings. However, the 1 Chronicles–Nehemiah account interprets Israel's and Judah's history as a series of divine punishments and blessings to even a greater extent than the Deuteronomist's record. For example, the Chronicler has a very high regard for David, Solomon, the Jerusalem temple, and the priestly community that served there. Furthermore, the Chronicler's respect for the Levites may be a reflection of the enhanced role played by the priestly community during the postexilic period.

The legislation contained in the sixth-century BCE Holiness Code (Lev. 17–26), with its revision of **Priestly** legal statutes and emphasis on the importance of maintaining ritual purity, helped to enhance the role of the priests who served as the judicial and religious leaders of the community. This collection of legal material provides further evidence of an appreciation in the postexilic period for the work of the priestly class. While still subordinate to the "sons of Aaron" (an interchangeable term for Zadokite priests), the Levites took charge of temple administration (2 Chron. 24:6, 11). Although they could not offer sacrifices, they had other worship-associated duties: cleansing of holy objects and chambers, the preparation of the showbread and cereal offerings, and service as a choir of thanksgiving during burnt offerings (1 Chron. 23:25–32).

The expansive role portrayed for the priests and Levites in Chronicles does not fully explain the initial difficulties the clergy had in establishing themselves in Judea. Like the other returnees, they would have had to work to gain acceptance from the authorities already in the land. For instance, Eliashib, the high priest, gave Tobiah the Ammonite a specially furnished chamber within the temple precincts (Neh. 13:4–5). This bestowal of favored status might have something to do with the meaning of Tobiah's name: "Yahu (or Yahweh) is my good." While Tobiah is described as an Ammonite, it could be that he had risen to prominence in Jerusalem and his family had some devotion to Israel's God. In this case, Eliashib's motives also may have been based on a desire to gain political and financial support from this important official for the Jerusalem priesthood. Whatever the case, Nehemiah, representing the strict Yahwism of the exile, refused to allow a foreigner and one who had actively worked against rebuilding Jerusalem's walls (Neh. 2:10), even one with a Yahwistic name, to have access to the temple and summarily expelled Tobiah the Ammonite from his apartment (Neh. 13:7–9). His reasoning for this action is based on citation of the law in Deuteronomy 23:3 and reflects a bureaucrat's use and reverence for the law as a model for behavior among the people he served.

As might be expected, a great deal of the returned exiles' energies was taken up with reopening the land to farming and rebuilding the temple and the city fortifications. The payment of tithes to support the work of the priesthood became secondary to these tasks and was simply not made in some years. Nehemiah found many Levites and singers who had left temple service in order to survive (Neh. 13:10). As might be expected of a conscientious administrator, he ordered that the regular tithes of grain, wine, and oil be brought to the temple storehouses. The responsibility for distribution of these commodities was then given to a committee of trustworthy priests and Levites (Neh. 13:12–13).

Worship in the Second Temple

Two factors direct much of the worship in the exile and Second Temple period. They are the emphasis on proper action, especially with regard to ritual purity, and the enhanced role of the priesthood in directing this proper action by the people. The Holiness Code of Leviticus 17–26 sets the standard for worship, ensuring ritual purity and orderly religious activities. Under this code of law, compiled during the postexilic restoration period, all worship was to be conducted with the proper solemnity by the priests. These individuals, in turn, were required to adhere to a strict code of ritual purity to maintain their holiness and thus qualify them to conduct the rituals when sacrifices were made (see Lev. 21).

Special care was taken to guarantee that sacred acts were performed at the proper time, using the prescribed sacrificial rituals. For example, the offering of the firstfruits, or a portion of the first gleanings from a harvest, was to be brought to the priest, who would ceremoniously raise it to God on the first day after the Sabbath (Lev. 23:9–11). Animal, grain, and drink offerings were then made (v. 13). Most important, eating from the firstfruits was forbidden before this set of sacrificial rituals was complete (v. 14). In this and other offerings, special attention was given to every detail to ensure that the ritual in no way resembled or could be construed as being tied to the idolatrous religions of Canaan or Mesopotamia (Lev. 18:1–5).

> ### Summary of the Holiness Code (Lev. 17–26)
> ### (Based on Patrick 1985, 155)
>
> - The place of sacrifice and subsidiary rules (Lev. 17)
> - The holiness required of Israel (Lev. 18–20)
>   - Prohibited sexual intercourse (Lev. 18)
>   - Commandments demonstrating the holiness of God (Lev. 19)
>   - Penalties for violation of religious and sexual prohibitions (Lev. 20)
> - Qualifications for priests and rules of offerings (Lev. 21–22)
>   - Physical and social qualifications for priests (Lev. 21)
>   - Rules of presentation and list of acceptable offerings (Lev. 22)
> - Calendar of annual festivals and daily ritual (Lev. 23:1–24:9)
>   - Cycle of festivals (Lev. 23)
>   - Oil and bread for the Holy Place (Lev. 24:1–9)
> - Remedial law for blasphemy and homicide (Lev. 24:10–23)
> - Sabbatical and jubilee years (Lev. 25)
> - Rewards and punishments (Lev. 26)

Sacrifice also served as a link with the past for the returned exiles. By reinstituting the major forms of animal and grain sacrifices, which could not be performed during the exile, the covenant was renewed and the temple worship of the monarchic period was restored. The major festivals that comprised the religious calendar (Lev. 23:15–44; Ezra 3:1–6) allowed the priests to display and reinforce their authority while at the same time strengthen the practice of the Yahweh cult. Individual vows and sacrifices, the consecration of houses or land, and the determination of assessments on property also involved the intervention of priests and further established a tie between the activities of the community and the priesthood (Lev. 27).

Within the laws of the sacrificial cult, proper observance of the Sabbath as a day of rest was of particular importance because it was one of those Jewish religious activities that was unparalleled among other people of the ancient Near East. Within the Priestly literature in the Bible, it set the Israelites apart from other peoples (Exod. 31:12–17; 35:1–2), just as it set the day apart in recognition of Yahweh's role as the creator (Gen. 2:1–3). The Sabbath functioned both as a weekly reminder of the covenant with God and as the basis for calculation of all religious festivals (Lev. 23). For high holy days, like the Day of Atonement, the Sabbath functioned as the model for proper behavior in which the people were to set aside all work and deny themselves through fasting while the priest made atonement for the sins of the people (Lev. 16:29–33). In the postexilic period, Sabbath observance became a hallmark of maintaining holiness among the people (Lev. 19:3, 30) and, by extension, the land (Lev. 26:34–43).

The major religious festivals were celebrated on the first day of each lunar month. The most important of these were the Passover and the Feast of Unleavened Bread in the first month (Lev. 23:5–8), the Feast of Trumpets in the seventh month (23:23–25), the Feast of Weeks at the beginning of the wheat harvest (23:15–21), and the Feast of Booths at the end of the harvest (23:34–36, 39–43). They comprised general convocations of the people to mark the yearly harvests and to memorialize the major events in the history of the people. With the restoration of the temple, the feasts also promoted an ingathering of Jews to Jerusalem from throughout the region and in later periods from throughout the Diaspora.

During the exilic and postexilic periods, several new feasts were instituted, and others were made more elaborate. For instance, Purim was a festival created to celebrate Esther's deliverance of the Jews from destruction in the Persian period (Esther 9:18–32). Another feast included in the religious calendar of this period was the Day of Atonement (Lev. 23:26–32). It is not mentioned in any preexilic text or in Nehemiah, but, like other feasts contained in the Priestly legislation of Leviticus, it may have its origin in the settlement period.

There are Near Eastern parallels to the events prescribed for the Day of Atonement. For instance, at the height of the temple's purification rituals during the Babylonian New Year festival, a ram is decapitated, and the body of the ram is thrown into the river while the head is cast into the "open country" (*ANET*, 333). The *mašmašu* priests involved in the ritual slaying are not allowed back into the temple precincts until after the temple has been completely purified. Whatever its origins, the Day of Atonement eventually became one of the most solemn rituals in the Jewish calendar. This yearly ritual (described in Lev. 16, including the earlier ritual of the "scapegoat" in vv. 3–10), observed on the tenth day of the seventh month, was designed to atone for the sins of the people in the previous year. Blood from the sacrifice of a bull and a goat was rubbed and sprinkled on the altar and within the Holy of Holies by the high priest. This double expiation restored the ritual purity of the sanctuary and of the nation for another year.

Within the strict system of laws developed in the period after the exile, attention was also given to protecting the individual and the community from all forms of contamination (see Lev. 10:10; Hag. 2:11–13). Thus, just as the animal or cereal offering had to meet the strict requirements for acceptability as sacrifices, associations (business and social) also had to be scrupulously correct. Every attempt was made to avoid the taint of the unclean and the foreign. In this regard, the genealogical system became extremely important as a means of determining membership in the temple priesthood (Ezra 2:1–63; Neh. 12:1–26) as well as proper or correct lineage for the rest of the people.

According to these statutes, lepers (all those with discolorations or "eruptions of the skin"), their dwellings, and their clothing were to be examined by the priests. They would be expelled from the community if no signs of healing were noted within seven days (Lev. 13–14). Similarly, menstruating women and men defiled by sexual or other body emissions were to be avoided until they had been cleansed through ritual purification and bathing (Lev. 15).

The degree of ritual purity required of individual members of the community was based on their family background and occupation. The high priest was thus required to guard himself against contamination even more strictly than lay members of the community (Lev. 21:10–15). As the only member of the nation who was permitted to enter the Holy of Holies (Lev. 16:2), it was imperative that he stand apart as a symbol of ultimate ritual purity. To a lesser degree, the other priests also practiced rites that kept them ritually pure so that they could perform their sacred duties. For instance, bathing of the body and clothing were required of priests after performing sacrifices (Num. 19:7–8).

Figure 4.7. Second Temple ritual bath near the Temple Mount

To determine who could freely participate in the ritual activities of the temple, the entire nation was divided according to the pattern set in the genealogical list in Nehemiah 7:6–60. The male population of Judah was therefore made up of the following classifications: priests, Levites, laypersons, converted Jews, men of uncertain descent, eunuchs, and non-Jews. To participate fully in the religious activities of the community, a person had to be able to provide proof of pure lineage and have no physical defect (see the alternative viewpoint in Isa. 56:3–8 that stresses Sabbath-keeping as a means of participation, even for eunuchs). Ezra 2:59–63 describes measures taken to deal with those who could not prove their descent.

The increased influence of the priesthood in the life of the returned exiles is reflected in the level of religious activity it generated. In addition to the reestablishment of the sacrificial practices, the use of the Psalms became even more formalized in Jewish worship. Part of creating the canon of sacred texts included organizing the Psalter into a songbook of the Second Temple. Many of the superscriptions attached to individual Psalms are an indication of the musical instruments used as well as instructions for choirmasters on the explicit tune to use when chanting the words (see Pss. 8, 22, 30, 42, 45). Thus the Chronicler's description of the musical guilds established in David's time (1 Chron. 25) probably reflects the situation in the period after the exile.

There was also an integration of new cultic practices and religious festivals into the service of worship. Continuity with past practices was a goal, but some changes were inevitable. Many of the new procedures are reflected in the Holiness Code (Lev. 17–26) that served as an outline for religious practice and ritual following the reconstruction of the temple in 515 BCE. The role of the priests continued to grow in importance during the Hellenistic and Roman periods. However, they increasingly had to cope with the political ambitions of their rulers as well as with competing philosophies and mystery religions introduced by the Greeks after the conquest of the Persian Empire by Alexander of Macedon in 331 BCE.

Discussion Questions

1. What can be said about life in exile in Mesopotamia?
2. What changes took place in Israelite beliefs and forms of worship as a result of the exile?
3. Did the policies of the Persian Empire benefit those who returned to Judea?

4. What challenges did the returned exiles face, and how did that influence their social customs?
5. Were the reforms and policies of Nehemiah and Ezra important to the survival and formalization of religious practices in Yehud?
6. What do the letters from the Jewish colony in Elephantine, Egypt, say about the establishment of Judaism outside of Judea?
7. To what extent did the construction of the Second Temple (515 BCE) influence worship and the development of postexilic Judaism?

Intertestamental and 5
New Testament Periods

Historical Introduction

This final chapter will focus on the transformations in Judea, Samaria, and the Galilee during the Hellenistic (331–67 BCE) and Roman (67 BCE–135 CE) periods. Attention will also be given to the origins of the Christian movement within its social and historical context. The primary factors responsible for these events are the introduction of **Hellenistic culture** after the conquest of the Persian Empire by Alexander the Great of Macedon, who ruled from 336 to 323 BCE, and the emergence of the Roman world empire in the period from about 150 BCE to 150 CE. Jewish resistance to these outside forces briefly allowed for an independent Jewish state to emerge (134–63 BCE). However, the **Hasmonean** (Maccabean) **kingdom** soon succumbed to the petty ambitions of its rulers and was eventually absorbed into the Roman domain.

The Levant (including Syria, Samaria, and Judea) had long been the victim of the ambitions of the Near Eastern superpowers in Egypt and Mesopotamia. Nevertheless, the Jews were able to maintain a basic continuity of belief and worship despite the pluralistic influences of the Assyrian, Babylonian, and Persian cultures. This can be seen in the efforts of the Babylonian king to assimilate the exiled Israelites in Daniel 1, 3, and 6. Although this book was composed in the time of the Maccabean Revolt (167–164 BCE), the model of courage exemplified by its four young heroes speaks of resistance to oppression and cultural assimilation in earlier periods as well.

Where earlier civilizations had failed, Hellenistic philosophies and Greek urban-based administrative policies succeeded in sparking a new set of priorities in Judaism. The sense of world culture implicit in Hellenism contributed to the creation of a new, Hellenized Judaism in Judea and the Galilee region and throughout the Diaspora communities. Thus, when the Romans came, many of the Jews were more open to the idea of dealing with the cosmopolitan attitudes of a world empire. They became a part of its commercial and social life and contributed to its blend of many cultures while maintaining their core identity.

The success of the Christian movement can also be attributed to the generally open social atmosphere first created by the Greeks and then perpetuated by the Romans. Popular philosophies such as Stoicism and Epicureanism were very attractive in the period from the first century BCE to the third century CE. Mystery religions like **Mithraism** were readily adopted by the Roman legionnaires, and their tenets were spread by soldiers, merchants, and traveling philosophers. In an empire where the only requirement was loyalty to Rome and the emperor, new ideas could take root with little hindrance. They were particularly attractive to the disenchanted, the disadvantaged, and the seeker after fresh knowledge. Relatively safe and well-constructed overland and maritime travel routes were a final ingredient in the phenomenal growth of Christianity, as well as many other new religions during this time.

Background to Hellenism: The Persian Period

While they were under the rule of the Persians, the Jews of the Diaspora as well as those who returned to Judea enjoyed nearly two hundred years of relative peace. This stability allowed returned Judean exiles to rebuild some of their destroyed towns and cities and reestablish basic economic stability within their province of Yehud (i.e., Judea). For instance, several hundred Yehud seal impressions on storage jar handles, which are found primarily only within the geographic confines of the province, speak to the organization of the economy and its resources. Within the constraints of a fairly small population, agricultural lands were returned to cultivation; industrial activity resumed after being largely dormant throughout the Babylonian exile in the areas of central and southern Judea.

Some emphasis on urbanization also returned during the Persian period, at least to the extent of a few towns like Jerusalem and some military outposts. With at least a portion of its walls rebuilt and the temple once again functioning as a center of religious activity, Jerusalem could provide a focal point for life and a model of urbanism for the other cities and towns of Judea. Persian authority throughout the empire and its improved roads assured a steady stream of foreign merchants into Judea and the creation of a slightly more cosmopolitan culture there. Contact with and a greater acceptance of the outside world during the Persian period made the eventual transition to Greek/Hellenistic political and cultural domination easier for many Jews.

The second major factor that influenced the development of Jewish culture during the Persian period was the elimination of the civil office of the king of Judah. One direct result of this political reality was the enhancement of the high priest's position in Jerusalem after the temple was rebuilt. In effect he became the titular religious and civic head of the Jewish community, bowing only to the authority of the Persian king and his governor. The high priest's position was confirmed by the Persian government (Neh. 13:30; Hag. 1:1) and was solidified by his control of the sacrificial cult and priestly community in Jerusalem.

According to tradition, the office was held by a member of the Zadokite priestly family, referred in the postexilic texts as the "sons" or "descendants of Aaron" (Lev. 1:7; 2:3; 3:3; Neh. 10:38; 12:47). Their family tie to preexilic temple worship provided legitimacy and a sense of continuity to the position of high priest (Hag. 1:12; Zech. 3:1–9; 6:11). However, because of the civil influence also wielded by this office, it became increasingly secularized. As a result, to serve as high priest or to be able to choose who would hold that post became a political prize.

A third important development during the Persian period was the continued effort to canonize the Hebrew Scriptures, which probably began during the monarchic period. While there is no direct evidence of when this formal process began, there are traditions about the collection of sacred writings, their preservation, and eventual restoration following the exile (2 Macc. 2:13–15; 2 Esdras 18:19–26). Acceptance of an authoritative body of law is presupposed by the Persian king's decree given to Ezra to teach and enforce that law (Ezra 7:25–26). However, the final form of the canon will not be certified for many centuries, and the evidence of the **Qumran** scrolls, which date to the period between approximately 150 BCE and 70 CE, demonstrates that there were variations within the tradition and text that had not been totally reconciled before the destruction of Jerusalem by the Romans in 70 CE.

Still the text-centered character of the postexilic Jewish culture added to the growth in the importance of the priestly community as well as their ability to interpret the law and carry out their cultic duties in the temple. Ultimately, the development of the canon of scriptures also helped to solidify the religious and ethnic identity of the people wherever there was a Jewish community. Its intent was to compile and edit both the oral as well as the written traditions of the people of Israel. After the traumatic experience of exile, the priests wanted to be certain that sacrifice and other cultic acts were performed regularly and correctly in the Jerusalem temple (Lev. 1–7). They hoped to ensure God's continued good will by a strict conformity to the law. Thus the law had to be written down and canonized into an authoritative document, the Torah, which could be consulted to prevent future mistakes or misunderstandings of what was expected. The result is the Holiness Code (Lev. 17–26), with a strict emphasis on ritual purity and recognition of God as the source of law and life. The compilation and editing process also sparked increased study of the text and the development of a group known as scribes or rabbis (teachers). They became authorities on the law and its interpretation and were consulted on these matters by the religious community (see John 1:38; 20:15–16).

A final development that can be ascribed to the Persian period is the political and social separation between the Jews of Judea and the Samaritans. This break has its roots both in the political conflicts between these two Persian provinces and in their individual religious differences. The returning exiles excluded Samaritans, who had not experienced the crucible of the exile, from assisting with rebuilding the Jerusalem temple (Ezra 4:1–3). Later, Nehemiah also stood up to Samaritan pressure against the rebuilding of the city's walls and denied that they had any "claim or historic right in Jerusalem" (Neh. 2:30).

With the Jews denying them participation in the Yahweh cult based in Jerusalem and calling them unfit because they had not experienced the exile, and because some were considered to be of mixed cultural heritage, it is no wonder that the Samaritans rejected Jerusalem as the true site of God's presence. Instead, under the leadership of Sanballat the Horonite, who was appointed governor of the province of Samaria prior to Nehemiah's arrival, they declared Mount Gerizim near Shechem to be their place of worship (see Gen. 12:6–7 and Josh. 24 for events justifying their position). In many ways this decision paralleled Jeroboam's efforts to separate from Jerusalem and establish his own sacred sites at Dan and Bethel (1 Kings 12:25–33). It is possible that through the marriage of his daughter to Jehoiada, the son of the high priest Eliashib (Neh. 13:28), Sanballat was also able to establish a legitimate priesthood to serve the shrine at Mount Gerizim.

Josephus recounts that in the fourth century, the Samaritans attempted to gain Alexander's political good will so that they could construct an alternative temple on Mount Gerizim in about 330 BCE (*Ant.* 11.8.321–24). However, the archaeological evidence is still in dispute, and given the discovery of inscriptions containing priestly names, it is possible that an initial sacred complex was constructed in the fifth century. In any case, it was later destroyed by the Hasmonean king and high priest John Hyrcanus in 128 BCE (*Ant.* 13.9.254–56). Indications that Mount Gerizim, with or without a formal temple, continued to be the focus of Samaritan worship in the first century CE are found in the Samaritan woman's statement to Jesus in John 4:20.

The Rise of Hellenism: Alexander and the Diadochoi

Following a series of campaigns in Greece and Anatolia from 336 to 335 BCE, Alexander of Macedon turned his full attention toward the Persian Empire. The first step was to free the Greek city-states of Asia Minor from Persian control. Then, in order to cripple the Persian navy, Alexander systematically besieged and captured the Persian strongholds along the Mediterranean coast. In 332 BCE, he entered Egypt unopposed, paid due respect to the Egyptian gods, and was crowned pharaoh. Continually pressuring the Persian armies, Alexander

Figure 5.1. Alexander the Great

eventually burned the Persian capital of Persepolis, and in the years from 330 to 323 BCE he completely broke their control over the Near East. His armies campaigned as far east as the Indus delta in western India. The breadth of his conquests set the stage for an entirely new period in that region's history. Alexander believed in the creation of a "world culture" based on Greek philosophy, law, political administration, and the foundation of Greek cities throughout the former Persian Empire. Hellenistic, Greek-like culture was eventually formed from the blend of Greek ideas and the customs and traditions of the areas into which they were introduced.

One sign of Alexander's determination to create such a synthesis of cultures can be seen in his inclusion of Greek scholars and scientists as part of his army's auxiliaries. These scholars assisted with the introduction of Greek as the principal political and economic language in conquered regions. They also studied local languages and customs, popularizing some of them among the Greeks and thereby speeding the process of cultural blending. Another and even more far-reaching contribution to the spread of Greek culture was the founding of many new cities, such as the Egyptian port city of Alexandria. The Greeks had established their society upon the polis, the political community of the city-state. Because Greek immigrants (many of them former members of Alexander's army) within the Near East were familiar with the polis, it became the primary vehicle for the transmission of their culture to the rest of the ancient world.

The speed with which Alexander conquered the Near East reflected his own genius as a military commander as well as the general discontent with Persian rule in several major regions of the empire, especially in Egypt and the Mediterranean coastal area north and east of Egypt. Pacification of these conquered areas was made even easier by retention of the Persian administrative structure. To maintain political stability, Alexander and his successors retained those officials who proved loyal to the new regime. The local economy was then stimulated by the introduction of Greek marketing techniques and fresh operating capital.

Following Alexander's death in 323 BCE, his generals divided up his empire among themselves. These **Diadochoi** (the Greek word means "successors") completed the process of pacifying conquered regions and introducing Hellenistic culture. Within the western reaches of the former Persian Empire, two of these generals eventually held sway over large territories. Ptolemy ruled Egypt, Syria, and Palestine, while Seleucus gained control over the provinces of Asia and Asia Minor. Their successors introduced typical forms of Greek culture: the gymnasium, the theater, the agora, and the social associations for professional, cultural, and religious groups. At the same time, these foreign rulers and their Greek subjects acclimated themselves to the patterns, ideas, and traditions of their new homes, forming a synthesized Hellenistic culture that would dominate the area until the coming of the Islamic conquest in the seventh century CE.

Tobiad Romance (Ant. 12.4.1–11) is Josephus's chronologically suspect account of Joseph, son of Tobias, whose tax-farming activities become the source of wealth and power for his family during the third and second centuries BCE. Related by marriage to the high priests, the Tobiads exercised great political influence.

During the early years of Greek rule, Judea saw no drastic cultural changes. The **Ptolemies**, whose primary purpose was to exploit the economic resources of their domain, chose not to impose Hellenistic ideas on the Jews, but they did introduce new coinage and kept a strong hand on business activities. The absence of the names of governors of Judea on coins may indicate that the Ptolemies did not appoint one, leaving the high priest in a stronger position to influence affairs within Judea. Temple worship continued unhindered, and the office of high priest exercised great authority in matters of religious practice. Hellenization was most popular among the generation following the conquest and among those who had contact with Jews in the Diaspora, such as the large communities in Antioch and Damascus. There were also obvious advantages for merchants and administrators who adopted Greek language and manners and could therefore deal more freely with new economic and political opportunities.

Competition between the Ptolemies and **Seleucids** for control of Syria and Judea heated up during the mid-third century BCE. Continual intrigue occurred as both sides tried to create or maintain support for their rule in this buffer region between their main holdings. When the greedy high priest Onias II took a pro-Seleucid position, refusing to pay tribute to the Ptolemaic government around 245 BCE, the battle for Judea began in earnest. Even members of the high priest's family chose sides; his nephew Joseph, the son of Tobias, remained loyal to the Ptolemies, procured from his uncle the position of envoy to the Egyptian ruler, and ultimately defused the crisis. As a reward, and with the aid of an exorbitant bid, Joseph was named chief tax collector of Syria, Phoenicia, and Judea, a post he held for over two decades. Josephus, in what is known as the *Tobiad Romance* (*Ant.* 12.4.1–11) records that Joseph's economic success caused the Tobiads to become the chief beneficiaries of Hellenization among the Jews.

Eventually, however, the Tobiads' political loyalties shifted after 200 BCE when the Seleucid king Antiochus III won the battle of Panias in northern Galilee over Ptolemy V and gained control over Judea and Jerusalem (*Ant.* 12.3.129–37). This battle changed the political balance, leaving the Ptolemies bottled up in Egypt and requiring a quick transfer of allegiance by the new high priest, Simon II (see Sir. 50:1–21), to Antiochus's camp. Complicating matters, Simon was the leader of the group that advocated strict adherence to Jewish tradition and Mosaic law, and as little Hellenization as possible. To obtain this group's support, Antiochus made a series of concessions to the leaders in Jerusalem. His edict forbade gentiles from entering the precincts of the Jewish temple. He also made grants of financial assistance to the Jerusalem temple and authorized an exemption from taxes for members of the priesthood and the council of elders, the **Sanhedrin** (*Ant.* 12.3.138–46).

These concessions and promises of religious freedom quickly evaporated as Antiochus became embroiled in the international ambitions of the Romans, coming to the aid of the embattled Greeks of Asia Minor. Roman territorial aspirations and military prowess were too much for both the Greeks and Antiochus. He was forced to sign a treaty in 188 BCE ceding to the Romans his territories in Asia Minor and sending twenty hostages to Rome. Among these hostages was his son, the future Antiochus IV. The loss of revenues from these areas forced Antiochus III to increase taxes. In his efforts to seek additional revenues, he plundered the temple of Bel in the Persian city of Susa, but he was killed during this campaign. Thus in 187 BCE, Antiochus III's eldest son, Seleucus IV, succeeded his father. Eventually, Seleucus IV sent his own son, Demetrius, to Rome in exchange for the release of Antiochus IV. When Seleucus was murdered by Heliodorus, his prime minister, Antiochus IV usurped the throne in 175 BCE.

The power struggle among the Seleucids apparently sparked a new wave of political shifts in Judea as various factions attempted to gain control of the position of high priest in Jerusalem. The intrigue begins when Onias III, Simon II's successor as high priest, has an argument with Simon, the "captain of the temple" (possibly its financial officer) over the administration of the city market (2 Macc. 3:4–8). Simon, in turn, goes to Apollonius, governor of Coele-Syria and Phoenicia, and tempts him with stories about the wealth in the Jerusalem treasury. Apollonius then sends his deputy Heliodorus to loot the temple, but Heliodorus, according to the account in 2 Maccabees 3:22–28, is miraculously thwarted by the appearance of supernatural beings. On the political level, Simon continues to slander Onias III, and the high priest then appeals to Seleucus IV for assistance (2 Macc. 4:1–6).

After Seleucus IV's death, Antiochus IV's attention is attracted by a huge bribe offered by Jason, Onias III's brother, in order to secure the high priesthood. Jason, whose non-Jewish name is an indication of his willingness to introduce Greek institutions, such as a gymnasium in Jerusalem, is able to purchase the office, and Antiochus ousts Onias in 175 BCE (*Ant.* 12.5.239; 2 Macc. 4:7–10). Onias apparently flees to Transjordan, where he continues to denounce the leaders in Jerusalem until he is murdered on Menelaus's orders in 172 BCE (2 Macc. 4:33–34).

As high priest, Jason hoped to further his own political position with Antiochus IV by transforming Jerusalem and the rest of Palestine into a Hellenized state. His model for this was the capital of the Seleucid kingdom, Antioch. To be sure, Jason's policy would have been welcome since Antiochus could use Jerusalem as a model of a Hellenized city and promote it as a bulwark against further revolts by the pro-Ptolemy supporters. First Maccabees 1:11–15 details Jason's role in carrying out Antiochus's policy of Hellenization. The text describes a group of "lawless men" as Hellenizers (Jews who supported the importation of Greek culture) who willingly violated the covenant in order to please the Greek king. Opposition to Hellenism became increasingly vocal when Jason built a Greek-style gymnasium in Jerusalem and encouraged the wealthy to enroll their sons in the *ephebeion* to train there to become citizens with a background in Hellenistic culture and sensibilities. One result was the effort by some Jews to "remove the marks of circumcision" in order to participate in the games (1 Macc. 1:14–15). Jason's policies are further criticized when temple priests started to attend sporting events rather than offering prescribed sacrifices (2 Macc. 4:10–15).

When Jason sends Menelaus, the brother of Onias III's old enemy Simon, to Antioch in 172 BCE with that year's tribute money, Menelaus takes the opportunity to put in his own bid for the high priesthood. Since it had now become a precedent to obtain the office of high priest through bribery, he succeeds by offering a payment of three hundred talents of silver more than Jason's promised amount. As a result, Jason is "driven as a fugitive into the land of Ammon," where he may have hoped to obtain support for a return to power (2 Macc. 4:23–26).

Menelaus, as high priest, only made matters worse, embezzling funds and stealing sacred vessels from the temple treasury to pay his debts to Antiochus IV (2 Macc. 4:27–32). When Onias III denounced him for doing this,

> The impact of Onias III's murder (2 Macc. 4:27–34) on the non-Hellenized Jewish community may have been the basis for apocalyptic references to the "anointed one" in Daniel 9:26 and the lamb (i.e., pious Jews) killed by ravens (i.e., Seleucids) in *1 Enoch* 90:8.

Figure 5.2. Antiochus IV
Epiphanes

Menelaus conspired with Antiochus IV's deputy, Andronicus, to have Onias murdered (2 Macc. 4:27–34). On his return from a campaign in Cilicia, Antiochus IV learns of the murder of Onias III and orders the execution of the dangerous Andronicus, eliminating a possible threat to the throne (2 Macc. 4:35–38). Meanwhile, in Jerusalem, Menelaus and his deputy, Lysimachus, have been committing further outrages (2 Macc. 4:39).

When Antiochus IV invades Egypt in 169 BCE and rumors circulate that he has been killed, the struggle between Jason and Menelaus for control of the office of high priest resumes. At one point Jason briefly captures the city of Jerusalem and drives out the Seleucid officials (2 Macc. 5:5–7). On his return from Egypt, Antiochus IV interprets these chaotic conditions as open rebellion, and he sends in troops to pacify the province. His efforts result in a brutal loss of life (2 Macc. 5:1–14, 23–26). Menelaus curries favor with the king by inviting Antiochus to carry off the vessels and treasures from the temple, and the king maintains Menelaus's rule as high priest (1 Macc. 1:20–24; 2 Macc. 5:15–16). However, Antiochus IV also appoints governors to keep a close watch on the territory, and he builds the Akra citadel. These actions are quickly followed by an anti-Jewish campaign designed, according to 2 Maccabees 6–7 (compare 1 Macc. 1:41–42), to make all of the people of the Seleucid realm "one people" and to cause them to renounce their old traditions and religion. Continued Roman pressure on Antiochus's kingdom may have increased his anger; however, the stipulations of his subsequent decree all suggest that his plan was to completely Hellenize the Jews, appointing Philip, a Phrygian, as governor and thus stripping Menelaus of some of his secular powers (2 Macc. 5:22–23). Their shrines and altars were defiled, and swine were sacrificed in the temple (see Dan. 11:31). Other ritual acts, like circumcision, were banned (1 Macc. 1:45–48).

Temporary Independence: The Hasmonean Kingdom

Antiochus's policies culminated in the construction of an altar to the Greek god Zeus Olympios in the Jerusalem temple (Dan. 11:31; 1 Macc. 1:54; Mark 13:14). This "abomination of desolation," combined with his other anti-Jewish measures, sparked a revolt in 167 BCE led by the priest Mattathias of the house of Hasmon. Reflecting the more conservative attitudes of the rural areas of Judea, the revolt began in the village of Modin, northwest of Jerusalem. Mattathias refused to obey the decree to sacrifice to idols and went so far as to kill the first Jew who attempted to obey this command (1 Macc. 2:13–26). His justification for the killing was the precedent set by Aaron's grandson Phinehas, who killed an Israelite for marrying outside the congregation (Num. 25:6–8). In both cases the principle involved obedience to the covenant and the purity of the nation.

With Antiochus treating the country as a royal fief and allotting parcels of land to his supporters (Dan. 11:39), Mattathias found it necessary to lead his five sons into the hill country, where they began to wage a guerrilla war against the Seleucids and their Hellenized supporters. The rebels, who were heavily burdened by Antiochus's imposition of heavy taxes, were joined by the traditionalists called the Hasidim, "holy ones" or "the Assembly of the Pious" (1 Macc. 2:29). These individuals saw the war as both a national struggle and a cultural one. Their adherence to the law, however, led to a massacre when a group of one thousand Jews refused to defend themselves from attack on the Sabbath (1 Macc. 2:33–38). This reluctance was eventually overcome as the idea of holy war made it possible to temporarily set aside legal restraints on combat and self-defense (1 Macc. 2:41).

Faced with a series of military defeats, just before his death Antiochus IV issued a royal letter in hopes of regaining some support in the area by granting the Jews the full right to "their own proper meats and [to] observe their own laws" (2 Macc. 11:27–33). That same year (164 BCE) Judas, Mattathias's oldest son, recaptures most of Jerusalem (1 Macc. 3:1–9) and justifies his title Maccabaeus, "the hammer," by his exploits. This title provides the name for the Maccabean Revolt as well as for the rest of Judas's family. The temple is re-dedicated, and restrictions on the practice of Judaism are removed, an event still celebrated today as the feast of **Hanukkah** (1 Macc. 4:41–58; 2 Macc. 10:1–8).

Final victory, however, was made possible by disputes within the Seleucid royal house. Since the death of Antiochus IV in 164 BCE, rival claimants to the Seleucid throne had attempted to outbid each other for the support of the provincial leaders. One of these claimants was Demetrius I Soter, who had been given as a hostage to the Romans by his father, Seleucus IV, in order to secure the release of his father's brother, Antiochus IV. After Antiochus IV's death, the army commander Lysias seizes Antiochus's young son, Antiochus V, from his foster uncle, Philip, and claims power. Meanwhile, Demetrius escapes from Rome and returns to the Seleucid realm. He proceeds to kill Antiochus V and Lysias and usurp the throne (1 Macc. 7:1–4; 2 Macc. 14:1–2; *Ant.* 12.4.189–13.3.79).

Among Demetrius's efforts to restore his influence in Judea was his appointment of Alcimus the Zadokite as high priest in 162 BCE (1 Macc. 7:9–15), but he only served for three years, and there is a break in the office for the next seven years. It is also during this time that Judas Maccabeus is killed in battle in 161 BCE. He is succeeded as the leader of the **Maccabees** by his youngest brother, Jonathan (1 Macc. 9:11–21, 28–31; *Ant.* 13.1.1). Demetrius's own rule (162–150 BCE) falters when Alexander Balas, claiming to be a son of Antiochus IV, changes his name to Alexander I Epiphanes and establishes a rival kingship in the Seleucid-controlled city Ptolemais. When Demetrius tries to reaffirm his power in Judea by allying himself with the battle-tested Jonathan Maccabaeus, he finds that Alexander has already done so. To underscore the legitimacy of his position as the true Seleucid ruler, Alexander appoints Jonathan a "friend of the king" and high priest in 152 BCE (1 Macc. 10:18–20).

It is interesting to note how Jonathan included his title as high priest in official diplomatic correspondence with the Roman Senate (1 Macc. 12:3) and with the Spartans (1 Macc. 12:6).

The transference of the high priesthood to the Maccabee family provides a turning point for their fortunes as political leaders in Judea, but it also relegated the priesthood to a lesser position and changed the rebel movement from one associated with religious motives to one based on political gain. Even the account in 1 Maccabees spends little time on Jonathan's duties as priest and instead focuses on his military and diplomatic efforts. Mostly what we learn about is Jonathan's ability to remain in the good graces of the Seleucid kings from one dynasty to the next and to have his appointment as ruler and high priest reconfirmed by Demetrius II (1 Macc. 11:30–37). The fact that there was opposition to Jonathan's becoming high priest may be found in the Qumran materials, where it is possible that he is identified with the "Wicked Priest" who "forsook God and betrayed the precepts for the sake of riches" (1QpHab VIII, 8–13).

Eventually, however, Jonathan became a victim of Seleucid intrigues (1 Macc. 13:12–23). He is captured and executed by the Syrian usurper Trypho (Diodotus) in 142 BCE. After Jonathan's death, the people proclaimed his brother Simon to be "their leader and high priest forever, until a faithful prophet should arise" (1 Macc. 14:41; *Ant.* 13.6.213). This appointment was particularly important since Simon, like Jonathan, was not of the Zadokite line and thus was not, according to tradition, entitled to hold the office of high priest. Josephus (*Ant.* 16.6.163) describes John Hyrcanus, the successor of Simon, as the high priest of "God Most High." The implication is that the Maccabees were attempting to justify their position as priests and civil leaders through a comparison with the Old Testament figure of Melchizedek, who was described as a king of Salem and priest of "God Most High" (Gen. 14:18).

Political developments and a shift in the people's expectations of a return of prophetic direction made Simon's appointment possible; the Hasmoneans, as they now called themselves, took full advantage of the situation. Indications are, however, that significant numbers dissented from the Maccabean claims to high priesthood. Documents associated with the **Essene** community (the *Manual of Discipline* and the so-called *Damascus Document* from the Cairo Geniza) indicate that during this period the Essenes' support for the Hasmoneans ceased, and a separatist nature developed in this group instead. The *Testament of Moses* (6:1–4), a document dating to the early first century CE, also contains a statement of discontent with the Hasmonean claims to both civil and religious authority.

Simon and his son, John Hyrcanus, continued to use the unsettled political situation in the Seleucid Empire to their advantage. In 141 BCE, Simon captured the Akra, the Seleucid fortress just to the south of the Temple Mount that had been a bastion of Seleucid control and a "thorn in the side" of the Maccabees (*Ant.* 12.5.252–53; 1 Macc. 13:49–51). It was then totally demolished to prevent its standing higher than the temple and to guarantee that it could never again be used against the people (*Ant.* 13.6.215–17). To add a further dimension of support, Simon, like his older brother Judas (1 Macc. 8:17–32), turned to Rome for support and obtained official recognition of his position from the Roman Senate in 138 BCE (1 Macc. 15:15–21). The Seleucids did attempt to reassert their power at the beginning of Hyrcanus's reign. However, according to Josephus (*Ant.* 7.3.393; 13.8.236–49), when Antiochus VII besieged Jerusalem, Hyrcanus bribed him to leave by giving up hostages and providing a ransom from David's tomb. During his long reign (134–104 BCE), Hyrcanus expanded his area of control, engaging in a campaign of territorial expansion. Moving north, he conquered Samaria and destroyed the Samaritan temple on Mount Gerizim (*Ant.* 13.10.275–81). In the south, he forced the Idumeans, living in the area once known as Edom, to convert to Judaism and to be circumcised (*Ant.* 13.9.257–58).

> Simon's eulogy (1 Macc. 14:4–15) contains utopian language of a time when "old men sat in the streets; they all talked together of good things" (v. 9a); peace was established in the land (v. 11); and "all the people sat under their own vines and fig trees" (v. 12; compare 1 Kings 4:25; Mic. 4:4; and Zech. 3:10).

Despite these accomplishments, Hyrcanus was not popular with all segments of his people. His Hellenized court and lifestyle were offensive to the stricter elements of Jewish society. One group, known as the **Pharisees**, demanded that he renounce the office of high priest and in one instance accused him of uncertain parentage, saying his mother had been a captive of Antiochus IV (*Ant.* 13.10.288–92). This did not prove to be a particularly damaging accusation, however, since Hyrcanus was able to rely on the support of the wealthier landowners and merchants. This group, known as the **Sadducees**, also controlled membership in the priesthood (*Ant.* 13.10.293–96). As Josephus notes, both of these groups eventually emerged as important elements in the political and religious history of the Jewish people (*Ant.* 13.5.171–73).

Hyrcanus's son, Aristobulus I, was the first to bear the title of king of Judea (*Ant.* 13.11.301). He continued his father's expansion policies in the north but died after only one year of rule in 103 BCE. He was succeeded by his brother Alexander Jannaeus. This particularly ambitious and cruel ruler used the support of the Sadducees and a company of mercenary troops to impose his rule on the people. The Pharisees, however, were ardently opposed to his position as high priest, ridiculing him as he officiated at sacrifices (*Ant.* 13.13.372). This precipitated a six-year civil war in which the Pharisees aligned themselves with the Seleucid king Demetrius III in an effort to depose Jannaeus (*Ant.* 13.13.376). Jannaeus managed to gain his revenge after surviving the Seleucid invasion. He systematically exterminated the leading Pharisee families, crucifying eight hundred of them and killing their wives and children during a banquet for his supporters (*Ant.* 13.14.380).

Figure 5.3. "The Treasury," a rock-cut structure at Petra

The potential problems of continuing this internal struggle against his own people took their toll on Jannaeus. On his deathbed he advised his wife and successor, Salome Alexandra (76–67 BCE), to make peace with the Pharisees. Alexandra appointed her older son, Hyrcanus II, a supporter of the Pharisees, as the new high priest, and she herself ruled as queen. However, her more energetic younger son, Aristobulus II, was not satisfied with this arrangement and, with the support of the Sadducees, precipitated a civil war in 67 BCE after Alexandra died.

During this period of political chaos, a new political climate and divisive affairs in Rome began to impact Judean politics. Seizing the opportunity to gain influence in Judean affairs, Antipater of Idumea advised Hyrcanus II to seek refuge with the Nabatean ruler Aretas III in Petra while he sought help in his struggle against Aristobulus II. His initial foray into politics soon paid dividends. The other new influence, and the decisive element in the dispute between the brothers, was an escalating civil war in Rome and the arrival in Jerusalem of the Roman general Pompey. The Roman Senate had established an alliance with the leaders of Judea as far back as the time of Judas Maccabeus (1 Macc. 8:17–32). Eventually, Roman interests in the Near East brought them into conflict with the Armenian king Mithridates. In 66 BCE, Pompey was sent to unseat him and protect the new Roman province of Syria. His success in this mission, based on exploiting the internal conflicts so ripe in the region, made Rome the emerging power in that area.

Thus, when Pompey arrived in Damascus, he was met by representatives of many of the small kingdoms of the Near East, including those representing both Hyrcanus II and Aristobulus II of Judea. Seeing that it was to his advantage, Pompey sided with Hyrcanus. Aristobulus was imprisoned, but his followers fortified the Temple Mount and held out against the assaults of the Roman forces for three months. When their position was finally overrun, a general slaughter, luridly described by Josephus, took place. Aristobulus was spared so that he could be taken as a captive to Rome as part of Pompey's triumphal procession (*Ant.* 14.4.69–79). Jewish reaction to these events may be found in the Pharisaic document *Psalms of Solomon* 2:26–32 (dating to about 40–30 BCE), which apparently refers to Pompey when it triumphantly describes the death in Egypt of the one who placed himself before God. What may be implied here is Pompey's reported desecration of the temple by entering the Holy of Holies (*Ant.* 14.4.72).

As a result of Pompey's intervention, Judea was added to the Roman province of Syria and was administered by Pompey's chief lieutenant, Gabinius. Hyrcanus II retained the title of high priest but not his royal designation or the political autonomy that went with it (*Ant.* 14.5.89–91). The country itself was divided into five districts, each centered on a major population center: Jerusalem, Jericho, Gazara (Gezer), Amathus (east of the Jordan River), and Sepphoris in Galilee (*Ant.* 14.5.91). The Romans also claimed all the cities in the north and in Transjordan, which had been ruled by the Hasmoneans but did not have large Jewish populations. Hyrcanus was reappointed as high priest, but with no claims of civil authority (*Ant.* 14.4.73–76).

For the next twenty years Judea was plagued by popular uprisings led by Aristobulus, who escaped from Rome with either Julius Caesar's or his sons' help in 56 BCE (*Ant.* 14.6.92). Hyrcanus and his Idumean adviser, Antipater, managed to survive these threats to their authority while playing a dangerous game of shifting allegiances with the Roman generals. This was complicated by the bloody civil war that was taking place between these Roman commanders in Italy. In 55 or 54 BCE, Hyrcanus's lack of real power was demonstrated when Rome's proconsul for Syria, Marcus Licinius Crassus, plundered the temple treasury (*Ant.* 14.7.105–9). By campaigning against the Parthians (successors of the Persians), Crassus was hoping to show that his abilities as a general matched those of his fellow triumvirate members, Julius Caesar and Pompey. His theft of sacred items from the temple helped fund this expedition, but all he accomplished in this exploit was a major defeat and his own death.

Crassus's death increased the tensions between Caesar and Pompey that eventually led to the climax of the Roman civil war. Antipater, governor of Idumea under Alexander Jannaeus, and Hyrcanus II supported Caesar. After Pompey's murder in Egypt in 48 BCE, they helped marshal support for Caesar among the Jews in Egypt. As a reward, Hyrcanus was appointed in 47 BCE as ethnarch of Judea, becoming for the first time both a civil as well as a religious leader. In addition, Caesar permitted the rebuilding of the walls of Jerusalem and promised the Jews free exercise of their religion (*Ant.* 14.8.143–44). Antipater received Roman citizenship and was named procurator of Judea by the Roman Senate.

Antipater's and Hyrcanus's good fortunes were once again upset when Caesar was murdered by members of the Roman Senate in 44 BCE. Seizing this as an opportunity for more independence, they supported one of the conspirators, Cassius, and helped him gather an army and funds by extorting new taxes from the people. During this time Antipater's son Herod emerged as a leader. Antipater appointed his eldest son, Phasael, governor of Jerusalem, and he appointed Herod to administer Galilee (*Ant.* 14.8.158). Herod became the head of the family after 42 BCE, when his father was murdered.

The rise of Mark Anthony as the new Roman power in the east and his triumph over Cassius simply meant a change of masters for Herod and his brother Phasael. They were appointed tetrarchs of Judea by Mark Anthony in 41 BCE (*Ant.* 14.13.326). Even with these changes, maneuvering for control of Syria and Judea did not cease. The Parthians now took advantage of Anthony's prolonged stay in Egypt and invaded Syria, installing Antigonus, the son of Aristobulus II, on the throne in Jerusalem. They also captured both Phasael and Hyrcanus II. Phasael committed suicide while in prison, and Hyrcanus II was mutilated (his ears were cut off) so that he could no longer serve as High Priest (according to the proscriptions of Lev. 21:16–23; *Ant.* 14.13.365–69).

Herod escaped by fleeing with his family to the fortress of Masada in the Judean desert. He then went to Rome, where his arguments and bribes convinced the Roman Senate to declare him king of Judea in 40 BCE (*Ant.* 14.14.381–85). It would take three years of fighting and another Roman siege of Jerusalem before Antigonus and his Parthian supporters could be defeated and Herod could begin his reign in 37 BCE. At Herod's request, the Roman general Sosius in Antioch beheaded Antigonus, effectively ending the Hasmonean line and opening the door for Herod's new ruling dynasty (*Ant.* 14.16.487–91).

Last Glimpses of Power: The Herods

Having obtained the rulership of Judea, Herod now plotted to legitimize his position and obtain the support of the people. This would not be easy since he was an Idumean, and his family had converted to Judaism at sword's point. Herod's first step was to tie himself to the Hasmoneans. Like David (1 Sam. 18:22–27; 2 Sam. 3:13–16), he allied himself to the family of the previous ruler, marrying Mariamme, the granddaughter of Aristobulus II. He also appointed her seventeen-year-old brother Aristobulus III as high priest, but when the young man's popularity began to grow, he quickly found it necessary to arrange his drowning in 35 BCE, thus eliminating the last of the Hasmonean line (*Ant.* 15.2.31–56). Herod's paranoia also claimed the life of Hyrcanus, now in his eighties.

Violent acts such as these characterized Herod's entire reign (37–4 BCE). Despite the continued good will of the Roman emperors and the expansion of his kingdom, the rule of terror spread. Eventually it claimed the lives of several of Herod's wives and sons, and many others whom he suspected of plotting against him (Matt. 2:16–18; *Ant.* 15.3.80–87; 15.7.222–39). The executions were so many that, upon signing the death warrant for one of Herod's sons,

Figure 5.4. The interior of the fortress at Herodium

Augustus Caesar remarked that it was better to be Herod's pig than his son (Macrobius, *Satur.* 2.4.11). Despite the tragedy of his personal life, Herod achieved real diplomatic triumphs, obtaining Octavian's (later named Augustus) support for his rule and reacquiring territory around Jericho and in Transjordan that had been lost to Cleopatra and Mark Anthony.

Herod's lasting accomplishments came in his building program. He styled himself as a Hellenistic prince, obligated by his position to rule as benefactor to his people. With this in mind, he constructed Judea's first port (Caesarea Maritima) and restored old cities (Samaria, renamed Sebaste, the Greek equivalent of "Augustus") with all the items considered necessary in a Hellenistic urban center: temples, theaters, and stadia. While he flattered Augustus Caesar with the names of these cities, Herod strengthened his own position by reequipping the strategic hilltop fortress of Masada, thirty-five miles south of Jerusalem in the rugged area west of the Dead Sea, and constructing an elaborate palace-fortress complex at Herodium, seven miles south of Jerusalem on the edge of the Judean desert.

> The Roman standard, also referred to as the *aquila* (eagle), was carried in processions and into battle by Roman legions. It represented the authority of the Senate and later the emperors and contained the abbreviation SPQR, "the Senate and the Roman people." The standard also contained the number and name of particular legions.

The crowning architectural achievement of Herod's career was the rebuilding of the temple in Jerusalem (*Ant.* 15.11.380–425). Its gold inlaid columns and massive construction (using blocks of stone weighing over 450 tons in the supporting platform of the temple complex) were designed to impress the Jews, but it never won their affection. He destroyed any credibility he might have had as a pious Jew by erecting temples to the Roman gods and by staging athletic games in Caesar's honor (*Ant.* 19.7.329; 15.8.268).

On Herod's death, riots erupted throughout Judea that had to be suppressed by the Roman legate of Syria, Varus. According to Herod's will, his kingdom was to be divided among three of his sons, Archelaus, Antipas, and Philip. The Roman Senate ratified the will and named Archelaus ethnarch (not a king) of Judea, Samaria, and Idumea, while his brothers were appointed tetrarchs of Galilee and Perea, respectively. Archelaus ruled ten years, relying on Varus's backing to control the office of high priest and to continue his father's building projects. In 6 CE, a delegation sent by both Jews and Samaritans convinced Augustus to exile Archelaus to Gaul (France), and Judea was annexed to the Roman province of Syria. A procurator was then appointed to serve as local administrator.

From 6 CE until 41 CE six Roman governors, or procurators, ruled Judea. Their administrative offices were in Caesarea Maritima on the coast, but they were required to attend major festivals in Jerusalem when the influx

Figure 5.5. Inscription bearing the name of the
Roman procurator Pontius Pilate, from Caesarea Maritima

of pilgrims created a dangerous situation for the Romans. The first of these procurators was P. Sulpicius Quirinius. He began his administration by ordering a census (*Ant.* 18.1.1–3; Luke 2:1–2), an action that led to armed rebellion throughout the province by people fearing higher taxes and labor service. He and his successors also controlled the appointment of the high priest. Quirinius placed Ananus (Annas in Luke 3:2) in the office, but his successor, Valerius Gratus, deposed Ananus in 15 CE and later appointed and deposed three other high priests.

The best known of the procurators was Pontius Pilate, who succeeded Gratus in 26 CE. Like his predecessors, he gave little attention to the traditions of the people he was ruling (Luke 13:1). Josephus mentions two examples of this lack of respect for the Jews. Early in his reign, Pilate ordered the Roman legionary standards brought into Jerusalem. These standards and an accompanying bust of Caesar (*Ant.* 18.3.55–59) represented the military occupation of the country and were also extremely offensive to the Jews, who forbade the worship of images. Some Jews demonstrated their disgust for what Pilate had done by lying down with their necks bared before the soldiers. They challenged the Romans to kill them since they would rather die than live in a city defiled by the presence of the standards (*J.W.* 2.9.169–74).

Perhaps in the hopes of restoring the people's confidence in his rule, Pilate proposed to build an aqueduct that would transport water to the growing population of Jerusalem. This backfired when he financed the aqueduct with funds (*corban*) from the temple treasury that were supposed to be restricted to religious projects (*J.W.* 2.9.175–77).

While these events were occurring in Judea, Herod Antipas continued to rule in Galilee. He had strengthened his position by marrying the daughter of Aretas IV, the king of the Nabateans. When he later divorced her in order to marry Herodias, the wife of his deceased half-brother Philip (Mark 6:17), that led to conflict with the Nabatean king, which resulted in a war and a defeat for Antipas in 36 CE. John the Baptist was one of the many voices raised against Antipas's illegal marriage (see Lev. 20:21). It was Antipas's fear of John's popularity (*Ant.* 18.5.118) and his desire to silence the voice of dissent that led to John's eventual execution (Mark 6:18–28). Antipas also showed his disdain for his more orthodox Jewish subjects by constructing his new capital city of Tiberias on the site of an ancient cemetery at the southern end of the Sea of Galilee. This act violated the Jewish law against contact with the dead and the burial of the dead within city walls (Num. 19:11; *y. Shebi'it* 9.1; *Ant.* 18.2.36–38).

Herod Antipas's dealing with the case of Jesus (Luke 23:1–25) played into the hands of the Sanhedrin council but also failed to gain him any more respect with the Jews. For instance, his placement of the inscription over the crucified Jesus, "This is the King of the Jews" (Luke 23:38), was an obvious attempt to humiliate them rather than Jesus. He was eventually ousted from his position in 36 CE after massacring a crowd assembled to hear a Samaritan prophet speak (*Ant.* 18.4.88–89).

A change came in the Judean political situation in 39 CE when the mentally unstable Roman emperor Caligula exiled Herod Antipas to Gaul. Caligula had given Herod Philip's lands to Herod Agrippa (a grandson of Herod the Great). When Antipas asked for the title of king, he was exiled, and Herod Agrippa was awarded his lands as well. Emperor Claudius (*Ant.* 19.5.274–75) later gave him control of Judea in 41 CE. Thus Agrippa controlled all the lands that his grandfather had ruled forty-five years earlier.

Herod Agrippa attempted to build support for his rule through strict adherence to the Torah. He also gave several gifts to the temple treasury, including the golden chain he had worn while a prisoner in Rome. Perhaps as another way of currying favor with the Pharisees, Agrippa persecuted the disciples of Jesus. James the brother of John was executed, and Peter was imprisoned (Acts 12:1–3). Shortly after this the king was stricken with a fatal illness. Tradition suggests that this was a result of his being proclaimed a god, but he may have succumbed, like so many others, to poison. He subsequently died while officiating at games held in the emperor's honor at Caesarea in 44 CE (Acts 12:21–23; *Ant.* 19.8.343–50).

Roman Rule and Jewish Protest: The First Jewish Revolt

Following Agrippa's death, the emperor Claudius once again placed Judea under the rule of a Roman procurator. In 50 CE, Agrippa's son, Agrippa II, was given the rule over Galilee, but he was thoroughly loyal to the Romans and became one more source of irritation for dissatisfied Jews. In the remainder of the country, those men appointed as procurators between 44 and 66 CE faced a difficult administrative task. Because they were more concerned with exploiting the resources of the territory rather than meeting the needs of the people, they were continually required to quell small rebellions and put down street riots caused by the people's desire to end Roman rule and presence in Judea. The **Zealot** movement, made up of disgruntled elements among the Jews (*J.W.* 4.3.158–61), was revived by the procurators' incompetency and eventually led to open revolt in the First Jewish War (66–74 CE). Periodic famines (*Ant.* 20.5.101), the provocative and insensitive actions of some Roman soldiers, and the teachings of a series of messiah figures who offered the people hope of independence and restored greatness all worsened the very volatile situation (*Ant.* 20.5.97–112).

One of the principal measures used by the procurators was to encourage the Jews to fight among themselves. The priestly nobility was in conflict with the Levites, and there were disputes between the supporters of the Herodians, the Hellenists, and the pious Jews. Divided, the factionalized Jewish community was unable to provide a common front against the Romans. In one case described by Josephus, Felix (procurator 52–60 CE) arranged the murder of the high priest Jonathan, hiring assassins from among the Zealots (*sicarii*, so named for the short, curved sword they carried) to mingle with the crowd during worship and kill him (*Ant.* 20.8.162–65). This provocative act was followed by an even more dangerous situation: an Egyptian prophet called for rebellion and promised to arrange the miraculous destruction of the walls of Jerusalem (*Ant.* 20.8.169–72; Acts 21:38).

These insurrections brought a swift and bloody reprisal on the Jews. They also painted every other noninstitutional speaker with the brush of sedition, as the apostle Paul discovered (Acts 21:37–40). He was subsequently brought before Felix by the Jewish high priest Ananias, but Felix suspended the trial (Acts 24:1–23). Paul was not sent to Rome for his hearing before Caesar until after Felix was succeeded by Festus in 60 CE (Acts 25:1–12). The narrator of Acts 25:3, 9 suggests that Festus conspired to have Paul assassinated on the way to Jerusalem as a part of the political maneuvering of a procurator who "wished to do the Jews a favor."

Festus died while in office in 62 CE. His death and the delayed arrival of his replacement, Albinus, contributed to inflaming an already anarchic period in which the high priest Ananus (probably an alternate spelling of Ananias) executed several of his political and religious enemies. Among his victims was James, the brother of Jesus and the head of the Christian community in Jerusalem (*Ant.* 20.9.197–200). Matters did not improve substantially when Albinus arrived. In exchange for bribes, he allowed the tithes of food from the threshing floor that were earmarked for the priests to be stolen. Albinus was also forced to submit to extortion by the *sicarii*, who kidnapped his servants and then demanded the release of their imprisoned fellows in exchange (*Ant.* 20.9.204–10).

Gessius Florus succeeded Albinus in 64 CE. He acquired this position as a result of his wife Cleopatra's friendship with Nero's wife (*Ant.* 20.11.252). Desiring to make the most financial gain he could from the procuratorship, Florus allowed the plundering of whole villages and took bribes from his political favorites (*J.W.* 2.14.278–79). Feeding upon the political climate of discontent that Florus had created, religious riots broke out in Caesarea over the obstruction of the entrance of the local synagogue due to the construction of workshops on an adjoining piece of land (*J.W.* 2.14.284–92). When Florus plundered the temple treasury, it became clear that he had no intention of providing either justice or fair treatment. With no indication from the emperor Nero that a replacement would be appointed, revolt became inevitable (*J.W.* 2.14.293).

The First Jewish War began in 66 CE with two acts of defiance by those hoping to oust the Romans from Judea. Eleazar, the son of Ananias the high priest, called on the sacrificial priests to refuse gifts or offerings from foreigners. This effectively ended the practice of sacrificing in honor of the emperor (*J.W.* 2.17.409). Many of the chief priests and Pharisees argued against this action (*J.W.* 2.17.410–16), fearing Roman reprisals toward the temple and the people. The inflammatory actions of both Florus and Eleazar's radical followers helped initiate the final confrontation with Rome.

The other act that precipitated the war was the capture of the Masada fortress by the rebel leader Menahem ben Hezekiah (*J.W.* 2.17.408). The Roman garrison was massacred and arms were distributed to the people with a call for a general insurrection (*J.W.* 2.17.433–34). What occurred, however, was not a united effort to throw off Roman rule but rather a confused period in which debtors rushed to burn contracts with the hope of breaking the hold of the elite over large tracts of land (*J.W.* 2.17.426–27). In the midst of the chaos, various Jewish factions claimed leadership. There were also some massacres of the Jewish populations of predominantly gentile cities like Caesarea, Scythopolis (Beth-shan), and the Decapolis cities in Transjordan (*J.W.* 2.18.457–80).

After the Roman forces under Cestius experienced some initial reverses, Nero appointed Vespasian and his son Titus with three legions and auxiliaries to

Figure 5.6. Aerial view of the ancient fortress of Masada, where 960 Jews reportedly committed suicide rather than fall into the hands of their Roman enemies. The stronghold is constructed atop a precipitous natural outcrop.

quell the Jewish revolt. From the start, some of the Jewish urban centers, including Sepphoris (*J.W.* 3.2.29–34), declared themselves loyal to Rome rather than join the revolt. The more systematic efforts of Vespasian and Titus led to the surrender of several towns (Tiberias), although some like Jotapata were besieged, and most of their defenders were killed (*J.W.* 3.6.127–339). Josephus himself was one of the Jewish commanders at Jotapata. He escaped the final fall of the city but was subsequently captured and became an advisor and seer for the Roman generals (*J.W.* 3.8.340–54).

Gradually all of the Judean countryside and the rebel fortresses (Gamala and Gischala) fell to the Romans. According to Talmudic tradition, one group of Jews, led by Rabbi Johanan ben Zakkai, escaped from the siege of Jerusalem and made a separate peace with the Romans in 68 CE, moving to the coastal town of Jamnia (*b. Git.* 56a–b). There they are said to have established a scholarly and commercial community that served as a center for the discussion of Jewish practices and law until the Bar Kochba Revolt (132–135 CE) caused them to scatter into the Galilee region. Other Jewish factions, like the Essenes of the desert settlement at Qumran, were scattered, and their villages were destroyed. The Qumran community did manage to hide their sacred books in mountain caves near their settlement. These **Dead Sea Scrolls** were discovered in 1947 and serve as one of the most important modern tools for studying the biblical text.

Jerusalem, overcrowded with refugees from all over Judea and divided into warring factions, finally came under siege in 70 CE. Vespasian had returned to Rome to become emperor after Nero's death, which left Titus to complete the mopping up of the insurrection. His efforts were facilitated by the fighting between the principal Jewish leaders John of Gischala, Simon bar Giora, and Eleazar (*J.W.* 5.6.248–74; 5.13.527–40). Five months of fighting and starvation gradually wore down the defenders. The end of the fighting finally came in early September 70 CE with the capture of the upper city (*J.W.* 6.10.435). Herod's temple as well as large portions of the city and its defenses were torn down at Titus's command, and a great slaughter of the population followed the siege. An encampment was constructed for the occupying Tenth Roman legion, but the city itself ceased to be a major Jewish population center (*J.W.* 7.1.1–12). All that remained of the revolt were some hilltop fortresses, and the last of these, Masada, fell in 74 CE after the 960 defenders, led by Eleazar ben Ya'ir, committed mass suicide rather than be captured by the Romans under Flavius Silva (*J.W.* 7.8.320–406). The official triumphal procession marking the fall of Jerusalem is commemorated on the Arch of Titus in Rome. It depicts the captured leaders as well as the sacred objects taken from the temple, the table of the bread of the Presence (Matt. 12:4) and the seven-branched menorah.

A Final Chapter: Bar Kochba and Diasporic Judaism

The fall of Jerusalem and the destruction of the temple ended the power of the Sanhedrin and the office of high priest (*Ant.* 20.10.224–51). Never again would the temple community dominate Jewish religion and thought. The total population of the country was reduced by as much as one-third through death and enslavement. Of course, the economy was thrown into chaos, with large tracts of land transformed into royal estates to be leased out for the profit of the emperor and Jewish farmers reduced to tenants. Jerusalem initially became the headquarters of the Tenth Legion, and the political status of the country was changed from a Roman province of the third category (ruled by a procurator) to the independent Roman province of Judea, administered by a governor of praetorian rank, who resided in Caesarea Maritima.

Separate centers of learning and worship, such as that established at Jamnia, represented post-70 CE Judaism: a Torah-centered, nonsacrificial religion led by the rabbis (teachers) and devoted to study of the law and the development of community purity and dietary standards. While the tradition that the Jamnian rabbis were responsible for developing the canon of Hebrew Scriptures is an exaggeration, it is likely that they discussed the canonicity of biblical books. The Roman emperors attempted to encourage this more peaceful form of Judaism while doing everything they could to destroy nationalism and messiah figures. An indication of their efforts is found in the writings of the early church historian Eusebius (*Eccl. Hist.* 3.12.19–20), who describes attempts by Vespasian and his son Domitian to hunt down members of the house of David.

A further step in this policy of preventing nationalism from recurring among the Jews was the rebuilding of Jerusalem by the emperor Hadrian in 130 CE. According to the historian Dio Cassius (*Vita Hadr.* 14.2), he constructed a Roman-style city and renamed it Aelia Capitolina. Other construction projects were also ordered at Caesarea and Sepphoris (later renamed Diocaesarea). Instead of quieting the Jews, however, this attempt to extinguish the traditional religious and political heritage of Jerusalem sparked the Second Jewish Revolt in 132 CE. Sources for this revolt and its primary causes are fragmentary, but they all seem to indicate that Jerusalem and rabbinic traditions, including circumcision, were still rallying points for rebellion.

The leader of the revolt was a messianic figure named Simon Bar Kochba (or Bar Koziba), who appears in rabbinic sources as Bar Kochba, "son of the star" (cf. Num. 24:17–19; *y. Ta'an.* 4.8.68d–69d). He drew support from those, like the famous Rabbi Akiba, who believed that Yahweh would use this man to rid their land of the hated Romans. For a brief time the rebels were successful. They reoccupied Jerusalem, set up a bureaucracy to govern the affairs of state, and reestablished the religious calendar of festivals. Coins were minted

Figure 5.7. Coins from the Bar Kochba period

during this period by the revolutionary government, bearing inscriptions such as "Year One of the Redemption of Israel" and "Year Two for the Freedom of Israel." They also refer to Bar Kochba as *nasi*, "prince," a title used in Ezekiel 37:24–25 to refer to an eschatological messiah/king figure of the line of David.

Such high hopes were dashed, although Rome did have to transport distant legions to the rebellious province to put down yet another Jewish war. Coins found in excavations dated to this period come from as far away as Britain and Germany, where the legionnaires were paid before they were shipped to the Near East. The Roman general Sextus Julius Severus was summoned by the emperor Hadrian from his station in Britain to recapture Jerusalem in 134 CE. He drove the rebels into the mountainous areas of the Judean wilderness, where some evidence of these fugitives has been found in the caves at Wadi ed-Daliyeh and Nachal Chever, south of En Gedi. Guerrilla warfare continued for another year until the fall of the last rebel stronghold of Bethar (about six miles southwest of Jerusalem) in 135.

Rabbinic tradition contends that Jerusalem fell on the same day, the ninth of Ab, that both the first and second temples were destroyed. True or not, this became the traditional fast day for ritually mourning these events. The surviving Jews, many of whom were sold as slaves, were expelled

Qumran texts also provide a mention of a messianic figure called the "Star from Jacob" (*Testament of Judah* 24), styled as the "scepter of my kingdom" who, when he comes, will "smite all the children of Seth" (*Damascus Rule* VII, 18–21).

from the restored Aelia Capitolina and from Judea in general (Eusebius, *Eccl. Hist.* 4.6.3). The expulsions also applied to Jewish Christians, thus leaving the gentile population to lead the church in that area. Hadrian continued his rebuilding of Aelia Capitolina and the other cities of the province, now renamed Syria Palestina ("land of the Philistines"). His plans included the construction of a temple to his personal god, Jupiter, over the site of Solomon's temple as well as on the site of the Samaritan shrine on Mount Gerizim.

With the death or exile of a large portion of the Jews from what is now termed Syria Palestina comes a shift in the history to **rabbinic Judaism**. Jews were scattered throughout the Roman Empire, joining earlier groups who had previously settled throughout the Mediterranean. Their synagogues became focal points for worship, study, and interpretation of the developing Hebrew canon of Scriptures. Jewish commentaries on Scripture were developed in succeeding centuries by scholars who placed more emphasis on the importance of oral law as an explanatory tool, producing the second-century CE **Mishnah**. Interpretative works during this period conclude in the sixth century with the closing of the Babylonian **Talmud**. Communities in Antioch, Corinth, and throughout Asia Minor proved to be both fertile ground for converts and a source of contention for Paul and the other missionaries of the Christian faith (Acts 14:1–2; 17:1–8; 18:1–4).

> The second-century BCE Jewish sage, Jesus ben Sira, warns his community in Jerusalem against forsaking "the law of the Most High God" (Sir. 41:8). However, he is familiar with Greek philosophy and makes use of its ideas while making his points about the superiority of Judaism. In this way he can argue that the lure of Hellenism is not worth abandoning the ancient faith in Yahweh.

Social Life

Alexander's conquests brought a new and vibrant culture to the urban centers of the Near East. Gradually it mixed with local customs and traditions, creating a Hellenistic culture. In general, this synthesis was beneficial for both. For the Jews, however, the introduction of Hellenism became a major source of controversy, dividing the people between the Hellenizers and the traditionalists. The resulting cultural conflict spilled over into economic, political, and religious areas. Explored below are those developments in everyday life that changed or became more focused as a result of the introduction of Hellenistic culture.

Cities and City Planning

At the center of Greek culture was the *polis*, or urban center. When Alexander's armies conquered the Near East, they established many new cities and rebuilt others. In part, this was a way of consolidating their control over the conquered areas, but it also fulfilled the expectations of Greek immigrants. Urban centers with gymnasia, theaters, and the *agora* (marketplace) were the basis of life wherever Greeks settled. A further sense of order was created in Hellenistic cities by the imposition, where possible, of the grid pattern of streets and buildings. The agora then served as the heart of the business district of the city with a variety of buildings and shops located on all four sides of a public square. Sometimes another agora was constructed within a quieter district of the city where temples were the focal point. This arrangement was not always possible in the older cities like Jerusalem, but where destruction or mass rebuilding had taken place (as in Herod's Sebaste/Samaria), the new pattern was employed by city planners. Smaller towns, like Cana, Gamla, or Chorazin, do not contain marketplaces or an agora during the first century CE.

In new cities, such as Herod the Great's administrative center and port, Caesarea Maritima (built between 22 and 10 BCE), the full range of Hellenistic construction and civic planning took place. The port, a vital strategic and economic link for relatively poor Judea, had a breakwater, docks, and quarters for sailors on leave. To satisfy his Hellenistic tastes and to please his Roman

Figure 5.8. Remains of private houses
at the site of the biblical town of Capernaum

masters, Herod built a temple to the deified Caesar in the unwalled city as well as a theater and amphitheater (*Ant.* 15.8.268). Some of the sanitation needs of the people were handled by an underground sewage system, and transportation was facilitated by an arrangement of parallel streets (*Ant.* 15.9.331–41).

Other than the palaces of kings and Roman officials and the homes of the wealthy, the majority of housing within the cities of Judea was overcrowded and not well constructed. Evidence at Capernaum, for example, suggests that private houses, set in blocks of four around a central courtyard, often consisted of one story, with a staircase on the outside wall leading up to a living area on the roof. They were crudely constructed of uneven blocks of basalt with little evidence of mortar to solidify the walls. Because of a lack of large wooden beams, the rooms tended to be less than eighteen feet wide, and the ceilings were quite low. There were small windows overlooking the courtyard, allowing some ventilation and providing a relatively cool dwelling in the often hot and humid climate of the Upper Galilee region. The floor was made of uneven basalt slabs, which could easily cause a stumble or the loss of some item, like a coin, between the cracks (Luke 15:8). The smaller population centers lack the aqueduct system built to supply a permanent source of water for larger cities like Sepphoris. Instead, villages continued to depend on household catch basins for rainwater or reservoirs on the crown of a hill that supplied communal drinking water for animals, doing laundry, and other needs.

> At issue in Pilate's use of temple funds for his aqueduct was the fact that these funds were considered to be *corban*, an offering reserved for God (see Mark 7:11–13). It is possible he had negotiated an agreement with temple officials to share the costs of the project, but it still proved provocative.

The new and expanded urban centers were designed to accommodate relatively large populations (perhaps as many as 60,000 to 120,000 in Jerusalem in the 30s CE). Such a large number of people (swelling dramatically during festivals like Passover) meant increased demands for water and food supplies. To meet the former need Herod initiated public works projects to construct new water channels and to stimulate a periodically stagnant economy. Even with these measures, however, it was standard for every home to have one or more rain-catching cisterns or pools. Perhaps hoping to curry favor with the Jewish population, Pontius Pilate constructed an aqueduct capable of supplying a continuous supply of fresh water to Jerusalem's inhabitants. However, because he used temple funds to support the project, it only resulted in riots by the outraged Jews (*J.W.* 2.9.175–77).

Archaeological surveys indicate that in the late Persian and throughout the Hellenistic periods, small, unwalled agricultural villages ringed the urban centers supplying the food and other farm products that the people of the cities consumed. These concentric circles of smaller communities produced the grains, meat, and oil that were the staple of the Jewish diet of the inhabitants of urban centers like Jerusalem. In their turn, the larger cities contained industrial districts for the manufacture of pottery, metal implements, woven cloth, and dyed material. There was continuous contact between these two population areas, but there were some very large differences between them in terms of their perspective on the political and social issues that seemed to consume the Hasmonean and Herodian rulers and the priestly community.

Urban-Based Bureaucracy

Helping to administer both the cities and the surrounding villages was a new group of court-appointed bureaucrats whose positions were owed to the rulers of Judea. Thus their loyalties centered on pleasing their Greek and Roman masters and adapting to some aspects of a foreign culture. In like manner the Hasmoneans and Herodians also employed a civil service to collect taxes and enforce order (Mark 6:21). This service gave many Jews the opportunity to move up socially, and in some cases they became quite wealthy and powerful. For instance, Zacchaeus, the chief tax official in the Jericho region, is said to have been very rich (Luke 19:2). He, like John, the port official at Caesarea mentioned in Josephus (*J.W.* 2.14.287), had taken advantage of the Roman system of tax farming. Under this system the tax collector was assigned a certain amount to collect and then was allowed to collect as much more as he could to cover administrative expenses. In addition, tolls were imposed on business activity (*Ant.* 17.8.205), which, along with taxes on agricultural yield, helped to fund some of Herod's building projects and other civic improvements by his successors.

By Jesus's time nearly all tax collectors, civil officials, and local judges (Luke 1:58–59) in Judea were Jews. Like the stewards who manipulated the day laborers and tenant farmers (Luke 16:1–8), these middle- and lower-level government employees, who accumulated fortunes, considered themselves socially above the masses. They were vilified for this (Luke 19:7; Matt. 11:19) and relegated to the same despised status as prostitutes and sinners (Matt. 21:31; Mark 2:16). Tensions between these officials, who were necessarily loyal to Rome, and other Jews were very real. The Pharisees especially are depicted several times in Luke's Gospel as openly disparaging those, like tax collectors, who work for the Romans (Luke 5:30; 7:34; 15:1; 18:10–14). In contrast, Jesus preached nonviolence, as when he defused the question of whether to pay tribute to Caesar in Luke 20:22–25 and preached the love of enemies (Matt. 5:44–45).

The temple also imposed an annual tax of a half-shekel on all adult Jewish males (Matt. 17:24–27). These funds allowed for the maintenance of the building, its grounds, and temple personnel. It also maintained a physical tie to Jews outside of Judea. In addition, the temple employed officers to police their grounds and uphold religious law. It is to the temple police and chief priests that Judas Iscariot goes to make his case against Jesus and to obtain compensation for his betrayal (Luke 22:4–6). These same officers were then employed to arrest Jesus (John 18:3).

Village Life

Despite the growth of urban centers and the incentives offered by jobs and occasionally better housing (see Herod Antipas's inducements to new settlers in Tiberias, *Ant.* 18.2.36–38), the majority of Judean Jews in Jesus's time still lived in small towns and villages. Like their ancestors, they had learned to accommodate themselves to their climatic conditions and to contend with variations in rainfall, the likelihood of insect infestations, and the scorching winds that blew in from the southern desert regions (Luke 12:54–55). Josephus wrote of the many villages in Galilee that were aided by the richness of the region's soil (*J.W.* 3.3.43). A conservative estimate of two hundred villages with populations of about five hundred each would total one hundred thousand peasant villagers inhabiting that area.

Life went on much as before in the villages, and even the pottery types remained much the same, consisting primarily of common, rough ware with just a few stylistic differences to distinguish the introduction of Persian or Hellenistic characteristics. Some towns like Cana (Khirbet Qana), Yodefat, and Gamla in the Galilee were built on hilltops, and their street patterns and domestic structures are a mixture of adaptation to the topography of the hill and some influences from the larger Hellenistic sites. Their houses tend to be clustered together, but that is more reflective of social connections than a defensive pattern. They lack a formal agora or marketplace, but it is likely that business activity took place in shops built into homes or at the entrance to the village marked by a standing stone or some other free-standing object. They are linked by trails rather than formal roads to nearby towns like Sepphoris and Tiberias, facilitating trade.

The effects of Hellenism were less pronounced in the villages than in the cities. Councils of elders continued to decide local matters (Matt. 10:17), although tax collectors and other government officials would have added another level of authority to their lives. Aramaic remained the common language in the villages, while Greek was the principal tongue for business, law, and everyday speech in the cities. The basic conservatism of the peasants in these small settlements meant a retention of older traditions and values that tied them more closely to pre-Hellenistic eras.

Those social activities that existed in the rural areas centered on family ties and seasonal religious festivals. Marriages were contracted between families, with a dowry contract serving as the binding document. The brides usually entered their husband's household during their teen years, while the men generally married in their late twenties. The marriage was celebrated with a wedding feast (Matt. 22:2; Luke 14:8). The ritual included the groomsman escorting the bride to the wedding (John 3:29), while the bridesmaids accompanied the bridegroom to the celebration (Matt. 25:1–12). A steward was placed in charge of the arrangements for the feast; he or she would orchestrate the festivities and parcel out the wine and other refreshments (John 2:8–10). To separate these activities and the guests from other gatherings, a special wedding garment was required for admission to the feast (Matt. 22:11–13).

Pilgrimages to Jerusalem to attend the Passover (Luke 2:41), the Feast of Tabernacles (John 7:2), and other major religious events (John 10:22, Hanukkah celebration) were the social highlight of the villagers' year. Religious obligations could be fulfilled while leaving enough time to shop, see family and old friends, and pass on to the young the importance of their cultural heritage (Luke 2:22–24). After the destruction of the temple in 70 CE, the synagogue—along with the law of the Torah—took the place of the Jerusalem cult community and functioned as a primary gathering place for the Jews of the Diaspora (Acts 13:14–15; 14:1; 17:1). Villagers who remained in Palestine retained the memory and image of the temple but had to content themselves with local celebrations of the Sabbath and seasonal holidays, along with an occasional trip to a nearby market center to break the monotony of village life.

Leisure

Leisure was a major pursuit in the urban centers and would have been a mark of rank and status for those who had the time to devote to activities unassociated with business or labor. The Greeks, and later the Romans, demanded the opportunities and pleasures of the gymnasium, stadium, and theater. Young men of the elite classes would attend the gymnasium to be educated in the Greek philosophers and poets, engage in a private workout in the nude (a source of tension for some Hellenized Jews who were identifiable by their circumcision; *Ant.* 12.5.240–41), and then bathe either to begin or to end a workday. This facility also provided a place to make social contacts, conduct club meetings, or participate in the activities of professional or private associations. This latter activity was another innovation of the Greek culture, which was very dependent on the development of social relationships.

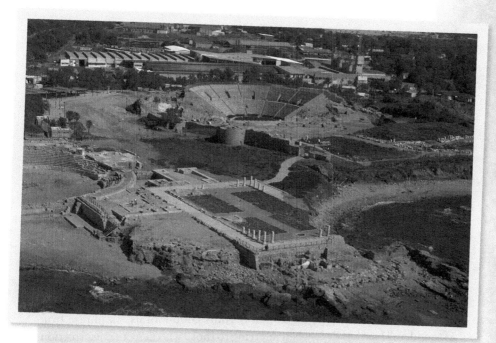

Figure 5.9. Aerial view of the theater, amphitheater, and Herod's palace at Caesarea Maritima

Businessmen, skilled workers, and even the poor formed these associations of social equals as a social outlet, to aid each other in commercial activity, civic responsibilities, and religious activities, and even to provide funds to ensure proper burial.

The stadium provided facilities for public athletic contests. For instance, the multipurpose amphitheater (50.35 m. wide and 265 m. long) constructed by Herod in Caesarea also could function as a hippodrome, accommodating horse and chariot races (*Ant.* 15.9.341; 16.5.137). Josephus describes plays, athletic and wrestling matches, chariot races, and battles between condemned convicts and animals in the Jerusalem theater-amphitheater. The winners of these contests received rich prizes and public recognition (*Ant.* 15.8.268–74). Since no confirmed trace of this facility has yet come to light, it is necessary to turn to the finely built theater excavated at Caesarea Maritima as a physical model.

There are frequent references in Josephus (*Ant.* 12.5.241; 19.8.343–45) and in the intertestamental literature to the use of public facilities by the Hellenizers (1 Macc. 1:14). For instance, the high priest Jason created a "gymnasium and *ephebeion*" (a municipal "finishing school" for young men) in Jerusalem as a mark of his commitment to Hellenism (2 Macc. 4:9, 12). The Hellenizers, who wished to adopt Greek culture and practice, were stronger in the cities. They freely attended dramatic events and participated in games such as foot races, wrestling, and other Olympian events. By the New Testament period, Paul could describe his ministry using the analogy of running a race in 1 Corinthians 9:24–27 or compare it to "fighting a good fight" in 2 Timothy 4:7. In these passages, however, he is speaking primarily to gentiles and Hellenized Jewish Christians. Many of the Jews in Judea were offended by the excesses of Herod in staging Greek games in Jerusalem. The naked performers and the gold and silver statuettes given to the winners caused a great uproar (*Ant.* 15.8.277–83).

Drama combined the study of Greek literature with live entertainment to enhance cultural life in the Hellenistic city. Regular performances of the Greek playwrights were held in the theaters, like the three-thousand-seat facility at Sepphoris in the Galilee, in the cities of the Decapolis in Transjordan, and all over the Near East, further educating the people in Greek values and philosophy. Paul's use of quotations from Greek plays reflects the great familiarity these dramas had in the Hellenized cities. Examples of this are found in 1 Corinthians 15:33, "Bad company ruins good morals" (a phrase from Menander, *Thais* frg. 218) when referring to those who deny the resurrection, and in Titus 1:12, "Cretans are always liars, evil beasts, lazy gluttons," using Cretans as a euphemism for Christian heretics (quoted from the sixth-century BCE philosopher Epimenides of Crete).

Public baths were also constructed to provide city dwellers with a familiar place to socialize, exercise, transact business informally, and engage in the hygienic pleasures of alternating hot and cold baths (*Ant.* 19.7.329). Since this required large quantities of water, aqueducts were constructed to bring water into the cities. Bathing facilities and health resorts, such as those at Tiberias and Calirrhoe, were constructed near natural hot springs (*Ant.* 17.6.171; 18.2.36). Herod included a bath complex in his royal palace at Jericho. Even Roman soldiers, while stationed at the Galilee city of Capernaum, built for themselves a separate bath facility in much the same design as ones excavated in other parts of the Roman Empire. Given the mixed population of Capernaum, it is unlikely that locals would have been welcome to share this bath with the Roman troops.

Separate bathing facilities (*miqva'ot*) for Jewish ritual cleansing (Lev. 15:5–11) became popular in the first century BCE, with seven hundred discovered so far in excavations in Palestine (see fig. 4.7, p. 202). While they are found in village sites, the best and largest examples are those associated with the priestly quarter in Jerusalem and at the Essene community at Qumran. Steps were provided to assist bathers to reach the water and immerse themselves. These, however, were not designed for social gatherings but for purifying the body before entering the temple or after it had been made impure by sexual activity or contact with the dead (Lev. 15:18; 17:15).

Education and Scholarship

Throughout the period from 350 BCE to 70 CE, traditional Jewish education in Hebrew and Aramaic continued to be conducted primarily in the home. Parents were responsible for providing at least a minimal if informal education, and it would be interspersed with vocational training providing the child with a trade or basic skills needed for life in a village. It is likely that some instruction was made available in the temple at Jerusalem (Luke 2:46) and in the local synagogues, but we lack sufficient evidence to determine its extent. During the first century BCE, urban upper-class sons were able to attend schools in which they received a basic level of Greek education (Philo, *Spec.* 2.228–30), but that was a source of contention among Jewish families who wished to limit Hellenistic influences (1 Macc. 1:11–15). Jewish tradition states that local schools for young children were created by the high priest in the first century CE (*b. B. Bat.* 21a), but again this represents a later and perhaps idealized view of the times. There is no scriptural evidence of this, however, except Jesus's demonstrated knowledge of the law (Luke 2:41–51) and his ability to read Hebrew even though he was only the son of a carpenter (Luke 4:16–17). Still, it should be noted that some Jews, like the apostle Paul, could reach a higher level of education (both in Jewish Scriptures and in Greek literature and philosophy) and were able to make use of formal rhetoric in speech and writing (2 Cor. 10:10; Gal. 1:14).

In the Diaspora, education for some Jews and for most of the Greek residents of Hellenistic cities took place in the gymnasium. The gymnasia not only included areas for physical education but also housed lecture halls where students could study Greek language and literature. They used the same handbooks on rhetorical style and writing exercises that were employed all over the Greco-Roman world. Lessons at the gymnasium were part of the *ephebeion*, an institution of higher education open only to wealthy future aristocrats. There were Greeks who, after secondary school, went on to train in medicine or the law, but for those whose families held high social standing, the *ephebeion* in Jerusalem, where Jews performed exercises in the nude and were educated in the ways of Hellenism, were labeled by the author of 2 Maccabees as "ungodly" (2 Macc. 4:9, 12–13).

One further accommodation to living in a Hellenistic environment was the translation of the Hebrew Scriptures by a group of scholars into Greek during the period after the second century BCE in Alexandria, Egypt. The Septuagint (abbreviated LXX) does not represent a separate canon of Scriptures from its Hebrew counterpart. It simply provided a vehicle for the Greek-speaking Diasporic Jews to study and use their Scriptures. As the writings of the first-century CE scholar **Philo of Alexandria** reflect, there is a mixture of

Figure 5.10. The Dead Sea Scrolls were discovered in caves in these cliffs.

Greek literature with the interpretation of the Hebrew Scriptures, and this contributed to the establishment of some new schools of thought on Jewish traditions. For instance, Philo, in his exposition on the Septuagint (Greek) translation of the Pentateuch, was heavily influenced by Platonism and Stoic philosophy, as is evident in his *Exposition of the Laws of Moses*. His discussion of *Logos* ("the Word") in relation to God's mental activity while in the act of creation can serve as a background (see *Opif.* 15–25; *Pirqe R. El.* 3) or at least a comparative study for the use of *Logos* in the opening of John's Gospel (1:1–14). Like the authors of the early Christian Scriptures, it is likely that Philo was more at home with the Septuagint version of the text, and he may have known little Hebrew.

The Dead Sea Scrolls discovered in the caves above the site of Qumran provide some indication that there is still some fluidity in the Hebrew texts in the first century CE that eventually would be formalized into a canon of Scripture in the period after the second century CE. There are variations between texts of the same books demonstrating multiple traditions, but there are indications of a growing formalization of the Hebrew script. It can therefore be said that on the basis of the Dead Sea Scrolls found at Qumran, what would become the Masoretic text of the Hebrew Bible in the sixth century CE was nearly set by the end of the first century CE.

After the destruction of the Jerusalem temple in 70 CE, the development of the Hebrew canon becomes obscured by the tradition that the burden of Jewish education and the preservation of the canon fell to a community of scholars who met at Jamnia (Yavneh). According to this tradition, they and their successors set a tone of instruction and study of the Scriptures in synagogues wherever Jews lived. Supposedly, the Jamnia rabbis deliberated throughout the period immediately following 75 CE and at least until the end of the Bar Kochba Revolt in 135. They are said to have compiled manuscripts and, in an exhaustive process of debate, to have determined which books should be included in the canon of scripture. Second Esdras 14:37–48 describes the re-creation of the traditional canon of twenty-four books and an additional seventy volumes of Deuteroncanonical/apocryphal wisdom. While there is no historical basis for this picture of an academy discussing the canon or making authoritative decisions on the shape of the canon, certainly some process did take place contributing to the text that would later be formalized after 500 CE through the efforts of another group of scholars known as the **Masoretes**. However, the Jewish rabbis did not ratify the books of the Deuterocanon/**Apocrypha** as part of the Hebrew canon for a variety of reasons, including the fact that they postdated the period of Ezra and reflected Hellenistic ideas. Another body of literature known as the **Pseudepigrapha** was also denied a place in the canon in large part because much of it was fictional commentary on biblical works and contained theological ideas not acceptable to the Jewish community. These sixty-five books, many produced during this time of Hellenistic synthesis, date well into the Roman era, and the early Christian community influenced some of these writings (*Testaments of the Twelve Patriarchs*). They contain folk stories, additions to canonical books, and the meditations of scholars and scribes in Palestine and the Diaspora. Examples of these works include *1 Enoch*, *Jubilees*, and the *Testament of Job*. Their worth was considered secondary to the text of the original body of Scripture. Their authorship was often uncertain, and, significantly, most were written in Greek.

Eventually, a dispute over the importance of these writings in relation to the canonical material arose among the Jews. Religious parties arose as a consequence of this issue. Josephus describes these various groups but gives only a tantalizingly small amount of information about them. He portrays the Pharisees as advocates of the free use of the interpretive material such as the oral Torah and the Mishnah as the equal of the canonical works (*Ant.* 18.1.11–23). They are described in Matthew 23:3 as sitting "on Moses's seat" and thus as precise interpreters of the law. The Pharisees are often paired with scribes in the New Testament, possibly indicating that the movement, unlike the priestly class, was open to non-Levites (Mark 2:16; Luke 5:30). The Essenes, who lived communally and refrained from the sacrifice of animals associated with the temple cult (*J.W.* 2.8.119; Philo, *Good Person* 75), speak critically in the Qumran texts of the Pharisees, referring to them as the "seekers after smooth things" (4Q169 3–4 I, 1, 2, 7), that is, persons who make their interpretations based on pleasing the mass of people. In contrast, the Sadducees, who were in control of the priestly establishment, argued for strict and exclusive use of the canonical books of the Torah to answer religious questions (*Ant.* 13.10.297) and denied the resurrection (Matt. 22:23–28).

After 200 CE more emphasis was placed by the rabbis on the study and reiteration of the legal pronouncements in the Scriptures. Local communities of scholars taught young men the Torah and expounded its meaning. This resulted in the compilation of the Mishnah under the direction of Rabbi Judah the Prince. It consists of sixty-three tractates or treatises comprising the consensus of rabbinic opinion on how the laws of the Pentateuch related to aspects of everyday life (agriculture, marriage, and ritual purity) in their time. Originating as oral interpretation, the written version of the Mishnah often includes both majority and minority perspectives on particular topics and rarely cites biblical verses, instead quoting rabbinic opinion on the law. Additional commentary on these legal treatises is contained in the Babylonian and Palestinian Talmuds, dating to the period of the mid-fourth through mid-sixth centuries CE. Commentary, or **midrash**, on nonlegal material, including legendary narratives of the lives of the major biblical figures in the Hebrew canon, is also contained in the Talmud.

Law and the Administration of Justice

There were several shifts of authority in the enforcement of the law during the Hellenistic and Roman periods. During portions of this era, foreign governments and their representatives imposed order, imprisoning offenders and carrying out capital punishment. At other times the Hasmonean government and the Sanhedrin council took primary responsibility for the administration of justice. In many cases little distinction was made between civil and religious law since the Torah imposed penalties for crimes against persons (theft, murder, adultery) as well as crimes against God (blasphemy, pagan worship).

There were several levels of judicial authority. Whether appointed by the Greeks, Hasmoneans, Herodians, or Romans, local courts handled local civil and criminal cases. In situations in which there was a dispute over land or property ownership, the services of a scribe or lawyer (Titus 3:13) might be employed to record and argue the case (1 Cor. 6:1). Many of these lawyers were associated with the Pharisees and scribes and were actually teachers or authorities on the Mosaic law (Matt. 22:34–36; Luke 5:17; 14:3). Jesus's various legal hearings before Caiaphas the high priest (Matt. 26:57–68) and before Pilate (Matt. 27:11–14) demonstrate that capital crimes and cases of treason or civil unrest brought the higher authorities based in Jerusalem or Caesarea to bear on the problem (*J.W.* 7.10.412–14). Clear-cut religious crimes were handled by the leaders of the local synagogue or by the high priest and the Sanhedrin (see the trial of Stephen and his stoning, Acts 6:8–13 and 7:54–58). For instance, some Sadducean members of the Sanhedrin had Peter and John arrested and tried for preaching the resurrection of the dead in Jesus's name (Acts 4:1–22).

Roman officials throughout the empire had jurisdiction to overrule local courts or to intervene in any case in which they were interested (see Herod's trial in *Ant.* 14.9.167–70). Thus, when the members of the Sanhedrin and their followers nearly came to blows over Paul's case, the Roman tribune took him to the local army barracks for safekeeping (Acts 23:6–10). Roman citizenship, which had been obtained by some of the people of the provinces, also figured in the process of justice. As a Roman citizen of Cilicia, Paul successfully avoided further prosecution by the Jewish leadership by appealing his case to Caesar. Despite his desire to do a favor for the Jews, Festus, the Roman procurator, was obliged by law to grant Paul's request (Acts 25:9–12).

Clothing and Personal Adornment

The wealthy and those involved in the government during the Persian period through the Roman era commonly adopted foreign clothing styles. Among those items of Persian clothing, most often adopted were riding trousers with boots and leggings and a high felt cap. Zephaniah's admonitions (1:8) against the wearing of "strange apparel" suggest that these fashions had become fairly widespread. With the coming of the Greeks, Persian garb was displaced.

At first there was some resistance among the Jews to Hellenistic fashions. For instance, one charge made against Jason, the high priest in the time of Antiochus IV, was that he forced the nobility of Jerusalem to wear a broad-brimmed hat associated with the cult of the Greek god Hermes (2 Macc. 4:12). It was not until the mid-Hasmonean period that Greek costume became common among the general population in Judea. Rejection of the new fashions was less common in the Diasporic communities like Alexandria. There the Jews quickly adopted the Greek styles of dress.

By the time of Jesus there was no stigma attached to wearing the *chitōn*, a long seamless tunic (John 19:23), with a cloak (*himation*, Matt. 27:31) and tassels (*kraspedon*) on the four corners of the hem (Matt. 23:5; Mark 6:56). There were often decorative bands on the *chitōn* that ran from the

Figure 5.11. Funerary relief showing a veiled wealthy woman from second-century AD Palmyra

shoulder to the hem. Foot coverings included the thonged sandal (*hypodēma*; Mark 1:7) as well as the Roman *calceus*, a shoe that covered the entire foot. During this period there was no formal headwear for men except for the embroidered caps of the priests (*Ant.* 3.7.157–58). The issue of women being required to cover their long hair with a veil is raised in 1 Corinthians 11:4–7. It is unlikely that Paul is instructing the Corinthian church to adopt a Jewish tradition (see 3 Macc. 4:6; *Ant.* 3.11.270 for this custom); Greek and Roman women also regularly covered their head with a veil (Tertullian, *Cor.* 4; Plutarch, *Quaest. rom.* 267a).

There are only a few specific items of jewelry mentioned in the New Testament (rings in Luke 15:22 and James 2:2; gold jewelry in 1 Pet. 3:3). However, archaeological discoveries have shown that the jeweler's art continued to flourish as it had in previous periods (see Isa. 3:18–21; Ezek. 16:11–13). Gold bracelets and clothes clasps encrusted with jewels, colored glass, and pearls have been uncovered, adding credence to the description of the woman in Revelation 17:4 and the "golden sash" in Revelation 1:13. Greek and Roman styles of jewelry were also borrowed, along with female hairstyles. First Timothy 2:9 contains Paul's admonition that women in the Christian community not adopt extravagant apparel, which he describes as "braided hair or gold or pearls or costly attire" (see Juvenal, *Sat.* 6; *T. Reu.* 5:1–5). Inscribed seals and rings used to stamp documents or possessions or to adorn fingers and toes are also common finds in the excavation of Roman occupation levels.

Although not specifically for adornment purposes, *tefillin* or **phylacteries** were commonly worn by devout men within the Jewish community. Remains of phylacteries have been found in the excavations at the Qumran community dating to the first century CE. Traditionally they consisted of black leather boxes, each containing four passages of Scripture: Exodus 13:1–10, 11–16;

Deuteronomy 6:4–9; 11:13–21. Based on injunctions in Exodus 13:9 and Deuteronomy 6:8 to keep the law constantly in the mind and heart, they were attached to the forehead and the left arm by leather straps. The phylacteries also became a source of excessive pride, according to Matthew 23:5, for some literally wore their religion on their sleeves.

Weapons and Warfare

The methods of warfare continued to become more sophisticated during the Hellenistic and Roman eras. This was due in large part to the introduction of new weapons (catapults, ballistae, and improved siege engines) by the Greek and Roman armies that conquered the area (*J.W.* 3.5.80). Acquiring skill with these new weapons and methods took time for the Jews. Their lack of basic military expertise resulted in a terrible massacre during the early part of the Maccabean Revolt. Being attacked on the Sabbath and refusing to break the Sabbath law, over one thousand were killed (*Ant.* 12.6.274–75). Subsequently, they set aside this law temporarily in times of national crisis (1 Macc. 2:29–41).

Open warfare against Antiochus IV's army of experienced soldiers, horsemen, and elephants (*J.W.* 1.1.41; 1 Macc. 6:33–39) was clearly impossible for the underequipped Jews. Better organization (1 Macc. 3:55–56), local intelligence networks (1 Macc. 5:24–29), and the guerrilla tactics of Judas Maccabeus and his brothers Jonathan and Simon finally outlasted the Seleucid forces (1 Macc. 9:65–69). Even after the Greek armies were expelled from most of Judea, the Jews' lack of skills in siege warfare meant that the Seleucid citadel in Jerusalem, the Akra, was not captured until 141 BCE (1 Macc. 13:49–52; *Ant.* 13.6.215–17).

In the Roman period there were numerous Jewish uprisings in addition to the two principal revolts of 66–70 and 132–135 CE. Weaponry for infantry in these conflicts generally consisted of the Greek or Roman short sword (*falcata*, 28 inches long) and javelin, a breastplate, shield, and helmet (Eph. 6:13–17; *J.W.* 3.5.94–95). Composite bows and slings were also employed for long-distance harassment of an enemy force. Daggers or short swords were often concealed under the garments of rebels and those like the *sicarii* who sought to instigate civil unrest (*J.W.* 7.10.409–12; *Ant.* 20.8.164–65; Matt. 26:51). The Roman cavalry carried pikes, a long sword (*spatha*), shields, and a quiver of throwing darts. Their horses were also partially armored (*J.W.* 3.5.96–97).

Throughout the New Testament period, the Romans were the unprecedented masters of warfare. They developed remarkable portable siege engines, catapults, and other ballistic weapons that could fling bolts, stones, and other projectiles with great force. The effects of their unparalleled organizational skills and expertise in siege warfare could only be delayed, not overcome (*J.W.* 3.5.70–101). Josephus's description of the siege of Jerusalem is a case in point. The Jews managed to burn the Roman siegeworks and battering rams. However, famine and loss of life during the many skirmishes eventually led to the fall of the city (*J.W.* 5.11.466–90).

Disease and Medical Treatment

During the early second century BCE, the Jewish sage Ben Sira described the physician as a partner with Yahweh in the healing process. He was to be given "his place" because his skill came from God, much as prophets had previously served as divine representatives whose relationship with God aided in their miraculous cures. The patient was to pray to God, but "there is a time when success lies in the hands of physicians, for they too pray to the Lord" to aid with the diagnosis (Sir. 38:12–14). Another common medical technician was the midwife, who provided care for pregnant mothers and assisted in birth (Gen. 38:28; Exod. 1:15–21). In contrast, the New Testament seldom gives such a positive endorsement of physicians or the practice of medicine (Luke 4:23 and 5:31 mention them proverbially) because of its emphasis on the healing character of God's Spirit. Luke is the most prominently mentioned physician (Col. 4:14), but of course he is a Greek.

Jewish physicians might well have had the same training as Luke, but it is likely that most of their medical knowledge had Egyptian or Greek origin. The Egyptians were the most advanced physicians in the ancient Near East. They treated injuries like broken limbs (Ezek. 30:21) and lanced boils to speed healing. In addition, they performed intricate surgeries including trepanning, boring through a skull to relieve the pressure of fluid built up after a concussion or as a result of a tumor. The contents of their medical treatises, which may have found their way into medical aphorisms (see 1 Tim. 5:23), display a general knowledge of herbal medicines for the relief of certain ailments such as indigestion, constipation, boils (2 Kings 20:7), and sleeplessness. Many times these cures, as Ben Sira notes (Sir. 38:1–15), were also accompanied by sacrifices, prayers, and incantations to invoke God's aid (compare the reassurance in Exod. 15:26).

In Judea and elsewhere there were doctors seeing patients with both physical and mental ailments they could not heal. The primitive (by modern medical standards) instruments and herbal remedies they used to diagnose and treat

> Jesus's ability to provide a cure is contrasted with the standard prophetic story in which the prophet serves as an intermediary for the deity. In Mark 1:40–42, Jesus is petitioned by a leper to cleanse him with the assurance this could happen "if you choose." Jesus takes pity on the man, and as the deity himself, simply says, "I do choose."

illness simply could not cope with many diseases. This is graphically illustrated in Mark 5:25–26 (paralleled in Luke 8:43–44), which tells of a woman who had suffered from a chronic form of hemorrhaging for twelve years and had spent all her savings on charlatans presenting themselves as physicians. With hope and resources waning, she sought out Jesus, whose reputation as a healer had grown throughout the country. When she touches the fringe of his garment (Luke 8:44), she demonstrates the emic (insider) belief in the healing power-by-association attached to the clothing of an important or pious person (compare Mark 6:56). This sort of desperation to find a cure is of course still a part of the medical scene today, with people traveling great distances in hopes of a wonder drug or a miracle at the hands of a faith healer.

It had also been standard procedure since the earliest periods of Jewish history to consult priests (Lev. 13:2–8) or prophets (1 Kings 14:1–3; 2 Kings 8:8) who would diagnose and cure disease (2 Kings 5:3). Although Jesus was not a priest, his stature as a prophet was accepted by many (Matt. 16:13–14), and this attracted those looking for the traditional curative abilities of the man of God (Luke 9:37–40; Acts 5:16). Such an attempt may be illustrated by the band of lepers that Jesus encounters as he travels between the Galilee and Samaria. They call out to him to have mercy, and Jesus instructs them, according to the law, to "go and show yourselves to the priests." They are subsequently declared "clean" (Luke 17:11–14). However, their physical cure is then contrasted with the spiritual cleansing of the one who returned to thank Jesus (17:15–19).

Demon possession is another instance in which disease is tied to spiritual rather than simply physical causes. These individuals were afflicted with both physical (blindness, Matt. 12:22; seizures, Matt. 4:24; Luke 9:39) and severe mental disorders (Mark 5:2–5) and thus were beyond the abilities of normal medical practitioners. The dialogue Jesus has with the possessing spirits in Mark 5:7–10 reflects an emic acceptance of possession that may puzzle modern (etic) understandings of mental disorders. In the text, however, spiritual beings recognize his power, just as Jesus's explanation in Matthew 12:25–32 differentiates his actions and his realm from that of Satan. There is no modern explanation for Jesus's casting out of demons. The mental distress these people manifested in the Gospels may have been purely psychological, or it may represent the Gospel writers' attempt to emphasize the messianic qualities of Jesus.

The other major source of cures and purification in ancient Judea was water, an element necessary in dealing with skin diseases and the impurities of bodily discharge (Lev. 13:6; 15:5–8). That also helps to explain why hot springs, such as those near Tiberias, became pilgrimage sites for the ill and the infirm. Herod is said to have sought a cure for intestinal distress at the warm baths at Calirrhoe near the Jordan River (*Ant.* 17.6.169–76). Similarly, a pool of water could become a place where the afflicted congregated and dipped themselves, hoping for a cure (see also Naaman's cleansing in the Jordan River in 2 Kings 5:10–14). Among the best known of these pools was that at Bethesda (or Bethzatha) near the Sheep Gate in Jerusalem. In John 5:2–7, this pool was said to be surrounded by the sick and the crippled who believed that the first to enter the water when its surface became troubled would be instantly cured. The movement of the water was probably due to the actions of an intermittent spring, but in antiquity this was attributed to the touch of an angel or other divine being.

Modern scholars have attempted to identify Bethesda through excavation as well as the use of ancient literary sources. The Copper Scroll from the Qumran community mentions a pool at Bethesda (3Q15 XI, 12), and Eusebius mentions two rain-fed pools frequented by the sick. The importance of the site as a healing center after Jerusalem became Aelia Capitolina (second century CE) is demonstrated by the discovery of votive offerings associated with the Roman cult of Asclepius unearthed by archaeologists. Although the number of ancient churches and other structures built over this area prevent a full tracing of the cisterns in question, it seems likely that those uncovered just north of the temple are the pools of Bethesda.

Figure 5.12. Remains of the Pool of Bethesda, Jerusalem

Burial Customs

The poor and the stranger normally were buried in unmarked, shallow graves (Luke 11:44) or in a "potter's field" (Matt. 27:3–8). The remains of most of these burials have long since disappeared, although occasionally new road construction will uncover these simple gravesites. Therefore our knowledge of burial customs in the Hellenistic and Roman periods is primarily based on the tombs of the more affluent or those who belonged to associations that provided proper burial for their members. Most of these individuals were interred in caves (John 11:38) or rock-cut tombs located outside the city walls, such as those in the Kidron Valley on the western slope of the Mount of Olives.

After death, the body was washed, its eyes were closed, and its mouth and other orifices were bound shut (John 11:44). A mixture of spices was applied to the body, perhaps as a form of preservation or perhaps to ward off the smell of decomposition for those who subsequently visited the tomb (John 11:39; 19:39–40). The corpse was then dressed in its own clothes or placed in a linen shroud (Matt. 27:59). Next a procession, including musicians, family, and (if the family could afford it) professional mourners, followed the remains to the tomb (Eccles. 12:5; Matt. 9:23). It was customary for mourners to continue to visit the tomb for thirty days to reanoint the body (Mark 16:1) or to check to be sure the person had not been buried prematurely (John 11:31).

Tombs varied in size and design, reflecting the wealth and influence of the family. The very elaborate tomb of Jason in Jerusalem, dated to the first century BCE, contains four outer chambers separated by stone doors and a burial chamber with ten radiating *loculi* (individual interment chambers carved into the wall so the body could be laid perpendicular to the wall). There is also a communal charnel chamber designed as the repository for the bones of earlier burials that had been displaced by more recent ones. This single-family tomb was fronted by a porch area and decorated with a pyramid-shaped monument (*nefesh*) that was placed over the gated entrance to the forecourt. The elements of this tomb seem particularly elaborate compared to the description of Joseph of Arimathea's garden rock-cut tomb with its sealing stone, in which the body of Jesus was laid (John 19:41; Matt. 27:59–60).

Some of the Herodian era and early first-century tombs, such as the recently discovered burial cave and ossuaries apparently belonging to the family of the high priest Caiaphas, show the wealth expended in building a tomb. Most contain carved limestone ossuaries (24 in. × 14 in. × 12 in.) in which the bones of several family members were placed, a practice that replaced the charnel chamber and its heaps of bones found in earlier tombs. The practice of *ossilegium* (bone gathering) was employed to make room for new primary burials in the tomb while retaining a place for the older remains within the confines

Figure 5.13. Kidron Valley tombs. From left to right: "Absalom's Tomb," Tomb of the Sons of Hezir, "Zechariah's Tomb"

of the tomb. The conditions of some of the skeletal remains from this period also show the unrest and conflict of the times. Some clearly reveal sword cuts, and one case of death by crucifixion has been discovered in a family tomb at Givat ha-Mivtar. In this instance an iron nail was driven through one of the victim's heel bones and twisted as it struck a knot in the cross.

Among the most spectacular of the Herodian era tombs in the Kidron Valley are those attributed by tradition to Zechariah, dated to the period of the fall of the temple, and Absalom, dated to the period just before 70 CE. They both include a *nefesh*, a pyramid-shaped monument considered a habitation for the soul of the deceased in Egyptian and other cultures, but simply as a memorial among the Jews (1 Macc. 13:27–30). The outsides of these tombs may have been whitewashed to note a recent burial and thus warn Jews to stay away from the contaminating contact with the dead (Matt. 23:27).

Economic Life

Trade Routes and the Means of Travel

Like the Persians before them, the international character of the Greek and Roman empires required reliable and well-kept travel and trade routes.

Since ancient times, regional travel had relied on the Via Maris, the King's Highway, and a system of roads that had expanded with the fortunes of the Israelite monarchy. With the coming of the Greeks and Romans, however, the network of trade routes throughout the Near East markedly expanded and improved. For instance, Pompey's swift rise to political power and notoriety in Rome came after he rid the Mediterranean Sea of pirates. Quick to recognize a commercial opportunity, Herod constructed an artificial harbor at Caesarea Maritima that for the first time provided a deep-water harbor and access to the Mediterranean trade for Palestine (*Ant.* 15.9.333–40).

Travel by land still had its dangers from robbers (Luke 10:30–36; 2 Cor. 11:26), but a real attempt was made by the Romans to keep roads open and free of bandits (Matt. 27:44). With travel to distant places becoming more feasible for larger numbers of people (Acts 16:4; 18:2) because of the imposition of the Pax Romana (a period of peace enforced by the Roman legions and fleets), a general upsurge in commercial activity took place. Along with this was an increase in cultural exchange as eager merchants carrying goods, gossip, and religious beliefs took the opportunity to travel these improved trade routes. Paul clearly took advantage of these routes during his missionary journeys, taking a Roman road from Antioch to Tarsus, Iconium, and Pisidian Antioch (Acts 15:41–16:6).

Wherever the Greek, Roman, or Jewish merchant went, he took with him his merchandise as well as his cultural heritage. Thus in every commercial center (Antioch, Corinth, Ephesus), ethnic communities were established. For the Jews this meant a synagogue with its governing body of elders, a school, and a network of families in whose houses travelers could stay without encountering the dangers associated with public inns or taverns. Thus these communities of Jews provided the first stop for Paul and the other early Christian missionaries (Acts 13:1–14:1).

> The contrast between the older, narrow paths and gates and the construction of wider roads and gateways provides the metaphorical basis for Jesus's admonition for Christians to choose the "narrow gate" and the hard road "that leads to life" (Matt. 7:13–14).

The means of overland travel included traditional pack animals, the donkey and camel, as well as two- and four-wheel carts. These latter vehicles, pulled by teams of oxen, were used to transport grain, olive oil, pottery, and building stones from one village to another and to urban markets from the farming villages. Wealthy travelers and government officials also used chariots. One example of this is found in Acts 8:26–29, where Philip meets the Ethiopian eunuch, who is riding in his chariot on the desert road between Gaza and Jerusalem.

The increasing wheeled-vehicle traffic required the construction of wider paths and broader, paved city-gate complexes. In heavy traffic zones, more than one lane was required to facilitate movement and prevent disputes between teamsters. Because these vehicles and traveling officials needed well-kept roads (Prov. 15:19), governments and perhaps even local authorities and associations must have regularly sent work gangs along the more traveled routes to clear away stones and other obstructions (Isa. 40:3–4; 62:10). Where a river had to be crossed, fords were identified, and in the Roman period flat stones were laid in the riverbed to smooth the way for wagon wheels.

The Persians had previously introduced a system of way stations every ten to fifteen miles along roadways throughout their vast empire. Hellenistic and Roman rulers continued this practice to facilitate the needs of travelers as well as the imperial postal system. One way that archaeologists are able to identify ancient roads today is through the discovery of Roman mile markers, which were set up by the rulers who ordered the roads to be built or repaired. These markers not only indicate the route but also, based on the name of the Roman emperor in the inscription, when it was constructed. Satellite photos have also provided remarkable images of the network of roads in antiquity, especially in the unpopulated areas of Saudi Arabia.

Travel by sea, although generally only during certain seasons of the year, became more common during this era (Acts 13:13; 15:39). Paul's journey described in Acts 27 provides a great deal of information on accommodation of prisoners and passengers on commercial ships. Despite ending in a shipwreck, their voyage is an excellent portrayal of the difficulties faced by an often-overloaded vessel whose principal means of forward motion was its sails, although most also had oars to assist them. Their first ship is described as being one that made calls at the ports of Asia, presumably transporting cargo and making deliveries along the way. At Myra, in Lycia, they transferred to an open-sea vessel from Alexandria. During this leg of the voyage, mention is made of sailing leeward of islands to avoid contrary winds; baggage, tackle, and finally cargo (wheat) are thrown overboard to lighten the ship when it had to run before a storm. The cupidity of the ship's owner, captain, and crew is displayed in their insistence on sailing in the stormy winter season (Acts 27:9–11) as well as in the crew's attempt to abandon ship during the storm, leaving the 276 passengers to fend for themselves (v. 30).

The very circuitous route of Paul's ship from Caesarea to Rome was typical of trading vessels. The war galleys of Rome of course took a more direct path and had several rows of oars to supplement the sails and to facilitate maneuvering. They were used to support and transport land troops and to carry messages quickly to the farthest corners of the empire. Paul, whose status as a prisoner did not warrant transport on a galley, had to rely on lesser and slower accommodations (Acts 28:11–13).

Weights and Measures

The commercial advantage of a standardized system of weights and measures was recognized very early in Israelite history. The standard *shekel* (a unit of measurement that weighed 11.4 grams and originally was a weight used on one side of a scale to balance against portions of a product on the other side) became the primary measuring unit in Israel. The shekel was borrowed from the Canaanites, who had borrowed it from the complex civilizations of Mesopotamia. As trade expanded into Egyptian territory, adjustments were made to provide equivalencies to the Egyptian measurement system. Weights uncovered by archaeologists at eighth- and seventh-century BCE Israelite sites show this development with Egyptian pictographic hieroglyphic symbols inscribed on metal balance weights.

Although somewhat cumbersome compared to modern Western standards of weights and measures, the shekel weight, when used consistently, provided a reasonably sound system for everyday commerce. Multiples or fractions of this weight (*beka* = half shekel; Gen. 24:22; Exod. 38:26) allowed for transference of goods and commodities with a reasonable expectation that a shekel's weight in one area would be a shekel's weight in another. Discrepancies did occur, of course, since some areas relied on a so-called "heavy" shekel while others used a "light" or "royal standard" shekel. Corruption was also a problem, as numerous references to the use of "false balances" show (Prov. 11:1; Hosea 12:7; Amos 8:5).

By the New Testament period, the older system of units of weight is more often expressed in terms of their monetary value rather than their weight on a scale, and exchange is more commonly based on coinage. The "ten thousand talents" owed by the debtor in Matthew 18:24 would be equivalent to sixty million denarii or fifteen million shekels. This incredible sum is equal to nearly 450,000 pounds, or 204 metric tons of silver. The Roman "pound" (*litra*) weighed approximately 326.4 grams (12 ounces) or ninety-six denarii, and when used to refer to ointments or perfumes reflected both their expense as well as their actual weight (see John 12:3; 19:39).

Volume measures again varied because of the differences between the Jewish system and the overlapping Greek and Roman systems. According to the terminology of Ezekiel 45:13–14, it seems the basic unit of dry measure was the *homer*, which was variously equated with thirty-two to forty gallons or 120 to 150 liters. The *cor* was equal to the homer and could be used for liquid measure as well. Its volume varied, with different sources describing it as equal to sixty gallons or 220 liters. This unit was then broken down with ten *baths* equal to one cor. The bath (= 22 liters or 6 gallons) was used to determine many smaller measures (1 Kings 7:26). The *log* (one-third of a quart or .3 liters) is the smallest unit mentioned (Lev. 14:10). Examining storage jars found at Tell Beit Mirsim inscribed with the word "bath" helped to demonstrate the approximate nature of this system of measurement. They have the liquid capacity of about 5.5 gallons, or 21 liters.

Roman measures used in the New Testament period include the half-liter (*sextarius*), the liter (*choinix* in Rev. 6:6), and the jar (*metrete*), which is the equivalent of 39 liters, or 10 gallons each. This measure is not to be confused with the "stone jars" of water mentioned in John 2:6 holding "twenty or thirty gallons," which were permanent storage jars, not intended to be transported. The pound of costly ointment (300 denarii), which Mary, the sister of Martha, used to anoint Jesus's feet probably weighed around 326.4 grams (John 12:3). This precious substance was equal in value to the yearly wage of the average worker (John 12:5).

Measurements of distance in Israel were based on the cubit (18 inches/.5 meters, or about the length of one's forearm), the span (about 9 inches/23 centimeters, about the span of one's hand), and the handbreadth (about 3 inches/8 centimeters, or about the width of one's palm). These units, like all others in antiquity, varied from place to place and over time (see the larger cubit of Ezekiel 40:5, which equaled 20.6 inches). The Roman cubit was approximately seventeen inches in length and was used to measure distance (John 21:8) and height (Rev. 21:17). A mile (Matt. 5:41) in Roman measure equaled a thousand paces (about 29.6 centimeters each) and was therefore equivalent to about 1,480 meters. In Near Eastern usage, the *stadion* (Luke 24:13; John 6:19) consisted of 7.5 *stadia*, or 3,263 cubits for each Roman mile. The fathom, mentioned in Acts 27:28 as a depth guide used by sailors, equaled 6 feet, or 2 meters.

Coins

Since the time of the Persians (sixth century BCE), the Near East had become increasingly reliant on a monetary economy (1 Chron. 29:7 and Neh. 7:70 mention the Persian daric). Minted coinage was introduced by the Lydians in the seventh century BCE and became widespread as both a form of payment and a visual expression of political power by the time of Alexander the Great. Standardization of weights and the certification of coinage size and weight with the royal Persian and later Alexandrian seal expedited commerce and facilitated trade between regions.

The fact that the Jews were allowed to coin money during the Persian period (fourth century BCE) is attested by the discovery of a number of small silver coins bearing the inscription "Yehud" (Judea). For large transactions and donations to the temple, the *mina* (727 grams) and the *talent* (43,620 grams) continued to be used (Ezra 2:69; 8:26), but the smaller shekel weight (11.4 grams) was more common in the marketplace. Most of these coins have been found within the geographic confines of Yehud, indicating that they were used for local transactions and would have only nominal value elsewhere.

The Greek rulers of Judea restricted the coining of money to their own mints, and during the Seleucid period of control after 198 BCE, coins appeared under Antiochus IV's mandate that included both a deified king and dedications to the Greek god Zeus. However, after the Maccabean Revolt (as they did during the Jewish revolts of 70 and 135 CE), the Jews once again began minting their own bronze and lead coins to proclaim their independence and to supplement the silver and gold coinage of the Hellenistic kingdoms. Greek inscriptions on these Jewish coins mention the Hasmonean kings Alexander Jannaeus and Jonathan and contain twin cornucopias as well as inscribed anchors and flowers.

Herod's mints in Tiberias and Jerusalem issued dated coins based on the Roman standard weights, and these coins refer to him as "king" while avoiding the depiction of human or divine images. The Roman procurators in Syria and Judea used imperial coinage supplemented by locally minted coins, which bore nonreligious symbols to prevent problems with the scrupulously monotheistic Jews. The silver *denarius* from Antioch or Caesarea and the *didrachma* of Tyre were commonly used to pay the annual temple tax. One of these was probably the coin mentioned in Mark 12:16, which is said to bear the likeness of Caesar.

By New Testament times a remarkable variety of Greek, Roman, and foreign coins were in circulation in Judea. This was due in part to the longevity of coins and the introduction of the coins issued to Roman soldiers, who brought them to Judea from all over the empire. Thus the thirty silver shekels given to Judas Iscariot (Matt. 26:15; equal to 120 *denarii* or four months wages) were most likely from Tyre or Antioch. Larger currency contained the image of the reigning emperor who had ordered it to be minted (Mark 12:16; Luke 20:24). These dated coins help archaeologists determine the chronology of levels within their excavations. When they are found embedded in particular levels or strata, they can aid in the determination of when walls were constructed or floors were laid.

The range of common coinage sizes and types runs from the Greek copper *lepton*, worth half a penny or 1/64 of a day's wage (the "widow's mite" in Mark 12:42; Matt. 5:26), to the shekel weight Greek silver *stater* (Matt. 17:27) and the Roman silver *denarius* (Matt. 22:20). The *denarius* in Matthew 20:2, however, was a smaller coin (worth about twenty cents), which apparently was the standard wage for day laborers. There was also a gold shekel worth fifteen silver shekels, equivalent to sixty days' labor. Larger weight currency included the *mina* (rendered in Luke 19:16–20 as a pound), worth a little over three months' wages, and the *talent*, worth more than fifteen years' labor (Matt. 25:15). The variations in the origin and value of these coins meant that many commercial transactions had to be facilitated by a "money changer" who could be found within the temple precincts (Matt. 21:12–13; John 2:14) or sitting in the city gate.

Because of the free use of many different currencies, money changers performed an essential service as middlemen amid the maze of coinage, exchanging foreign coins for the silver *didrachma* of Tyre that was used exclusively to pay the temple tax (*Ant.* 3.8.194–95; see the command in Exod. 30:13–15). A fee of between 4 and 8 percent was charged for this service. They also acted as bankers, paying interest on money left in their charge (Matt. 25:27). These commercial transactions and the sale of sacrificial animals within the outer precincts of this holiest of places contributed to an atmosphere more attuned to the secular marketplace. In the only instance of real anger exhibited by Jesus, he violently demonstrates his desire for reform of a bankrupt system and reacts to this greedy display and the collaboration of the priests with the Romans by "cleansing the temple" (Matt. 21:12–13; Mark 11:15–17; Luke 19:45–46; John 2:13–22).

Urban Industry and Professions

Skilled and service industries dominated the workforce in the cities of Judea and the larger Greco-Roman world. To publicly declare their power and perhaps to soften tensions in the region where they held authority, royal

Figure 5.14. Inscription from Corinth with the name "Erastus," probably the city treasurer mentioned in Romans 16:23

and administrative patrons spent great sums on public works projects, employing large numbers of masons and other skilled workmen. For example, in Corinth a Latin inscription of the mid-first century CE states, "Erastus laid this pavement at his own expense, in appreciation of his appointment as aedile [an official of the city]." This may be the same man mentioned in Romans 16:23 as city treasurer of Corinth.

The idea of patronage, of leaving a permanent monument to one's own service to the people, and the honor to be gained from beautifying a city motivated many such individual acts by the wealthy and powerful. The Herods were no exception. Herod the Great practically rebuilt Jerusalem and endowed temples and other buildings throughout Judea and the Near East. His sons followed his example, as the monumental structures emerging in excavations at Caesarea Maritima and Caesarea Philippi (Banias) attest. Josephus, taking note of this activity and the desire of the Herods to memorialize their rule, described Herod Agrippa as being "by nature very beneficent, and liberal in his gifts, and very ambitious to oblige people with such large donations; and he made himself very illustrious by the many chargeable presents he made them. He took delight in giving, and rejoiced in living with good reputation" (*Ant.* 19.7.328).

The Herods did produce a remarkable number of beautiful public buildings. However, the large numbers of workmen attracted to these projects were eventually left without employment when the building boom ended. Their discontent and lack of hope eventually contributed to the heightened passions that exploded in the Jewish revolt of 70 CE. While cottage industry was the typical pattern in the villages, in the cities large-scale finishing and manufacturing took place. Woolen thread, spun by village women, was woven into cloth on looms in the garment district of Jerusalem, near the Dung Gate (*J.W.* 5.8.331). Tailors were also available to cut and sew this cloth into finished garments (Matt. 11:8), and fullers could dye or bleach them (Mark 9:3). Pottery, tempered metal utensils (Isa. 54:16; Sir. 31:26), and weapons were all made and sold in the shops of Jerusalem (Luke 22:36).

The presence of tanners in major cities ensured the manufacture of leather goods (Acts 9:43), although the tanning process was conducted outside the walls because of the noxious smells and resulting residue. Paul learned the trade of tentmaking and leatherwork as a young man in Tarsus and continued to earn his living at this trade during his missionary journeys (1 Thess. 2:9; 1 Cor. 9:6). Working gave him a recognized status as well as the opportunity to associate with other urban craftsmen and thus make useful contacts wherever he went (Acts 18:3).

The wagonloads of grain transported from the surrounding villages were baked into bread (*Ant.* 15.9.309–10; Jer. 37:21), and butchers provided freshly slaughtered meat for the city's inhabitants. The large number of olive trees

There has been some speculation among scholars that the frequent mention of day laborers in the New Testament is an indication of an elite-oriented society in which small farmers are forced off their holdings (contrast Mark 10:29) and must resort to tenant farming or becoming day laborers. While the poor in the form of beggars are clearly evident (Mark 10:46; Luke 18:35), and it is not improbable that landlords took advantage of the pool of day laborers to assist with the harvest (Matt. 20:1), we do not have sufficient information to make broad statements about the overall economy of this period.

growing in Judea and the vicinity of Jerusalem (Acts 1:12) provided enough oil that it could be exported. Spices and ointments to anoint the body were commonly available (Mark 14:3–5; 16:1; John 12:3) and may have either been refined or prepared in Jerusalem (Sir. 49:1).

Village Economy

Rural life and economic activity were still based on the small family land holding and the cooperative efforts of the community (1 Cor. 9:10). Jesus frequently drew from simple agricultural scenes and pastoral activity to make his point in telling parables (the sower in Matt. 13:3–9; the reaper in John 4:36). John the Baptist speaks of Jesus himself as a diligent winnower who clears his threshing floor, gathers wheat into the granary, and burns the chaff (Luke 3:17). Produce from plots of land, often on terraced hillsides, fed the family, village, and nearby urban centers. A portion also went for taxes (*Ant.* 14.10.202–6), a burden that could impoverish small farmers in bad agricultural years. Some villages, such as Capernaum, located on the shore of the Sea of Galilee, based their economy and a portion of their diet on fishing (Luke 5:2–11; John 21:5–13).

Due to economic hardship and political changes, sections of the better land came into the hands of absentee landlords. On several occasions they gained ownership through the patronage of the Herods (*Ant.* 15.1.2) or the Romans. They used tenant farmers (Mark 12:1) or day laborers to work the land (Matt. 20:1) and employed stewards to manage the affairs of their estates (Luke 16:1). Like the growing population of unemployed craftsmen and laborers, these landless or poverty-stricken peasants also became discontented with their economic helplessness (Matt. 20:1–16; Mark 12:2–9). During the First Jewish Revolt in 69–70 CE, many of them formed a portion of the rebel forces. Depending upon the size of the village, some manufactured goods would have been produced by local craftsmen. Tiny, insignificant Nazareth (John 1:46) was probably pleased to have the services of the master carpenter Joseph and his son (Mark 6:3). Their workshop probably produced new baskets, chests, and furniture and repaired old ones. In addition, they would have been responsible for transporting and installing ceiling beams in most of the village homes (compare the work of teams of carpenters who helped rebuild Jerusalem's gates, Neh. 3:3–6). Local potters undoubtedly worked in these villages as well (Sir. 38:29), although the finer ware and Greek and Cappadocian imports would have been purchased in the cities.

Religious Life

The temple that was rebuilt in Jerusalem with the financial assistance of the Persian government (515 BCE) provided Jews with a renewed focus for their religion. Although temple worship and religious life were not perfect (Isa. 58:1–9; Mal. 2:1–3), a symbol of restoration was created that served communities of Jews throughout the Near East and beyond. During his reign, Herod created a much more magnificent structure encompassing the Persian-period structure, and for a time it must have been a source of pride and unity. Aside from the regular rites of sacrifice, the physical aspect of Jewish devotion to the temple is seen in regular pilgrimages (Acts 2:5) and in the payment of the annual temple tax by all adult males (Matt. 17:24). With religious rites and instruction in the hands of the priests and without a monarchy to rival their authority, the power of the priesthood grew to new heights. However, an increasing number of Jewish sects also grew out of their discontent with the priestly monopoly over the temple and over theological disagreements regarding such things as resurrection from the dead (*Ant.* 18.1.11–25).

Priests and Temple

Worship in the postexilic temple in Jerusalem was formalized with the Zadokite priesthood in strict control (Ezek. 44:15). Their role during the Second Temple period (515 BCE to 70 CE) was one of responsibility and regulation. For example, they were responsible for reinitiating and maintaining the intricacies of the sacrificial cult and ensuring that the religious calendar of festivals was celebrated. They probably controlled the orchestration of temple music and other lesser rites as well (1 Esd. 5:59–61). Levites who returned from the exile or who had remained in Judah during the Babylonian captivity were granted some responsibilities for the maintenance of the temple complex but were not allowed to participate in formal sacrificial activities (1 Chron. 16:24–27). In addition to performing their cultic duties, the priests also regulated certain aspects of life, such as marriage (Ezra 9–10) and the types of work activities that could be carried out on the Sabbath (Neh. 13:15–22).

In the Second Temple period it once again became customary to make pilgrimages to Jerusalem to attend the three major religious festivals: Passover (John 11:55), the Feast of Weeks (2 Macc. 12:31), and the Feast of Booths

(John 7:2; 2 Macc. 1:9). The temple treasury grew with the donations of these pilgrims and the annual temple tax, making it the wealthiest institution in the country. This wealth became an attractive target during the Seleucid period when Antiochus IV plundered the temple (1 Macc. 1:20–23; 2 Macc. 5:15–21). With so much cash coming into its coffers, the temple must have served as a bank, lending out sums to finance business and to stimulate the economy by increasing the amount of money in circulation.

The power and prestige of the temple and the priestly community eventually led to political involvement. The Hellenized high priest Jason helped to precipitate the Maccabean Revolt of 167 BCE with his introduction of Greek customs and acceptance of Antiochus IV's tribute demands (2 Macc. 4:7–17). Following the revolt, the Hasmoneans gained control of both the office of high priest (1 Macc. 14:17) and the secular leadership: "The Jews and their priests have resolved that Simeon should be their leader and high priest forever" (1 Macc. 14:41–45). Their control of these offices continued until Herod obtained the status of king from the Romans, and thereafter he handpicked the high priests to ensure his political control over them and the temple (*Ant.* 15.3.39–41).

Herod's attempt to control the priests and the people also included his construction of a newly designed and expanded temple over the one built by Zerubbabel in the Persian period. Construction began in Herod's eighteenth year as king and continued for forty-six years (20 BCE–26 CE; John 2:19–20).

Josephus, who saw this temple before its destruction, provides a detailed description of its structure and appearance (*Ant.* 15.11.380–425). A large area was cleared around the temple, and a huge, walled platform (approximately 1,440 feet long and 960 feet wide) was constructed as a base for the temple and its adjoining buildings. Massive blocks of limestone enclosed the slope, and the Antonia Tower was founded on the northwest corner to house a Roman garrison and to serve as the residence of the Roman procurator when he was in Jerusalem (*Ant.* 15.11.409). Gates were built in all four walls, with a huge staircase leading up to those on the south side.

Zechariah, the father of John the Baptist, was a member of one of the Levite clans. Because there were so many Levites in Jerusalem, lots were drawn to determine when during the year they would serve and what task each would perform. Zechariah was chosen by this process to burn incense in the temple (Luke 1:8–10).

The older shrine was preserved until the walls of the new building enclosed it (*Ant.* 15.11.389). Priests who had been trained as stonemasons then dismantled it. Although the new sanctuary was patterned after Solomon's temple, its Greco-Roman colonnades and the lavish use of gold-decorated roofs and columns displayed a Hellenistic influence. The holy site had been preserved and fortified, but the new temple was as much a testament to Herod's power and wealth as it was to the people's devotion to Yahweh.

Figure 5.15. Herod's Temple, the temple platform, and the Antonia Fortress (top right) are visible in this section of the 50:1 scale reproduction of the first-century CE city of Jerusalem now on display at the Israel Museum in Jerusalem.

Despite Herod's political motives in rebuilding the temple, the Jews accepted the structure itself, and it is described as a central feature in the religious life of the people in the New Testament. Its precincts included several distinct enclosures leading inward to the Holy of Holies. Only priests could enter the inner areas, but ritually pure Jews and their wives could enter the outer temple or porch (*Apion* 2.103–5). Women and those inflicted with infectious diseases, however, were not allowed in the area immediately outside the temple proper, where sacrifices were conducted on the altar.

Gentiles were restricted to the outermost part of the temple enclosure. Inscriptions that warned non-Jews, on pain of death, to proceed no further were written in Greek and Latin and set into the wall near the gate leading inward (*Ant.* 15.11.417). Excavators have discovered such an inscription dating to about 20 BCE, written in Greek. It was probably from Solomon's Porch (John 10:23) on the eastern side of this outer zone. Also in an area on the outskirts of the Temple Mount, where their activities could not pollute the purity of the inner courts, was the large area from which Jesus drove the money changers in Matthew 21:12–17.

Jewish Religious Factions

While there were many religious and political factions in Judea during the period from 200 BCE until the end of the first century CE, the four "philosophies" singled out by Josephus as the most influential were the Sadducees, the Pharisees, the Essenes, and the Zealots. Drawing most of their support from the wealthy and influential families of the community, the Sadducees sat on the Sanhedrin council and generally supported the policies of the Romans as a way of preventing conflict that could further ravage the nation (John 11:49–50). Although they were Hellenized in some of their manners of dress and custom, they rejected the use of anything other than the Pentateuch (Torah) in matters of law and favored harsher punishments than the other factions (*Ant.* 13.10.293–95). The Sadducees also rejected the idea of a resurrection of the dead, saying that the soul died with the body and that humans had complete free will to determine their own fate during life (*Ant.* 18.1.16; Mark 12:18).

Originating as a distinct group during the Hasmonean period, the Pharisees appear to have had a broader base of support among the people than the Sadducees. This may have been due to their advocacy for more lenient punishments for crimes (*Ant.* 13.10.294), their belief in a resurrection of the dead, and their belief in an eternal punishment of the wicked (*Ant.* 18.1.14–15; Matt. 23:6–8). One indication that this latter idea was fairly widespread among the people may be Martha's statement to Jesus that Lazarus would "rise again in the resurrection at the last day" (John 11:24). Jesus also uses the theme of

Figure 5.16. Remains of the Qumran settlement buildings

the resurrection of the dead in a statement dealing with the judgment of the righteous and the unrighteous in John 5:28–29.

The Pharisees also differed philosophically from the Sadducees in their acceptance of both free will and fate as factors influencing human lives (*Ant.* 18.1.13). Perhaps the most fundamental difference, however, between Pharisee and Sadducee lay in the former's equal acceptance of oral tradition and the Torah to interpret the law (*Ant.* 13.10.297–98). Jesus seems to take a similar position in Matthew 5:21–48, where he quotes several of the commandments from the Sinai code and then expands upon them. In this way he establishes himself as legitimate interpreter of the oral tradition on the issues of law and personal behavior.

On the other hand, in Mark 7:8, Jesus tells the Pharisees, "You leave the commandment of God, and hold fast the tradition of men." At first this statement seems to validate the Sadducean position regarding the sanctity of the Torah as the basis of interpretation of the law. His intent, however, was to point out the ways in which they had overburdened the original purpose of the law by demanding strict adherence to every aspect of ritual practice. In this case, a son could find a loophole in the law and deny his parents the support they were due under the law (Exod. 21:17) by declaring property or income to be *corban* and thus restricted as "an offering to God" (Mark 7:9–13).

The Pharisees are generally portrayed as the opponents of Jesus in the New Testament, but Paul continues to identify himself as a Pharisee after his conversion (Acts 23:6). At times, Jesus highlights the positive character of the Pharisees' teachings and strict adherence to the law, and in Matthew 23:3 he tells the disciples and the crowd to "do whatever they teach you and follow it." However, he then takes note of their hypocritical nature in not practicing what they themselves teach.

The Essenes are not mentioned by name in the New Testament, and thus our chief sources of information on them are Josephus and the scrolls produced by the Essene community at Qumran near the Dead Sea. Founded to protest the usurpation of the high priesthood by Jonathan Maccabaeus in 152 BCE, the Essenes separated themselves from what they considered to be the corrupt, impure nature of the temple's sacrificial cult. Like the Pharisees, they also believed in the resurrection and in rewards for a righteous life. Some chose to found separate settlements like the wilderness community at Qumran. According to the scrolls, the "Teacher of Righteousness" led them there so that they might live in the proper way, free from the contaminating influences of the less ritually pure Jews. This group is said to have lived a strict and regimented life, sharing their wealth with the community and practicing celibacy. The cemetery, however, does attest to the fact that females and children were a part of the community. Other groups of Essenes continued to live in cities like Jerusalem, where they engaged in their rituals of purification and performed private sacrifices (*Ant.* 18.1.18–22).

Josephus's "fourth philosophy," the Zealots, was founded in 6 CE by Judas of Galilee (Acts 5:37) in response to the imposition of a census by the Romans (*Ant.* 18.1.23–25). There were several other rebel groups in Judea, variously known as Zealots or *sicarii*, who participated in guerrilla tactics and the public assassination of officials (*J.W.* 7.8.262–70). They had no common agenda and can only be tied to Judas's ideas, not his leadership. It seems that the Zealots were closely affiliated with the Pharisees and their beliefs in upholding the Jewish law, and one, Simon, became a member of Jesus's group of disciples (Luke 6:15). However, they were more of an extremist group, violently demonstrating their opposition to Roman taxation and assuring the people that God would come to the aid of his faithful worshipers. Their fanaticism led them to engage in terrorist acts against the Romans, and they found it difficult to maintain alliances with other Jewish opposition groups. Eventually their revolutionary activities culminated in the ill-fated defense of Masada in 74 CE where their mass suicide ended the movement.

Sanhedrin

In addition to the priestly community and the various religious factions, there was another major religious body that influenced life in Jerusalem. This was the Sanhedrin, a council made up of seventy-one members and chaired by the high priest. This group is described in Mark 15:1 and Luke 19:47 as including "the chief priests and the scribes and the leaders of the people." Similar councils of elders were organized during the Hasmonean period and were charged with a variety of duties, including tax collection and dealing with legal disputes (*Ant.* 14.9.167–80). After Herod became king, however, he killed all but one of its members for putting him on trial for murder, and presumably he replaced them with men who could be controlled more easily (*Ant.* 14.9.175–76).

In the New Testament period council membership included both Sadducees and Pharisees (Acts 23:6). At that time the Sanhedrin's jurisdiction apparently extended only over religious matters. For instance, the members, chaired by the high priest Caiaphas, deliberated over what to do about Jesus after he raised Lazarus from the dead (John 11:47). Later, during his trial, the Sanhedrin consists of the chief priests, scribes, and elders, who hear the testimony of witnesses and question Jesus before turning him over to Pilate for trial (Matt. 26:59–68; Mark 14:53–15:1). Some within the Sanhedrin arrested Peter and John for preaching in the temple, and the whole council then questioned them, asking, "By what power or by what name did you do this?"

Figure 5.17. The partially reconstructed synagogue at Capernaum, built on the site of the synagogue where Jesus read the Scriptures

(Acts 4:7). Their power to punish the evangelists was limited by popular opinion, since these men had performed confirmed miraculous healings; thus they simply warned them not to speak in Jesus's name (Acts 4:18). The Sanhedrin also found it difficult to speak with a united voice against the teachings of the Christians since some members of the council, the Pharisees, believed in the resurrection of the dead, while the Sadducean members did not (Acts 23:7–9; *Ant.* 18.1.14, 16).

Synagogue Worship and Leadership

During the time that the Jerusalem temple was still in existence, the synagogue served as a secondary place of worship in Judea. Its primary function was to serve as a place of prayer and study of the sacred Scriptures. It originated in the Diasporic communities of Egypt and Mesopotamia and spread into Judea with the establishment of the Hasmonean kingdom. While we lack archaeological evidence to confirm this, it is likely that during the New Testament period a synagogue was built in every Judean village and city of any size. Many synagogues were indistinguishable from houses, so it is difficult to differentiate the two. Still, there are a few in Masada, Gamla, and Modi'in that have been identified as such by archaeologists because of their size, orientation, decoration, or inclusion of a *miqvah* (ritual bath).

Thus Jesus is said to have begun his ministry in the Nazareth synagogue (Luke 4:16–21) and later used the Capernaum synagogue to open his activities in the Galilee region (Mark 1:21–28). Throughout the rest of the ancient world, wherever there was a community of Jews, the synagogue provided a meeting place as well as a seat for the study of Scriptures and for nonsacrificial worship. Paul would have received his early Septuagint training in the synagogue in Tarsus before coming to Jerusalem for advanced Hebrew studies with the scholar Gamaliel (Acts 22:3). After his conversion to Christianity, he first went to the synagogues of the Diaspora before taking his message to the gentiles (Acts 18:1–6).

Sabbath worship in a synagogue varied from place to place but generally included the recitation of the *Shema'* (confession of faith, Deut. 6:4–5), Scripture readings from the Law and the Prophets, prayer, thanksgiving, and individual exhortations (Acts 13:15). Some of the rites associated with temple worship were also transferred to the synagogue after 70 CE, although not animal sacrifice. These places of worship were open to all people during services, and they did attract some pious Greeks interested in the moral teachings of the Jewish law (*J.W.* 7.3.45). Some converted to Judaism (Acts 13:43) or were among the group known as the "God-fearers" (Acts 13:16, 26, 43; 14:1). Many of these same people were later converted to Christianity by Paul and the other apostles (Acts 17:4).

Synagogue leadership was not in the hands of priests. Lay officials and a council of elders (Mark 5:22, *archisynagōgos*) directed synagogue worship, supervised maintenance of the building, and enforced the rules of the congregation. Sometimes an attendant or deputy aided the head of the synagogue (Luke 4:20). It was their responsibility to discipline members who disobeyed some aspect of the law (Luke 13:14). Paul's statement that he had five times received thirty-nine lashes at the hands of the Jews probably refers to synagogue justice (2 Cor. 11:24).

Presumably some early converts to Christianity maintained their membership in the local synagogue (James 2:2). Being Jews as well as Christians, they may have blended into the life of the congregation or perhaps shared the building with the Jews. The antagonism of some Jews against Christian converts (Acts 13:45; 14:2; 17:5–9) suggests, however, that this sort of arrangement did not last long, and Christians were probably forced to meet in private homes and their own house churches (Rom. 16:5; Acts 20:20).

These early Christian congregations worshiped according to the pattern set in Acts 2:42: "They devoted themselves to the apostles' teaching and fellowship, to the breaking of bread and the prayers." Various talents of the members were used in worship and in the governance of the community (Rom. 12:3–8). The letter to Titus 2:5–9 describes the qualities needed by elders and other leaders of the church, but for them to survive and prosper, all of the adult members were to serve diligently as good examples to each other and to the outside community.

The Jewish Revolt in 66–74 CE and the Bar Kochba revolt in 132–135 CE drastically changed the demographic character of Judea, with Jerusalem as well as many Jewish villages being destroyed. Many of the survivors were sold into slavery, and eventually the Roman emperor Hadrian banned Jews from living in Palestine. That meant in essence that Jewish belief and thought shifted to the Diaspora. The synagogue became the focal point for worship, and the local rabbi and the elders became the intellectual leaders for these scattered communities.

Christians were also heavily impacted by the occasional shifts in official policy toward various religious groups within the Roman Empire. Paul's experiences with the Roman legal system are a reflection of the concern Rome held for potentially troublesome religious movements (Acts 23:23–25:21). As a result, Christian worship often had to maintain a low profile while facing opposition from civil and religious authorities (Acts 14:19; Heb. 12:7; James 1:2–4). Some groups in Rome even resorted to seeking out hiding places in the burial chambers of the ancient catacombs to perform their rites. Their situation and their ability to worship publicly remained tenuous until the fourth century, when the emperor Constantine recognized Christianity as the official religion of the empire.

Discussion Questions

1. To what extent should the accounts in Josephus's works and the books of Maccabees be used to reconstruct the history of the intertestamental period?

2. How much of an influence was Hellenism on Judaism in the period from 300 BCE to 100 CE?

3. In what ways did Hellenism transform the architecture and social world of Judea?

4. Was the Maccabean Revolt a positive or a negative development for the Jews in Judea?

5. Why did Judaism split into rival parties of Sadducees, Pharisees, and Essenes?

6. Is there a separation between health care and religious belief in the New Testament period?

7. How did the Pax Romana and the establishment of international trade routes affect the economic life and transmission of ideas in the Levant?
8. Do Jesus's parables provide a useful glimpse into the everyday life of the people in first-century CE Judea?
9. Why were the Jews continuously in revolt against the Romans during the first and second centuries CE?

Glossary

anachronism: A detail or word in a story that does not fit the time period of the story itself but often reflects the time in which the story is composed (see Gen. 11:28; Exod. 13:17).

'Apiru: See *Habiru*.

Apocrypha: *See* **Deuterocanonical books**.

ark of the covenant: The gold-covered box created to house the Ten Commandments. It is carried by the Levites and is kept in the Holy of Holies of the tabernacle during the wilderness period.

ashlar masonry: A building practice that incorporates dressed stones that are worked smooth on all six sides in the manner of Canaanite-Phoenician architecture.

bullae: Hardened clay seal impressions that contain the emblem, symbol, or name of an official who has sent a sealed document.

canon: Those books designated by a faith community as Scripture and as the written standard for faith and practice.

carbon 14: Dating of organic remains using the computation of the atomic half-life of an isotope of carbon.

casemate wall: Two parallel walls connected by short perpendicular walls forming a series of rooms, or casemates, in a city wall; sometimes filled with rubble to strengthen the structure during a siege; also used for storage, as back rooms for houses built inside the city wall, or for warehouses and shops.

chiefdom: A political arrangement that unites, sometimes temporarily, an association of tribal groups under the leadership of a war chief, whose responsibility is to lead warriors into battle or deal with some other crisis; may be a step toward nationhood.

circumscription: A physical circumstance, such as natural resources or political encapsulation, that limits a group's ability to expand beyond its boundaries.

covenant: Any contractual agreement, but within the Bible a contractual agreement between Yahweh and the chosen people that promises them land and progeny in exchange for their exclusive worship and obedience.

Covenant Code: One of the seven bodies of Israelite law (Exod. 20:18–23:33), it is considered to be the oldest. It contains both casuistic (case law) and apodictic (command) forms of legal pronouncement.

covenant renewal ceremony: A ritual mentioned as occurring several times and led by Israelite leaders to reinforce the importance of the people's covenant with Yahweh (see Exod. 24:1–8; Josh. 24:1–28).

Day of Atonement: As described in Leviticus 16, this fast day is set aside for the annual cleansing of the tabernacle, including the Holy of Holies. It occurs on the tenth day of the seventh month. The ritual includes the transmission of Israelite sin onto the scapegoat, which is then driven into the wilderness (Lev. 16:7–10).

Dead Sea Scrolls: The scrolls discovered in the caves near Qumran on the northwestern shore of the Dead Sea beginning in 1947. These scrolls include the oldest copies of the Old Testament/Hebrew Bible books that have been found to date. They are dated to the period from the second century BCE to the first century CE.

Deuterocanonical books: The seven to fifteen books (e.g., 1 and 2 Maccabees, Judith, and Baruch) written between 300 BCE and 100 CE that are contained in the Septuagint (Greek) and the Vulgate (Latin) and are accepted as authoritative by Roman Catholics and the Eastern Orthodox but not by Protestants and Jews.

Deuteronomic Code: A late seventh-century BCE law code (Deut. 12–26) that updates some of the legal stipulations found in the earlier Covenant Code and that may be associated with Josiah's reform movement.

Deuteronomistic Historian: The name given to the unknown author(s) or editor(s) of the long and complex history found in Deuteronomy through 2 Kings called the Deuteronomistic History. This retrospective viewpoint is characterized by a strict moralism and a view of Israelite history in which the people continually fail to obey the covenant and therefore deserve Yahweh's punishment.

Diadochoi: The generals of Alexander the Great who succeeded him as ruler in the territories they had conquered together. Among the most important are Ptolemy in Egypt and Seleucus in Mesopotamia.

Diaspora: The scattering of the people of Israel and Judah throughout the countries and regions of the Near East following the destruction of Samaria (721 BCE) and Jerusalem (587 BCE). The term has subsequently been applied to the scattering of the Jews throughout the Roman Empire following the destruction of Jerusalem in 135 CE.

Diasporic Judaism: The life and practice of Jews outside of Palestine. The major impetus for the development of the **Diaspora** is the Babylonian exile. Diasporic Judaism found continued vitality among Jews who remained in the lands of the exile or who emigrated from Palestine in the centuries following the exile. This Diasporic Judaism was transmitted when some of the exiles returned to Judah (later Israel).

divination: The practice of using a variety of means and props to communicate with the gods or the dead.

emic: Describes an "insider" perspective based on being a part of a particular culture and time period.

enacted prophecy: A prophecy that includes an action by the prophet designed to attract attention and reinforce the message.

endogamy: The practice and policy of marrying only within one's own identifiable group.

Essenes: A Jewish sect described by Josephus and commonly thought to have built the Dead Sea community at **Qumran** and to have produced the **Dead Sea Scrolls**. They withdraw from active participation in the Jerusalem cult to protest the Hasmoneans' usurpation of the high priesthood in 152 BCE.

etic: Describes an "outsider" or observer process and is subject to the degree of objectivity that the researcher can apply to the text and to available archaeological data.

etiology: Story designed to explain the origin of an event, the background of a place name, or the basis for a tradition.

everlasting covenant: A pledge made by God to David in which Yahweh promises that there will always be a king of the line of David ruling in Jerusalem (2 Sam. 7:7–17).

exogamy: Marriage outside the kinship or social group.

Fertile Crescent: Region that begins on the eastern shore of the Mediterranean Sea and curves like an inverted quarter moon ending at the Persian Gulf; includes the major river valley cultures of Egypt and Mesopotamia; developed high civilizations around 3000 BCE.

four-room house: A style of house common during the Iron Age in Canaan; two-story dwelling with a ground floor made up of a long central room with a ceiling two stories high, surrounded by partitioned rooms on three sides.

glacis: Fortification of clay and stone slope built up against the face of a city wall and sometimes plastered over to present a smoother, less scalable surface.

Habiru (*'Apiru*): A term used in Mesopotamian and Egyptian texts for stateless persons. Sometimes the ethnic term "Hebrew" is identified with *Habiru*, but this is unlikely.

Hanukkah: The festival that commemorates the rededication of the temple in 165 BCE after the initial victory of the **Maccabees** over the Seleucid Greeks during the Maccabean Revolt.

Hasmonean kingdom: Independent Jewish kingdom founded in 142 BCE by Jonathan, brother of Judas Maccabeus. It lasts several tumultuous generations until the Roman general Pompey absorbs Judea into the Roman Empire in 63 BCE.

hegemony: A political situation in which a powerful nation or empire exercises extensive influence over the policies and actions of neighboring states.

Hellenistic culture: Following Alexander of Macedon's (Alexander the Great) conquest of the Near East, Greek cultural ideas, architecture, and philosophy are introduced in these regions creating a synthesis that contains aspects of both Greek and Near Eastern culture.

henotheism: Belief in the existence of many gods combined with the choice to worship only one of them.

ḥerem: An element of "holy war" in Israelite warfare that requires the complete destruction of all persons, animals, and property as a dedicatory sacrifice to Yahweh.

high place: *Bamah* (pl. *bamot*) in Hebrew; a hilltop used as a local shrine.

Holiness Code: A portion of the **Priestly source** (Lev. 17–26), probably dating to the fifth century BCE, that reiterates the command to "be holy" and is concerned with matters of **ritual purity**.

Holy of Holies: That holiest portion of the tabernacle, and later the Jerusalem temple, that houses the **ark of the covenant**. Only the high priest is allowed to enter this sacred precinct.

Hyksos: A label meaning "rulers of foreign lands" applied by the Egyptians to foreign invaders who conquered and ruled Lower (northern) Egypt during the Fifteenth Dynasty (ca. 1650–1550 BCE). They were expelled by Ahmose, the founder of the Eighteenth Dynasty, restoring Egyptian rule.

khirbet: Small rural settlement with a limited number of occupational strata. Contrast this with the "tell" of a city or town that has many strata.

Levant: Geographical term describing the lands that border the Mediterranean Sea from modern Turkey to Egypt.

levir: The brother or nearest male relative who has the obligation to impregnate the childless widow of his deceased brother or relative (so that she will have a child to continue the line of her late husband) and to provide for her needs.

levirate obligation: A legal arrangement based on the obligation of the brother or nearest male relative to provide a deceased kinsman with an heir (see Gen. 38:1–11). The brother or relative is required to impregnate the widow and to provide for her needs. The resulting child is legally considered the child of the dead man. Procreation is required, but an actual marriage tie is not necessary.

Maccabees: Based on the name of their leader, Judas Maccabeus, the term applies to the Hasmonean rebels who revolted against Seleucid rule in Judea in the second century BCE.

Masoretes: Jewish scholars who in about 500 CE added a vowel pointing system to the Hebrew text of the Bible in order to facilitate its pronunciation. They also developed procedures to detect and prevent as many scribal errors as possible as they copied the manuscripts of the Hebrew text.

midrash: Taking its cue from explanations and comments within the biblical text, the rabbinic midrash provides commentary on the Hebrew Bible, with particular emphasis on Torah law and teaching. Its purpose is to fill in interpretive gaps in the text left by the biblical writers.

Mishnah: Second-century CE Jewish compilation of sixty-three tractates or treatises of written commentaries on the Torah (Pentateuch); known as the "oral Torah"; represents the consensus of rabbinic opinion on how the laws of the Pentateuch related to aspects of everyday life in their time such as agriculture, marriage, and **ritual purity**.

Mithraism: A religion and an offshoot of Persian religion from the first century BCE to the fourth century CE; adopted by Roman legionnaires and spread by soldiers, merchants, and traveling philosophers.

ostracon (pl. **ostraca**): Broken piece of pottery used to record a message or inscription.

pastoralism/pastoral nomadism: A form of human activity based on seasonal movement of flocks of sheep and goats from one pasture area to another. This lifestyle is described in the ancestral narratives.

Pharisees: A Jewish sect described by Josephus and the New Testament, known for their beliefs in an afterlife and the acceptance of both oral tradition and the canonical Scriptures as authoritative.

Philo of Alexandria: A first-century CE Jewish philosopher and teacher who composed treatises on the law and on the life of Moses, working from the

Greek translation of the Pentateuch (**Septuagint**). His familiarity with and use of Greek thought provides insights into the intellectual and religious life of Greek-speaking Jews during the Hellenistic and early Roman imperial periods.

phylactery (Hebrew *tefillin*): A black leather box containing four passages of Scripture attached to the forehead and the left arm by leather straps; based on injunctions in Exodus 13:9 and Deuteronomy 6:8 to keep the law constantly in the mind and heart; worn by devout men in the time of Jesus.

Priestly source: According to source-critical scholars, the Priestly writers represent one of the postexilic editors of the biblical text. Their contribution is evident primarily in sections dealing with sacred ritual and the role of the priestly community (in particular in Exodus, Lev. 1–16, and Numbers).

Pseudepigrapha: Sixty-five books dating to the Hellenistic and Roman periods, they are denied a place in the canon because of their fictional commentary and generally unacceptable theological ideas. These books include *Testaments of the Twelve Patriarchs*, *1 Enoch*, *Jubilees*, and *Testament of Job*.

Ptolemies: Descended from Alexander of Macedon's general Ptolemy, this dynasty of rulers of Hellenistic Egypt held sway until the death of Cleopatra VII in 30 BCE. They competed with the Seleucid rulers for control of Syro-Palestine and ultimately lost control of the area after the battle of Panias in 200 BCE.

Qumran: A settlement at the northwestern end of the Dead Sea believed to have been established by **Essenes** and closely associated with the **Dead Sea Scrolls**.

rabbinic Judaism: A form of Judaism that emerged with the destruction of the temple in 70 CE and the scattering of the Jewish people. Its primary premise is that Moses was given both a written and an oral form of the law. Between 200 and 600 CE, this movement produced a number of interpretative works (**Mishnah** and **Talmuds**) that helped to shape Judaism throughout the Middle Ages.

ritual purity: The steps taken to transform persons or objects into a "clean" or "pure" religious state. Impurity can be caused by contact with the dead or the diseased, through bodily emissions, or through eating certain forbidden foods. Some individuals, like the high priest, must maintain an even higher level of ritual purity in order to carry out sacred duties.

Sadducees: A Jewish sect described by Josephus and the New Testament that dominated the ritual activity of the Jerusalem temple during the period from 200 BCE to 70 CE. They did not believe in an afterlife and only accepted the canonical Scriptures as authoritative.

Sanhedrin: The supreme council in Jerusalem made up of the most powerful and influential leaders and active during the first century CE.

satrap: Provincial governor ruling one of the segments of the Persian Empire.

Sea Peoples: A term used for groups of invaders who, about 1200 BCE, attacked many of the population centers along the eastern Mediterranean coast, weakening both the Egyptian and Hittite Empires and destroying the port of Ugarit. Some, later known as the Philistines, settled along the southern coastal plain of Canaan.

Second Temple period: The period in Jewish history following the construction of the Second Temple in Jerusalem (515 BCE) until the destruction of Herod's temple in Jerusalem in 70 CE by the Romans.

Seleucids: Rulers of the successor kingdom of "Asia" including Mesopotamia, Syria, and, after 200 BCE, Judea. They were successors of Seleucus, one of Alexander of Macedon's generals (*see* **Diadochoi**).

Septuagint: The Greek translation of the Hebrew Bible by the Jews of Alexandria, Egypt, in the fourth through second centuries BCE, which contains the Apocrypha (*see* **Deuterocanonical books**) and is abbreviated LXX for the seventy scribes thought to have produced it.

Shasu: Tribes of lawless nomadic herders and quarrelsome sedentary farmers mentioned in Egyptian records, who inhabited land from the eastern Delta region to Gaza between 1500 and 1150 BCE.

Sheol: Hebrew word meaning "pit," the abode of the dead. According to the Old Testament/Hebrew Bible, both the righteous and the wicked go there after death. There is no indication in the Hebrew tradition of punishment or reward and little indication of anything that happens in Sheol. Older translations of the Bible often translate *Sheol* as "hell," but that is incorrect.

Shephelah: The low hills in western Canaan separating the coastal plains from the central hill country to the east.

sicarii: A group of Jewish rebels who emerged during the turbulent first century CE. They used guerrilla tactics and carried out brazen assassinations of Roman sympathizers. During the First Jewish Revolt they captured Masada and were besieged by a Roman army until they committed mass suicide rather than be captured.

stele: Inscribed monument usually carved on a stone or pillar and erected to commemorate a military victory or other important event.

stratigraphy: In archaeology, the succession of occupation layers revealed by excavations that can be used for dating artifacts.

stratum: A distinct layer of occupation within the mound of a **tell**.

superscription: The rubrics of instruction found at the beginning of many of the Psalms that detail instrumentation or the tune to be used in performing the psalm.

synagogue: A gathering place for Jewish worship, study, and the public reading of the Scriptures. First- and second-century CE archaeological evidence has been found in Judea and the Galilee. Both Jesus (Matt. 4:23) and Paul (Acts 9:20) are described as teaching in the synagogues during their ministries.

tabernacle (tent of meeting): The portable sanctuary created during the wilderness wandering to house the **ark of the covenant** and to serve as the place for sacrificial offerings (Exod. 25–31; 35–40).

Talmud: The rabbinic schools of thought that flourished in Babylonia between 200 and 600 CE focused on an intensive study and argumentation over the interpretation of the commentary on law known as the **Mishnah**. Their comments and stories about the rabbis who produced them form the corpus of the Babylonian Talmud.

tell(s): An English word derived from Arabic, referring to an artificial hill that is created by the successive layers or strata of occupation on a site. Extensive layers suggest an ancient town or even a city rather than a rural village (*see* **khirbet**).

tent of meeting: *See* **tabernacle**.

teraphim: The image of a household god or patron spirit that would represent the good fortune of the household and would be inherited by the heir.

theocratic: A form of government led by religious leaders and whose laws are based on religious principles.

theodicy: An explanation for God's actions; most often found in the words of the prophets.

theophany: The appearance of God to a human being.

transhumance: Seasonal herding by select members of a family on pastures both near and far from their settlement, while the majority of the population is occupied primarily with agriculture.

Zealots: A militant, nationalistic Jewish sect described by Josephus that opposed Roman occupation of Judea.

Annotated and Select Bibliography

Any serious student of the world portrayed in the Bible should seek out additional resources to further their study. Below is an annotated list of some additional resources as well as a listing of those works that I have found particularly helpful in the creation of this edition. This short guide is arranged in categories of reference works and then more specific items to assist you to obtain several levels of information from the simplest to the most complex.

Study Bibles

The study Bible is a good solution for those who want to have additional information available with the notes on each page providing quick insights and historical data. Those recommended include:

The Catholic Study Bible (NABRE). Oxford: Oxford University Press, 2011.
The HarperCollins Study Bible (NRSV). San Francisco: HarperOne, 2006.
Jewish Study Bible (NJPS). Oxford: Oxford University Press, 2004.
New Interpreter's Study Bible (NRSV). Nashville: Abingdon, 2003.
New Oxford Annotated NRSV Bible with Apocrypha. 3rd ed. Oxford: Oxford University Press, 2001.
Oxford Study Bible (REB). Oxford: Oxford University Press, 1992.

Bible Atlases

In order to obtain more information on historical geography or about a particular site mentioned in the Bible, a Bible atlas is an excellent resource.

An atlas can provide much more commentary on the topographical and climatic character of Syria-Palestine and the ancient Mediterranean world. Bible atlases come in a variety of price ranges and formats. For instance, the *Hammond Atlas of the Bible Lands* (New York: Hammond, 2008) and the *Bible Atlas and Companion* (Uhrichsville, OH: Barbour, 2008) are inexpensive but serviceable atlases. Slightly more expensive, but also in paperback, is the *Oxford Bible Atlas*, 4th ed. (Oxford: Oxford University Press, 2009). The model for most modern reference atlases is Y. Aharoni, M. Avi-Yonah, and A. Rainey, *The Macmillan Bible Atlas*, 3rd ed. (New York: Macmillan, 1993).

Several atlases, like *The Harper Atlas of the Bible* (San Francisco: Harper-One, 2008), C. Rasmussen, *Zondervan Atlas of the Bible* (Grand Rapids: Zondervan, 2009), and A. Rainey and R. S. Notley, *The Sacred Bridge* (Jerusalem: Carta, 2006), have spectacular color pictures and excellent discussions of geography. However, they are all fairly expensive, and this expense must be weighed against the need to purchase other resources. Bible dictionaries and commentaries do deal at least somewhat with biblical geography and usually contain a set of color maps.

For more detailed study of specific aspects of historical geography, the following resources would be helpful:

Brisco, Thomas C., and V. Brisco. *Holman Bible Atlas: A Complete Guide to the Expansive Geography of Biblical History*. Nashville: Broadman & Holman, 1999.

DeVries, LaMoine F. *Cities of the Biblical World*. Peabody, MA: Hendrickson, 1997.

Dorsey, D. A. *The Roads and Highways of Ancient Israel*. Baltimore: Johns Hopkins University Press, 1991.

Hutton, Jeremy. "'Bethany beyond the Jordan' in Text, Tradition, and Historical Geography." *Biblica* 89 (2008): 305–28.

Kallai, Zecharia. *Historical Geography of the Bible: The Tribal Territories of Israel*. Jerusalem: Magnes, 1986.

Matthews, Victor H. "Back to Bethel: Geographic Reiteration in Biblical Narrative." *JBL* 128 (2009): 151–67.

One-Volume Bible Dictionaries

The single-volume Bible dictionary is an excellent resource to obtain thumbnail sketches on every person or place mentioned in the Bible. Those recommended are:

Baker Illustrated Bible Dictionary. Grand Rapids: Baker Books, 2013.

Eerdmans Dictionary of the Bible. Grand Rapids: Eerdmans, 2000.

HarperCollins Bible Dictionary. Rev. ed. San Francisco: HarperOne, 2011.

Holman Illustrated Bible Dictionary. Rev. ed. Nashville: Holman, 2003.

Multivolume Bible Dictionaries

A multivolume reference work will be the most comprehensive and the most expensive of these study aids. There are currently two excellent multivolume dictionaries available, although *The Anchor Bible Dictionary* in six volumes (New York: Doubleday, 1992) is now dated. More up-to-date is *The New Interpreter's Dictionary of the Bible*, 5 vols. (Nashville: Abingdon, 2006–9). Both are also available on CD-ROM. Most student questions can be answered by using either of these dictionaries, and the bibliographies at the end of most articles are particularly helpful for further study of specific items.

Archaeology

For those who wish to gain a more detailed understanding of archaeological methods and the results of recent excavations in biblical lands, there are a number of reference works and monographs to choose from. For the beginner, recommended are:

Benjamin, Don C. *Stones and Stories: An Introduction to Archaeology and the Bible*. Minneapolis: Fortress, 2009.

Ben Tor, A. *The Archaeology of Ancient Israel*. New Haven: Yale University Press, 1994.

Laughlin, J. *Archaeology and the Bible*. London: Routledge, 1999.

Comprehensive, but dated, reference works include:

Levy, T. E., ed. *The Archaeology of Society in the Holy Land*. London: Continuum, 1998.

Meyers, Eric, ed. *Oxford Encyclopedia of Archaeology in the Near East*. 5 vols. Oxford: Oxford University Press, 1997.

Stern, Ephraim, ed. *The New Encyclopedia of Archaeological Excavations in the Holy Land*. Jerusalem: Carta, 1993.

For the purposes of further study and as a reflection of the works consulted in the production of this new edition, the following monographs and articles are recommended:

Bloch-Smith, Elizabeth, and Beth A. Nakhai. "A Landscape Comes to Life: The Iron Age I." *NEA* 62 (1999): 62–92, 101–27.

Callaway, Joseph A. "A Visit with Ahilud." *BAR* 9, no. 5 (1983): 42–53.

Charlesworth, James H., ed. *Jesus and Archaeology*. Grand Rapids: Eerdmans, 2006.

Crossan, John D., and Jonathan L. Reed. *Excavating Jesus: Beneath the Stones, Behind the Texts*. San Francisco: HarperCollins, 2001.

Currid, James D. *Doing Archaeology in the Land of the Bible: A Basic Guide*. Grand Rapids: Baker, 1999.

Dever, William G. *What Did the Biblical Writers Know and When Did They Know It? What Archaeology Can Tell Us about the Reality of Ancient Israel*. Grand Rapids: Eerdmans, 2001.

Finkelstein, Israel. *The Archaeology of the Settlement of Israel*. Jerusalem: Israel Exploration Society, 1988.

Hoffmeier, James K. *Israel in Egypt*. New York: Oxford University Press, 1997.

Jeremias, J. *Jerusalem in the Time of Jesus*. Philadelphia: Fortress, 1969.

Kenyon, Kathleen. *Digging Up Jerusalem*. New York: Praeger, 1974.

Laughlin, John C. H. "On the Convergence of Texts and Artifacts: Using Archaeology to Teach the Hebrew Bible." In *Between Text and Artifact: Integrating Archaeology in Biblical Studies Teaching*, edited by Milton C. Moreland, 115–32. Leiden: Brill, 2004.

Levy, Thomas E., ed. *The Archaeology of Society in the Holy Land*. New York: Continuum, 1998.

Magness, Jodi. *The Archaeology of Qumran and the Dead Sea Scrolls*. Grand Rapids: Eerdmans, 2002.

Mazar, Amihai. *Archaeology of the Land of the Bible, 10,000–586 BCE*. New York: Doubleday, 1990.

Meshorer, Yaakov. *Ancient Jewish Coinage*. New York: Amphora, 1982.

Meyers, Eric M., ed. *The Oxford Encyclopedia of Archaeology in the Near East*. 5 vols. New York: Oxford University Press, 1997.

Rast, Walter E. *Through the Ages in Palestinian Archaeology*. Philadelphia: Trinity, 1992.

Stern, Ephraim. *Archaeology of the Land of the Bible: The Assyrian, Babylonian, and Persian Periods (732–332 BCE)*. New York: Doubleday, 2001.

———. *The Material Culture of the Land of the Bible in the Persian Period 538–332 BC*. Warminster, UK: Aris & Phillips, 1982.

Vaughn, Andrew G., and Ann E. Killebrew, eds. *Jerusalem in Bible and Archaeology*. Atlanta: Society of Biblical Literature, 2003.

Wilkinson, John. *Jerusalem as Jesus Knew It: Archaeology as Evidence*. London: Thames & Hudson, 1978.

Collections of Ancient Near Eastern Texts in Translation

Throughout this volume you will encounter references to ancient texts that either parallel or provide comparative data to biblical narratives or legal statements. The following monographs and multivolume reference works are sources for these translated texts, and serious students should consider obtaining some of them or spending time with them in the library.

Avigad, Nahman. "The Epitaph of a Royal Steward from Siloam Village." *IEJ* 3, no. 3 (1953): 137–52.

Coogan, Michael. "Life in the Diaspora: Jews at Nippur in the Fifth Century BC." *BA* 37 (1974): 6–12.

Coogan, Michael, and Mark Smith. *Stories from Ancient Canaan*. 2nd ed. Louisville: Westminster John Knox, 2012.

Dalley, Stephanie. *Myths from Mesopotamia*. Oxford: Oxford University Press, 2009.

Gabbay, Uri. "Dance in Textual Sources from Ancient Mesopotamia." *NEA* 66, no. 3 (2003): 103–4.

Greenstein, Edward L., and David Marcus. "The Akkadian Inscription of Idrimri." *JANES* 8 (1976): 59–96.

Hallo, William W., and K. Lawson Younger Jr., eds. *The Context of Scripture*. 3 vols. New York: Brill, 1997–2002.

Lichtheim, Miriam. *Ancient Egyptian Literature: A Book of Readings*. 3 vols. Berkeley: University of California Press, 1975–80.

Matthews, Victor H., and Don C. Benjamin. *Old Testament Parallels: Laws and Stories from the Ancient Near East*. 3rd ed. Mahwah, NJ: Paulist, 2006.

Moran, William L. *The Amarna Letters*. Baltimore: Johns Hopkins University Press, 1992.

Na'aman, Nadav. "The Contribution of Royal Inscriptions for a Re-evaluation of the Book of Kings as a Historical Source." *JSOT* 82 (1999): 3–17.

Nissinen, Marti. *Prophets and Prophecy in the Ancient Near East*. Atlanta: Society of Biblical Literature, 2003.

Porten, Bezalel. *The Elephantine Papyri in English: Three Millennia of Cross-Cultural Continuity and Change*. Leiden: Brill, 1996.

Pritchard, James. *Ancient Near Eastern Texts Relating to the Old Testament*. Princeton: Princeton University Press, 1969.

Roth, Martha T. *Law Collections from Mesopotamia and Asia Minor*. 2nd ed. Atlanta: Scholars Press, 1997.

Histories of Israel and the Ancient Near East

Turning now to monographs and reference works that assist with further study of the history of Israel in its ancient Near Eastern context, the following are grouped by time period and are among the works consulted in the creation of this new edition. You will note that many of them are collections of articles on particular time periods and that collections of this type are becoming more typical rather than the creation of comprehensive histories that quickly are superseded by new discoveries.

Coogan, Michael D., ed. *The Oxford History of the Biblical World*. Oxford: Oxford University Press, 1998.

Hayes, John H., and J. Maxwell Miller. *Israelite and Judean History*. 2nd ed. Louisville: Westminster John Knox, 2006.

Matthews, Victor H. *A Brief History of Ancient Israel*. Louisville: Westminster John Knox, 2002.

———. *Studying the Ancient Israelites: A Guide to Sources and Methods*. Grand Rapids: Baker Academic, 2007.

Moore, Megan B., and Brad E. Kelle. *Biblical History and Israel's Past: The Changing Study of the Bible and History*. Grand Rapids: Eerdmans, 2011.

Redford, Donald B. *Egypt, Canaan, and Israel in Ancient Times*. Princeton: Princeton University Press, 1992.

Snell, Daniel C. *Life in the Ancient Near East*. New Haven: Yale University Press, 1997.

Histories of the Exilic and Persian Periods

Albertz, Rainer. *Israel in Exile: The History and Literature of the Sixth Century BCE*. Atlanta: Society of Biblical Literature, 2003.

Berquist, Jon L., ed. *Approaching Yehud: New Approaches to the Study of the Persian Period*. Atlanta: Society of Biblical Literature, 2007.

———. *Judaism in Persia's Shadow: A Social and Historical Approach*. Minneapolis: Fortress, 1995.

Betlyon, John W. "A People Transformed: Palestine in the Persian Period." *NEA* 68 (2005): 4–58.

Briant, Pierre. *From Cyrus to Alexander: A History of the Persian Empire*. Winona Lake, IN: Eisenbrauns, 2002.

Carter, C. E. *The Emergence of Yehud in the Persian Period: A Social and Demographic Study*. JSOTSup 294. Sheffield: Sheffield Academic Press, 1999.

Coggins, Richard J. "The Origins of the Jewish Diaspora." In *The World of Ancient Israel*, edited by Ronald Clements, 163–81. Cambridge: Cambridge University Press, 1989.

Hoglund, Kenneth. *Achaemenid Imperial Administration in Syria-Palestine and the Missions of Ezra and Nehemiah*. Atlanta: Scholars Press, 1992.

Kalimi, Isaac, ed. *New Perspectives on Ezra-Nehemiah: History and Historiography*. Text, Literature, and Interpretation. Winona Lake, IN: Eisenbrauns, 2012.

Kuhrt, Amélie. "The Cyrus Cylinder and Achaemenid Imperial Policy." *JSOT* 25 (1983): 83–97.

Levin, Yigal, ed. *Judah and Its Neighbours in the Persian and Early Hellenistic Periods*. New York: T&T Clark, 2007.

Lipschits, Oded, Gary N. Knoppers, and Rainer Albertz, eds. *Judah and the Judeans in the Fourth Century BCE*. Winona Lake, IN: Eisenbrauns, 2007.

Lipschits, Oded, and Manfred Oeming, eds. *Judah and the Judeans in the Persian Period*. Winona Lake, IN: Eisenbrauns, 2006.

Yamauchi, Edwin M. *Persia and the Bible*. Grand Rapids: Baker, 1990.

Zadok, Ran. *The Jews in Babylonia during the Chaldean and Achaemenian Periods*. Haifa: University of Haifa Press, 1979.

Histories of the Intertestamental and New Testament Periods

Collins, John J. *Between Athens and Jerusalem: Jewish Identity in the Hellenistic Diaspora*. New York: Crossroad, 1983.

Feldman, Louis H., and Galia Hata, eds. *Josephus, the Bible, and History*. Detroit: Wayne State University Press, 1989.

Grabbe, Lester L. *A History of the Jews and Judaism in the Second Temple Period*. Vol. 1, *Yehud: A History of the Persian Province of Judah*. New York: T&T Clark, 2004.

———. *Judaism from Cyrus to Hadrian*. 2 vols. Minneapolis: Fortress, 1992.

Harrison, Robert. "Hellenization in Syria-Palestine: The Case of Judea in the Third Century BCE." *BA* 57 (1994): 98–108.

Jonker, Louis, ed. *Texts, Contexts and Readings in Postexilic Literature: Explorations into Historiography and Identity Negotiations in Hebrew Bible and Related Texts*. Tübingen: Mohr Siebeck, 2011.

Koester, Helmut. *Introduction to the New Testament: History, Culture, and Religion of the Hellenistic Age*. 2 vols. Philadelphia: Fortress, 1980.

Levine, Lee I. *Judaism and Hellenism in Antiquity: Conflict or Confluence?* Peabody, MA: Hendrickson, 1998.

Malina, Bruce J. *Christian Origins and Cultural Anthropology*. Atlanta: John Knox, 1986.

———. *The New Testament World: Insights from Cultural Anthropology*. Atlanta: John Knox, 1981.

Meeks, Wayne A. *The First Urban Christians: The Social World of the Apostle Paul*. New Haven: Yale University Press, 1983.

Schäfer, Peter. *The History of the Jews in the Greco-Roman World*. New York: Routledge, 2003.

Smallwood, E. Mary. *The Jews under Roman Rule: From Pompey to Diocletian*. Atlanta: SBL Press, 2015.

Tcherikover, Victor. *Hellenistic Civilization and the Jews*. New York: Atheneum, 1970.

Since so much of this volume is concerned with discussing various aspects of the social world and domestic life depicted in the biblical narrative and ancient Near Eastern texts, the following group of studies is useful for those who wish to learn more about architecture, aspects of honor and shame, commercial activity, and family life.

Bunimovitz, Shelomoh, and Avraham Faust. "Ideology in Stone: Understanding the Four-Room House." *BAR* 28, no. 4 (2002): 33–41, 59–60.

Clark, Douglas R. "Bricks, Sweat and Tears: The Human Investment in Constructing a 'Four-Room' House." *NEA* 66, no. 1/2 (2003): 34–43.

Cohen, Shaye J. D., ed. *The Jewish Family in Antiquity*. Atlanta: Scholars Press, 1993.

Court, John, and Kathleen Court. *The New Testament World*. Englewood Cliffs, NJ: Prentice-Hall, 1990.

deSilva, David A. *Honor, Patronage, Kinship and Purity: Unlocking New Testament Culture*. Downers Grove, IL: InterVarsity, 2000.

Green, Joel B., and Lee M. McDonald, eds. *The World of the New Testament*. Grand Rapids: Baker Academic, 2013.

Hanson, Kenneth C., and Douglas E. Oakman. *Palestine in the Time of Jesus: Social Structures and Social Conflicts*. Minneapolis: Fortress, 1998.

King, Philip J., and Lawrence E. Stager. *Life in Biblical Israel*. Louisville: Westminster John Knox, 2001.

Magness, Jodi. *Stone and Dung, Oil and Spit: Jewish Daily Life in the Time of Jesus*. Grand Rapids: Eerdmans, 2011.

Matthews, Victor H. "Entrance Ways and Threshing Floors: Legally Significant Sites in the Ancient Near East." *FEH* 19 (1987): 25–40.

Matthews, Victor H., and Don C. Benjamin. *Social World of Ancient Israel, 1250–587 BCE*. Peabody, MA: Hendrickson, 1993.

McNutt, Paula. *Reconstructing the Society of Ancient Israel*. Louisville: Westminster John Knox, 1999.

Meyers, Carol. *Discovering Eve: Ancient Israelite Women in Context*. New York: Oxford University Press, 1991.

Nakhai, Beth A. "Contextualizing Village Life in the Iron Age I." In *Israel in Transition: From Late Bronze II to Iron IIa (c. 1250–850 BCE)*. Vol. 1, *The Archaeology*, edited by Lester L. Grabbe, 121–37. New York: T&T Clark, 2008.

Osiek, Carolyn. *What Are They Saying about the Social Setting of the New Testament?* New York: Paulist Press, 1984.

Osiek, Carolyn, and David L. Balch. *Families in the New Testament World*. Louisville: Westminster John Knox, 1997.

Perdue, Leo G., Joseph Blenkinsopp, John J. Collins, and Carol Meyers. *Families in Ancient Israel*. Louisville: Westminster John Knox, 1997.

Reinhardt, Wolfgang, and Andrew Warren. "The Population Size of Jerusalem and the Numerical Growth of the Jerusalem Church." In *The Book of Acts in Its Palestinian Setting*, edited by Richard Bauckham, 237–65. Grand Rapids: Eerdmans, 1995.

Reviv, Hanoch. *The Elders in Ancient Israel*. Jerusalem: Magnes, 1989.

Roetzel, Calvin J. *The World That Shaped the New Testament*. Atlanta: John Knox, 1985.

Rousseau, John J., and Rami Arav. *Jesus and His World*. Minneapolis: Fortress, 1995.

Stager, Lawrence E. "The Archaeology of the Family in Ancient Israel." *BASOR* 260 (1985): 1–35.

Also of importance in any study of the ancient world is to examine developments in science and technology. Studies on health care, industrial and agricultural implements and methods, and horticulture are found in this collection.

Avalos, Hector. "Ancient Medicine: In Case of Emergency, Contact Your Local Prophet." *BRev* 11, no. 3 (1995): 27–35, 48.

———. *Health Care and the Rise of Christianity*. Peabody, MA: Hendrickson, 1999.

Avigad, Nahman. "Jerusalem Flourishing—A Craft Center for Stone, Pottery, and Glass." *BAR* 9, no. 6 (1983): 48–65.

Biggs, Robert D. "Medicine, Surgery, and Public Health in Ancient Mesopotamia." In *Civilizations of the Ancient Near East*, edited by Jack M. Sasson, 1911–24. Peabody, MA: Hendrickson, 1995.

Borowski, Oded. *Agriculture in Iron Age Israel*. Winona Lake, IN: Eisenbrauns, 1987.

Hepper, F. Nigel. *Baker Encyclopedia of Bible Plants*. Grand Rapids: Baker, 1992.

Kinnier Wilson, J. V. "Medicine in the Land and Times of the Old Testament." In *Studies in the Period of David and Solomon and Other Essays*, edited by T. Ishida, 337–65. Winona Lake, IN: Eisenbrauns, 1982.

McNutt, Paula. *The Forging of Israel: Iron Technology, Symbolism, and Tradition in Ancient Society*. Sheffield: Sheffield Academic Press, 1990.

Muhly, James D. "How Iron Technology Changed the Ancient World—And Gave the Philistines a Military Edge." *BAR* 8, no. 6 (1982): 40–54.

Powell, Mark. "Weights and Measures." In *Anchor Bible Dictionary*, edited by David Noel Freedman, 6:897–908. New York: Doubleday, 1992.

Stieglitz, Robert R. "Long-Distance Seafaring in the Ancient Near East." *BA* 47, no. 3 (1984): 134–42.

Walsh, Carey E. *The Fruit of the Vine: Viticulture in Ancient Israel*. Winona Lake, IN; Eisenbrauns, 2000.

Zias, Joseph. "Current Archaeological Research in Israel: Death and Disease in Ancient Israel." *BA* 54 (1991): 146–59.

Zohary, Michael. *Plants of the Bible*. Cambridge: Cambridge University Press, 1982.

The history of the Levant has been marked by almost continuous warfare as the super powers in Egypt and Mesopotamia attempted to gain access to the major trade routes and control the area of Syria-Palestine. The royal annals of kings in the Bible and elsewhere are filled with details about methods of warfare and their effect on the peoples who faced the brunt of invading armies. Here is a representative sample of works dealing with this important topic.

Bleibtreu, Erika. "Grisly Assyrian Record of Torture and Death." *BAR* 17, no. 1 (1991): 53–61, 75.

Graham, Philip. "Weapons and Warfare in Ancient Syria-Palestine." In *Near Eastern Archaeology: A Reader*, edited by Suzanne Richard, 184–92. Winona Lake, IN: Eisenbrauns, 2003.

Kelle, Brad E., and Frank R. Ames, eds. *Writing and Reading War: Rhetoric, Gender and Ethics in Biblical and Modern Contexts*. Atlanta: Society of Biblical Literature, 2008.

Niditch, Susan. *War in the Hebrew Bible: A Study in the Ethics of Violence*. New York: Oxford University Press, 1993.

Wernick, Nicholas. *Warfare in the Ancient Near East to 1600 BC: Holy Warriors at the Dawn of History*. London: Routledge, 2006.

Yadin, Yigael. *The Art of Warfare in Biblical Lands in the Light of Archaeological Discoveries*. London: Weidenfeld and Nicolson, 1963.

Religion plays a huge role in the life of the ancient Israelites. Large sections of this volume have dealt with methods of sacrifice, worship practices, and the changes that took place over time, eventually evolving into two major world religions: Judaism and Christianity. The following studies have contributed to our discussion and would be helpful for further study.

Collins, John J. *The Apocalyptic Imagination: An Introduction to Jewish Apocalyptic Literature*. Grand Rapids: Eerdmans, 1998.

———. *Jewish Wisdom in the Hellenistic Age*. Louisville: Westminster John Knox, 1997.

Gottwald, Norman K. *The Tribes of Yahweh: A Sociology of the Religion of Liberated Israel 1250–1050 BCE*. Maryknoll, NY: Orbis, 1979.

Grabbe, Lester. *An Introduction to Second Temple Judaism*. New York: Continuum, 2010.

Haran, Menahem. *Temples and Temple Service in Ancient Israel*. Oxford: Clarendon, 1970.

Hengel, Martin. *Judaism and Hellenism*. Philadelphia: Fortress, 1981.

Hess, Richard S. *Israelite Religions: An Archaeological and Biblical Survey*. Grand Rapids: Baker Academic, 2007.

Hurowitz, Victor. "Inside Solomon's Temple." *BRev* 10, no. 2 (1994): 24–37, 50.

Keel, Othmar, and Chris Uehlinger. *Gods, Goddesses, and Images of God in Ancient Israel*. Minneapolis: Fortress, 1998.

Lang, Bernhard. "Afterlife: Ancient Israel's Changing Vision of the World Beyond." *BRev* 4, no. 1 (1988): 12–23.

Neusner, Jacob. *From Politics to Piety: The Emergence of Pharisaic Judaism*. Englewood Cliffs, NJ: Prentice Hall, 1973.

Rahmani, L. Y. "Ancient Jerusalem's Funerary Customs and Tombs, Part Three." *BA* 45, no. 1 (1982): 43–53.

———. "Ossuaries and Ossilegium (Bone-Gathering) in the Late Second Temple Period." In *Ancient Jerusalem Revealed*, edited by H. Geva, 191–205. Jerusalem: Israel Exploration Society, 1994.

Saldarini, Anthony J. *Pharisees, Scribes, and Sadducees in Palestinian Society: A Sociological Approach*. Grand Rapids: Eerdmans, 2001.

Shanks, Hershel. "The Tombs of Silwan." *BAR* 20, no. 3 (1994): 38–51.

Smith, Mark S. *The Origins of Biblical Monotheism: Israel's Polytheistic Background and the Ugaritic Texts*. New York: Oxford University Press, 2001.

Theissen, Gerd. *Sociology of Early Palestinian Christianity*. Philadelphia: Fortress, 1978.

VanderKam, James C. *The Dead Sea Scrolls Today*. Grand Rapids: Eerdmans, 2010.

———. *From Joshua to Caiaphas: High Priests after the Exile*. Minneapolis: Fortress, 2004.

Zevit, Ziony. *The Religions of Ancient Israel: A Synthesis of Parallactic Approaches*. New York: Continuum, 2001.

Yet another aspect of ancient Israel's cultural heritage has been the development of law and its relationship to social justice and the maintenance of an ordered existence. The studies listed below are representative of a multitude of works on this subject.

Boecker, Hans J. *Law and the Administration of Justice in the Old Testament and Ancient East*. London: SPCK, 1980.

Derrett, J. Duncan M. *Law in the New Testament*. London: Darton, Longman & Todd, 1970.

Hecht, Neil S., Bernard S. Jackson, and Stephen M. Passamaneck, eds. *An Introduction to the History and Sources of Jewish Law*. Oxford: Clarendon, 1996.

Levinson, Bernard M. *Deuteronomy and the Hermeneutics of Legal Innovation*. New York: Oxford University Press, 1997.

Matthews, Victor H. "The King's Call to Justice." *BZ* 35 (1991): 204–16.

———. "The Social Context of Law in the Second Temple Period." *BTB* 28 (1998): 7–15.

Patrick, Dale. *Old Testament Law*. Atlanta: John Knox, 1985.

Weinfeld, M. *Social Justice in Ancient Israel and in the Ancient Near East*. Minneapolis: Fortress, 1995.

Westbrook, Raymond, and Bruce Wells. *Everyday Law in Biblical Israel: An Introduction*. Louisville: Westminster John Knox, 2009.

Willis, Timothy M. *The Elders of the City: A Study of the Elders-Laws in Deuteronomy*. Atlanta: Society of Biblical Literature, 2001.

Index of Subjects

circumcision, 16, 27, 41, 89, 194, 213, 214, 229, 236
circumscription, 93
cisterns, 56, 63, 163, 233, 248
city gate, 5, 25, 43, 61, 68, 73, 102, 112, 113–16, 121, 134, 162, 165, 178, 187, 189, 192, 248, 251, 256, 257, 259, 260, 261
climate, 8, 11, 14, 20, 32, 59, 182, 233
clothing, 2, 19, 20, 21, 78, 114, 123, 126–30, 134, 136, 137, 202, 243, 244, 247
Code of Hammurabi, 37, 141, 143, 145, 146, 148
coins, 130, 190, 192, 193, 195, 211, 229, 230, 233, 253–56
concubines, 38, 79, 98, 147, 149
conquest period, 2, 41, 48–53, 64, 85, 86, 93, 95, 98, 109
cosmetics, 63, 124, 130, 131, 193
covenant, 4, 11, 16, 22, 23, 29, 37, 38, 41, 54, 72–74, 81, 86, 89, 93, 95, 140, 145, 148, 152, 155, 156, 161, 182, 191, 197, 200, 213, 215
   "everlasting covenant," 99, 100, 105, 121, 155, 171
Covenant Code, 82, 140, 141, 147
covenant renewal ceremony, 86, 168, 182, 191
crucifixion, 250
curse, 139, 146
Cyrus Cylinder, 165, 170, 174, 175

Damascus Document, 217
dance, 62, 132
Day of Atonement, 88, 200, 201
Dead Sea Scrolls, 228, 240, 241
Decalogue, 73, 140
deportation, 107, 140, 149, 164, 165, 170, 171, 173, 182
Deuteronomic Code, 140, 147, 148, 159
Deuteronomistic Historian, 92, 93, 95, 101, 102, 104, 105, 107, 109, 140, 141, 146, 150, 152, 155, 157, 158, 172, 198
Diaspora, 174, 177, 179, 182, 183, 190, 193, 195, 196, 201, 206, 207, 211, 236, 239, 241, 266, 267
diplomat, 129, 216, 222
disciples, 225, 263, 264
disease, 32, 37, 76, 83, 118, 123, 126, 133, 134, 135, 136, 160, 171, 246, 247, 261
divination, 80, 154, 155
divine warrior, Yahweh as, 52, 64
divorce, 144, 181, 190, 191, 224
drama, 237, 238
dyes, 7, 70, 123, 126, 129, 131, 234, 257

economics, 11, 13, 14, 18, 19, 24, 26, 34, 40, 48, 49, 54, 75, 76, 93, 101, 102, 105, 114, 119, 124, 130, 140, 147, 156, 165, 178, 184, 191, 192, 207, 210–12, 231, 232, 250–59, 268
Edomites, 186
education, 72, 239, 240, 241
Egyptians, 7, 11, 19, 20, 23–25, 45, 49, 50, 52, 54, 61, 102, 103, 109, 114, 122, 125, 131, 132, 139, 146, 171, 177, 179, 183, 193, 195, 196, 209–11, 225, 246, 250, 253
elders, 24–26, 28, 54, 61, 70, 72–76, 78, 79, 93, 94, 98, 99, 103, 114, 115, 119, 142, 155, 190, 191, 212, 235, 251, 264, 266, 267
Elephantine letters, 170, 183, 195, 196, 204
emic, 1, 14, 247
endogamy, 6, 34, 36, 37, 75, 190
entertainment, 24, 56, 130, 131, 132, 238
Enuma Elish, 69
ephod, 87
Ephraimites, 65, 85, 97
Epicureanism, 207
Essenes, 217, 228, 238, 242, 262, 263, 267
etic, 11, 14, 247
etiology, 41
euphemism, 41, 44, 64, 89, 238
excavation, 4, 5, 13, 17, 52, 53, 57, 69, 86, 88, 102, 111, 113, 117, 118, 121, 122, 123, 137, 139, 151, 170, 172, 178, 187, 230, 238, 244, 248, 255, 257
exile, 64, 110, 125, 140, 150, 156, 159, 165, 168–75, 177–81, 183–86, 189–91, 193–201, 203, 204, 206–9, 231, 259. See also Babylonian captivity; deportation

Feast of Tabernacles, 104, 182, 236
festivals, 62, 104, 105, 108, 109, 119, 131, 132, 143, 144, 149, 150, 152, 158, 172, 174, 200, 201, 203, 222, 229, 233, 236, 259
First Jewish Revolt, 225, 226, 227, 258
food, 24, 32, 43, 55, 64, 84, 93, 123, 124, 126, 136, 139, 163, 173, 177, 226, 233
four-room house, 57, 122
frankincense, 7, 83, 123, 131
funeral, 136, 142

gentiles, 212, 227, 231, 238, 261, 266
geographic reiteration, 40, 85, 86, 98
geography, 6–11, 13, 14
Gezer Calendar, 59, 63
Gibeonites, 53, 137
glacis, 112, 162
"God-fearers," 266
grapes, 32, 33, 55, 61, 62, 84

Greeks, 69, 168, 176, 182, 189, 190, 193, 203, 206, 207, 209–14, 231, 232, 234, 236–40, 242–46, 250, 251, 253, 255, 259, 260, 266
gymnasium, 211, 213, 236, 237, 239

Habiru, 50, 51. See also *'Apiru*
hair, 20, 129, 131, 148, 149, 155, 191, 244
Hanukkah, 215, 236
Hasidim, 215
Hasmoneans, 216, 217, 219, 220, 221, 234, 242, 243, 255, 260, 262, 264, 265. *See also* Maccabees
health care, 4, 33, 123, 133, 134, 135, 238, 267
hegemony, 108, 109
Hellenizers, 213, 231, 237
herding, 18, 26, 29, 30, 31, 39, 53, 54
ḥerem, 65, 72, 95
high place(s), 41, 88, 104, 105, 107, 108, 109, 119, 149, 150–54. See also *bamah/bamôt*
Hittites, 25, 36, 48, 102, 143, 160
holiday, 84, 124, 178, 236
Holiness Code, 140, 159, 160, 198, 199, 200, 203, 208
Holy of Holies, 119, 201, 202, 219, 261
honor, 27, 38, 42, 72, 78, 136, 148, 173, 183, 222, 225, 226, 257
hospitality, 3, 35, 40, 42, 43, 44, 58, 84
human sacrifice, 40, 41, 78, 84, 154
Hurrians, 48
Hyksos, 19, 49, 52

Idumeans, 217, 219, 221
Iliad, 69
immigrants, 22, 23, 24, 25, 27, 28, 35, 54, 210, 232
industry, 256, 257
inheritance, 22, 34, 37, 38, 46, 71, 78, 79, 80, 81, 103, 144, 145

Jebusites, 92, 99, 111, 157, 196
jewelry, 21, 36, 114, 124, 126, 130, 192, 193, 244

"King's Call to Justice," 146, 147
Kuntillet 'Ajrud Inscription, 152

labor service contract, 36, 37, 60
land purchase, 26, 28, 61, 80, 98, 111, 145, 157
language, 20, 23, 49, 51, 169, 182, 190, 210, 211, 217, 235, 239
law, 2, 3, 18, 21, 22, 24, 37–39, 43, 60, 70–73, 76, 78–80, 83, 85, 87, 88, 101, 108, 114, 121, 126, 129, 134, 137, 140, 141, 143–48, 150, 152, 156, 158–60, 165, 168, 177, 179, 180,

182, 193–96, 198–201, 208, 210, 212, 215, 224, 228, 229, 231, 235, 236, 239, 241–43, 245, 247, 262–64, 266
leprosy, 134, 135
levirate obligation, 38–39, 76, 78–79
Levites, 71, 83, 84, 87, 101, 104, 105, 108, 122, 141, 142, 149, 158, 159, 160, 178–82, 184, 185, 191, 195–99, 203, 225, 242, 259, 260

Maccabees, 170, 206, 215, 216, 217, 245, 255, 260, 267. *See also* Hasmoneans
Manual of Discipline, 217
Mari texts, 17, 18, 30, 33, 60, 129, 144, 145, 154, 155
markets, 111, 114, 116, 117, 124, 131, 192, 210, 212, 232, 235, 236, 251, 255, 256
marriage, 4, 27, 33–39, 44, 46, 73, 75, 76, 78, 79, 96, 97, 101–3, 131, 142–44, 176, 179, 181, 190, 191, 194, 195, 209, 211, 224, 236, 242, 259
Medes, 108, 164
medicine, 63, 134, 135, 239, 246
mercenaries, 97, 160, 218
Merneptah's stele, 51
Mesha Inscription, 106
messengers, 76, 129, 136, 161, 184
messiah, 105, 225, 229, 230
Midianites, 41, 62, 67, 70, 74, 82, 87
midrash, 242
midwife, 77, 246
miqvah/miqva'ot, 238, 265. *See also* ritual purity
Mishnah, 231, 241, 242
Mitannians, 19, 48, 49, 102, 103
Mithraism, 207
Moabites, 67, 75, 106, 147, 190
mōhar, 27
mourning, 21, 132, 136, 137, 138, 182, 191, 230
Murashû documents, 169, 170, 184
music, xiv, 96, 131, 132, 133, 203, 249, 259

Nabateans, 218, 224
Nazirite, 74, 78

olive oil, 33, 57, 63, 64, 251

palaces, 5, 7, 20, 69, 101, 111, 117, 118, 119, 121, 151, 165, 173, 189, 222, 233, 237, 238
Passover, 41, 84, 89, 109, 122, 158, 201, 233, 236, 259
patronage, 158, 257, 258
Pentateuch, 240, 242, 262

Index of Personal Names

Isaac, 4, 21, 25, 28, 31, 32, 33, 34, 35, 36, 40, 41, 43, 44, 98
Isaiah, 107, 121, 130, 135, 136, 139, 156, 185
Ishbosheth, 97, 98, 142

Jacob, 4, 16, 20, 26, 27, 28, 30, 31, 32, 36, 37, 38, 40, 41, 42, 44, 45, 75, 80, 82, 85, 89, 98, 230
Jael, 67
Jehoiakim, 109, 110, 164, 171
Jehoshaphat, 106, 117, 132, 141
Jehu, 105, 106, 107, 127, 130, 137, 153, 156
Jephthah, 65, 66, 74, 78, 84, 85, 89, 97
Jeremiah, 61, 101, 110, 122, 130, 131, 134, 136, 140, 145, 148, 173, 186, 194, 195
Jeroboam, 103, 104, 105, 109, 125, 128, 137, 149, 152, 154, 158, 209
Jeroboam II, 106
Jesus, 209, 224, 225, 226, 234, 235, 239, 243, 246, 247, 249, 251, 254, 256, 258, 261–66, 268
Jezebel, 130, 137, 142, 145, 156
Joab, 97, 98, 99, 100, 112, 128, 142, 160
Joshua, 4, 5, 52, 67, 68, 70, 74, 80, 85, 93, 95
Josiah, 108–10, 121, 122, 137, 140, 142, 150, 152, 153, 154, 158, 159, 171, 197
Judah (person), 21, 38, 39, 44
Julius Caesar, 219, 220

Laban, 35, 36, 37, 38, 40, 42

Marduk, 69, 174, 183
Mark Anthony, 220, 222
Mephibosheth, 99, 100
Micaiah, 155, 156
Michal, 98
Moses, 41, 64, 70, 71, 74, 77, 78, 81, 82, 89, 90, 138, 141, 155, 241

Naaman, 135, 248
Nabonidus, 173, 174
Nathan, 99, 100, 136, 155
Nebuchadnezzar, 109, 110, 145, 164, 168, 173, 174, 183
Nehemiah, 168, 169, 173, 176–79, 185, 187, 189, 190, 191, 192, 195, 198, 199, 201, 204, 209
Nero, 226, 227, 228

Omri, 105, 106, 107, 111, 125, 126
Othniel, 76

Paul (apostle), 226, 231, 238, 239, 243, 244, 251, 252, 257, 263, 266, 267
Peter (apostle), 225, 243, 264
Philo, 239, 240
Pompey, 219, 220, 251
Pontius Pilate, 223, 224, 233, 243, 264

Rachel, 28, 31, 36, 37, 38, 77
Rebekah, 21, 22, 28, 35, 36, 37
Rehoboam, 100, 102, 103, 104, 105, 125
Ruth, 73, 75, 78, 79

Samson, 65, 67, 74, 75, 80, 84
Samuel, 74, 75, 78, 85–88, 93–96, 99, 101–3, 120, 126, 128, 135, 144, 155, 156
Sanballat, 170, 177, 178, 179, 190, 209
Sarah, 24, 25, 32, 38, 43, 44, 98
Saul, 20, 57, 60, 68, 70, 71, 74, 76, 80, 85, 86, 92–98, 105, 117, 118, 120, 126, 128, 130, 135–38, 145, 151, 161, 197
Sennacherib, 64, 69, 108, 127, 150, 162, 163, 171
Shalmaneser III, 20, 106, 107, 127, 161
Shalmaneser V, 164
Shimei, 100
Simon Bar Kochba, 229
Solomon, 49, 93, 99–103, 105, 107, 112, 117–20, 125, 128, 131, 141, 142, 146, 147, 149, 152, 157–61, 170, 171, 190, 197, 198, 231, 260, 261

Tiamat, 69
Tiglath-pileser III, 107
Titus, 227, 228

Uzziah, 59, 106

Vespasian, 227, 228, 229

Zadok, 100, 101, 196, 197
Ziba, 99
Zimri, 125, 126, 161

Index of Place Names

Index of Scripture
and Other Ancient Writings

Leviticus

1–7 208
1–10 82
1–16 274
1:3–9 83
1:3–17 159
1:7 208
1:10–13 83
1:14–17 83
2:1–16 83
2:3 208
3:3 208
3:15 83
3:16 159
4:2 83
4:3 83
4:4–10 83
4:6–7 159
4:15–20 83
4:22–24 83
4:24–26 83
4:29–31 83
5:7–13 83
5:11 159
6 83
6:10 82
7:1–21 83
7:11–14 83
7:15–18 83
10:1–3 83
10:10 159, 201
12 83
12:1–6 118
13 118
13–14 134, 160, 202
13:1–11 134
13:2–8 247
13:6 247
13:47–59 126, 134
14:10 254
15 83, 202
15:5–8 247
15:5–11 238
15:18 238
15:19–24 118
16 201, 270
16:2 202
16:3–10 201
16:7–10 88, 270
16:29–33 200
17 200
17–26 140, 198, 199, 200, 203, 208, 272

17:15 238
18 200
18–20 200
18:1–5 199
19 200
19:3 201
19:10 125
19:29 152
19:30 201
19:31 80
20 200
20:21 224
21 199, 200
21–22 200
21:10–15 202
21:16–23 220
21:17–21 118
22 200
23 200
23:1–44 84
23:1–24:9 200
23:5–8 201
23:9–11 199
23:13 199
23:14 199
23:15–21 201
23:15–44 200
23:23–25 201
23:26–32 201
23:34–36 201
23:39 104
23:39–43 201
24:1–9 200
24:10–23 200
25 200
25:4 62
26 200
26:34–43 201
27 200

Numbers

6:2–21 74
12:10 134
14:33 77
16:30 80
18:30 62
19:7–8 202
19:11 224
21:21–32 89
21:25 54
21:32 54
23:1–2 83
24:17–19 229

25:1–9 134
25:6–8 215
27:1–11 37, 71
27:4 78
28:11–15 151
29:12 104
30:2 85
31:9–12 69
32:24 55
35:9–34 142
36:1–13 78

Deuteronomy

1:9–18 141
4:9–14 72
4:41–43 142
5:11–21 140
5:12–15 148
5:26 80
6:4–5 266
6:4–9 245
6:8 245, 274
6:20–24 72
7:3 181
7:5 153
7:13 63
8:7–8 64
8:9 55
11:13–21 245
12 196
12–26 108, 121, 140, 150, 159, 270
12:2–3 88
12:2–4 108, 150
12:3 153
12:5 171
12:13–14 108, 140, 157
12:15–27 159
12:21–27 140
12:29–13:18 150
12:29–14:2 150
13–14 152
13:16 117
14:1 136
14:3–8 159
14:29 197
15:12 148
15:12–15 147
15:12–18 140
15:16–17 148
16:1–17 84, 159
16:2 171
16:2–17 108

1 Kings

1:8 197
1:29–30 100
1:34 155
1:43–48 100
1:45 155
2:5–7 128
2:11 98
2:13–25 100
2:26 101, 197
2:26–27 100
2:28–34 100
2:35 158, 197
3:1 101, 142
3:2 104, 119
3:4 41
3:9 141
3:16–28 141
4:1–19 120
4:1–21 99, 101
4:7 101
4:7–19 160
4:10 123
4:25 217
4:26 161
4:27–28 124
5:1–7:51 99
5:3 157
5:4–6 157
5:7–12 101
5:13–17 111
5:13–18 147
6 118
6–7 119
6:1 49
6:5 119
6:7 157
6:23–28 119
7 99
7:1–12 118
7:13–51 118
7:21 119
7:26 253
8:1–6 119
8:37 134
8:54–66 158
8:62–66 158
9:11 118
9:15 124
9:15–19 102, 112, 124
9:20–21 147
9:22 124, 147

9:26–28 102
10:1 132
10:2 114, 131
10:10 131
10:22–29 118
10:25 126
10:26–29 102
11:1–8 142
11:1–13 102, 146
11:4–8 152
11:6–8 158
11:14–20 102
11:28 103, 125
11:29 126
11:29–31 103, 128
11:29–33 125
11:34–39 105
11:40 103, 125
12:4 102
12:12–20 125
12:16 100, 103
12:20 103
12:25–33 104, 121, 149, 209
12:27 124
12:28–29 154
12:28–33 158
12:31 105, 152
12:32 104
12:33 104
13:2 137
13:31 137
13:33 158
14:1–3 247
14:10 123
14:11 137
14:16 105
14:22–24 152
14:23 104, 153
14:25–26 103, 104
15:8 138
15:11–15 95
15:26 3
16:4 107
16:8–22 105
16:9 161
16:9–10 125
16:10–16 107
16:11 125
16:15–20 125
16:21–22 125
16:24 111
16:31 105, 142, 152
16:31–33 142

16:32–33 152
17:14–16 61
17:17–24 135
17:21 135
17:24 135
18:4 156
18:13 143
18:19–45 152
19:15–16 155
20:1–34 106
20:23–30 162
20:31–32 137
20:34 116, 124, 192
21:1–4 145
21:3 26
21:4 145
21:8–12 145
21:13–14 145
21:15–19 146
21:23 156
21:24 119, 137
22:1–4 106
22:1–8 152
22:1–36 106
22:5–6 155
22:5–28 156
22:10 61, 111, 113
22:10–12 117
22:29–35 161
22:29–36 162
22:29–40 156
22:31–34 161
22:39 121
22:43 104

2 Kings

1:2 134
1:8 128
3 9
3:2 153
3:4–27 106
3:7 161
3:25 69, 163
3:25a 163
3:25b 161
3:27 41
4:10 58
5:3 247
5:5 129
5:10 135
5:10–14 248
5:15 135
6:8–7:16 106

Deuterocanonical/Apocryphal Works

1 Esdras

3:1–5:6 170
5:59–61 259

2 Esdras

14:37–48 241
18:19–26 208

1 Maccabees

1:11–15 213
1:14 237
1:14–15 213
1:20–23 260
1:20–24 214
1:41–42 214
1:45–48 214
1:54 214
2:13–26 215
2:29 215
2:29–41 245
2:33–38 215
2:41 215
3:1–9 215
3:55–56 245
4:41–58 215
5:24–29 245
6:33–39 245
7:1–4 215
7:9–15 215
8:17–32 217, 219
9:11–21 216
9:28–31 216
9:65–69 245
10:18–20 216
11:30–37 216
12:3 216
12:6 216
13:12–23 216
13:27–30 250
13:49–51 217
13:49–52 245
14:4–15 217
14:9a 217
14:11 217
14:12 217
14:17 260
14:41 216
14:41–45 260
15:15–21 217

2 Maccabees

1:9 260
2:13–15 208
3:4–8 212
3:22–28 212
4:1–6 213
4:7–10 213
4:7–17 260
4:9 237, 239
4:10–15 213
4:12 237, 243
4:12–13 239
4:23–26 213
4:27–32 213
4:27–34 213, 214
4:33–34 213
4:35–38 214
4:39 214
5:1–14 214
5:5–7 214
5:15–16 214
5:15–21 260
5:22–23 214
6–7 214
9:13 11
10:1–8 215
11:27–33 215
12:31 259
14:1–2 215

3 Maccabees

4:6 244

Sirach

27:4 61
31:25 62
31:26 257
38:1–15 246
38:12–14 246
38:29 259
41:8 231
48:17–19 163
49:1 258
50:1–21 212

Pseudepigrapha

1 Enoch

90:8 213

Psalms of Solomon

2:26–32 219

Testament of Judah

24 230

Testament of Moses

6:1–4 217

Testament of Reuben

5:1–5 244

Dead Sea Scrolls

1QpHab

VIII, 8–13 216

3Q15

XI, 12 248

4Q169

3–4 I, 2 242
3–4 I, 7 242

Damascus Rule

VII, 18–21 230

Josephus and Philo

Josephus

Against Apion

2.103–5 261

Jewish Antiquities

3.7.157–58 244
3.8.194–95 256
3.11.270 244
7.3.393 217
9.14.277–91 164
11.1.8 184
11.5.173 10
11.8.321–24 195, 209
12.3.129–37 212
12.3.138–46 212
12.4.1–11 211, 212
12.4.189–13.3.79 215

12.5.239 213
12.5.240–41 236
12.5.241 237
12.5.252–53 217
12.6.274–75 245
13.1.1 216
13.5.171–73 218
13.6.213 216
13.6.215–17 217, 245
13.8.236–49 217
13.9.254–56 209
13.9.257–58 217
13.10.275–81 217
13.10.288–92 217
13.10.293–95 262
13.10.293–96 217
13.10.294 262
13.10.297 242
13.10.297–98 263
13.11.301 218
13.13.372 218
13.13.376 218
13.14.380 218
14.4.69–79 219
14.4.72 219
14.4.73–76 219
14.5.89–91 219
14.5.91 219
14.6.92 219
14.7.105–9 220
14.8.143–44 220
14.8.158 220
14.9.167–70 264
14.9.167–80 243
14.9.175–76 264
14.10.202–6 258
14.13.326 220
14.13.365–69 220
14.14.381–85 220
14.16.487–91 220
15.1.2 258
15.2.31–56 221
15.3.39–41 260
15.3.80–87 221
15.7.222–39 221
15.8.268 222, 233
15.8.268–74 237
15.8.277–83 238
15.9.309–10 257
15.9.331–41 233
15.9.333–40 251
15.9.341 237

15.11.380–425 222, 260
15.11.389 260
15.11.409 260
15.11.417 261
16.5.137 237
16.6.163 216
17.6.169–76 247
17.6.171 238
17.8.205 234
18.1.1–3 223
18.1.11–23 241
18.1.11–25 259
18.1.13 263
18.1.14 265
18.1.14–15 262
18.1.16 262, 265
18.1.18–22 264
18.1.23–25 264
18.2.36 238
18.2.36–38 224, 235
18.3.55–59 224
18.4.88–89 224
18.5.118 224
19.5.274–75 224
19.7.328 257
19.7.329 222, 238
19.8.343–45 237
19.8.343–50 225
20.2.38–39 11
20.5.97–112 225
20.5.101 225
20.8.162–65 225
20.8.164–65 245
20.8.169–72 225
20.9.197–200 226
20.9.204–10 226
20.10.224–51 229
20.11.252 226

Jewish War

1.1.41 245
2.8.119 242
2.9.169–74 224
2.9.175–77 224, 233
2.14.278–79 226
2.14.284–92 226
2.14.287 234
2.14.293 226
2.17.408 227
2.17.409 226
2.17.410–16 226
2.17.426–27 227

2.17.433–34 227
2.18.457–80 227
3.2.29–34 228
3.3.43 235
3.5.70–101 246
3.5.80 245
3.5.94–95 245
3.5.96–97 245
3.6.127–339 228
3.8.340–54 228
4.3.158–61 225
5.6.248–74 228
5.8.331 257
5.11.466–90 246
5.13.527–40 228
6.10.435 228
7.1.1–12 228
7.3.45 266
7.8.262–70 264
7.8.320–406 228
7.10.409–12 245
7.10.412–14 243

Philo

De opificio mundi (On the Creation of the World)

15–25 240

De specialibus legibus (On the Special Laws)

2.228–30 239

That Every Good Person Is Free

75 242

Other Greek and Latin Works

Dio Cassius

Vita Hadriani (Life of Hadrian)

14.2 229

Eusebius

Ecclesiastical History

3.12.19–20 229
4.6.3 231

Herodotus

Histories

5.52–53   188

Juvenal

Satires

6   244

Macrobius

Saturnalia

2.4.11   222

Menander

Thais

Frg. 218   238

Plutarch

Quaestiones romanae et graecae (Roman and Greek Questions)

267a   244

Tertullian

De corona militis (The Crown)

4   244

Rabbinic Works

Babylonian Talmud

Baba Batra

21a   239

Gittin

56a–b   228

Jerusalem Talmud

Shebi'it

9.1   224

Ta'anit

4.8.68d–69d   229

Pirqe Rabbi Eliezer

3   240

Papyri

Elephantine Papyri

TAD A4.7   195

Ancient Near Eastern Texts

Amarna Tablets

EA 29   102
EA 67:17   96
EA 71:21   96
EA 73:28   96
EA 74:29   96

Aqhat

KTU 5:5–8   114

Code of Hammurabi

30   145
57   30
117   147
130   143
138   144
141   144
142   144
167   79
170   79
171   79
172   76
195   71
226   148
227   148, 149
261   36, 37
264   37
265   37
266   37
267   37

Epic of Gilgamesh

13:79–84   136

Laws of Eshnunna

19   73

Mari Texts: ARM and ARMT

A. 1968   154, 155
4:1.10–28   145
6:45.7–10   129
10:7   155
14:22.4–11   29, 30
14:80.4–10   60

Middle Assyrian Laws

A.33   76
A.40   21
A.45   76
A.55   143

Sumerian Laws

7   27

Image Credits

Photo on page 181 Israel Museum, CC0 / Wikimedia Commons.

Photo on page 210 Carole Raddato, CC BY-SA 2.0 / Wikimedia Commons.

Photo on page 232 Fallaner, CC BY-SA 4.0 / Wikimedia Commons.

Photo on page 244 Public Domain / The MET, purchase 1902.

Photo on page 250 ArtMediaFactory / shutterstock.com.

Photo on page 262 Aprilphoto / shutterstock.com.